The International Law Standard
in Treaties of the United States

The International Law Standard in Treaties of the United States

By

Robert Renbert Wilson

HARVARD UNIVERSITY PRESS
Cambridge, Massachusetts
1953

Distributed in Great Britain by
Geoffrey Cumberlege
Oxford University Press
London

Library of Congress Catalog Card Number 53–5063
Printed in the United States of America

TO

M. VAN N. W.

PREFACE

Begun as a very restricted inquiry into the use of the term "international law" or "law of nations" in treaties of the United States, this study became somewhat broader as it developed. Considerations which figured in this broadening were especially (1) the realization that the standard might be implied in treaty provisions in which the term "international law" itself did not appear, and (2) the realization that a state's position with respect to the standard might appear from what it advocated (perhaps as a statement of existing law, as well as law for the future), even if it were unsuccessful in such advocacy. As a matter of organization, however, it seemed useful to look primarily at provisions making specific mention of the standard, while not leaving out of account some developments (involving other perfected treaties) in which the standard was a significant factor in diplomacy or in judicial interpretation.

This book does not purport to be in any sense a study of all the international law which treaties of the United States express. To try to summarize all of that law in a single volume would doubtless be impracticable. Nor does the plan include a detailed statement, in connection with every treaty in which the term "international law" appears, of what the substantive content of the law was on particular points at the time—the complete law, for example, on such a broad subject as neutral rights and duties. In certain instances an attempt has in fact been made to indicate briefly what the law was at the given times. The essential object, however, has been the more modest one of seeing how treaty engagements of the United States have, ordinarily through express terms in the instruments, been related to the law as a whole, and of providing a basis for judging the relative emphasis upon the standard as well as the utility of the method used in these treaties. Limitation to perfected international agreements which the United States has accepted has excluded developments relating to such recently or currently important topics as human rights or the international control of atomic energy.

In the carrying out of the plan of the study, more than a textual commentary frequently became necessary, since even familiar expressions in treaties are not self-defining.[1] Determination of the significance of the use of even such a term as "the law of nations" may, in particular situations, necessitate consultation of the records of negotiations, hearings, legislative discussions, and often examination of tribunals' decisions. Most of the evidence consulted in the investigation was in printed form, although in some instances I have depended upon unpublished diplomatic correspondence and other manuscript records. For the period through 1863 the monumental volumes on United States treaties edited by David Hunter Miller have furnished much valuable information.

With the idea of bringing the investigation as nearly up to date as was practicable, I have tried to deal with relevant treaty developments up to about the middle of 1951.

The study is not essentially one in diplomatic history, although it has seemed necessary in the course of it (as, for example, in connection with Pinckney's treaty, 1795, and the Treaty of Washington, 1871) to trace diplomatic developments in some detail where they throw light upon what the United States did concerning the standard. In this connection I am heavily indebted to the authors of many monographs, some on the history of particular treaties and others on certain phases of American foreign relations. I have also made use of numerous special studies, as well as standard treatises, on international law. Although, obviously, a treaty reference to "international law" may conceivably have significance for private international law as distinct from public, I have endeavored to present only the public international law aspects.

[1] Cf. the statement of a committee member (not an American) at the Hague Codification Conference of 1930: "When once a treaty has been concluded, no one reads the reports, for treaties live of themselves and, if they are not clear enough to meet the needs of life, hardly any reference is made to the reports. The reports . . . explain how and why certain agreements are reached; but . . . we ought not to exaggerate their value" (*Minutes of the Third Committee: Responsibility of States*, p. 45).

Chapter I presents a general statement and a classification. Chapters II through V deal principally with illustrative instances of effort for, and actual inclusion of, provisions concerning the standard as they came to appear in perfected international agreements, and also, in many cases, with the interpretation and application of the provisions. The history of the Kellogg-Briand Pact, in which a specific mention of the standard does not appear, but the bearing of which upon whatever is done about the standard in the field of pacific settlement has, since the Nuremberg trials, become rather evident, illustrates that both diplomatic and judicial pronouncements may assume practical importance.

The table of United States treaties in Appendix I does not include all treaties that would fall within the classification of Chapter I, section 4, but only international agreements that are specifically referred to or cited in the present study. Where a provision concerning the law appears in each of a number of treaties in identical form (as, for example, in the bilateral arbitration treaties of the pattern which the United States began to use in 1928 in its relations with European and Asiatic states), particular treaties in the group are subjects of discussion only where the record of negotiation or application throws some light upon attitude, purpose, or legal effect.

In Appendix II there is material drawn from the treaty practice of six states other than the United States. Limitations of plan have permitted only brief commentaries on portions of texts, for the purpose of comparing with language used in United States treaties. Without discounting in any sense the importance of treaty usage to be discovered in agreements made by smaller states, I have thought it useful for the present purpose to compare uses of the standard by the United States only with those by the other major states selected. In this Appendix, citations are to official collections of the respective countries or to standard general collections of treaty texts.

The idea which gave rise to the study here undertaken dates from the first of several periods of work, under temporary appointment, in the Department of State, when there first came to my attention the number and variety of specific references in treaties to international law. Subsequent periods of government work involving specialization on a particular type of treaty have impressed upon me the possible usefulness of an attempt to clarify the manner in which the standard has been used. In this connection I have had the privilege of discussion with many persons whose interest in treaties is more than a mere academic one. Opinions and conclusions which I have expressed are, however, my own, and in no sense official.

I am indebted to the Research Council of Duke University for funds used for research assistance and in the preparation and publication of the manuscript. Officers of the Duke University Library, of the Library of Congress, of the Division of Historical Policy Research of the Department of State, of the National Archives of the United States, and of the Pan American Union have through their courtesy facilitated the research. The editor-in-chief of the *American Journal of International Law* has kindly permitted the reproduction in this book of certain materials the substance of which originally appeared in articles in that journal. Condensations of some parts of the material were used in lectures given at the Universities of Istanbul and Ankara in 1948 and published in Turkish and English in 1949 by the Turkish Institute of International Law under the title, *Andlaşmalarda Devletler Umumî Hukuku* (*International Law in Treaties*).

My colleague Professor R. Taylor Cole of Duke University has put me in his debt by reading an early draft of the manuscript and making useful suggestions for its improvement. My thanks are due to Dr. David R. Deener, sometime Research Associate in the Duke University Department of Political Science, for his most valuable counsel and research assistance, and to Mrs. David R. Deener for her excellent work in typing the manuscript. I express to the Harvard University Press my high appreciation of the consideration and courtesies shown me in connection with publication; I am particularly indebted to Miss Elizabeth Treeman of the Press for her editorial work and for her many helpful suggestions. Mr. Claude S. Phillips, Jr., has rendered assistance of great value in the correction of proofs.

Robert R. Wilson

Durham, North Carolina
February 26, 1953

CONTENTS

The International Law Standard in Treaties of the United States

Chapter I

INTRODUCTION

"International law is the standard of conduct of States in their reciprocal relations." Reaffirmed as a principle in the Bogotá Charter of the Organization of American States, this proposition invites analysis from the point of view of the treaty relations, as well as other relations, of states. If they have any legal quality, treaties are not made in a vacuum. Viewed as a background against which all international agreements are made, international law becomes something more than a set of understandings "to which all nations subscribe, but to which only a few adhere."[1] Seen from the point of view of preëxisting rules, treaties afford means of affirming these rules, or of adapting, varying, suspending, or supplementing them in the relations of the parties *inter se*. The manner in which they have done so will appear from the treaty practice of a particular state, such as the United States.

There have been various attempts to discern "principles" of American diplomacy in terms of broad policies which the country has followed and reflected in its treaties. Overstatement of the part which the United States has had in the development of an international legal system based on these principles is not, however, conducive to understanding. Broad claims, such as that the "ideals of the United States in international law" have been "wiser and more altruistic than those of any other great power,"[2] are not very helpful. Of American policies it has been suggested that, while "deliberately conceived from egoistic national con-

[1] As suggested by a member of Congress in 1939 (84 *Congressional Record* A3107).

[2] Statement made before the House Committee on Foreign Affairs, *Hearings on . . . a Third Hague Conference for codification of international law*, 69th Cong., 1st Sess. (1926), p. 53. The same speaker conceded that criticism might be made of some of the country's *conduct*.

siderations," they have proved to have a high international value.[3] It is not necessary to review here the well-known record of these policies in their actual application in order to emphasize that they, and not mere zest for legal abstractions, furnished occasion for the treaties. Nonetheless, when the latter refer, explicitly or implicitly, to the body of legal rules comprising international law, the precise purpose and effect of such references becomes a proper subject of legal inquiry.

It has often been pointed out that, in one sense, any binding agreement, even a bilateral one, "makes" law (the so-called "particular international law") for the subjects to it—in accordance with the theory of the autonomy of the subjects' will in relation to contracts[4]—aside from the preëxisting law against the background of which the treaty is made. It may also be noted that any treaty mention of such matters as jurisdiction, extradition, or recognition would extend to considerable areas of the law. In general, the present inquiry will, however, be restricted to treaties which make reference to the law in more direct, specific terms. "International law" then becomes, itself, a term in treaties.

In the present chapter it is proposed to consider (1) the way in which considerations other than legal ones enter into this process, (2) characteristics of the customary law which may be incorporated by such a treaty reference, (3) the nature and form of references, (4) a classification of the references, and (5) some factors which seem to make the position of the United States, with respect to the law thus referred to, a special one.

1. EXTRALEGAL FACTORS AFFECTING TREATIES

The weaknesses of the treaty system, which involves contractual arrangements between entities whose individual interests the agreements may serve temporarily, have received attention

[3] Pitman B. Potter, *Doctrines américaines de droit international* (1937), p. 25. On the view that it is now futile to try to construct international law on individual state interests, see Gerhart Niemeyer, *Law without Force* (1941), *passim*.

[4] Cf. Lazare Kopelmanas, "Custom as a Means of the Creation of International Law," *British Year Book of International Law*, XVIII (1937), 127, 150.

not merely from jurists but from observers of social processes generally.[5] Obviously, matters of great international importance are likely to present questions other than those of law. Particularly when there is a large measure of popular control over and influence upon foreign policy, decisions recorded in treaties may frequently be compromises, even on such a point as that of adherence to preëstablished rules of law. Changing power relationships, economic factors, and new conceptions of what the national interest requires, naturally enter in.[6]

Whether the occasion for treaties is to promote freedom of commercial intercourse, or to establish respect for individual human rights, or to secure a greater use of pacific methods of settling international disputes, or to develop in a particular hemisphere a system of neighborliness consistent with a universal legalism,[7] much besides the legal considerations may demand

[5] See, for example, P. W. Bridgman, *The Intelligent Individual and Society* (1938), p. 241.

[6] Cf. John Donaldson, "Fundamentals of the Foreign Economic Processes and Policies of the United States," *Weltwirtschaftliches Archiv*, XXX (1929), 49–77; Jesse S. Reeves, "The Interrelation of the Domestic and Foreign Policies of the Nation," *Annals of the American Academy of Political and Social Science*, vol. 218 (November 1941), pp. 1–8; Carl J. Friedrich, *Foreign Policy in the Making* (1938), ch. IV; George H. Blakeslee, "The Foreign Policy of the United States," in Quincy Wright (ed.), *Interpretations of American Foreign Policy* (1930), p. 3.

[7] On the matter of a legal particularism in the region, Secretary of State Charles Evans Hughes said: "The law of nations is of universal application. Consequently it is not suggested that there exists an American international law as distinct from that which necessarily prevails throughout the society of civilized states. There are, however, legal problems which are peculiar to the States of the American continents. In the formulation and advocacy of proposals designed to make clear the application of the principles of international law to those problems there are reasons for their particular consideration by American States; for they have a distinctive interest in a cause peculiarly their own" (*Papers relating to the Foreign Relations of the United States* [hereafter cited as *For. Rel.*], 1925, I, 303). Along the same line Secretary Cordell Hull said: "These principles upon which we have built our inter-American life are no exclusive property of the continents of the Americas. They are not peculiar to this hemisphere. They are universally applicable and are open to universal adoption. . . . The international law to which we submit ourselves is not an international law of the Americas alone but is the law of civilized nations everywhere throughout the earth" (*Department of State Bulletin*, April 17, 1943, p. 323). One of the more recent formulations of American "principles" is that in chapter II of the Charter of the Organization of American States, signed at the Bogotá Con-

primary attention. On the other hand, even such a policy as that expressed in the Monroe Doctrine is not unrelated to the law. For, while the Doctrine in its beginnings was more a matter of single state policy than international agreement, it rested, as Elihu Root once pointed out, upon the right of self-protection, and that right is recognized by international law.[8] Treaties have, of course, commonly reflected positions of relative dominance, economic difficulties, or temporary exigencies of the parties.[9] If the making and enforcement of the agreements often involve political uses of legal arguments, questions of law may not in fact be the principal consideration. At the same time there may be, and has been in the diplomacy of the United States, a "conception of legality" [10] which plays a real part.

The relative emphasis upon things other than law may naturally depend upon the urgency of the matter (as in a situation of widespread insecurity) or upon whether there is moral ground for action not clearly permitted by already accepted rules. If law is "essentially a living and changing compromise between stable order and the necessity of social change," [11] it is never static. Adherence to it does not imply that its subjects will not seek to change it. Benjamin Franklin and his colleagues recognized this when they put the question, "Why should not this law of nations go on improving?" [12] The achieving of "fixity of principles," an expression which Earl Russell for the British Foreign Office used in writing to Charles Francis Adams, American minister at London, in 1861,[13] need not imply that the principles will be unchangeable. The General Assembly of the United Nations in its

ference, 1948; text in *Report of the Delegation of the United States to the Ninth International Conference of American States* (1948), Department of State publication 3263, p. 168. See note 86 *infra*.

[8] *For. Rel.*, 1929, I, 717.

[9] Cf. G. B. de Mably, *Le Droit public de l'Europe* (1761 ed.), 1, 16–18.

[10] John Bassett Moore, *The Principles of American Diplomacy* (1918), p. 424.

[11] Percy Corbett, "Conflicting Theories of International Law," *Proc. Amer. Soc. Int. Law*, 1940, p. 101. Cf. Carleton Kemp Allen, *Law in the Making* (1939 ed.), p. 40.

[12] *Diplomatic Correspondence of the United States of America from September 10, 1783, to March 4, 1789* (1833), II, 237.

[13] Francis Wharton, *A Digest of the International Law of the United States* (1886), III, 288.

actions looking to the progressive development as well as codification of international law, and the International Law Commission itself, has proceeded upon the assumption that there can be improvement through conscious effort. Even aside from efforts for progressive development, however, there may be treaty uses of the general body of the law. The primary motivation for such uses may be political or economic considerations rather than any desire to extend the domain of law.

2. CUSTOM AS AN ELEMENT

The meaningfulness of treaty references to international law as a standard rests in large part upon the fact that customary rules still comprise a very great part of the law.[14] Among the chief questions that have been raised in this connection are those of how customary rules emerge, the method of their recognition, the advantages that have been claimed for them over written rules, and the way in which customary rules may be changed.

It has been common to say that usage crystallizes into law through the conviction that conformity to the rule has become obligatory, the *opinio juris sive necessitatis*. As one authoritative

[14] H. A. Smith (ed.), *Great Britain and the Law of Nations*, II (1935), v. Among the studies bearing on the subject of this section are the following: Jean Collette, *Les Principes de droit des gens dans la jurisprudence de la Cour Permanente de Justice Internationale* (1932), pp. 25 *et seq.*; J. Kosters, "Les Fondements du droit des gens," *Bibliotheca Visseriana*, IV (1925), 1–275; Gilbert Gidel, "Droits et devoirs des nations; la théorie classique des droits fondamentaux des états," *Recueil des cours*, X (1925), 541–597; Arnold Raestad, "'Droit coutumier' et 'principes généraux' en droit international," *Nordisk Tidsskrift For International Ret*, IV (1933), 61–84; Lazare Kopelmanas, "Custom as a Means of the Creation of International Law," *Brit. Year Book Int. Law*, XVIII (1937), 127–151; Fred Castberg, "La Méthodologie du droit international public," *Recueil des cours*, XLIII (1933), 313–381; Robert Redslob, "Considérations sur les fondements du droit des gens," *Revue de droit international et de législation comparée*, XIV (1933), 488–513; Yvon Gouet, *La Coutume en droit constitutionnel interne et en droit constitutionnel international* (1932); G. Gianni, *La Coutume en droit international* (1931); Maurice Bourquin, "Règles générales du droit de la paix," *Recueil des cours*, XXXV (1931), 5–227; S. Séfériadès, "Aperçus sur la coutume juridique internationale et notamment sur son fondement," *Revue générale de droit international public*, XLIII (1936), 129–196; Karl Strupp, "Les règles générales du droit de la paix," *Recueil des cours*, XLVII (1934), 263–586.

writer has put it, customs are manifestations of certain exigencies of communal life and from them have resulted the fundamental principles of law.[15] Without here attempting such a distinction as that between normative rules and constructive rules, or that between norms for acting and norms of acting, it is possible to regard as binding those rules whose satisfactory and reasonable character has caused them to be regularly identified with international duties, or to be "found" by tribunals. The tribunals' findings "attest," but do not "make," the law.

Even with the assumption of complete good faith, to suppose that there can be something approaching complete clarity of substantive rules based upon custom is hardly reasonable. The function of the judge assumes great relative importance, and the weakness of a system of international law which has traditionally required no state to refer questions for interpretation to an outside agency, without its consent in the particular case, becomes apparent. The movement for obligatory arbitration in the late nineteenth and in the twentieth centuries has depended for its justification upon the belief that, even if there is, before an adjudication, lack of agreement about what a customary rule is, the rule can either be found and applied by arbitrators or declared not to exist in a form that would justify the tribunal's holding the respondent state to compliance with it.[16] Distrust, and unwillingness to repose the necessary confidence in judges (who might seem to acquire the additional role of legislators),

[15] Dionisio Anzilotti, *Cours de droit international* (1929), I, 66 *et seq.* Cf. Allen, *Law in the Making*, pp. 86–87, to the effect that customs establish themselves because they fit the economic convenience of the most powerful caste, and not because they correspond with any conscious, widespread necessity. This statement was not made specifically as to law in the international community.

[16] For an instance in which, in a note to Great Britain, the Russian government urged, with respect to a particular subject matter, the "absence of universal binding . . . rules," see *Parliamentary Papers*, Cmd. 1874 (1923). At the time of the United States Senate's action in 1946 on acceptance of the Optional Clause of the Statute of the International Court of Justice, the Senate rejected an amendment introduced by Senator E. D. Millikin which would have provided that adherence would "not apply to disputes where the law necessary for decision is not found in existing treaties and conventions to which the United States is a party and where there has not been prior agreement by the United States as to the applicable principles of international law."

has impeded the movement.[17] With recognition of the part which adjudication can play in the development, it has been said that so-called customary law is often not so much the product of state practice as it is the product of tribunals.[18]

An advantage sometimes claimed for judge-declared law over written law is that of its greater malleability and adaptability to a changing milieu. A recent authoritative appraisal of the law in general has proceeded upon the assumption that while general principles are fairly well understood, the particular manner of application is the subject of wide disagreement.[19] This might be illustrated in the concept of denial of justice, questions relating to which have arisen in widely differing forms.[20] In the case of the laws of war, technological development may outdistance effort to provide law in conventional form, and if the latter is thought to be the only law that exists, much conduct may go unregulated. Even concerning the concept of aggression, developing ideas and practice have not quickly found expression in definitive language.

That a customary rule may become universally obligatory by virtue of a *general* practice; that international obligations can be in the form of customary and treaty rules for some states while in force only as customary rules for others; and that when recognition of a customary rule has become sufficiently general, the rule's binding force may apply to a state not theretofore actually applying it, seem clear. In the case of the *Paquette Habana*,[21] there was application in the Western Hemisphere of a rule that had theretofore apparently been judicially applied only to Euro-

[17] On the supposed inutility of referring to arbitration questions as to which the substantive law is a matter of dispute, see John Westlake, "International Arbitration," *International Journal of Ethics*, VII (1897), 1, 14. Cf. Hans Kelsen, "Compulsory Adjudication of International Disputes," *Amer. Jour. Int. Law*, XXXVII (1943), 397–406.

[18] Raestad, "'Droit coutumier' et 'principes généraux' en droit international." Cf. J. L. Brierly, *The Law of Nations* (1949 ed.), p. 62.

[19] *Survey of International Law in relation to the Work of Codification of the International Law Commission*, U.N. Publication A/CN.4/I (November 5, 1948).

[20] See the statement of John Bassett Moore at the Fourth International Conference of the American States, 1910, Sen. Doc. 744, 61st Cong., 3d Sess., p. 24.

[21] 175 U.S. 677 (1900).

pean situations.[22] There must, of course, be adequate evidence that the custom has really become so generally followed that there is no longer reasonable doubt about its jural force. International tribunals, as also national prize courts, have sometimes discovered international customary law from an examination of the practice of substantially all the states.[23] Regional arrangements may develop that are consistent with international law,[24] but the mere invocation of custom that is observed by only a few states, on a regional basis or otherwise, cannot supplant, except as between those states and perhaps within limitations, a rule recognized as binding by the greater part of the nations of the world.

There is, of course, the possibility that the tribunal may find no customary rule sufficiently well established to impose a duty upon a respondent state. In the *Lotus* case, for example, the Permanent Court of International Justice found that no norm existed which could be successfully invoked by the complainant state.[25] Criticism of the decision has brought out that the Court inferred the existence of a rule of international law from the absence of protest against a general practice, and that it seemed to base an international custom upon the mere nonexistence of a

[22] Through diplomatic effort, a practice long observed in a particular region may secure extraregional recognition, as was apparently the case with respect to the Latin American practice concerning asylum in embassies and legations, which was invoked as to persons in Spain during the civil strife in that country from 1936 to 1938 (N. J. Padelford, *International Law and Diplomacy in the Spanish Civil Strife* [1939], pp. 157–168). In its judgment of November 20, 1950, in the Colombian-Peruvian case concerning asylum, the International Court of Justice said, concerning the first submission of the Colombian Government, that "it is not possible to discern . . . any constant and uniform usage, accepted as law, with regard to the alleged rule of unilateral and definitive qualification of the offence." At another place in its opinion, the Court found evidence to show that "asylum as practised in Latin America is an institution which, to a very great extent, owes its development to extralegal factors. The good-neighbor relations between the republics, the different political interests of the governments, have favoured the mutual recognition of asylum apart from any clearly defined juridical system" (*I.C.J. Reports*, 1950, pp. 277, 286).

[23] See, for example, the *Carthage*, G. G. Wilson (ed.), *Hague Arbitration Cases* (1915), pp. 353, 365; the *Odessa*, L.R. (1916), 1 A.C. 145; the *Zamora*, L.R. (1916), 2 A.C. 77; the *Hakan*, L.R. (1918), A.C. 148.

[24] See note 7, *supra*.

[25] P.C.I.J., series A, no. 10 (1927).

norm.[26] Neither analogies from private law nor broad authorizations for courts to apply "general principles of law" have seemed to provide escape from a large measure of deference for a state which declines to be bound by a rule that cannot be shown to have been established by custom or convention.

When law is so largely based in custom, the manner in which customary rules change becomes important. In theory, modification implies consent, or at least acquiescence, on the part of all parties to whom the law is applicable. In practice, tribunals appear to employ common-sense methods of ascertaining whether there has been a variation in what custom has established. There is, naturally, room for jurists to disagree on the adequacy of evidence. The latter may show that a customary rule has been replaced by a conventional one rather than by a new customary rule.[27]

The manner in which the United States once appealed to law and principle to challenge an established usage appears from the controversy concerning the Danish Sound Dues.[28] In this instance, an American Secretary of State (Abel Parker Upshur) had reported to President Tyler that Denmark could not demand the tolls "upon any principle of natural or public Law." [29] More than a decade later an English spokesman declared, however, that the Danes' right to levy the charges had been recognized by the European powers and had "become part of the international law of Europe." [30] Some five years later another American Secretary of State (James Buchanan) asserted that under the "public law of nations" the navigation of the two seas involved was free and

[26] On the question of whether the successful exercise of powers can eventually transform simple tolerance into a permissive rule of law, and whether abstention from an exercise of jurisdiction—where abstention was motivated by admission of a *duty* to abstain—can itself provide the basis for a customary rule, see Collette, *Les Principes de droit des gens*, pp. 24 *et seq*.

[27] On the principle of desuetude, applicable to customary international law, see Georg Schwarzenberger, *International Law*, I (1949), 199.

[28] On the history, see Charles E. Hill, *The Danish Sound Dues and the Command of the Baltic* (1926).

[29] *Annual Message of the President to Congress*, Sen. Doc. 1, 28th Cong., 1st Sess. (1843), p. 20.

[30] The Earl of Clarendon's statement (46 *British and Foreign State Papers* 661).

the navigation of the channel joining them ought also to be free.[31] The United States submitted that what the Danes claimed by "immemorial prescription" and "immemorial usage" was inapplicable to Americans, since the levies conflicted with "natural privileges and international law." Secretary William Learned Marcy declared, in an instruction of July 18, 1853, that "these ancient customs have in many instances been found to be inconsistent with rights now generally recognized in the more liberal and reasonable practice of commercial nations." [32] President Pierce in his annual message of the following year advanced the legal argument that Denmark's collection of the tolls was sanctioned, not by general principles of the law of nations, but by special conventions.[33] In the course of the negotiations Denmark sought to maintain its position by appeal to sovereignty, usage, prescription, the interest of other powers in preventing Denmark from assenting to the proposals of the United States, and "old" rights as against what was demanded on the basis of new international law.[34]

3. NATURE AND FORM OF REFERENCES TO THE LAW

From the foregoing section it will appear that the rules comprehended in a treaty reference to "international law" or the "law of nations" may sometimes be difficult to discern. By a general mention of them a treaty may emphasize their existence, without by any means clarifying their substantive content. Mere emphasis does not, however, exhaust the possibilities. The United States officially expressed to the United Nations in 1946 its feeling that "international law is already sufficiently developed to serve as a guide and basis in international relations." [35] Agreements may specify the standard as that which is to be applied

[31] D. H. Miller (ed.), *Treaties and Other International Acts of the United States of America*, VII (1942), 530.

[32] *Ibid.*, pp. 534–535.

[33] James D. Richardson, *A Compilation of the Messages and Papers of the Presidents, 1789–1897*, VI, 2812.

[34] Miller, *Treaties*, VII, 542, 564.

[35] From the Acting United States Representative to the United Nations to the Secretary-General, in connection with acceptance of the Optional Clause of the Statute of the International Court of Justice (61 *Stat.* 1219).

in various situations. Alternatively, they may make mention of the standard in the course of registering assent to rules as parts of the law, or may implicitly subscribe to the standard when recording the assent of parties to a suspension of its operations in their relations *inter se.*

Investigation reveals over two hundred references in terms to the "law of nations" or "international law" (or clear equivalents of these terms) in intergovernmental agreements to which the United States has become a party.[36] If to the number indicated there be added instruments in which there are indirect or implied references to the body of custom, usage, or precedent, the total would be even greater. Difficult to classify are some early treaty provisions which look to assurances of legal treatment of, for example, persons, goods, or vessels. When it is specified that legal procedures shall be applied, the texts do not always indicate clearly whether the latter shall conform to national law merely, or to international law, or to both. Thus, the first commercial treaty which the United States made (with France, signed February 6, 1778) provided that ships and nationals of one party that might come upon the coasts of the other party were to be treated according to "general rules." [37] Unless the contrary appears from the contexts or from records of the parties' intentions, such words as "rights," "lawful," or "unlawful," when used in an international agreement,[38] would presumably mean legality in the international, rather than in the merely national, sense. A provision that nationals of one state shall recover from another state on claims according to the "acknowledged practice of civilized nations" [39] might reasonably be con-

[36] See Appendix I. In the present chapter the term "treaty" is ordinarily used in the generic sense.

[37] Miller, *Treaties,* II (1931), 25, art. 28 (26). In early treaties which the United States made with the Netherlands, Sweden, and Prussia, respectively, there were stipulations that the legality of prizes should be decided conformably to "laws and regulations," the parties to make such laws and regulations as they should judge necessary.

[38] See article XIV of the 1805 treaty with Tripoli (8 *Stat.* 214), article XXV of the 1783 treaty with Sweden (8 *ibid.* 60), article I of the 1831 convention with France (8 *ibid.* 430).

[39] Article V of an agreement of December 23, 1826, with Hawaii. There is doubt whether this ever became a perfected treaty (Miller, *Treaties,* III [1933], 271).

strued to mean that law should be applied, in view of the fact that the functions of claims commissioners usually are essentially judicial.[40]

Assurance that procedures should be essentially orderly rather than arbitrary was apparently the object of some early treaty clauses. Thus the earliest agreements with Prussia set forth that seizures, detentions, or arrests should be only by order or authority of law.[41] Undertakings with various American republics in the first half of the nineteenth century required that the trial and judgment of vessels be according to law.[42] Somewhat less clear is the reference, in the third of the separate articles subjoined to the first treaty between the United States and Sweden, to "illicit commerce contrary to the principles of neutrality," [43] a wording which raises, among others, the much-discussed question of whether the carriage of contraband by neutral vessels has traditionally been forbidden by international law or simply made risky by that law. A treaty project referring to the "acknowledged practice of enlightened nations" [44] would seem to comprehend at least a part of what was covered in "customs and usages, consecrated amongst civilized communities from time immemorial."

Less broad and more technical than the body of law just referred to are the rules sometimes the subject of reference in international administrative agreements.[45] The basic objectives sought through such conventions are illustrated in the statement (on the Convention on Civil Aviation) that the Chicago Conference of 1944 produced "a complete modernization of the basic public

[40] See Chapter II, section 3, *infra*.

[41] The requirement that a party follow "the regular course of proceedings usual in such cases" would presumably mean at least nondiscriminatory treatment as compared with that accorded to nationals (or goods or vessels) of other states (8 *Stat.* 84, 162; article XVI of each treaty).

[42] Illustrated in the treaty of 1825 with the Central American Federation (8 *Stat.* 322).

[43] Treaty cited in note 38, *supra*.

[44] Miller, *Treaties*, V, 626.

[45] Illustrated in the Convention for the Protection of Submarine Cables, 1884, in the fifth article of which the parties agree that their ships when carrying cables shall conform to rules concerning signals (24 *Stat.* 989). On the history of the convention, and especially the American attitude, see Keith Clark, *International Communications* (1931), ch. III.

international law of the air." [46] The "principles" of such agreements are commonly accompanied by, or by provisions for the making of, more detailed rules. Thus the multilateral agreement concerning safety of life at sea, signed May 31, 1929, referred in the preamble to the establishment of uniform principles and rules, and there were specific provisions for the formulation, in concerted action, of regulations.[47] An indirect reference to international law is illustrated in the 1937 multilateral convention on Inter-American Radio Communication, which mentions the "sovereign right of all nations to the use of every radio broadcasting channel." [48] National courts take cognizance of the evolution of rules that may be applicable in litigation growing out of such incidents as collisions at sea,[49] while pronouncements by international tribunals may, of course, furnish incentive and guidance for the projection of new international regulations.[50] Finally, within the framework of the broad principles in a multilateral convention, there may be provisions looking to adaptations to the needs of particular regions or of particular groups.[51]

4. CLASSIFICATION OF TREATY REFERENCES BY SUBJECT MATTER

Grouped according to their substantive content, treaty provisions specifically mentioning the "law of nations" or "international law" (or seeming by clear implication to refer to this standard)

[46] *Proceedings of the International Civil Aviation Conference, Chicago, November 1–December 7, 1944,* Department of State Publication 2820, I (1948), 3.

[47] 50 *Stat.* (2) 1122.

[48] 53 *Stat.* (3) 1593, 1596 (art. 11, par. 1). Reservation of rights under preëxisting general law may, of course, be accomplished through reservations. Cf. a provision in an agreement between the United States and Canada in 1939, whereby the "rights" enjoyed by the national defense services of either party state were not to be lessened (53 *Stat.* [3] 2157).

[49] Illustrated in the *Scotia,* 14 Wall. 170 (1871).

[50] See, in this connection, Philip C. Jessup, "The Growth of the Law," *Amer. Jour. Int. Law,* XXIX (1935), 495–499, on developments following the *Lotus* case decision.

[51] For example, the international radio conference at Washington in 1927 sought to provide in the convention the "fundamental" law, with the expectation that separate agreements would be made for special purposes, specific regions, or particular groups of states (Clark, *International Communications,* p. 208).

fall into eight categories. The first of these, which includes approximately one third of the total, concerns the peaceful settlement of international disputes or the settlement of claims. The parties commonly make mention of the law as a standard for the guidance of tribunals, as the field of law in which arbitrators must be competent, or, more frequently, as that in accordance with which differences are to be settled. In some instances the law is not the only standard specified, and sometimes agreements record acceptance of a liability wider than that which international law imposes.[52] Arbitration being regarded, especially by Anglo-American jurists, as a judicial process, and not one for "splitting the difference," it is natural to find in treaties on this subject emphasis upon the law as a factor.

Approximately one fifth of the treaty references to the law of nations occur in extradition agreements which include, in the list of extraditable crimes, piracy as defined by that law. As is well known, the subject of piracy has received considerable attention in the literature on public international law. One of the still controversial questions is that of whether piracy is an international law crime or whether that law simply allows jurisdiction to be exercised by a state, on the "universality" principle, regarding persons or ships that would not otherwise be properly the objects of jurisdiction by the state. The latter alternative would leave to the national lawmakers the function of making the described conduct a crime. In 1820 Justice Joseph Story, with Chief Justice John Marshall concurring, concluded that piracy depended for its definition and punishment "not upon the particular provisions of any municipal code, but upon the law of nations." He added that "its true definition by that law is robbery upon the sea." [53] There was to be strong support for this

[52] See Chapter II, section 3, *infra*. For an instance of treaty interpretation which sought to avoid a narrowing of "the general right now supposed to have pre-existed under the law of nations," see 1 *Op. Atty. Gen.* 520. The particular provision involved was in article 28 of the Jay Treaty (8 *Stat.* 116, 129).

[53] 5 Wheat. 153. See also Benjamin M. Ziegler, *The International Law of John Marshall* (1939), ch. X. For a summary of the holdings by the same court, see James J. Lenoir, "Piracy Cases in the Supreme Court," *Amer. Jour. of Crim. Law and Criminology*, XXV (1934–35), 532–553.

position in subsequent writing of jurists.[54] However, differences of opinion about which law (national or international) makes piracy a crime has apparently not caused serious impediments to the operation of extradition treaties.[55] The United States has, on occasion, refused to accept a too-inclusive definition of the offense. It has, for example, withheld approval of the designation by other states of insurgent vessels as piratical, insisting, rather, that the character of the vessels and the actions of those operating them should determine whether their character was piratical under the law of nations.[56] It would appear that the customary mention of piracy as defined either by municipal law or by the law of nations would be the most inclusive manner in which this particular crime could be covered in an extradition treaty.[57] In the treaty practice of the United States there have, however, been exceptions to the rule of mentioning the law of nations in connection with the definition of piracy,[58] and the record of negotiations in such instances does not suggest that the parties considered the omission as seriously limiting the coverage of the treaties.[59]

[54] J. B. Moore, *A Digest of International Law* (1906), II, 951; Judge Moore's statement in his dissenting opinion in the *Lotus* case (P.C.I.J., series A, no. 10, at pp. 70, 71). Cf. Gilbert Gidel, *Le Droit international public de la mer*, I (1932), 307.

[55] By the law of the United States there may be imprisonment for life of one convicted of committing on the high seas piracy as defined by the law of nations, if such person is later brought into or found in the national territory (18 U.S.C., sec. 481). An earlier law (1819) had provided for the death penalty. See 14 *Op. Atty. Gen.* 286. That piracy is not an international law crime is the principle accepted in the Harvard Research Draft Convention on Piracy (*Amer. Jour. Int. Law*, XXVI [1932], Supp., 759–760).

[56] *For. Rel.*, 1884, p. 297, and 1885, p. 920. The foreign states concerned were Haiti, Colombia, and Venezuela, respectively.

[57] See Harvard Research Draft Convention and Comment on Jurisdiction with Respect to Crime, *Amer. Jour. Int. Law*, XXIX (1935), Supp. 445.

[58] Some of the older commercial treaties which contained clauses concerning extradition did not include "piracy as defined by the law of nations." This wording is not included in the treaty with Switzerland, signed May 14, 1900, or in that with Turkey, signed August 8, 1923 (49 *Stat.* [2] 2692, 2694).

[59] This applies to negotiation of the treaty with Switzerland signed March 14, 1900. Wording with regard to "piracy as defined by the law of nations"

About one seventh of the specific mentions of the international law standard are in provisions relating to war and neutrality. They occur in connection with such different things as treatment of prisoners of war, reprisals, contraband, and prize law. In their treaties of the eighteenth century the United States and Prussia provided that rules concerning prisoners of war were to be as sacredly observed as the "most acknowledged" articles in the "law of nature or nations." [60] The treaty of Guadalupe Hidalgo, 1848, provided that persons who had been paroled, and also escaped prisoners of war, were to be dealt with according to the laws of war.[61] With various Latin American states the United States contracted not to resort to war or to reprisals for treaty violations unless justice and satisfaction were denied "in violation of the laws and of national right." [62] There are a number of mentions of international law in the Hague Conventions of 1899 and 1907, perhaps the most frequently referred to being that in

---

was not in the draft treaty as proposed by Switzerland and seems not to have been suggested, at least in writing, by the United States (MS., U.S. Department of State, Switzerland, Notes, vol. IV [July 1, 1893, to September 31, 1897], February 6, 1896; Notes to Switzerland, vol. I, notes of January 18, 1898, and April 18, 1899; Notes, Switzerland, vol. V [January 1, 1898, to July 31, 1901], March 12, 1899, and August 1, 1899). In the discussion with Turkey in 1923 concerning an extradition treaty, after the Turkish government had proposed that the language on the point in question should follow that of the Swiss-American convention already referred to, the Department of State indicated the desirability, "for the sake of uniformity," of following generally the phraseology of the convention with Paraguay, signed March 26, 1913 (which did mention the law of nations), but assented to a draft without this particular wording (Department of State files 211.67/2, 211.67/3, 211.67/4 [National Archives]).

[60] Article XXIV of each treaty (cited in note 41, *supra*). The 1799 treaty refers to the "law of nature and nations."

[61] 9 *Stat.* 922. Somewhat comparable are provisions in the Red Cross Convention of July 27, 1929 (47 *Stat.* 2074). Article II provides that combatants falling into the hands of the enemy are prisoners of war and subject to international law. Article XVII, paragraph 6, provides that the requisitioned means of transportation shall be subject to international law. As to clauses in the convention on prisoners of war, see Chapter V, section 1, *infra*.

[62] See, for example, article 37, paragraph 3, of the 1870 treaty with El Salvador (18 *Stat.* [3] 725). The Spanish text (which is also authentic) reads, "con violación de las leyes y del derecho internacional." A similar provision is in an earlier treaty with the same state (10 *Stat.* 891) and in the 1846 commercial treaty with New Granada (9 *Stat.* 881).

the preamble of Hague Convention IV of 1907.[63] Contraband of war was often listed in early treaties; without listing, the Havana Convention on Neutrality in Maritime War, 1928, referred to search of a ship for the purpose of ascertaining whether its cargo might be "prohibited by international law." [64] In peace treaties made with some of her former enemies in the Second World War, the United States secured the right to examine prize court decisions or orders of those states involving ownership rights of American nationals, and to recommend that revision be undertaken of such decisions or orders as might not be in conformity with international law.[65]

A fourth category of provisions comprise those whereby the parties agree that international law shall be the standard of treatment to be accorded by each party, in its territory, to (1) the public agents or (2) the nationals, of the other party. As to the first, treaty practice has been marked by a rather careful distinction between diplomatic agents and consular officers. On the treatment to be accorded to diplomatic agents, there is a body of law which is well known. When, nearly a century ago, an American negotiator was asked by Japanese officials the question, "What kind of thing is the law of nations?" his reply was largely in terms of diplomatic privileges and immunities.[66] A Soviet ambassador seventy-seven years later suggested that an ambassador was to some extent a proof of the existence of international law.[67] The method of incorporating by reference in

[63] In the revised Geneva Convention Relative to the Treatment of Prisoners of War, August 12, 1949, comparable language appears, not in the preamble, but in article 142, which relates to denunciation of the Convention. By the final paragraph of this article, denunciation "shall in no way impair the obligations which the Parties . . . shall remain bound to fulfil by virtue of the principles of the law of nations, as they result from the usages established among civilized peoples, from the laws of humanity and the dictates of the public conscience" (Department of State publication 3938, General Foreign Policy Series 34 [1950], p. 138). A similar provision is in each of the other three basic instruments signed at the same conference.

[64] 47 *Stat.* (2) 1989. See Chapter V, section 3a, *infra*.

[65] See Annex XVII of the Treaty with Italy, 61 *Stat.* 1369; Annex VI of the Treaty with Roumania, 61 *ibid.* 1799.

[66] Miller, *Treaties*, VII, 1095.

[67] *Proc. Amer. Soc. Int. Law*, 1934, at p. 195 (remarks of Ambassador Troyanovsky).

treaties the body of law applicable to diplomatic privileges and immunities has been used by the United States particularly in its relations with states in the Far East, the Middle East, and the Near East.[68] In the period when extraterritoriality existed in many countries, this may have been due in part to the desirability of including, as nearly as possible, all rules in effect between the parties in written undertakings, and in part to the idea that, international law having existed primarily between states of Christendom, it was sometimes needful to make clear that a wider application was intended.[69] With the passing of extraterritoriality, or, in other instances, the recognition of new statehood, written agreements could emphasize the new, mutual rights and duties under the law.[70] That usage, rather than law, was some-

[68] In 1854 a Chinese officer observed, in regard to certain negotiations with representatives of the Western state, that, "in the conduct of questions arising out of intercourse with foreign nations, the authorities of China rested entirely on the treaty. Things beyond the treaty they ignored, nor would they undertake the responsibility [attaching to them]" (English translation in Sen. Ex. Doc. 30, 36th Cong., 1st Sess., p. 460).

[69] See the statement of an American minister, as quoted by the Attorney General in 1855: "The states of Christendom are bound together by treaties, which confer mutual rights and prescribe reciprocal obligations. They acknowledge the authority of certain maxims and usages, received among them by common consent, and called the law of nations; but which, not being fully acknowledged and observed by the Mohammedan or Pagan states . . . is, in fact, only the international law of Christendom" (7 *Op. Atty. Gen.* 497–499).

As early as 1858, in negotiations with the Japanese leading to the treaty of July 29, 1858/March 19, 1859 (12 *Stat.* 1051), an American representative (Townsend Harris) argued from rights under the general law of nations. When the Japanese objected to his proposal that consuls, as well as the American minister and consul general, be given reception at all ports that were to be opened by the treaty, Harris answered that what he asked "was simply the right, which was enjoyed, by all Consuls, under the laws of Nations," and that "to insert a clause limiting them, to the bounds of their respective Consular Districts, would be an abandonment of . . . their undoubted rights." When references to consuls were left out of the treaty, Harris sought to emphasize that this was not an abandonment of a right. To the Japanese he said that, since the visit of Perry, they had "gradually been adopting foreign ways" and that there was no reason why they should not concede the point at issue (Miller, *Treaties,* VII, 1069, 1095, 1139, 1161, 1162).

[70] Illustrated in executive agreements with Persia, 1928 (U.S. Executive Agreement Series no. 19), with Saudi Arabia, 1933 (*ibid.,* no. 53), and Afghanistan, 1936 (*ibid.,* no. 88), the Agreement of Friendship and Commerce with Yemen, 1946 (Treaties and Other International Acts Series

times specified, even regarding diplomatic agents, is illustrated in the Sino-American commercial treaty of 1903.[71]

In the case of consular officers, while there are some exceptional instances in which privileges and immunities under international law are referred to, it has been a more common practice to rely upon most-favored-nation clauses or provisions requiring conformity to established *usage*.[72] That this would not rule out the law applicable is suggested by an opinion on the consular convention with France, signed February 23, 1853, by which consuls were to receive the privileges "usually accorded" to their offices.[73] Of this, Attorney General Caleb Cushing wrote

---

[hereafter T.I.A.S.], 1535), the Treaty of General Relations with The Philippines, 1946 (*ibid.*, 1568), the Agreement of Friendship and Commerce with Nepal, 1947 (*ibid.*, 1585), and in the Treaty of Friendship, Commerce and Navigation with China, 1946 (*ibid.*, 1871).

[71] 33 *Stat.* 2208. It appears, from the record of negotiations, that neither international law nor international usage was referred to in the first article of the draft originally presented by the United States. The Chinese desired revision of this draft so as to make the right of diplomatic representation reciprocal, and, when the Americans agreed, this desire seems to have led to the insertion of "international custom" in the first sentence. The Chinese also wished to withhold the right, which the Americans had requested, for United States diplomatic agents to communicate with the governors-general and lieutenant-governors, provincial governors, imperial residents, and military governors of dependencies of the Chinese Empire. In that connection it was proposed to make reference to "international law" in the second paragraph, and the treaty was initialed with this phrase included. As the treaty was finally signed, the wording was changed so that the reference in each of the two places, perhaps for the purpose of avoiding the use of two different standards, was made to read "international usage." Department of State files, T[reaty] C[ommissioners] no. 61 (to Conger, April 24, 1903, Legation Archives, Peking, Inventory 524), no. 62 (Minutes of Treaty Meeting April 17, 1903, Miscellaneous Letters to April, 1903, pt. II), no. 66 (Minutes of Treaty Meeting of April 29, 1903, Miscellaneous Letters cited, pt. I), and no. 87 (also T. C. to Conger, September 29, 1903, in Legation Archives, Peking, Inventory 524).

[72] A recent illustration is in article I, paragraph 2, of the consular convention which the United States signed with Costa Rica on January 12, 1948, which provides for most-favored-nation treatment (T.I.A.S. 2045). See also the consular convention signed with the Philippines, March 14, 1947, art. XIV (T.I.A.S. 1741).

[73] 10 *Stat.* 992. See also article VI of the treaty for relinquishment of extraterritorial rights in China (cited in note 79, *infra*), which provided for consular privileges and the exercise of consular functions in accordance with "modern international usage."

that "by the Consular Convention, and *by the law of nations without it,* the consul represented . . . his country," and "each nation does *by the general rule of public law* . . . concede to the consuls of the other a certain authority of discipline." [74]

As to ordinary nationals of one state in the territory of another, mentions of the international law standard have occurred especially in establishment clauses, and particularly those relating to the protection of persons and property, in commercial treaties. Beginning with the treaty of friendship, commerce, and consular rights signed with Germany on December 8, 1923, and extending through the treaty of friendship, commerce, and navigation signed with Ireland on January 21, 1950, sixteen out of the seventeen general commercial treaties which the United States signed (counting as a separate instrument from the Polish treaty the one concluded for Danzig) contained provisions whereby the nationals of each party were to enjoy, within the territory of the other, for their persons and property, the degree of protection required by international law.[75] There is some variation in the phraseology,[76] which ordinarily is in a context relating to "the most constant protection and security" and to compensation

[74] 8 *Op. Atty. Gen.* 76, 83 (italics inserted).

[75] The treaties include those with the following states, the date shown in each case being that of signature: Germany, 1923 (44 *Stat.* [3] 2132); Hungary, 1925 (44 *ibid.* [3] 2441); Estonia, 1925 (44 *ibid.* [3] 2379); El Salvador, 1926 (46 *ibid.* [2] 2817); Honduras, 1927 (45 *ibid.* [2] 2618); Latvia, 1928 (45 *ibid.* [2] 2641); Norway, 1928 (47 *ibid.* [2] 2135); Austria, 1928 (47 *ibid.* [2] 1876); Poland, 1931 (48 *ibid.* [2] 1507); Danzig, 1934 (48 *ibid.* [2] 1680); Finland, 1934 (49 *ibid.* [2] 2659); Siam, 1937 (53 *ibid.* [3] 1731); Liberia, 1938 (54 *ibid.* [2] 1739); China, 1946 (T.I.A.S. 1871); Italy, 1948 (*ibid.* 1965); Ireland, 1950 (*ibid.* 2155). The commercial treaty which does not refer to international law is that with Uruguay, signed in 1949 (Sen. Ex. Doc. D, 81st Cong., 2d Sess.). See Chapter III, section 1b, *infra.*

The preambular reference to international law in the treaty of establishment between the United States and Turkey, signed October 28, 1931, and references to "rights accruing by treaty or otherwise," as in the commercial treaty with Finland, cited above, may be noted. (On the former, see Chapter III, section 1a, *infra*).

[76] In the first thirteen of the treaties referred to in the preceding note, companies are not mentioned, in the parts of the treaties referred to, separately from nationals. In the last three, companies are covered by specific language, without leaving their inclusion to be implied.

for property that is expropriated. The manner in which the international law standard in such clauses is related to others, such as that of national treatment, is to be discussed later.[77]

Recent treaties providing for the termination of extraterritorial privileges have contained, sometimes with specific reference to the treatment of foreigners, various provisions as to international law. Thus the Montreux Convention of May 8, 1937, states in the preamble the purpose of establishing, between Egypt and the other states concerned, relations which shall be based on "ordinary international law." By the second article, foreigners resident in Egypt are to come under Egyptian legislation, subject to international law.[78] The treaty of January 11, 1943, in which the United States relinquished extraterritorial rights in China, provides in the first article that American nationals in China are to be subject to Chinese jurisdiction "in accordance with the principles of international law and practice." The seventh article records the parties' agreement to negotiate a modern commercial treaty "based upon the principles of international law and practice as reflected in modern international procedures." Pending the conclusion of such a treaty, questions coming up were (in accordance with this article and the notes exchanged) to be decided "in accordance with generally accepted principles of international law and with modern international practice."[79]

In a fifth category fall clauses making mention of the international law standard in relation to maritime and fluvial frontiers, and navigation rights. In one instance the occasion is application of the law to a change of an international boundary, in another the application of the principle of free navigation of international waterways; in still others, the law is referred to in connection with the parties' agreement on the three-mile limit as marking

[77] Chapter III, section 1, *infra.*

[78] 53 *Stat.* (3) 1647, 1653. The text of the treaty recorded the understanding that legislation applicable to foreigners in Egypt would "not be inconsistent with the principles generally adopted in modern legislation." In an accompanying declaration, Egypt disclaimed any intention to discriminate against foreigners after the time limit set for termination of extraterritorial rights. See, in this connection, J. Y. Brinton, "Egypt: The Transition Period," *Amer. Jour. Int. Law,* XXXIV (1940), 217–218.

[79] 57 *Stat.* (2) 767.

the proper (in the sense of legally established) extent of territorial waters.[80]

Another category of treaty references includes those found in certain multilateral conventions between states in the Western Hemisphere. As is well known, the Convention of August 23, 1906, for the establishment of an inter-American law commission,[81] has led to the formulation of drafts on various subjects. More particularly, there have been some direct references to international law in such instruments as the Convention on Rights and Duties of States, 1933,[82] the declaration concerning intervention in the Buenos Aires Convention of 1936,[83] the General Treaty of Inter-American Arbitration, 1929,[84] the Anti-War Treaty of October 10, 1933, [85] and the Bogotá Charter of the Organization of American States, 1948.[86]

The smallest group of treaty references includes two from treaties of the late eighteenth century and two from those of the nineteenth.[87] They have to do with the binding force of international agreements under conditions of hostilities, and prescribe simply that, in time of war, the sanctity of designated treaty articles shall be measured by observance of international law.

In a miscellaneous category may be placed various other references to the standard, such as one recognizing that inter-

[80] See Chapter III, section 2, and Chapter IV, section 2, *infra.*

[81] 37 *Stat.* (2) 1554.

[82] 49 *Stat.* (2) 3097.

[83] 51 *Stat.* 41. See Chapter IV, section 1b, *infra.*

[84] 49 *Stat.* (2) 3153.

[85] 49 *Stat.* (2) 3363.

[86] See articles 5(a), 6, 7, 9, 10, 67, and 71. In the Final Act of the Conference, the text of the Charter is referred to as containing "all the doctrines, principles, purposes, practices and accomplishments that have governed the peaceful relations of the peoples of America, and that constitute an advanced form of international law which the continent has contributed to the progress of the juridical and political culture of the world" (section I). Other references to international law are in sections XXXII and XXXV of the Final Act, and in article XXXI(b) of the Pact of Bogotá (as also in reservations to the Pact by the United States and Nicaragua, respectively).

[87] Treaties of 1785 and 1799 with Prussia (cited in note 41, *supra*), article XXIV in each case; treaty of Guadalupe Hidalgo (cited in note 61, *supra*), article XXII, paragraph 3; 1871 commercial treaty with Italy, 17 *Stat.* 845, article XXI, paragraph 2.

national law fixes domestic jurisdiction,[88] another in which the United States agreed to conform to international law in its action with respect to Cuba,[89] and a treaty assurance to the United States that Dominican courts would determine rights according to international law.[90] A provision which became the subject of a considerable discussion was that in the Gadsden Treaty whereby the United States sought the right to protect rights of certain of its nationals when it should feel "sanctioned and warranted by the public or international law."[91] There are, finally, the United Nations Charter, with its preambular reference to sources of international law, in addition to its mentions of the law in connection with peaceful means of settling or adjusting international disputes or situations which might lead to a breach of the peace, and the various references to the law in the Statute of the International Court of Justice.

5. SPECIAL ASPECTS OF UNITED STATES PRACTICE

In the foregoing sections sufficient examples have been noted to indicate that the international law standard has been specified in treaties which related to a wide variety of subjects. Of course, other states besides the United States have in their treaties referred to the international standard.[92] Possible justification for singling out this country for special consideration lies in (1) the environmental and human factors in the country's development, (2) the relatively strong emphasis upon legality in its constitutional system, and (3) its steadily increasing material power and consequently increasing responsibility. If the distinctive qualities observable in the role of the United States with respect to inter-

[88] Declaration accompanying the treaty relating to insular possessions in the Pacific, December 13, 1921 (43 *Stat.* [2] 1646), and reservation of the United States to the treaty.

[89] Treaty of Peace with Spain, December 10, 1898 (30 *Stat.* 1754), article I, paragraph 2.

[90] Instrument recording ratification of the plan of evacuation, signed June 12, 1924 (44 *Stat.* 2193, at 2209).

[91] See Chapter IV, section 1a, *infra*.

[92] See, for a comparative view of certain of these, Appendix II.

national law can be ascribed at least in part to its geographic situation and to the ethnic composition of its population,[93] it may also be possible to show that, believing strongly in the rule of law in their domestic affairs, its policy makers have not unnaturally thought internationally in terms of legality and not merely of power. If, in the past, particularly by reason of its fortunate situation, its advocacy of particular principles or rules has been in large measure a matter of conscious choice rather than compulsion, the positions which it has taken in regard to the standard which is international law would seem to merit some special attention. The significance of anything the United States may do by way of applying or emphasizing the law presumably increases with its growing responsibilities.

A mere classification of treaty references to the law, without a more detailed examination of illustrative situations which provided occasion for some of these references, would be of small value. The essential purposes and the legal effects of certain references will be the object of inquiry in following chapters. In some instances it will be desirable to consider how definite a body of law there was in existence at the given times, and in other instances to try to see what the substantive rules on particular matters actually were. The illustrative situations have been grouped under headings corresponding to commonly followed broad classifications.

[93] As suggested by G. G. Wilson, "The United States and International Law," *Proc. Amer. Soc. Int. Law*, 1936, pp. 14, 16.

Chapter II

PACIFIC SETTLEMENT

Mentions of international law are to be expected in undertakings for the keeping of the peace and for resort to peaceful processes for settling disputes. Such undertakings may record the duty of abstaining from the use of unlawful, or the permissibility or duty of using lawful, means. In the absence of an international legislature, indications of what these means are must come from other sources. Mere treaty statement of them is not to be considered apart from other evidences (since tribunals, foreign offices, and international conferences have important roles), but such statement serves a useful purpose. Treaty makers have sometimes made very general reference to international law and to what it authorizes or permits. Or, they may indicate what shall *not* be considered unfriendly acts—as in connection with the use of good offices under the Hague Convention for Pacific Settlement of International Disputes. The first of these methods of referring to the law is illustrated in a number of treaties to which the United States has become a party.

Outside the scope of the present inquiry are treaty clauses which declare merely that there shall be peace between the parties, a form of statement which American treaty makers have frequently employed.[1] General references to international law and to the peaceful processes which are consonant with it occur in bilateral and in multilateral agreements for the employment of specific procedures in the settlement of disputes. They take the form of (1) broad declarations committing the parties to employ

[1] An example is in the first article of the convention of September 30, 1800, with France: "There shall be a firm, inviolable, and universal peace, and a true and sincere Friendship between the French Republic, and the United States of America, and between their respective countries, territories, cities, towns, and people without exception of persons or places" (Miller, *Treaties*, II, 458).

the means which the law permits, (2) clauses indicating what questions are to be considered as proper for adjudication, (3) prescriptions of bases for awards, and (4) special provisions, in claims conventions, concerning the law as to exhaustion of local remedies.[2]

1. GENERAL COMMITMENTS TO USE LEGAL MEANS

Formal declarations that party states will abide peacefully by the rules of established law, as a matter of public policy and legal obligation, do not necessarily go very far. They may be in such vague and nebulous phrases that there is no very perceptible inroad upon the system which has traditionally permitted war as a "lawful" procedure. The preamble of Hague Convention I of 1907, for example, mentioned respect for the empire of law, appreciation of international justice, and the principles of right,[3] but from the same conference emanated conventions which recognized, at least by implication, that by declaring war states might acquire rights against other states (even rights against those states not participating in the war). The implied acknowledgment of the legality of war as an instrument of policy led to the criticism that much of the work of the Hague Peace Conferences was a labor of futility.[4]

[2] Omitted from classification here, because of their minor importance, are provisions referring to the law as a field of knowledge in which members of commissions should be proficient. That, particularly among Continental European jurists, arbitration has sometimes been regarded as something besides a strictly judicial procedure, is well known. See, for example, the remarks of Umpire Gutierrez of the Spanish-Venezuelan Commission in the *Padrón* case (Jackson H. Ralston, *Venezuelan Arbitrations of 1903*, Sen. Doc. 316, 68th Congress, 2d Sess. [hereafter cited as Ralston's *Report*], at pp. 927, 930). The theory of a "tribunal of conscience," as there outlined, would not seem to be consistent with the prevailing Anglo-American conception of arbitration. Cf. *American-British Claims Arbitration . . . Report of Fred K. Nielsen*, 1926 (hereafter cited as Nielsen's *Report*), p. 54. See also the statement that some opinions of international tribunals reveal, in the author's opinion, a lack of comprehension of the nature of international law and of the method of ascertaining the existence of rules, in Fred K. Nielsen, *International Law Applied to Reclamations* (1933), p. 7.

[3] 36 *Stat.* 2199. For the view that clauses in a preamble may create legally binding obligations, see Paul You, *Le Préamble des traités internationaux* (1941).

[4] See, for example, Salvador de Madariaga, *The World's Design* (1938), p. 116.

With the initiation of the movement for the renunciation of war as an instrument of national policy, there began to be more committal pronouncements in treaties. The Pact of Paris (1928), by its second article committing the parties not to seek the settlement of disputes except by pacific means, perhaps marks the most spectacular and universal effort in this general direction.[5]

Although there is no specific reference in the Pact to international law, its interpretation in relation to that standard was to have far-reaching importance. Secretary of State Frank B. Kellogg thought that it was desirable to make the Pact brief and direct. To the French ambassador, on February 27, 1928, he wrote: "If . . . such a declaration were accompanied by definitions of the word 'aggressor' and by exceptions and qualifications stipulating when nations would be justified in going to war, its effect would be very greatly weakened and its positive value as a guaranty of peace virtually destroyed. The ideal which inspires the effort . . . is arresting and appealing just because of its purity and simplicity."[6]

In the course of the conversations with the United States out of which the Pact finally came, the French government emphasized that the treaty must not come into effect until accepted by all or substantially all of the powers of the world. On this point the American Secretary of State said, in a telegram to the American ambassador in Paris on April 23, 1928, that, while it had from the beginning been the hope of the United States that the instrument should be world-wide in its application, it was clearly preferable "not to postpone the coming into force . . . until all the nations of the world can agree upon the text of such a treaty and cause it to be ratified." The United States, he said, was "not willing to jeopardize the practical success of the proposal . . . by conditioning the coming into force of the treaty upon prior universal or almost universal acceptance."[7] In

[5] See, generally, David Hunter Miller, *The Peace Pact of Paris* (1928); James T. Shotwell, *War as an Instrument of National Policy and Its Renunciation in the Pact of Paris* (1929); John E. Stoner, *S. O. Levinson and the Pact of Paris* (1943).

[6] *For. Rel.*, 1928, I, 10.

[7] *Ibid.*, p. 38.

a telegram to the American ambassador in London on May 9, Kellogg emphasized that, while each government was consulting its legal advisers, the main question was not "juridical" but "political." [8] He thought that a conference of jurists was unnecessary and undesirable, and that, as he expressed it in a telegram to London three days later, a commission of jurists, "if they got together, would spend their time trying to find out some reason why it could not be done." [9] In a conversation with the Japanese chargé on June 12, 1928, the American Under Secretary of State indicated that, in their consideration of the treaty, American representatives "would not be disposed to listen very much to jurists. This was not that kind of treaty." [10] Nearly a month later the Secretary of State expressed the hope that "legalistic efforts to justify in advance the violation of the proposed renunciation of war treaty" would not be permitted to "obscure the issue or delay the conclusion" of this treaty.[11] The selection of the original signatories caused some difficulty, but the chief advocate made it clear that the plan was to submit the Pact, after signature, to every country and extend an invitation to each one to become a party.[12] Thus the Secretary of State said, in a telegram to the American ambassador in Argentina, on October 25, 1928:

> I believed that if a treaty could be entered into between the principal Powers of Europe which was simple and did not involve any complicated system of sanctions or agreement to punish violators, that it would be readily accepted as a principle of international law by all the world.[13]

At the time of the visit of the British Prime Minister in the following year it was reported to have been officially agreed that the Pact marked a "new starting point for international negotiations for the preservation of peace," [14] and in 1930 the Acting Secretary of State referred to "our assumption" that the Kellogg Pact "marked a new era in international relations." [15] Two years later Secretary of State Henry L. Stimson spoke of

[8] *Ibid.*, p. 58.
[9] *Ibid.*, p. 63.
[10] *Ibid.*, p. 85.
[11] *Ibid.*, p. 103.
[12] *Ibid.*, p. 99.
[13] *Ibid.*, pp. 223–224.
[14] *Ibid.*, 1929, III, 5.
[15] *Ibid.*, 1930, I, 40.

his "efforts to make it a real and effective treaty instead of a mere concurrent expression of a pious intention."[16] The effort had been to "transpose into international law" the proposition inherent in the Pact, which, it was suggested, would mean that no nation could continue to benefit from belligerent rights or those of neutrals, and that recognition would be denied to what had been obtained in violation of the Pact.[17]

Of the many interpretive statements which the treaty elicited, perhaps the most cynical was the suggestion that the whole undertaking had had the effect of "outlawing" only *declared* wars. There seems to have been a widely held opinion during the first decade after its signature that, while the treaty might have considerable moral force, its legal force was very limited because of the absence of any indication of what the parties to it were obliged to do by way of enforcement.[18] As is well known, there were in this decade relatively frequent proposals of plans for "implementing" the Pact. Among the most widely publicized unofficial statements were the Budapest Articles of Interpretation (1934), approved by the International Law Association.[19] However, down to the beginning of the Second World War, there continued to be much skepticism about the legal value of the formal renunciation of war. In the later period of the gradual formation of a front against states which had flouted the principle of the treaty, this view appears to have yielded to the idea that there was an important legal quality in the instrument. Thus, long before the Nuremberg trials applied the idea, and even before the United States became a belligerent in the war, Justice Robert H. Jackson of the United

[16] *Ibid.*, 1932, I, 250.

[17] *Ibid.*, p. 360.

[18] Prolonged discussions in regard to the legal force and effect of reservations, such as that concerning the so-called British Monroe Doctrine and that concerning self-defense, marked the early history of the Pact. See, for example, the Report of the Senate Foreign Relations Committee on some of the legal points, in 70 *Cong. Rec.* 1730 (January 15, 1929). Particularly after 1929 there arose the question of the extent to which a nation signatory to the Pact would be justified, if it were not itself the immediate victim of aggression, in taking against the aggressor measures which, except for the Pact, would not be legal.

[19] See Chapter V, section 3a, *infra*.

States Supreme Court, in an address before the American Bar Association, said, concerning the Pact:

> This treaty . . . was not wholly sterile despite the absence of an express legal *duty* of enforcement. It had legal consequences more substantial than its political ones. It created substantive law of national conduct for its signatories and there resulted a *right* to enforce it by the general sanctions of international law.[20]

It would be difficult to show the extent to which such ideas had permeated legal thinking before the conclusion of hostilities in the Second World War. It remained for the spokesman for the United States at the International Conference on Military Trials, held in London in the summer of 1945, to take the position that unless the Pact had altered the status of wars of aggression it had no meaning at all and came close to being an act of deception. The agreement was regarded as "one in a series of acts which have reversed the viewpoint that all war is legal and have brought International Law into harmony with the common sense of mankind, that unjustifiable war is a crime." In the course of the conference sessions, Mr. Jackson observed: "If we go back to the pre-Briand-Kellogg pact days, there is no doubt that for a period of international law all war-making was legal . . . [The Kellogg-Briand] treaty and the acts which followed it did something to the law of war, and that change is what we stand on."[21] The American position thus came to be that of charging aggression, and of bringing the Nazi leaders to trial because of their illegal acts, while others, such as the French, just wished "to show that the Nazis were bandits."[22] "Crimes against peace" were distinguished in article 6(a) of the Nuremberg charter.

The tribunal at Nuremberg, while not relying solely upon the Pact of Paris to answer the defense argument that by the time

[20] *Amer. Bar Assn. Jour.*, XXVII (1941), 690–693, at p. 691. With this may be contrasted E. M. Borchard's opinion in the same year that "the Kellogg Pact has no legal force whatever" (*Amer. Jour. Int. Law*, XXXV [1941], 622).

[21] *Report of Robert H. Jackson, United States Representative to the International Conference on Military Trials, London, 1945* (1949), Department of State Publication 3080, pp. 52, 337.

[22] *Ibid.*, pp. 381–382.

of World War II the making of aggressive war was not an international crime, held that its charter was expressive of international law which existed at the time the charter was concluded, and went on to say of the principal instrument relied upon:

> The nations who signed the Pact or adhered to it unconditionally condemned recourse to war for the future as an instrument of policy, and expressly renounced it. After the signing of the Pact, any nation resorting to war as an instrument of national policy breaks the Pact. In the opinion of the Tribunal, the solemn renunciation of war as an instrument of national policy necessarily involves the proposition that such a war is illegal in international law; and that those who plan and wage such a war, with its inevitable and terrible consequences, are committing a crime in so doing. War for the solution of international controversies undertaken as an instrument of national policy certainly includes a war of aggression, and such a war is therefore outlawed by the Pact.[23]

It has already been seen that there were other multilateral agreements which the United States signed and which did make reference in terms to what was established as "law" and as lawful means. The General Treaty of Inter-American Arbitration, January 5, 1929, contains a preambular statement of the purpose to "strengthen the permanent reign" of law.[24] The Argentine Anti-War Treaty of October 10, 1933, commits the parties to the settlement of disputes by the pacific means having the sanction of international law, and refers separately to the political, juridical, or economic means which that law authorizes.[25] References to international law in the Montevideo Convention

[23] *Trial of the Major War Criminals before the International Military Tribunal, Nuremberg, 14 November 1945–1 October 1946*, I (1947), 220. See also Chapter V, section 3b, *infra*.

[24] 49 *Stat.* 3153.

[25] 49 *Stat.* 3363. The last-mentioned reference to the general law (in article III) specified that in the event any party state does not comply with the treaty, the other parties are to use the means described. Among the other mentions of the general law in the treaty are the reference in article VII to tribunals or supreme courts of justice competent to interpret the law, and that in article X, paragraph 3, to the non-finality of considerations or conclusions concerning the law as these might appear in conciliators' reports. When adhering, the United States stated in a reservation that it did not waive any rights under international law (49 *Stat.* 3374).

on Rights and Duties of States will be the subject of later discussion.[26] Desire for clarification of legal obligations which the United States and other American republics had assumed under various treaties led to the making of the Buenos Aires Convention to Coördinate, Extend, and Assure the Fulfillment of the Existing Treaties, signed December 23, 1936. The Anti-War Treaty of October 10, 1933, was integrated with the new instrument, and there was again formal reference to the means having the sanction of international law as those to be used exclusively by the contractants in relation with other parties to the treaty. There would not appear to have been a complete breaking away from traditional rules which might imply the legality of war and the duty of impartial treatment of belligerents by neutrals.[27] Reservations did not clarify the situation. Even if they had done so, their force and effect, so far as the United States was concerned, would have to be considered in the light of the accompanying declaration, which stated that reservations to the convention did not constitute amendments to the text, and that reservations, interpretations, and definitions by separate governments were for the benefit of the latter and not intended to be controlling on the United States.[28]

From the records of the conferences of Washington (1929), Montevideo (1933), and Buenos Aires (1936), it appears that there was an intention on the part of the delegates to do more than pay mere lip service to the "principles of international law" and to go farther than a mere formal endorsement of the means which that law permits. In connection with his list of eight "vitally important principles and proposals for a comprehensive peace program and peace structure," Secretary Hull said at the Buenos Aires Conference that international law "should be re-

[26] Chapter IV, section 1b, *infra*.

[27] The anticipation of neutrals' use of the sanctions of international law was not followed by any specification in the treaty of what those means were. Presumably they would never include force, in the first instance, or until a state should forfeit the benefits of the convention by itself using the means not sanctioned by the law.

By the terms of the Coördinating Convention, the 1936 agreement which proscribed intervention (discussed in Chapter IV, section 1b) was not to change collective treaties which were in force.

[28] Text in Chapter V, section 3a, *infra*.

established, revitalized and strengthened."[29] The cautiously phrased provisions of some of the conventions, and particularly the form of reservations by the United States, seemed to reflect a desire to conserve as much as possible of the stabilizing influence of traditional international law, while at the same time moving toward a system of greater security. A fundamental principle of that system would be the branding of aggressive war as illegal and the legalizing of at least permissive sanctions against it (on the part of states that were not the victims of aggression in the first instance). The transition was necessarily difficult and called forth some critical suggestion that the policy of the United States was essentially one of violating previously established international law.[30]

That the newer type of multilateral treaties have not had the effect of freezing the rules of the law of nations (particularly those of adjective law) as they existed at any one time, may be safely assumed. They have sought, rather, to promote the fundamental purposes of the law to which they made reference, and have identified those purposes with the ideal of peace.

The experience of the Second World War was followed by further formal expressions of American solidarity. The Final Act of the Chapultepec Conference on Problems of War and Peace, 1945, set forth that the peoples of the Americas were "sincerely devoted to the principles of international law" and listed principles which the American republics had been incorporating in their international law.[31] The Final Act of the Inter-American Conference for the Maintenance of Continental Peace and Security, held at Rio de Janeiro in 1947, reiterated "confidence

[29] *Department of State Press Releases,* vol. XV, no. 375, p. 432 (December 5, 1936). See also comment by George A. Finch, "Secretary of State Hull's Pillars of Enduring Peace," *Amer. Jour. Int. Law,* XXXI (1937), 688–693.

Before the Pan American Union on April 14, 1938, President Roosevelt characterized national and international law and morality not as the "restraints of weaklings" but as the "signs of serene strength" (Samuel I. Rosenman, ed., *The Public Papers and Addresses of Franklin D. Roosevelt,* 1938 vol. [1941], p. 220).

[30] Cf. E. M. Borchard, "War, Neutrality and Non-Belligerency," *Amer. Jour. Int. Law,* XXXV (1941), 618–625.

[31] 60 *Stat.* 1837.

in the principles of justice and international law" and referred to peace as "the realization of justice . . . guaranteed by law"; and in the first article of the Inter-American Treaty of Reciprocal Assistance, the parties condemned war and undertook in their international relations "not to resort to the threat or the use of force in any manner inconsistent with the provisions of the Charter of the United Nations or of this Treaty."[32] While the Pact of Bogotá, signed in 1948 and designed to replace eight prior multilateral agreements on pacific settlement, refers directly to international law only with respect to questions arising under that law, it does (subject to an article concerning the right of individual or collective self-defense as provided for in the Charter of the United Nations) bind the parties "to refrain from the threat or the use of force, or from any other means of coercion for the settlement of their controversies, and to have recourse at all times to pacific procedures."[33]

2. CRITERIA FOR DISTINGUISHING JURIDICAL QUESTIONS

The idea that some questions over which states have disputes are justiciable, and that others are not, fits in conveniently with the consent theory of international law. It is consistent with the notion of a body of rules which is relatively narrow in its range and with the conclusion that there are many questions that arise for which international law affords no solution because the states have never consented to extend the law to the subject matter involved. Certain economic relations of states have, for example, been thought to fall within this category.[34]

Although there have been sharp attacks upon the notion that there are questions which because of their nature are non-justiciable, that notion would seem to be at least implicit in the

[32] *Report of the Delegation of the United States to the Inter-American Conference*, Department of State Publication 3016 (1948), pp. 52, 53, 60.

[33] *Report of the Delegation of the United States to the Ninth International Conference of American States*, Department of State Publication 3263 (1948), p. 187.

[34] See the statement by the Permanent Court of International Justice, P.C.I.J., ser. A/B, no. 46, p. 162; and remarks of E. M. Borchard, "The Resurrection of International Law," *Proc. Amer. Soc. Int. Law*, 1923, pp. 69–70.

provisions of typical arbitration treaties of the United States. The common formula of these instruments puts within the category of justiciable those questions which by their nature are susceptible of decision by an application of international law.[35]

The limiting effect of defining justiciable questions is further emphasized by the inclusion of a provision reserving from adjudication "domestic jurisdiction questions." Such a provision is an indirect reference to the general law. There has been some variation in the form of statement. When a bilateral arbitration treaty, such as those which the United States made with many non-American states in 1928, 1929, and 1930, specifies that its provisions "shall not be invoked in respect of any dispute the subject matter of which . . . is within the domestic jurisdiction of either of the High Contracting Parties,"[36] the exception is a very wide one, since practically any question which might come up would be in some sense relatable to domestic jurisdiction. For example, it has been suggested that confiscation of alien-owned private property would not be technically justiciable if a domestic law of the state authorized it.[37] If excepted questions are those which are "solely," "essentially," or "exclusively" within the domestic jurisdiction, the reserve clause is far less limiting in its effect. However, even when such qualifiers are left out, there are, presumably, some ascertainable limits to the category of questions within domestic jurisdiction. When the United States was negotiating one of its arbitration treaties of the newer type with Turkey, the ambassador of that country presented a text referring to the term "domestic jurisdiction" as including "all matters pertaining to the right of sovereignty, to the principles of fundamental laws, to differences the settlement of which is left by international law to the exclusive competence

[35] On the use of "equity" in such treaties, see section 3, *infra*. See, in Hersch Lauterpacht's edition of L. F. L. Oppenheim's *International Law* (6th ed., vol. II [1940], p. 4n), the statement concerning "at least three meanings" on the basis of which the distinction between the two principal categories of disputes can be and has been understood.

[36] The model for this group of treaties was the one with France, signed February 6, 1928 (46 *Stat.* 2269). There were similar agreements with more than a score of European states.

[37] Chandler P. Anderson, "The Scope and Character of Arbitration Treaties," *Proc. Amer. Soc. Int. Law*, 1929, p. 114.

of each state, particularly matters concerning emigration, nationality and the customs régime, as well as all questions predicated upon national jurisdiction." This was later changed so as to include only "questions of sovereignty and all differences the settlement of which is left by international law to the exclusive competence of each state," but further negotiations did not result in the signing of an arbitration treaty.[38]

Article 15 of the League of Nations Covenant distinguished matters which by international law were "solely within the domestic jurisdiction." [39] Somewhat more specific was the description, in the General Treaty of Inter-American Arbitration, 1929, of controversies which are "within the domestic jurisdiction of any of the Parties to the dispute and are not controlled by international law." [40]

A possible effect of this difference in wording (from that in bilateral arbitration treaties with European states) was to create a different jurisdictional base in relation to arbitration commitments with American republics and with states outside the Western Hemisphere.[41]

Any reference in an arbitration treaty of the United States to international law for the purpose of designating justiciable disputes should be viewed in relation to the policy which the country has followed in regard to arbitration in general. It is common knowledge that the United States, long an advocate of the arbitral method of settling disputes, has in the past advocated arbitration that is voluntary, not obligatory—the latter type being distinguished by the fact that commitments to arbitrate antedate the occurrence of the disputes.[42] Outside of a few exceptional cases, such as the reference of the *Pious Fund* cases with Mexico and of the *I'm Alone* question with Canada, the

[38] *For. Rel.*, 1928, III, 949–950.

[39] In a statement that has been much quoted, the Permanent Court of International Justice said that the question of what is "solely a matter of domestic jurisdiction" is essentially a relative one, depending upon the development of international relations (P.C.I.J., ser. B, no. 4, p. 24).

[40] 49 *Stat.* 3153.

[41] Note 37, *supra*. And see the position taken by the Netherlands (*For. Rel.*, 1930, III, 623).

[42] Robert R. Wilson, "Reservation Clauses in Agreements for Obligatory Arbitration," *Amer. Jour. Int. Law*, XXIII (1929), 68–93.

American government has instituted arbitral proceedings under the terms of specific reference agreements which postdate the occurrence of the dispute, and not merely under general arbitration engagements. The United States Senate long asserted its function of passing upon each particular reference (to arbitrators) of any question, as well as its function of approving the general arbitration treaty in the first instance.[43] This was forcefully illustrated in the action by the Senate on the Treaty of Inter-American Arbitration, when it was made clear that the special agreement (of reference) was to be made in each case by the President, and then only with the advice and consent of the Senate.[44] Under such a reservation, omission of such a word as "solely" from the descriptive clause concerning matters of domestic jurisdiction would not seem to make any great practical difference. Any tribunal would have been, as was emphasized with respect to the Permanent Court of International Justice during the Senate debates in 1935 concerning adherence by the United States, one to which this country could go, but not one to which it could ever be brought against its will.

A practice of permitting reference of any dispute to arbitration only through a special agreement which shall take the form of a treaty places emphasis upon the general principle of customary international law that no state is bound to arbitrate any matter against its will.[45] Omission from the general arbitration treaties of the clause requiring that every *compromis* must be a formal treaty would not necessarily assure arbitration, but the legal obligation to refer (at the request or application of either party) would rest more definitely upon each party. Whether the obligation would be discharged by action of the executive alone, or by the executive with advice of a legislative

[43] Robert R. Wilson, "Clauses Relating to Reference of Disputes in Obligatory Arbitration Treaties," *Amer. Jour. Int. Law*, XXV (1931), 469–489.

[44] 79 *Cong. Rec.* 4753–54. The treaty, signed January 5, 1929, was approved by the Senate on April 1, 1935 (49 *Stat.* 3153).

[45] See the statement of the Permanent Court of International Justice in its advisory opinion concerning Eastern Carelia (P.C.I.J., ser. B, no. 5, p. 27). "It is well established in international law that no State can, without its consent, be compelled to submit its disputes with other States either to mediation or to arbitration, or to any other kind of pacific settlement."

body, would be a matter of constitutional arrangement and not one governed by international law. Elimination of the requirement of any *agreement* for the reference of any particular dispute (other than that in the general commitment, such as states commonly make when accepting the Optional Clause of the International Court of Justice), and the substitution therefor of the method of simple application by either party, means a far-reaching change. The old method, along with the plan of describing excepted questions and not leaving to the arbitral agency the authority to decide whether a particular dispute came within the exceptions, made consent to the particular proceedings a condition precedent of *any adjudication*. The abandonment of that method represents an essential step in the development of effective international organization.[46] As is well known,[47] the United States has, since 1946, moved forward toward a new policy. Some progress in that direction had been made even before 1946.[48] It is obvious that an applied standard will become more normal as individual states give up the right to be final authoritative interpreters of treaties for themselves, and the role of interpreter is transferred to international agencies having behind them the combined will and collective authority of all or the greater part of the community of states.

In its bilateral arbitration treaties of the type dating from 1928, the United States sought to keep in uniform style the agreements with non-American states. To the Polish minister, Secretary Kellogg wrote, "It is the desire of this Government that there should be uniformity in the series of treaties which it is now negotiating, and whenever a Government has requested an alteration . . . I have asked that it recede from the request in the interest of uniformity." [49] To the American ambassador in Turkey, he telegraphed, "Modification of, or addition to, the texts of the treaties . . . so as to meet the susceptibilities and

[46] See, on the relative importance of this step in the development of an effective international system, Hans Kelsen, "Compulsory Adjudication of International Disputes," *Amer. Jour. Int. Law*, XXXVII (1943), 397–406.

[47] See notes 67, 68, and 69, *infra*.

[48] Note 66, *infra*.

[49] *For. Rel.*, 1928, III, 759.

apprehensions that are peculiar to one or more countries would render impossible execution of this Government's program for negotiating treaties . . . which are substantially identical with all other governments outside of Latin America."[50] The American effort was not completely successful. Denmark, while accepting what the United States proposed, would have preferred a less limited treaty; the Spanish ambassador, under instructions, replied that his country, having "adopted . . . as a standard for a treaty of arbitration one that embraces all the disputes and conflicts, without any exception whatsoever," could not sign a treaty which, in the opinion of the Spanish government, did not "respond to the breadth of judgment that . . . inspired its international attitude"; Siam preferred a less limited treaty of arbitration.[51]

The formula in what the United States proposed, describing justiciable questions in terms of law,[52] occasioned some difficulties in the negotiations. For example, the Polish government proposed to substitute for the words "law or equity" the words "international law and custom." Replying to this suggestion, the Secretary of State said:

> The term "international law" is less inclusive than the term "law," and I feel that it would be inadvisable to adopt language which would

[50] *Ibid.*, p. 947.

[51] *Ibid.*, II, 719; III, 748, 880. See also *For. Rel.*, 1929, III, 760, 762–767.

[52] The formula, as it appears in the treaty with France, is as follows: "All differences relating to international matters in which the High Contracting Parties are concerned by virtue of a claim of right made by one against the other under treaty or otherwise, which it has not been possible to adjust by diplomacy, which have not been adjusted as a result of reference to the above-mentioned Permanent International Commission, and which are justiciable in their nature by reason of being susceptible of decision by the application of the principles of law or equity, shall be submitted. . . ."

The General Treaty of Inter-American Arbitration (note 44, *supra*) does not contain the words "or equity" as they are used in the bilateral arbitration treaties with European states. When in the course of the negotiation of some of the bilateral treaties, there was a reference to the Inter-American Treaty as being, in some respects, preferable to what the United States proposed for inclusion in the bilateral ones, representatives of the United States pointed out that at that time the Inter-American Treaty had not yet been approved by the United States Senate. (It was approved on April 1, 1935.)

have the effect of restricting the criterion by which the parties to the proposed treaty must determine whether a particular dispute is or is not justiciable.[53]

The Netherlands government desired a rewording which would leave out the word "equity," the latter being objectionable as "a juridical notion which does not seem well-defined to non-Anglosaxon minds."[54] The Czechoslovak foreign minister preferred to substitute for the word "equity" the words "international law," since under Czechoslovak law "equity" conveyed a different connotation. To this the Secretary of State replied that he did not believe that differences in existing definitions of equity were grounds for concern.[55]

In the course of the negotiations with Sweden, the minister of that country raised the question of whether the words, "and which are justiciable in their nature by reason of being susceptible of decision by the application of the principles of law or equity," did not give to each party a "further opportunity" to declare any concrete dispute to be outside the scope of the treaty. The United States representatives failed to see how the words, if properly construed, would afford such an opportunity. The Swedes then suggested that the words quoted were superfluous, since differences of a legal nature were adequately comprehended in the language concerning a claim of right made by one party against the other party. The position of the United States was that the definition of disputes was as broad as that in the 1908 (Root) arbitration treaties and that, since the exceptions were narrower, the new treaties marked an advance.[56]

[53] *For. Rel.*, 1928, III, 758.

[54] *For. Rel.*, 1930, III, 623. The Polish government, suggesting that the imprecision of the term "equity" was susceptible of misunderstanding, had observed that "principles of equity could not be invoked by a court of arbiters to supplement or override generally recognized principles of international law" (the Polish minister to the Department of State, *ibid.*, 1928, III, 763).

[55] *For. Rel.*, 1928, II, 687.

[56] *For. Rel.*, 1929, III, 708–710. There also arose in these negotiations the question of whether reference of a dispute to the Conciliation Commission to be established between the two countries was to be a condition precedent to arbitration. The United States did not construe the original language to require such a reference but agreed, at Sweden's request, to a slight change of wording to cover the point.

When, in the course of negotiations with his country, the German ambassador inquired whether the words quoted above regarding justiciability were to be understood as an interpretation and not a modification of the term "claim of right" in the same article, the Department of State replied, in part, as follows:

The definition of a justiciable question in Article I must be taken as a whole, that is to say, to come within the scope of the arbitration treaty a difference must at one and the same time relate to an international matter, be based upon a claim of right and be justiciable in its nature by reason of being susceptible of decision by the application of the principles of law or equity. To illustrate: a question arising under a treaty or under well settled principles of international law. If the question comes within this definition, it could not be excluded from arbitration because one of the parties might claim that it involves national honor or vital interests.[57]

In a communication to the Japanese Embassy, the Department of State said, concerning the scope of differences which the parties would be committed to refer under the new form of agreement, that this would be substantially the same as under the 1908 (Root) treaty. It added, "In both cases only differences of a legal or justiciable nature are referable. However, the draft Treaty is broader in scope, because the reservations described in Article II are more definite and limited than the reservations set forth in Article I of the Convention of 1908." As to the force and effect (upon article I) of the reservations in article II, the communication said:

The reservations enumerated in Article II of the draft Treaty operate in part to clarify and define the scope of the Treaty by excepting from arbitration non-justiciable questions. For example, Article II Clause (a) of the draft Treaty, exempting domestic questions, is implicit in Article I, which limits the scope of arbitration to international justiciable questions. However, the reservations operate to except from arbitration the enumerated categories of questions, whether justiciable or non-justiciable in character.[58]

[57] *Ibid.*, II, 866. The German ambassador's comments on the first reservation of article II of the draft treaty, made in an informal memorandum, are at pp. 864–865 of the same volume.

[58] *Ibid.*, 1928, III, 145. The memorandum also said, "All international disputes of a legal or justiciable nature, not specifically excepted in Article II, are subject to arbitration under the provisions of the draft Treaty" (*ibid.*, p. 146).

The Department expressed the opinion that the word "otherwise" in the first article of the standard treaty denoted "a claim which might arise under any established principle of international law"—a point which was to come up two years later in connection with an attempt to codify a part of international law.[59] In response to the Japanese inquiry whether the words "principles of law or equity" in the same article meant to include the general principles of justice as accepted both in international and domestic law, and whether "equity" was to be understood as synonymous with *ex aequo et bono,* the Department's memorandum submitted the following:

> The word "equity" is used in Article I to describe one branch of jurisprudence recognized by civilized nations as part of the general principles of objective law. The draft Treaty contemplates that a question is justiciable when it is susceptible of solution by the application of objective principles of law or equity. Consequently, the term "equity" is not to be understood to be synonymous with the term "ex aequo et bono" (in justice and good dealing), a subjective and variable standard depending upon the individual conscience of the judge.[60]

[59] The committee of the Hague Conference for the Codification of International Law, 1930, which considered the subject of responsibility, had as a basis for discussion a statement referring to responsibility resulting from treaties "or otherwise." There was extended discussion of the meaning of these words, in the course of which some delegates referred to article 38 of the Statute of the Permanent Court of International Justice (*Minutes of the Third Committee,* League of Nations document C.351(c).M.145(c). 1930. V). A subcommittee which studied the matter submitted this text: "The expression 'international obligations' in the present Convention means obligations resulting from treaty, custom or the general principles of law, which are designed to assure to foreigners in respect of their persons and property a treatment in conformity with the rules accepted by the community of nations" (*ibid.,* p. 112). A Roumanian delegate's proposal to insert the word "indisputably" before the word "accepted" was rejected, as was a Latvian representative's amendment which proposed the substitution of the words "in conformity with the rules of law" for the words "the rules accepted by the community of nations" (*ibid.,* p. 161).

[60] *For. Rel.,* 1928, III, 146. See note 51, *supra,* and discussion of equity, in connection with the bases for awards, found in section 3 of this chapter.

Negotiations with the Japanese did not lead to a perfected arbitration treaty. Shortly before the date of the memorandum referred to above, the Japanese chargé had informed the Under Secretary of State that his government was inclined to suspend action on the arbitration and conciliation treaties until some agreement was reached on the multilateral pact for re-

The general position taken by the United States in these bilateral negotiations was that international law is limited in its scope and that it does not pervade all phases of public international life—or, to put it another way, that regarding some subject matters the law merely prescribes that each state shall decide for itself.[61] This does not necessarily mean, of course, that the scope of the law is static. In the light of what the Permanent Court of Justice said concerning domestic jurisdiction questions,[62] the precise legal effect of a provision for applying the standard might not always be the same over the life of an arbitration treaty of long duration. A development of community rights may affect application.[63] To one of the parties with which it made a bilateral arbitration treaty in 1928, the United States through its Secretary of State observed that, "the present treaty, when effective, must, of course, be construed in accordance with international practice." [64]

In one sense, any question which treaty makers agree to have arbitrated thereby becomes "justiciable," and in such an undertaking as that in which it accepted membership in the International Labor Organization,[65] the American government assumed certain obligations regarding the obligatory jurisdiction of an international tribunal, without specific reserves as to the "justiciability" of matters referable or the requirement of another formal treaty before the court could exercise its jurisdiction.[66]

---

nunciation of war. The American position was that there was no such connection between the two "operations" as to make one at all contingent upon the other (*For. Rel.*, 1928, I, 85–86).

[61] A strong argument against the validity of the concept of nonjusticiable questions is that of Hersch Lauterpacht in *The Function of Law in the International Community* (1933).

[62] See note 39, *supra*.

[63] In its opinion concerning the jurisdiction of the European Commission of the Danube, the Permanent Court of International Justice concluded that a community agency had jurisdiction, although a riparian state (Roumania) insisted that it had not merely withheld its consent, but had regularly taken occasion to make that fact known (P.C.I.J., ser B, no. 14).

[64] *For. Rel.*, 1928, III, 760.

[65] 49 *Stat.* (2) 2712.

[66] See Manley O. Hudson, "The Membership of the United States in the International Labor Organization," *Amer. Jour. Int. Law,* XXVIII (1934), 669–682.

In the light of these considerations, the role of the United States in the decision of the question of whether the International Court of Justice should have a general "compulsory" jurisdiction and the action thereafter taken toward accepting the jurisdiction become central elements in the policy following World War II with respect to the standard which is international law. Reservation by the United States of the right to withhold from reference to the Court "disputes with respect to matters which are essentially within the domestic jurisdiction of the United States . . . as determined by the United States"[67] would not seem to mark a departure from the assumption on which rested its arbitration treaties of the preceding two decades. Consistency of the reservation which the United States has made—and which has subsequently been followed in acceptances of the Optional Clause by certain other states—with the basic plan of the Court (specifically, with paragraph 6 of article 36 of its Statute) may conceivably become the subject of judicial decision.

In the meantime, the United States, while entering into certain bilateral treaties (as well as some multilateral ones) with compromissory clauses that did not include a reservation of "domestic jurisdiction" questions,[68] has in such a conference as that at Bogotá in 1948 consistently held to the idea of "nonjusticiable" questions. In accord with its "basic policy . . . designed to achieve general recognition of the rule of law in international relations," it proposed that, "in all cases based upon claims of legal right," the American states agree in the Pact of Bogotá to accept the jurisdiction of the International Court of Justice as obligatory

[67] On the adoption of the reservation, and the probable legal force and effect of it, see Francis Wilcox, "The United States Accepts Compulsory Jurisdiction," *Amer. Jour. Int. Law,* XL (1946), 699–719; Lawrence Preuss, "The International Court of Justice, the Senate, and Matters of Domestic Jurisdiction," *ibid.*, pp. 720–736.

[68] This applies particularly to the first several commercial treaties which the United States signed after the cessation of hostilities in World War II. On the consistency of these with the action of the Senate in approving acceptance of the Optional Clause, see the statement of the Department of State in *Hearings . . . on a Treaty of Friendship, Commerce and Navigation between the United States of America and the Republic of China,* 80th Cong., 2d Sess. (1948), pp. 29, 30. This statement drew attention to the fact that there was a precedent in articles 84 and 86 of the International Civil Aviation Convention (T.I.A.S. 1591).

without the necessity of special agreement between the parties in individual cases. The United States proposed to "draw a distinct line between controversies which depend for their solution upon the interpretation of existing rules of law and those which, in effect, seek changes in legal relationships." The Pact, as finally approved by the Conference, provided for reference to the International Court of Justice of a dispute not resolved through the process of conciliation. It further provided that the parties were obligated to submit to arbitration any controversy which the Court should declare itself to be without jurisdiction to hear and adjudge, but the United States in its reservation made clear that submission on its part to arbitration should be dependent upon the conclusion of a special agreement between the parties to the case. Article V of the Pact excluded from the procedures accepted in the treaty "matters which, by their nature, are within the domestic jurisdiction of the state," and provided for submission to the International Court of Justice (if the parties disagreed concerning the point) of the question of whether a controversy concerned such a matter. However, the United States reservation provided that acceptance by this country of the compulsory jurisdiction of the Court should be "limited by any jurisdictional or other limitation contained in any Declaration deposited by the United States under Article 36, paragraph 4, of the Statute of the Court, and in force at the time of submission of any case." [69]

From the foregoing it will appear that, so far as the United States is concerned, there have not yet been worked out criteria, aside from those to be applied by the country itself, for distinguishing "legal" from "nonlegal" questions under all circumstances. At Bogotá the United States delegation was unwilling to undertake an "advance commitment" of "unlimited scope" which was deemed likely to "imperil existing legal relationships which constitute a stabilizing influence of major importance in international relations." [70] The full force and effect of what is said in article II, paragraph 7, of the United Nations Charter con-

[69] *Report of the Delegation . . . to the Ninth International Conference of American States*, pp. 42, 43, 187, 193, 200. (On reservation concerning local remedies, see pages 73–74, *infra*.)

[70] *Ibid.*, p. 50.

cerning "matters which are essentially within the domestic jurisdiction of any state" are yet to be determined.[71] Recent study has shown that, in actual application, the paragraph has been construed in a realistic manner which may prevent it from working, in matters of really international concern, a paralysis of international political bodies.[72]

3. BASES FOR AWARDS

It would appear from what has been said concerning the official position of the United States as to the nature of the arbitral process, that treaty makers might properly make clear that awards should be upon the basis of international law. Such references do in fact occur in numerous American treaties, the mention of the law being frequently in combination with such words as "justice" and "equity."

Particularly in the early days of the republic it was sometimes difficult for American negotiators to get provisions into the treaties which would direct the settlement of claims in accordance with the law of nations. The diplomatic history of two early treaties with Spain, that of Friendship, Commerce and Navigation, 1795,[73] and that of Indemnification, 1802,[74] will illustrate. Before the

[71] The mentioned paragraph of the Charter does not come within the type of treaty provisions with which this study is primarily concerned, since there is no specific reference in it to international law. At the San Francisco Conference, when an effort was made to include in article II, paragraph 7, wording which would have said, in effect, that the questions reserved were those which according to international law were within the domestic jurisdiction, the opposition relied in part upon the argument that omission of reference to international law would have no effect, since that law was the only criterion that could be applied, and in part upon the thought that international law was subject to constant change, as a result of which it escaped definition and should not, therefore, be listed as the criterion (UNCIO doc. 1019, I/1/42, June 16, 1945, pp. 2, 5–6; and doc. 1167, I/10, June 23, 1945, p. 4).

[72] See especially Lawrence Preuss, *Article 2, Paragraph 7 of the Charter of the United Nations and Matters of Domestic Jurisdiction* (1949), *passim.*

[73] 8 *Stat.* 138, 150. Article XXI refers to "justice, equity and the law of nations."

[74] 8 *Stat.* 198. This treaty refers to excesses committed by individuals "contrary to the laws of nations." By the second article, commissioners were to judge "according to the laws of nations and existing treaty, and with the impartiality justice may dictate."

former treaty was signed, the Spaniards proposed to divide cases involving captures of American vessels into two groups corresponding to time "epochs." They wanted to have ships which had been taken during the first of these epochs judged according to the marine ordinances and the general orders communicated at the time (presumably communicated to the Spanish forces). Thomas Pinckney, American minister, sent to Manuel de Godoy, the Prince of the Peace, on October 20, 1795, the following observations on the point:

> I am mortified . . . that your Excellency proposes to divide the war which has just been terminated into two epochs and that the American vessels which have been detained by those of Spain during that war should be differently treated according to the time at which they were taken, as it seems to me that Justice which should govern the conduct of nations toward neutral flags is always the same, and ought not to be liable to the variations of time or circumstances. It is very clear that the U.S. were as much neutral and as friendly to Spain at the beginning of the war as after the 1st of April last, and that consequently they should expect similar treatment at both epochs. That which is at least certain is that at all times they ought to be treated according to the law of nations, and I conceive I have proved very clearly what those laws are in this subject in my official letter of the 20 Sept. last and in order to avoid repetitions I take the liberty of requesting your Excellency to recur to that letter for the reasons upon which our claims are based.[75]

[75] MS., Department of State, 6 Despatches, Spain (enclosure in Pinckney's despatch of October 28, 1795, to the Department of State). Pinckney subjoins some "specific propositions founded upon justice and the law of nations as now established by the consent of a great majority of the nations of Europe and adopted by Spain herself." The propositions as outlined allowed the condemnation of a vessel as prize only for contraband carriage or blockade running, stressed the effectiveness of a blockade as a condition of its legality, and would have limited contraband to articles comprised under that description in article 24 of the Anglo-Spanish Treaty of May 23, 1667, or article 24 of the Franco-American commercial treaty of 1778. The French text of Pinckney's letter of September 20, 1795, referred to in the quoted despatch, is in the same volume. The letter refers to the rules in the maritime conventions which were set up in 1780, accepted first by the states of the north, and later adopted by a decisive plurality of the nations of Europe, including Spain. They comprised, Pinckney wrote, a "code respectable dicté par la sageuse et la modération," and had had the support of the "Puissances les plus respectables de l'Europe." With one exception, the great commercial powers of the two hemispheres had agreed that the code thus formulated "doit être le droit des gens à cet regard."

The Prince of the Peace touched but lightly on the dynamic qualities of the law of nations when, in his reply of two days later, he wrote to Pinckney in part as follows:

> You . . . conclude by repeating that all the detentions of the said vessels should be decided agreeably to the principles which you lay down as most consonant to the interests of the States and conformable to the laws of nations. Without waiting to prove to you the *modifications which according to the same law of nations those principles are susceptible of,* I only inform you that the vessels detained before the 1st of April must be judged like all those of the other powers according to the maritime ordinance (ordinancá de corso) of the 1st of May 1794 a general law comprehending the U.S. as well as all others until the special exception in their favor on the 6 April last by just considerations toward France.[76]

The American minister insisted, in turn, that the propositions that he had previously outlined were "founded upon principles already recognized" by Spain and the United States. He observed that, where there was a difference of opinion between two independent powers, it was "a happy circumstance if they can have recourse to principles already admitted by both parties, without the one being obliged to give up his opinion or to sacrifice his rights to the other." [77] In the end the negotiators inserted in the treaty the now familiar formula which refers to "justice, equity and the law of nations."

In the course of the negotiations in 1802, the question arose of Spain's responsibility for damage done to American vessels in Spanish waters by French privateers. Pedro Cevallos, the Spanish plenipotentiary, declared that such captures did not impose upon the Spanish government any further obligation than to declare them of no effect, whenever the circumstances which constituted the illegitimacy of the capture should be proved in a competent tribunal. He deduced this proposition from the principle that no sovereign was responsible for the wrongs done by the subjects or members of another. He told the American minister, Charles Pinckney, that examples inconsistent with this principle owed their existence to temporary circumstances and "could

[76] 6 Despatches, Spain, English translation of communication of October 22, 1795 (italics inserted).

[77] *Idem* (Thomas Pinckney's communication of October 23, 1795).

never destroy the rules of the law of nations."[78] It was finally agreed that commissioners to be appointed under the treaty should decide, according to the law of nations and the existing treaty, whether there had been illegal acts committed by Spanish subjects against American citizens or by American citizens against Spanish subjects. After signing the treaty Pinckney sought to justify his acceptance of its terms even if they did not include the desired provision concerning Spanish liability for French spoliations in Spanish jurisdiction.[79] (As it was, differences between the two countries during the two decades following caused long delay in the Spanish government's ratification of the 1802 instrument, which finally took place on July 9, 1818.)

It may be questioned whether a treaty reference to the law of nations concerning neutral rights and duties, or concerning state responsibility for public acts of belligerents within its territory, in 1795 or 1802, could have been declaratory of a set of rules very clearly established. The position and influence of Great Britain had to be taken into account, for example, when there were claims that the rules of the Armed Neutrality of 1780 were already established rules of international law. The American plenipotentiary in the two instances mentioned sought official endorsement of rules which seemed to have received sufficiently wide, although not universal, acceptance. In these cases, as in many others, the treaty negotiators did not adopt any rules short of the law of nations (such as national marine ordinances), but subscribed to a vague general formula as the basis for future awards.

That a formula which is not precise may occasion some difficulty will appear from proceedings which followed the conclusion of another treaty with Spain a few years later. A group

[78] *Idem* (communication of June 26, 1802, to Charles Pinckney).

[79] *Idem*, Pinckney's despatch of August 15, 1802. The sixth article of the treaty contained the following: "It not having been possible for the said Plenipotentiaries to agree upon a mode by which the . . . Board of Commissioners should arbitrate the Claims originating from the excesses of foreign Cruizers, Agents, Consuls or Tribunals in their respective Territories, which might be imputable to their two governments, they have expressly agreed that each Government shall reserve (as it does by this Convention) to itself, its Subjects or Citizens respectively, all the rights which they now have & under which they may hereafter bring forward their claims at such times as may be most convenient to them."

of claims grew out of acts of American forces in East and West Florida in 1812–13, 1814, and 1818. The second of these three "invasions," in particular, raised questions of customary international law of war. The depredations alleged to have been carried out by General Jackson's troops occurred after the Spanish authorities in West Florida had proved unable to prevent violation of their territory by the British, who were at the time the enemies of the Americans. In the case of the Seminole war, Jackson took the position that the Spanish were bound by their treaty of 1795 with the United States to keep Indians within their territory at peace with the Americans, but that the Spanish had demonstrated their inability to do this, and therefore the United States forces could rightfully take measures that were necessary, even within Spanish territory. The claims which had developed became the subject of article IX of the 1819 treaty between the United States and Spain, which contained the following:

> The high contracting parties, respectively, renounce all claim to indemnities for any of the recent events or transactions of their respective commanders and officers in the Floridas.
>
> The United States will cause satisfaction to be made for the injuries, if any, which, *by process of law,* shall be established to have been suffered by the Spanish officers, and individual Spanish inhabitants, by the late operations of the American army in Florida.[80]

In 1823 an act of Congress authorized and directed judges of superior courts at St. Augustine and Pensacola to pass upon claims brought in accordance with the ninth article of the treaty. Another section of the same act provided that these courts should report such decisions to the Secretary of the Treasury, who, if satisfied that awards were "just and equitable, within the provisions of the said treaty," should pay the amounts. In the exercise of revisory power believed to have been conferred by the act, Secretaries of the Treasury rejected awards for acts committed in 1812–13 and 1814.[81] Subsequently there were appeals

[80] 8 *Stat.* 252, 260 (italics inserted).

[81] Secretary William Harris Crawford rejected the awards growing out of the 1814 incidents on the ground that the law of nations justified Jackson's entry into West Florida in that year and that the claim therefore did not fall within the terms of the treaty. Secretary Richard Rush excluded awards on claims which had arisen in 1812–13, since he took the position that actions in those years were not within the description of "late" opera-

to Congress in the claimants' behalf. The meaning of the ninth article of the 1819 treaty became the subject of discussion. One point which came into question was the effect of the word "late" as it occurred in the text.[82]

After Congress passed the Act of June 26, 1834[83] (which authorized the Secretary of the Treasury to pay amounts that judges in Florida had awarded on the 1812–13 and 1818, but not the 1814, claims), there were some awards by judges in addition to those which had previously been made. On these awards also the Secretary of the Treasury exercised a revisory power; he laid down certain descriptions of claims which he thought the 1834 act did not authorize him to pay, and he excluded interest on the claims. This matter of interest furnished occasion for an appeal to internationally binding rules rather than to municipal ones. The Spanish minister to the United States in 1849 (Calderón), said that he considered the judgments of the courts in Florida "to be in conformity with the express stipulations of the treaty and the public law which controls such decisions."[84] An argument in behalf of the claimants was that the Spanish term "legalmente" (the equivalent of the English "process of law") in the last paragraph of the ninth article required a *judicial* as distinct from an executive determination of the claims; it would follow that, even if usage of the Treasury Department concerning domestic claims did not allow payment of the interest, such usage could not be controlling for the purpose of settling these claims, which must come under the law of nations and the treaty.[85] Attorney General John J. Crittenden, in an opinion in 1851 on the meaning of the words "process of law" as used in the ninth article, said:

> The compacts of nations can be governed only by the laws of nations, and these require that the language of such compacts should be interpreted according to its proper general sense, as understood by the civilized world, and regardless, of course, of any different or special

tions referred to in article IX of the treaty (Moore, *International Arbitrations,* V, 4525).

[82] See H. Rep. 16, 20th Cong., 1st Sess., referred to in Moore, *International Arbitrations,* V, 4527.

[83] 6 *Stat.* 569.

[84] Moore, *International Arbitrations,* V, 4530.

[85] *Ibid.*

signification which local laws or local usage may have given to its words or terms. . . . For it is a consequence most clear and palpable . . . that these words "by process of law," as terms used in the treaty, must be interpreted according to the laws of nations, and *not* according to our municipal code. . . . My opinion is, that they do imply and mean *some legal proceeding—some* mode of judicature in and by which the injuries, alluded to in the same clause of the treaty might be "established," and the damages resulting from them awarded or adjudged to the injured parties.[86]

The Attorney General did not find that the revisory function which the Secretary of Treasury had exercised was inconsistent with the treaty's requirement of "process of law."[87] The United States Supreme Court had, in the meantime, held that it lacked jurisdiction to hear an appeal from a ruling which a federal court judge in Florida had made under the Act of 1834.[88] Six years later the Court of Claims, by a divided vote, found that it could not give relief to the claimants.[89] Execution of the ninth article of the 1819 treaty was a matter which hindered the realization of the most amicable relations between Spain and the United States during the greater part of the century.

The meaning of a term such as "process of law" would have to depend upon the intention of the treaty makers. Use of the expression in a most general sense would seem to import substantive as well as procedural requirements. Where either international or municipal law may figure as substantive factors in the execution of provisions, it would perhaps be clearer to specify that there shall be decisions according to "applicable law"—as was done when the United States concluded a convention with the Netherlands, March 18, 1938, concerning arbitration of a difference relating to payment for certain military supplies.[90]

[86] 5 *Op. Atty. Gen.* 333, 338. Attorney General Caleb Cushing referred to this opinion with approval in 1854 (6 *ibid.* 533).

[87] For an interpretation of "process of law" as meaning no technical requirement, but laws passed for the purpose, see Sen. Misc. Doc. 55, 36th Cong., 1st Sess., referred to in Miller, *Treaties,* III, 63.

[88] *United States* v. *Ferreira,* 13 Howard 40 (1851).

[89] Case of Robert Harrison, Sen. Misc. Doc. 45, 34th Cong., 3d Sess.; Moore, *International Arbitrations,* V, 4531.

[90] 53 *Stat.* (3) 1564, 1566 (art. III, par. 2). On the meaning of "due process of law," as used in certain commercial treaties, see Chapter III, section 1, *infra.*

In general, clauses relating to bases of arbitral settlement (whether of disputes that are essentially between states, or groups of claims brought in behalf of nationals, or of specific claims brought in behalf of nationals of one signatory against the government of the other) fall into three categories: (1) those which specify only international law; (2) those which in terms specify something other than international law, for example, "justice," "equity," "public law," or the law of municipal courts; (3) those which specify international law and equity (and perhaps justice). An examination of illustrative provisions in each of these categories can be usefully supplemented by reference, in some cases, to pronouncements of arbitrators who have given effect to the provisions.

Perhaps the simplest method of directing application of existing rules of law is that which the United States and Great Britain used in the first two articles of their agreement of April 11, 1908, concerning the United States–Canadian boundary, when they directed that the arbitrator should determine rights arising under international law.[91] The Geneva Tribunal which made the award in the *Alabama* claims had an authorization to apply stated rules (the parties having disagreed on whether these rules were declaratory of preëxisting law) and international law not inconsistent with these rules.[92] A treaty such as that relating to Spitzbergen, signed February 9, 1920, may look to the establishment of a tribunal which shall take into consideration, *inter alia,* "any applicable rules of International Law."[93] The Hague Conventions for the Pacific Settlement of International Disputes (1899 and 1907) both contain, in the section relating to arbitral procedure, authorization for a tribunal which functions for the settlement of a dispute to declare its competence in applying the "principles of international law."[94] Party states may simply express

[91] 35 *Stat.* 2003, 2004, 2007 (art. I, par. 4, and art. II, par. 7). The question of the allocation of certain islands was to be referred for decision under special rules provided and "under the recognized principles of international law not inconsistent therewith."

[92] See Chapter V, section 2, *infra.*

[93] 43 *Stat.* 1892 (Annex 2, 9a). For example of an award based on a "literal and grammatical" interpretation of an article in the Treaty of Ghent, see Miller, *Treaties,* III, 106, 134.

[94] Article 48 of the 1899 Convention, and article 73 of the 1907 one.

in the preamble of a bilateral treaty the desire to end their differences in accordance with international law,[95] a form of statement which may be considered in relation to the prevailing principle that no state may without its consent be obliged to submit its disputes to adjudication.[96]

Where a treaty authorizes the application of international law as a basis for an award, this authorization would extend to procedural as well as substantive rules. Recent research has shown that there has been developed what virtually amounts to customary law in the matter of evidence before international tribunals, and that, by analogy to a common rule of statutory construction, parties may be considered as having contracted in contemplation of the existing practice.[97] An arbitrator who fails to follow well-established usage in the matter of evidence is likely to receive criticism.[98]

The second category of clauses comprises those which, in providing for arbitral settlement, have not in terms mentioned the law of nations or international law as the basis for awards. The first article of the Anglo-American Claims Convention of February 8, 1853, specified justice and equity as that in accordance with which the commissioners should declare that they would decide.[99] Article XII of the Treaty of Washington, 1871,[100] pro-

[95] Illustrated in a treaty of January 23, 1925, with the Netherlands, 44 *Stat.* (3) 2007.

[96] See note 45, *supra.*

[97] Durward V. Sandifer, *Evidence before International Tribunals* (1939), pp. 30, 333. The author admits that it might be going too far to say that, in the absence of agreement, a tribunal is bound to follow these customary rules.

In the *Parker* case, the Mexican-American General Claims Commission said that the greatest liberality would obtain in the admission of evidence, and that municipal restrictive rules of adjective law or evidence could not be introduced or given effect by clothing them with such phrases as "universal principles of law," "general theory of law," and so forth (*Opinions of Commissioners,* Docket no. 127). See also A. H. Feller, *The Mexican Claims Commissions, 1923–1934* (1935), pp. 258–259.

See, in this general connection, the reference in 1928 to "well-established international practice in reference to claims," in connection with Sino-American claims adjudications (*For. Rel.,* 1928, II, 357).

[98] See, for example, Philip C. Jessup, "The Palmas Island Arbitration," *Amer. Jour. Int. Law,* XXII (1928), 735–752.

[99] 10 *Stat.* 988.

[100] 17 *Stat.* 863.

vided that the arbitrators were to decide "to the best of their judgment, and according to justice and equity." [101] The fact that even under this formula the arbitrators made awards in accordance with what they found to be international law indicates that that law is not excluded as a basis because of the parties' failure to make specific reference to it.

It is true that the use of terms logically distinguishable from international law has sometimes led to differences of opinion. For example, article IV of the French-American Treaty of January 15, 1880, set forth that "the Commissioners . . . shall . . . make and subscribe a solemn declaration that they will impartially and carefully examine and decide, to the best of their judgment and according to *public law, justice* and *equity,* without fear, favor or affection, all claims within the description and true meaning of Articles I and II." [102] In the claim which France brought in behalf of Virginie Dutrieux, there was a question of war damage (by bombardment at Charleston, South Carolina) and an admission by the applicant state that there was no remedy at international law. Counsel for the memorialist argued, however, that the phrase "public law" was distinguishable from "international law" and that it was the intention of the contracting parties that the commission should recognize all equitable claims. The respondent government's agent submitted that the words "public law" were equivalent to "international law" and that the commission had an authorization to allow only such claims as would, under the law of nations and usage under it, be recognized as "just and equitable." In spite of the applicant state's submission that the "enlightened parties" to the treaty of January 15, 1880, had, in a broad and civilized spirit, agreed to forego the setting up of narrow, jealous objections which earlier and less advanced ages would have sanctioned as justifiable obstacles in the way of common justice, the tribunal sustained the demurrer and did not allow the claim.[103]

[101] The commissioners functioning under this formula had occasion, in the course of their work, to make certain rulings concerning exhaustion of local remedies, which are referred to in section 4, *infra.*

[102] 21 *Stat.* 673 (italics inserted).

[103] *French-American Claims Commission, Report by George S. Boutwell,* House Ex. Doc. 235, 48th Cong., 2d Sess. (1885), pp. 116–117. On the

A question concerning the scope of "public law," as the term occurred in the treaty, was before the same commission in a somewhat different form when the French government claimed in behalf of Henri Dubos, a French newspaper writer whom General Benjamin F. Butler had arrested and imprisoned during the period of martial law at New Orleans in 1862. The applicant state submitted that the General's "pretended" martial law was illegal "bluster." The tribunal considered the right to establish martial law, the manner of its enforcement, and the right of a foreign government to claim damages in behalf of its nationals who had been punished for alleged offenses during the period of martial rule. The claim was for $26,000 plus interest. The commission awarded $800 plus $849.86 interest. The reason for the award was not a finding of lack of authority to proclaim martial law, for the arbitrators held that there was a legal right to declare it. As the American commissioner (A. O. Aldis) said, dissenting, it was a right which the United States Supreme Court had upheld and which was therefore a part of the "law of the United States." The institution of such rule, during either civil or foreign war, was not in conflict with international law. The majority of the commissioners found, however, that in this case the commanding general had violated without necessity his own regulations.[104]

The same commissioners considered, in the claim of Elise Lebret, the question of the nationality of a married woman according to "public law." The American commissioner, after reviewing the naturalization laws of Great Britain, Italy, Russia, Prussia, Spain, and the United States, and noting that these agreed substantially in having the nationality of the wife follow that of her husband (whether this be the nationality at the time of marriage or one subsequently acquired), and that this was true regardless of the wife's consent, said:

> The argument on behalf of the claimant, that the law of the United States must be held invalid by international law, because the wife's

general status of alien-owned property in a theater of war, see *Spanish Treaty Claims Commission, Documents and Opinions* (1904–1910), II, 104.

[104] Boutwell's *Report*, pp. 93–94, 217–228. See also, on the *Dubos* case, Robert R. Wilson, "A Case of International Responsibility during Martial Rule," *Amer. Jour. Int. Law*, XXXVI (1942), 657–661.

consent is necessary to her change of citizenship after marriage, is fully answered by the practice and laws of the great powers. Indeed, this legislation of the great civilized states of the world establishes the doctrine that by public law the consent of the wife is not necessary, and that such laws of naturalization are valid, bind all subjects to their jurisdiction, and are to be respected by all other states.

It may be added that no state in the world has ever declared *by express legislation* that the wife's consent is necessary.

Even if one power, like France, were by express statute to declare that if the husband change his nationality after marriage it should not change or affect the nationality of the wife, that could not change the public law of the world or annul the laws of other states. . . .

I cannot see that there is any equity or justice in calling her French.[105]

In the protocols under which the Venezuelan claims commissions functioned early in the twentieth century, there was provision for settlements "upon a basis of absolute equity, without regard to objections of a technical nature or of the provisions of local legislation." Of this, Umpire Frank Plumley of the British-Venezuelan Commission said, in the *Aroa Mines* case:

International law is not in terms invoked in these protocols, neither is it renounced. But . . . since it is a part of the law of the land of both Governments, and since it is the only definitive rule between nations, it is the law of this tribunal interwoven in every line, word, and syllable of the protocols, defining their meaning and illuminating the text; restraining, impelling, and directing every act thereunder.

. . . . .

The phrase, "absolute equity," used in the protocols the umpire understands . . . to mean equity unrestrained by any artificial rules in its application to the given case.

Since this is an international tribunal established by the agreement of nations there can be no other law, in the opinion of the umpire, for its government than the law of nations; and it is, indeed, scarcely necessary to say that the protocols are to be interpreted and this tribunal governed by that law, for there is no other; and that justice and equity are invoked and are to be paramount is not in conflict with this position, for international law is assumed to conform to justice and to be inspired by the principles of equity.

. . . . .

[105] Boutwell's *Report*, Appendix, Exhibit D, pp. 203, 205.

The guide, commonly safe and constant and usually to be followed, is international law. But if in the given case, not easily to be assumed, it should occur that its precepts are opposed to justice, or lead away from it, or are in disregard of it, or are inadequate or inapplicable, then the determination must be made by recourse to the underlying principles of justice and equity applied as best may be to the cause in hand. The umpire will apply the precepts of international law in all cases where such use will insure justice and equity for this reason, if for no other—that well-defined principles and precepts which have successfully endured the test of time and the crucible of experience and criticism are safe in use, and should never carelessly be departed from in order that one may step out into a way unknown to walk by a course unmarked. But these precepts are to be used as a means to the end, which end is justice.[106]

The American-Venezuelan Commission also had occasion to assign meaning to the words "absolute equity" in the protocol. In the *Heny* case, Umpire C. A. H. Barge denied controlling weight to the rule (which, it had been argued, was in accordance with the "principles of law generally adopted by all nations and also by the civil law of Venezuela") that contracts of the kind under consideration by the tribunal could only obtain value against third parties by being made public in accordance with the local law.[107] When, on the other hand, the umpire (Barge) in the *Orinoco Steamship* case seemed to take the position that the protocol of February 17, 1903, authorized his making an award without the restriction of fixed rules, the United States protested that there had been disregard of the terms of the protocol and that the award contained essential errors of fact and law which would make it invalid under the principles of international law. After extended negotiations, Venezuela and the United States on February 13, 1909, signed a protocol whereby another arbitral tribunal was to decide first (before it should consider the merits of the case) whether the decision of Umpire Barge was

[106] Ralston's *Report*, pp. 386–387. The tribunal found that the *Aroa Mines* supplementary claim was based wholly on the seizure of property by revolutionists without proof of any fault on the part of the established (respondent) government.

[107] Ralston's *Report*, p. 23. In the *Rudloff* claim, the tribunal exercised a right to determine whether the provision of a contract which required that all disputes be submitted to local (Venezuelan) courts was equitable under the circumstances. It found that the provision operated inequitably (*ibid.*, pp. 182, 194).

void "in view of all the circumstances and under the principles of international law." The tribunal of the Permanent Court of Arbitration did not sustain the Venezuelan argument that the umpire could not have departed from any binding rules (on the supposition that under the language of the 1903 protocol the parties had given the commission unlimited discretion).[108] The United States contended successfully that this country's practice of inserting comparable wording in past arbitral agreements had not worked such a result as to give arbitrators complete discretion.[109]

If parties to a treaty do not necessarily exclude international law as a basis for arbitral awards merely by failure to refer to it in terms in the general agreement or in the instrument of submission, they may do so by express treaty provision for the application of other rules. Perhaps the best example is the provision for bases of awards by the German-American Mixed Claims Commission after the First World War. Umpire Edwin B. Parker said in the *Trudgett* case, which had to do with liability for detention of civilians of enemy nationality:

> It will not be profitable here to consider the legality or illegality as tested by rules of international law of such capture, confinement and detention. As this Commission has . . . held, Germany's liability in cases presented here is determined not by rules of international law but by . . . the Treaty of Berlin irrespective of the legality or illegality of the act complained of.[110]

[108] Ralston's *Report* at pp. 75, 84–85; James Brown Scott, *Hague Court Reports* (1916), p. 226. William Bainbridge, American commissioner in the *Orinoco* case before the American-Venezuelan commission, argued that the parties had not given the commission unlimited discretion. He submitted that, when the parties included the clause mentioning "absolute equity," they had in mind the "substance," not the shadow, of justice; he thought they had sought to make remedies dependent, "not upon the niceties of legal refinement, but upon the very right of the case" (Ralston's *Report*, p. 75). See reference to the point in a later adjudication (Nielsen's *Report*, p. 58).

Another case before the Venezuelan commission, in which there was application of international law although there had been no specific mention of it in the protocol, was the claim of the American Electric and Manufacturing Company (Ralston's *Report*, p. 36).

[109] See the summarized statement of the law, to which the tribunal applied its ruling, in L. B. Orfield, "Equity as a Concept of International Law," *Kentucky Law Journal*, XVIII (1929–30), 120.

[110] *Decisions and Opinions* (1925–26), 819–820, Docket no. 4890. See also Wilhelm Kiesselbach, *Problems of the German-American Claims Com-*

Local law may become a factor of some importance, either by virtue of arbitrators' interpretation of their "charter" or by more specific authorization in an international agreement. The umpire of the Mexican-American commission under the treaty of 1839 felt that, in such a matter as the measurement of damages, principles of local law should serve as a guide, "in so far as they do not infringe the general principles recognized in the law of nations." [111] A recent example of authorization by the parties is in the convention of April 15, 1935, in which the United States and Canada agreed that commissioners who were to arbitrate the questions concerning the smelter at Trail, British Columbia, should apply the law and practice followed in dealing with cognate questions in the United States.[112] With the concurrence of the agents of both parties, the arbitrators adopted, as a rule for their guidance, the proposition that, "with regard to any matter as to which express provision is not made in these rules, the Tribunal shall proceed as international law, justice and equity may require." In the course of its decision the tribunal, after observing that the fourth article of the convention did not bind it to apply national law and practice *to the exclusion* of international law and practice, said:

> It is further to be noted that the words "the law and practice followed in the United States" are qualified by "in dealing with cognate questions." Unless these latter words are disregarded, they mean a limitation of the reference to national law. What this limitation is,

---

mission (1930), *passim.* The liability, which was broader than international law would have imposed, was to be computed in terms of money by ordinary legal methods. In determining the nationality of claimants, the commission had occasion to apply international law, although, in its Administrative Decision no. V, it laid down certain rules not identical with those usually applied. See E. M. Borchard, "The Opinions of the Mixed Claims Commission, United States and Germany," *Amer. Jour. Int. Law,* XIX (1925), 133, 139–140.

[111] Quoted after Marjorie M. Whiteman, *Damages in International Law* (1937), II, 855. The convention had provided for adjustment of claims according to the principles of justice, the law of nations, and the treaty of amity and commerce between the parties. On the "controversy" as to whether the commission was a judicial or a diplomatic agency, see Frederick S. Dunn, *The Diplomatic Protection of Americans in Mexico* (1933), and J. B. Moore, *International Arbitrations,* II, 1216.

[112] 49 *Stat.* 3245. The provision is in article IV.

becomes apparent when one refers to the questions set forth in the previous article. These questions are questions of damage caused by smelter fumes, of indemnity therefor, of measures or regime to be adopted or maintained by the Smelter with or without indemnity or compensation. They may be questions of law or questions of practice. The practice followed, for instance, in injunctions dealing with problems of smelter fumes may be followed *in so far as the nature of an arbitral tribunal permits*. But the general questions of law and practice, such as the authority of the *res judicata* and exceptions thereto, are not "cognate questions" to those of Article III.[113]

A treaty authorization in broad terms (concerning bases for awards) may furnish support for a ruling on a point for which there is no clear rule of international law, even without a direct application of municipal law. Thus in the case of *Spader* and others before the American-Venezuelan commission, the arbitrators, holding that a right unasserted for over forty-three years could hardly in justice be called a "claim," said:

> It is doubtless true that municipal statutes of limitation can not operate to bar an international claim. But the *reason* which lies at the foundation of such statutes, that "great principle of peace," is as obligatory in the administration of justice by an international tribunal as the statutes are binding upon municipal courts.[114]

It remains to consider the force and effect, as declarations of existing international law, of those treaties of the United States in which the parties have specified not only that law but also "equity" (and sometimes also "justice") as the basis for awards. It has been seen that the linking of "justice, equity and the law of nations" goes far back in the history of American claims conventions,[115] and that at the present time the standard bilateral arbitration treaties which the United States has with non-American countries define justiciability in terms of susceptibility of decision by application of the principles of "law or equity."[116] The effect of using "equity" in such agreements has occasioned

[113] *Amer. Jour. Int. Law,* XXXV (1941), 684, 698 (first italics inserted).

[114] Ralston's *Report,* p. 162. On the extent to which any state which is party to a case involving the law of diplomatic protection may find it possible to derive from established legal rules and principles answers that accord with its own material interests, see Dunn, *Diplomatic Protection,* pp. 426–427.

[115] See notes 73 and 74, *supra.*

[116] See notes 54 and 55, *supra.*

differences of opinion, and arbitrators have sometimes thought that their mandate was wide enough to enable them to make rulings which, if they were adhering to strictly legal rules resting upon clear consent or treaties, they would not have been able to make.[117]

Under the formula of the Jay Treaty prescribing "Justice Equity and the Laws of Nations," [118] arbitrators found that there were limits within which they must stay in measuring damages. For example, in the case of the *Neptune,* a vessel which had been seized and later restored but awarded only freight, demurrage, expenses, and the invoice price plus a mercantile profit of 10 per cent (which was less than the value of the cargo at London or Bordeaux), Commissioner Christopher Gore said:

> By comparing the rule adopted by the board with the doctrines of Grotius, Pufendorf and Vattel, we shall find that it is conformable to justice, equity, and the law of nations as understood by those celebrated writers; and it is presumed that this is the rule prescribed to belligerents, and with which alone neutrals are under any moral obligation to be content. If there is any principle that authorizes a belligerent to seize on the property of a neutral, on condition of paying him the original cost, and all expenses actually incurred, with interest, and which deems such to be a just and adequate compensation, it must arise from the voluntary or conventional law of nations. The law of nations, as derived from the general principles of justice and equity, states a different doctrine.[119]

Under the 1868 claims convention with Mexico, arbitrators were to decide "according to public law, justice and equity." [120] An analysis of their work has revealed some lack of clarity about their precise function.[121] In one case Umpire Francis Lieber doubted whether his authority was restricted to that of deciding

[117] On the general subject, see especially Karl Strupp, *Das Recht des Internationalen Richters, nach Billigkeit zu entscheiden* (1930); Orfield, "Equity as a Concept of International Law," pp. 31–57, 116–140. See also note 143, *infra.*

[118] Miller, *Treaties,* II, 245, 252 (art. VII).

[119] J. B. Moore (ed.), *International Adjudications, Ancient and Modern,* Modern Series, IV (1933), 372.

[120] 15 *Stat.* 679–680.

[121] Frederick S. Dunn (*Diplomatic Protection,* pp. 96, 228) thinks it difficult to show that, in dealing with such matters as denial of justice and exhaustion of local remedies, the commissioners consistently applied established principles of law to the exclusion of other things.

according to law and equity, or whether it might be exercised in "conciliatory arbitraments"; he was willing to be governed in the matter by the conclusion of the two commissioners.[122] In a case involving seizure of American-owned tobacco in Mexico, Lieber ruled that, according to all the facts known to the arbitrators and according to "public justice," the claimants were entitled to an award.[123] In another case he said that the commission was "not a link in the common administration of justice, in the one or the other country, nor bound by anything but by the principles of justice and equity, progressively acknowledged by the jurisprudence of our whole race, and the law of nations of that same race."[124]

The British-American claims settlements under the special agreement signed at Washington on August 18, 1910, were to be made "in accordance with treaty rights and with the principles of international law and of equity."[125] In two of the cases before them which have been widely discussed, the commissioners had occasion to define the scope of their authority. In the claim of the *Eastern Extension, Australasia and China Telegraph Company, Ltd.*, the tribunal decided, in disposing of a British argument that in the absence of any rule of law governing the matter of cable cutting the arbitrators had a duty to frame a new rule, that it had no such duty; it was of opinion that principles of international law existing in 1898 were sufficient for decision of the case.[126] In the *Cayuga Indians* case, commissioners felt justified, on the basis of general principles of justice, in awarding $100,000, although the respondent state's defense seemed to be adequate if tested by strict law.[127] The American agent in the last mentioned arbitration has subsequently suggested that "such

[122] *Ibid.*, p. 96. The case was that of *Schaben* v. *Mexico*, Docket no. 100.

[123] *Ibid.*, p. 208 (case of *Samuel A. Belden* v. *Mexico*, Docket no. 131).

[124] *Ibid.*, p. 212, 213 (case of *Mather and Glover* v. *Mexico*, Docket no. 178).

[125] 37 *Stat.* (2) 1625.

[126] Nielsen's *Report* (1926), pp. 79–81. With this may be compared an award under the American-Peruvian convention of January 12, 1863 (Moore, *International Arbitrations*, II, 1629).

[127] Nielsen's *Report*, p. 307. The commissioners referred to the provisions of numerous arbitration treaties which link "equity" with the law in specifying bases of settlement.

handsome relative terms as 'equity' and 'justice'" be eliminated from arbitral agreements.[128]

The sequel to arbitral settlement of the *Norwegian Ships* case in 1922 also furnished occasion for discussion of the bases of an award. Operating under a special agreement of August 22, 1921, which authorized them to decide, "in accordance with the principles of law and equity," claims of Norwegians growing out of the requisitioning of vessels by the United States as a belligerent, the tribunal said:

> The words "law and equity" used in the special agreement of 1921 cannot be understood here in the traditional sense in which these words are used in Anglo-Saxon jurisprudence.
>
> The majority of international lawyers seem to agree that these words are to be understood to mean general principles of justice as distinguished from any particular system of jurisprudence or the municipal law of any state.[129]

The United States agent (William C. Dennis) reserved all rights of his state "arising out of the plain and manifest departure of the award from the terms of submission," and, while the United States subsequently paid the award, it informed Norway that it could not accept as proper or satisfactory in international arbitrations the mode by which the tribunal assessed damages or the absence of a reasoned statement indicative of the methods of their computation.[130]

There will naturally be differences of opinion between individual arbitrators in the matter of their attitude toward the application of law, international and national.[131] If a tribunal tends to

[128] Fred K. Neilsen, *International Law Applied to Reclamations* (1933), p. 72.

[129] *Amer. Jour. Int. Law,* XVII (1923), 362, 384.

[130] *For. Rel.,* 1923, II, 617–618, 626. As to the claim made, in substance, that the arbitrators had disregarded principles of law and equity and proceeded upon an erroneous rule of their own making, Secretary of State Hughes concluded that the argument was not so clearly established that the United States could assume that an impartial tribunal would decide that the award was invalid upon this ground (*ibid.,* pp. 621–622).

[131] The question of interest on claims awards may figure in such differences, particularly where equitable considerations influence arbitrators. The French-Mexican commission for the settlement of French claims arising out of revolutionary disturbances in Mexico had occasion to consider the interpretation of "equity" as the word occurred in the second article of the

take a too broad view of its jurisprudence, there are likely to be protests from the agent of the state against which an award is given. There is illustration of this in the history of the American-Panamanian Claims Commission under the conventions of July 28, 1926, and December 17, 1932. The parties, employing a familiar formula, authorized decisions "in accordance with the principles of international law, justice and equity." Of this authorization, the tribunal said that there was no reason to go into the question of whether these terms embodied an indivisible rule or meant that international law, justice, and equity had to be considered in the order in which they were mentioned, because either of these constructions led to the conclusion that the commission should be guided by "broad conceptions" rather than "narrow interpretations." [132] The comment which was made on

---

convention, which article the tribunal said should "être résolu en conformité à des principes admis par le droit international." On the matter of interest payments, President Verzijl concluded that there should be a different rule according to whether Mexico was or was not liable *under international law*. If Mexico was not so liable, there was to be no interest, unless payment of an award were unreasonably delayed past the date to be agreed upon. As to compensation for requisitioned property, Verzijl did not interpret Hague Convention IV of 1907, Annex 53, paragraph 3 (referring to the payment of the amount due) to imply interest. If this were not true in respect to international war, *a fortiori* it would not be true for civil war; there should not, therefore, be interest on this type of award except from the date of it. The same rule was applied with regard to *delits* by either government or revolutionary forces (the date to be fixed in view of the awards as a whole). On contract debts, however (particularly forced loans such as were prohibited by the French-Mexican treaty of November 27, 1886), there was to be interest at 6 per cent from the date on which the reclamation was brought to the attention of the Mexican government or made the occasion for action before the commission (*La Réparation des dommages causes aux étrangers par les mouvements révolutionnaires: Jurisprudence de la commission franco-mexicaine des réclamations* [1933], pp. 135, 138–140).

In the course of its opinion in the claim of *Jean Baptiste Caire*, the commission said: "When a State declares voluntarily its willingness to indemnify claimants beyond the limits of international responsibility, the general principles of customary international law, governing claims, apply here too" (*Jurisprudence de la commission franco-mexicaine des réclamations*, pp. 207–226; *Annual Digest*, 1929–30, p. 146).

[132] *Comisión General de Reclamaciones entre Panamá y Estados Unidos de América* (1934), Registro no. 1 (the *Perry* claim). The Spanish words from which the English ones are a translation are, respectively, "conceptos amplios" and "interpretaciones restringidas."

this by Bert L. Hunt, agent for the United States, included the following:

That provision of the arbitral convention which required that the awards be rendered "in accordance with the principle of international law, justice and equity," is not novel. It has been used in a considerable number of previous conventions. While these terms may be susceptible of varying interpretations, it would seem that the intention of the contracting parties in using those provisions should not be difficult of discernment. International law, as an independent jurisprudence, is of course very immaturely developed. A large percentage of cases coming before international tribunals for solution involve questions which are impossible of adjudication in accordance with what can be said to be clearly defined and definitely recognized principles of international law, or even with a line of accepted adjudications in identical cases. Each such case involves, therefore, the adaptation of old principles to new sets of facts or the evolvement of new principles through the process of deduction from the principles generally applied in relatively analogous circumstances. In other words, international law, as generally accepted, is inadequate to all present requirements. It requires clarification, extension, and broadening in practically every case. It is therefore in process of rapid evolution. Governments, recognizing that arbitral tribunals about to be created by them will be called upon to decide unformulated issues, have included in their arbitral conventions provisions requiring that the tribunals, when searching for new principles to be applied to new states of fact or when applying recognized principles to unprecedented circumstances, attune their broadening interpretations to recognize "*principles*" of equity and justice.

. . . When *recognized* principles of international law are found inadequate to the decision of *unprecedented* cases, analogous principles are to be applied, such analogies to be formulated, however, with recognized "*principles*" of justice and of equity as the guides in this respect. This it is believed has been the, perhaps unvoiced, reasoning of those who have concluded the conventions containing the provision here in question.[133]

[133] *American and Panamanian General Claims Arbitration . . . Report of Bert L. Hunt* (hereafter cited as Hunt's *Report*), Department of State Arbitration Series 6 (1934), pp. 82–83. The agent added to his statement the observation that contesting parties would usually feel that they had a right to have the boundaries between the right and wrong of their controversies determined carefully in strict accordance with international law, if there be such law. If "liberality" be admittedly used in applying existing law, the agent said, dissatisfaction would be inevitable on the part of those who might feel that their interests had been adversely affected by such liberality. Logical deduction and analogy, allowable only outside

The same tribunal's jurisprudence came into question in the *Manzo* claim,[134] a case which involved principles of municipal law in relation to international liability, and in which the commission awarded $2,500 against the United States. Characterizing the basis of the award as somewhat obscure, the American agent said, on the point of whether the arbitrators had applied "international law, justice and equity":

> The question involved . . . was . . . whether or not there was international responsibility on the part of the Government of the United States for the alleged negligence of a laborer foreman, which negligence

the field of recognizable law, must be in strict accordance with the recognized "principles" of justice and equity.

[134] *Comisión General de Reclamaciones* (1936), Registro no. 21. The injured Panamanian was a boy who was a water carrier for the Municipal Engineering Division of the Isthmian Canal Commission in 1905. He was hurt while oiling sheaves. The practice of allowing him to oil was equivalent to directing him to do so, and it was found to be negligence *per se* to employ so young a child (between ten and thirteen years of age) as an oiler of heavy machinery. In the course of its opinion the commission said (at p. 694, document cited): "The principal point argued by the parties is whether the case is governed by the municipal law of Panama, which gave private persons the right to sue the Government in tort, or by the municipal law of the United States, which did not give such a right. It is the opinion of the Commission that the liability in this case does not depend upon the decision of this question. Manzo's injury was brought about by the negligent conduct of an agent of the United States."

An executive order of the President of the United States made the Civil Code of Panama effective in the Canal Zone on May 9, 1904. Congress confirmed this by an act of August 24, 1912 (37 *Stat.* 560). In the case of *Panama Railroad Company* v. *Bosse* (249 U.S. 41, at pp. 43–44), the Supreme Court said that the executive order was "merely the embodiment of the rule that a change of sovereignty does not put an end to existing private law." Counsel for the United States in the *Manzo* case argued that, while municipal law remained in force as it had under the former sovereign, relations *between the inhabitants and the government* of the new sovereign state were changed. The agent of Panama had cited no provision of the Civil Code to prove that the United States was subject to suit or answerable in damages for injuries suffered by one of its employees. A commentator on Colombian law, whose work was cited, had said that the states or political entities were liable for damages caused by their agents or employees. (The respondent state did not admit that there had been any such injury.) The American agent submitted that relations between a government and its employees were obviously among the "fundamental principles" which, in the case of every government, must be governed solely and exclusively by its own law in such matters and could not be governed by the law of the former sovereign (Hunt's *Report*, p. 693).

may or may not have been responsible for the injury to the claimant, another employee in the Canal Zone. Whether there was causative or contributory negligence on the part of the injured claimant did not appear from the evidence. The Commission, in searching for the proper law to apply in the case, dismissed at once the municipal law of both the United States and Panama. There would appear to be no well-defined principles of international law regulating the relations of "master and servant" as between governments and their employees, and the Commission appears to have so found.

Had the Commission then stated that there was no controlling principle of international law or municipal law applicable to the case and that, under authorization of the convention, it intended to apply *in lieu* thereof some defined "principles" of "justice and equity," one might have understood the logic of the process, while perhaps disagreeing with the determination of legal liability in that manner in this class of cases.[135]

The American agent's criticisms, in the paragraphs just quoted, are more pertinent by reason of the fact that, in other claims cases, the American-Panamanian Commission seemed to adhere rather strictly to rules of positive law, national or international. For example, in the *Agnes E. Brown* claim, concerning which the American agent says that the tribunal acted virtually as a municipal court and applied local law applicable to an alleged breach of contract, the arbitrators apparently did not think there was any occasion for application of the principles of "justice and equity"—"although," the agent continued, "the claimant had been induced by the defendant Government to go to a foreign country, although she had discharged her duties satisfactorily, and although she had been summarily discharged and left without employment, income, or return transportation, because of the expression to her superior officer of certain views regarding school matters which were considered to be prohibitively political in character." [136] In the *Shearer* claim, in which the agent of the United States submitted that the Panamanian government had taken over, along with the claimant's land, valuable improvements thereon without making any compensation, the tribunal

[135] Hunt's *Report*, pp. 695–696.

[136] *Ibid.*, p. 95. The American agent took this to indicate the tribunal's view that resort to principles of "justice and equity" was allowable only in the absence of clearly recognizable principles of law.

applied only the letter of the local law, without apparent equitable considerations of the spirit thereof.[137]

The foregoing brief survey of the application which certain international commissions have made of treaty clauses in which there are mentions of the general law emphasizes that that law is the normal basis for arbitral awards. There have been other treaties of the United States in connection with which there have been references to international law as affording bases of awards of national (or "domestic") rather than international claims commissions. When, in a treaty settlement, the United States has accepted a lump sum in satisfaction of claims of its nationals against a foreign government over a given period, there has sometimes been express stipulation in the agreement that the United States will itself settle the claims involved.[138] It remains, in such a case, for Congress to create the machinery and direct the bases of settlements to be made. Under these conditions, there is no strictly legal restriction upon Congress in the performance of its function, that is, nothing which requires that the legislative body instruct commissioners to apply international law. In actual practice, a standard formula has come to direct settlements, that is, the disbursement of money received from the foreign state, according to justice, equity, the law of nations, and pertinent conventions. A study of the jurisprudence of fourteen "domestic" agencies of this kind which the United States used between 1803 and 1902 revealed evidence of the acceptance of funds as trusts, the understanding being that disbursement of them should be in accordance with principles.[139] Since in the discharge of these trusts the government is essentialy compensating individuals for losses due to violation of international law, the ultimate effect of the treaties and of the adjudications pursuant to them is to affirm

[137] The tribunal said: "La Comisión . . . es de opinión que el Agente de los Estados Unidos no hâ demostrado que la ley panameña no requería en la época de que se trata como condición para comenzar a contarse el período de posesión para la prescripción ordinaria, la transmitación de la posesión por medio del registro de la escritura pública" (*Comisión General de Reclamaciones* [1936], Registro no. 3, p. 111).

[138] See, for example, the Treaty of 1898 with Spain, 30 *Stat.* 1754, 1757–58.

[139] Robert R. Wilson, "Some Aspects of the Jurisprudence of National Claims Commissions," *Amer. Jour. Int. Law,* XXXVI (1942), 56–76.

the rules of that law existent at the time the respective causes of action arose.[140]

Whether references to international law occur in general commitments to keep the peace, in treaties of arbitration or judicial settlement, in *compromis* for the submission of questions between governments, or in conventions for the settlement of claims of individuals against governments, three general observations seem to be pertinent, on the basis of American treaty practice. The first is that such provisions, however vague they may seem in some cases, signify at least nominal endorsement of the principle of legality, as distinct from purely arbitrary, capricious or opportunistic procedures in international relations.[141] The second is that, since the law is not static, the precise legal effect of application of a formula such as that which has become common in general arbitration conventions would not necessarily be the same at different times over the life of an international agreement of long duration. The third is that, when a mention of international law occurs in connection with a mention of "equity" or "justice" or both of these terms, the effect in general has not been to authorize departures from the law.

The third of these points has occasioned some controversial discussion, both by agents who have appeared before tribunals and by publicists. It has been seen that, in many cases, the specification of international law apparently had the effect of emphasizing what would presumably have gone on even without this mention in the treaties. Even when there is no specific directive to arbitrators to make their awards according to law, the United States seems to have proceeded upon the assumption that proceedings would be judicial.[142] Where treaties of the United

[140] See also Public Law 455, 81st Cong., 2d Sess., authorizing the International Claims Commission to apply, in the settlement of claims that were originally against Yugoslavia, provisions of the applicable claims agreement and "the applicable principles of international law, justice and equity."

As suggested in the article referred to in the preceding note, such affirmation would be more true for substantive than for adjective law, since, in regard to the latter type of rules, there would be greater possibility of divergence between different national commissions.

[141] The force of the statement is conditioned by the prevailing official view as to the scope of the law. See note 34, *supra*.

[142] See notes 99 and 100, *supra*. See also Manley O. Hudson, *International Tribunals* (1944), p. 100.

States have referred to equity in connection with international law, those applying the provisions have had to interpret the authorizations, and, in general, they have done so with caution. As between the use of equity in the sense of something that is independent and in the sense of something "dans les limites et l'atmosphère du droit,"[143] the latter has received approval. If arbitrators have tended to identify equity with analogy,[144] the formulas which have become familiar in American treaties do not clearly seem to have been intended, so far as the United States was concerned, to authorize something entirely separable from international law. Diplomatic exchanges in connection with the making of the standard arbitration treaties which the United States signed with non-American states, beginning in 1928, support this view.[145]

4. RECLAMATIONS: EXHAUSTION OF LOCAL REMEDIES

The settlement of claims is normally in accordance with the standard which is international law. It is, of course, possible for states to waive their rights under that law, while not denying its

[143] The expression was used by Eugène Borel in 1934 in a report to the Institute of International Law on the subject "La Competence du juge international en equité," *Annuaire*, XXXVIII (1934), 199. The reporter submitted that equity could play a role *infra legem*, or, if need be, *praeter legem*, without the pretension of operating *contra legem*. In observations on the report, the question was introduced of whether some of the language of article 38 of the Statute of the Permanent Court of International Justice was distinguishable from the words "law or equity" as they occur in bilateral treaties of the United States (*Annuaire*, XXXVIII, 232–233). The report emphasizes that there is a difference in the meaning of "equity" in Anglo-American usage and "equité" as used in continental European countries and in Latin America. The observations of Karl Strupp (*ibid.*, pp. 245–249) were directed especially to the notion of equity in the sense of something "accessoire" and as something "indépendante."

It is beyond the scope of the present study to attempt a comparative analysis of the general problem as it exists in international and in municipal jurisprudence. An intimation of its reality in the latter sphere appears in a statement by Justice Felix Frankfurter in a case involving the payment of interest on local tax refunds to American Indians: "Instead of choosing a rigid rule, the Court has drawn upon those flexible considerations of equity which are established sources for judicial law-making" (308 U.S. 343, at 350, referring also to 135 U.S. 271, 281, and 232 U.S. 261).

[144] Orfield, in *Kentucky Law Jour.*, XVIII (1934), 124, 126–128.

[145] See note 60, *supra*.

applicability. Thus in their claims convention signed January 26, 1950, the United States and Panama, recording their recognition of the desirability of eliminating from their relations with each other any cause for difference, agreed to dispose of a group of claims which had been outstanding for a considerable time "on an equitable basis and without reference to the legal aspects." One of these claims having been the subject of a prior decision by its Supreme Court, Panama made clear that it was not ignoring or disregarding this decision, which set forth "the legal aspects of the matter." Furthermore, the parties recorded that any other unsettled claims on behalf of nationals of either country against the government of the other country, "whether arising under the provisions of agreements between the two countries or under general principles of international law, are not affected by the provisions of this Convention." [146]

Without shifting from the international law standard as a basis for settling a claim on its merits, parties may waive a particular defense under that law. In United States practice this has sometimes been done with regard to the rule requiring the exhaustion of local remedies before the case may properly come before an international tribunal. There is general agreement upon the existence of this rule, which has frequently been a subject of discussion. One view is that it is a convenient device for foreign offices rather than an "imperative" rule controlling the jurisdiction of international tribunals.[147] Its controlling force, however, has now come to be established upon the basis of practice which has developed into an element of customary law.[148] The Permanent Court of International Justice applied the rule in its judgment of February 28, 1939, in the *Panevezys-Saldutiskis Railway* case between Estonia and Lithuania.[149] The four dissenting judges did not deny existence of the rule as an element of international law, although one of them (W. J. M. van Eysinga) thought that an agreement for compulsory arbitration without condition would

[146] T.I.A.S. 2129.

[147] Jackson H. Ralston, *International Arbitration from Athens to Locarno* (1929), pp. 60–61.

[148] Cf. Alwyn V. Freeman, *The International Responsibility of States for Denial of Justice* (1938), p. 413.

[149] P.C.I.J., ser. A/B, no. 76, p. 4.

necessitate a specific reservation by parties if they wished to maintain the rule of local remedies.[150] Of the nature of the rule, Judge Manley O. Hudson, dissenting, said in part:

> It is a very important rule of international law that local remedies must have been exhausted without redress before a State may successfully espouse a claim of its national against another state. This is not a rule of procedure. It is not merely a matter of orderly conduct. It is a part of the substantive law as to international, i.e. State-to-State, responsibility. If adequate redress for the injury is available to the person who suffered it, if such person has only to reach out to avail himself of such redress, there is no basis for a claim to be espoused by the State of which such person is a national. Until the available means of local redress have been exhausted, no international responsibility can arise.[151]

That the rule is a fundamental one is apparent, since without it any injury which an alien suffered would be, not merely potentially but actually, a proper occasion for a demand for damages. Evidence of the reality of the rule is to be had from American arbitral practice.[152] It also figured in international conference discussion at the Bogotá meeting of American republics in 1948.[153]

[150] *Ibid.*, p. 37: "Compulsory arbitration, accepted unconditionally, constitutes an exception to the applicability of the local remedies rule."

[151] *Ibid.*, p. 47. Judge Hudson added that the rule was not one of thumb, to be applied in a more or less automatic fashion; in each case, he pointed out, account is to be taken of circumstances surrounding the means of redress, and "the facts may justify an international tribunal in saying that international responsibility has arisen even though local remedies have not been exhausted" (*ibid.*, p. 48).

[152] For illustrative instances in which arbitrators have given effect to the general rule, see awards of Sir Edward Thornton, umpire, in the cases of *Alfred A. Green & Company* v. *Mexico* and *Benjamin Burn* v. *Mexico* (Moore, *International Arbitrations,* III, 3139, 3140), and the award of the arbitrator in the claims of *Charles Oberlander* and *Barbara M. Messinger* against Mexico (*For. Rel.,* 1897, p. 382). See American references to the rule, in relation to Mexican-American claims, in *For. Rel.,* 1912, pp. 939, 944, 945. See also the argument of Fred K. Nielsen in the *Hawaiian Claims* cases before the British-American tribunal under the special agreement of August 18, 1910 (Nielsen's *Report,* p. 143).

[153] The United States did not accept article VII of the Pact of Bogotá, which sets forth that the parties bind themselves not to make diplomatic representations to protect their nationals, "or to refer a controversy to a court of international jurisdiction for that purpose, when the said nationals have had available the means to place their case before competent domestic courts of the respective states." By its reservations the government of the United States "maintains the rules of diplomatic protection, including the rule of

One of the questions which has engaged the attention of commissioners (for example, those who functioned under article XII of the Treaty of Washington, 1871) is that of whether a claimant must not only have gone to local courts, such as a prize court of first instance, but must actually have taken his case on appeal as far as he could go in municipal courts.[154] When respondent states have used the plea of nonexhaustion of local remedies, arbitrators have sometimes disposed of it by concluding that the very fact of submission has attested the will of the two governments to arbitrate without having the process impeded by the application of this jurisdiction-limiting rule.[155] In the early case of *The Sally (Hayes, Master)* Commissioner William Pinkney argued vigorously that, while by the agreement the local judicial remedy was to be tried, there was no justification for holding the claimant to a long-delayed procedure of exhausting local remedies, if he had not been guilty of laches.[156] Not only on this point but also on the flexibility of the local-remedies rule in general, it is to be expected that there will be some divergences of view between different arbitral boards and between different members of a particular commission.[157] There is a question of whether

---

exhaustion of local remedies by aliens, as provided by international law" (*Report of the Delegation of the United States to the Ninth International Conference of American States,* pp. 50, 51, 188, 200).

[154] The tribunal referred to examined carefully each individual case in which appeal had not been taken and, while not dismissing them automatically, considered whether there were reasonable grounds for nonexhaustion of rights to appeal (Moore, *International Arbitrations,* III, 3152–3159).

[155] Illustrated in the *Lacaze* case between France and the Argentine Republic in 1864 (Albert G. de Lapradelle and Nicolas Politis, *Recueil des arbitrages internationaux,* II [1924], 298; referred to in Freeman, *International Responsibility,* pp. 412–413). See also the cases cited in *Amer. Jour. Int. Law,* XXIII, Spec. Supp., at p. 154. Cf. note 150, *supra.*

[156] Moore, *International Arbitrations,* III, 3108–3115; Henry Wheaton, *Some Account of the Life, Writings and Speeches of William Pinkney* (1826), pp. 349–354. In this case, the provision of the Jay Treaty was interpreted so as to give the arbitrators competence, even though local remedies had not been exhausted, where it appeared that claimants had not been guilty of laches.

[157] That decisions of the same commission may show discrepancies on the point is shown by F. S. Dunn in comments on the work of the American-Mexican claims commission under the treaty of 1868 (see note 121, *supra*). In the case of *Mather and Glover* v. *Mexico,* Umpire Lieber made an award

the standard of international responsibility for protection of foreigners and their property is capable of application everywhere in exactly the same way. Arbitrators have frequently had to pass upon the adequacy of particular local remedies, but no clear-cut formulas seem to have evolved.[158]

As to the advisability or utility of relaxing the rule which requires exhaustion of local remedies, there has not been agreement. One view is that, since the rule is perhaps the best-established one applicable to the general subject of responsibility, and since it definitely serves to promote convenience through facilitating the tasks of diplomats,[159] no good purpose is served by a waiver of the right to use it as a defense. An opposing view is that it is desirable for states to make treaties in which they agree that no case shall be dismissed on the ground of the rule, since such provisions facilitate the redress of wrongs and are in harmony with enlightened principles of comity in international relations.[160] Although the former would seem to be the sounder view, it is not necessary to settle the question in examining some actual instances of treaty waivers.

One of the occasions on which the United States agreed not to apply the rule of local remedies in the regular way had to do with the special agreement of August 18, 1910, for the arbitration of claims with Great Britain.[161] In this instance, while the parties did not set aside the rule in express terms, they left it to the arbitrators to decide, as one of the equities of the case, the effect of any claimant's failure to seek redress through local courts.

---

to claimants who had not exhausted their local remedies (Docket no. 178). In another case before the commission, the Mexican brief characterized as a "dishonorable international condition" a failure to apply the rule (*Gibbs, Executor* v. *Mexico*, Docket no. 134). See Dunn, *Diplomatic Protection*, pp. 212, 228.

[158] Freeman (*International Responsibility*, p. 418) cites the *Montano* case between Peru and the United States (Lapradelle and Politis, *Recueil*, II, 271; Moore, *International Arbitrations*, II, 1630) as showing that the rule of local remedies has flexibility which makes it adaptable to practical needs.

[159] Clyde Eagleton, *The Responsibility of States in International Law* (1928), p. 102. Cf. Herbert W. Briggs, "The Settlement of Mexican Claims Act of 1942," *Amer. Jour. Int. Law*, XXXVII (1943), 231.

[160] Nielsen, *International Law Applied to Reclamations*, p. 70.

[161] 37 *Stat.* (2) 1625.

Following the agreement, the terms of submission, July 6, 1911, contained in their third article the following:

> The Arbitral Tribunal shall take into account as one of the equities of a claim to such extent as it shall consider just in allowing or disallowing a claim, in whole or in part, any failure on the part of the claimant to obtain satisfaction through legal remedies which are open to him or placed at his disposal, but no claim shall be disallowed or rejected by application of the general principle of international law that the legal remedies must be exhausted as a condition precedent to the validity of the claim.[162]

Arbitrators did not interpret and apply this authorization in such a way as to disregard completely the rules regarding exhaustion of local remedies. In connection with Canadian claims for refunds of duties despite the statute of limitations applicable thereto, occasion arose for the arbitrators to consider the force

[162] In a communication to the British ambassador dated March 4, 1911, the Department of State proposed, as one of the terms of submission, the rule that "the inclusion of a claim in any of the following Schedules shall operate as a bar to a plea in defense thereto that the legal remedies provided by municipal law have not been exhausted or that the claim is now pending before a municipal tribunal of competent jurisdiction." The British in turn suggested, as a substitute for this wording, the statement that "the Commission shall take into account to such extent as they shall consider just any admission of liability by the Government against whom a claim is put forward or any failure on the part of claimant to obtain satisfaction through legal remedies which were open to him or which were placed at his disposal."

The Department of State felt that this language would allow the commission to disallow a claim by application of the general rule of international law, whereas the understanding had been that jurisdiction of the tribunal was not to be limited by application of the technical rules of international law except as such claims were barred by previous treaties. The desire was, "in order to expedite the settlement of a claim which might properly be prosecuted through the channels of national justice", to withdraw it from the jurisdiction of municipal courts and allow the international tribunal to decide it on its merits. Mere inclusion in the schedule, however, would not accomplish this, as the commission "would be bound to apply the accepted rule." While insisting on the nonapplication of that general rule, the Department recognized that laches might become material in mitigation of an indemnity, and was willing to have the fact of failure to prosecute a claim in municipal courts presented to the tribunal as a matter of evidence, but requested provision that no claim should be disallowed or rejected by application of the international law principle. Agreement was apparently reached through informal discussion. Department of State files 441.11A/86; 441.11A/92, nos. 58, 1159; 441.11A/101, nos. 114, 1193 (National Archives).

and effect of their instructions. British counsel in this case argued:

> In view of . . . paragraph 3 . . . of the terms of submission, we believe that this Tribunal must consider these claims in precisely the same manner as would a court of the United States have considered them had they been presented there within that time.
>
> In other words, we are not asking that these Canadian citizens be accorded any different rights from any one else except to this extent that when these claims were referred to this Tribunal the United States of America did waive one defense, and that was the defense of the statute of limitations.[163]

The agent for the United States replied to this, in part, as follows:

> The plea that legal remedies must be exhausted may, of course, be said to be a substantive defense, because it is a well-known rule of international law that a claimant against a foreign country is not entitled to the intervention of his own government unless he has exhausted his legal remedies in the country against which he makes claim. Nevertheless, I think the plea may also be spoken of as something of a technical plea. . . . The plea is not concerned with the broad, fundamental question, with its various ramifications, whether a wrong was committed by the respondent government under international law.
>
> . . . . .
>
> I will waive, for the time being, all contention that there is the strongest possible equity against these claimants, and I will proceed on the theory that the well-known rule with regard to the necessity for the exhaustion of legal remedies is completely wiped out by article 3 in terms of submission, which, according to the construction of both Governments, evidently is not entirely wiped out.[164]

In deciding this case the tribunal looked to the applicability of Section 2931 of the Revised Statutes, as interpreted by the United States Supreme Court in a decision some four decades before.[165] It ruled that the plea of claimants' ignorance of United States law could not be sustained, and that the submission of the claims to the tribunal by the government of the United States constituted no implied waiver and did not operate to take them out from under the ordinary statutory provisions.[166]

[163] Nielsen's *Report*, p. 350.
[164] *Ibid.*, pp. 360, 361.
[165] *Aronson et al.* v. *Murphy, Collector*, 115 U.S. 579 (1885).
[166] Nielsen's *Report*, p. 362.

In the *R. T. Roy* case, adjudicated under the same agreement, the tribunal decided in a way to suggest that it did not attach great weight to the declaration, in the terms of submission, that "no claim shall be disallowed or rejected by application of the general principle . . . that the legal remedies must be exhausted as a condition precedent." The claim grew out of the seizure of a vessel of American registry which had been fishing in waters of Lake Huron *allegedly* within Canadian jurisdiction. If, on the question of fact, the place of arrest were not within the jurisdiction which the respondent state claimed, it would seem to be extraordinary to remit the claimants to the exhaustion of remedies within that jurisdiction. Even aside from this point, the criticism of the American agent, who considered that the commission had disposed of the case as if the general rule of international law had not been eliminated by the arbitral agreement, seems well founded.[167]

When setting up the General Claims Commission with Mexico under the convention of September 8, 1923, the United States again approved a plan of waiving rights under the rule concerning local remedies. Claims to be arbitrated were those which had arisen since July 4, 1868, excluding claims which the parties provided for in the Special Claims Convention. Article V of the convention relating to general claims contained the following:

> The High Contracting Parties, being desirous of effecting an equitable settlement of the claims of their respective citizens thereby affording them just and adequate compensation for their losses or damages, agree that no claim shall be disallowed or rejected by the Commission by the application of the general principle of international law that the legal remedies must be exhausted as a condition precedent to the validity or allowance of any claim.[168]

Three years before the signing of this convention, the confidential agent of the government of Mexico had informed the Secretary of State of the United States (Bainbridge Colby) that Mexico could not but feel deeply grieved over the charge that

[167] *Ibid.*, p. 406. The tribunal did not meet the question of what authority it had, under the terms of the agreement, to dismiss the claim because of a failure to resort to local remedies.

[168] 43 Stat. 1730 at 1734.

she intended to disavow her obligations. He made the point that President Adolfo de la Huerta, as well as President-elect Alvaro Obregón, had on repeated occasions declared publicly that Mexico would respect all rightful claims and would submit to the recognized principles of international law.[169] It soon became apparent that resumption of diplomatic relations between the two countries was to be dependent upon some satisfactory arrangement concerning claims. Negotiations to this end went on in Mexico City between May 14 and August 15, 1923. In the course of these meetings Charles B. Warren, one of the American negotiators, suggested that "when any loss or damage of any nature has been or may hereafter be suffered by any citizen of the United States, in whatever form his interest may be held, the General Claims Commission, to be created if this exchange of views and statements culminates in the resumption of diplomatic relations between the two countries, should have jurisdiction, *without limiting in any manner its general jurisdiction,* to hear and determine all such claims and to fix the damages sustained and the compensation to be paid therefor." [170] The conversations brought out that approval by the United States of a recommendation of the commissioners would "depend upon the signing and ratification of a general claims convention creating a commission *with the necessary jurisdiction.*" [171] Negotiations looking to claims settlements were successful.

In the general claims convention which the parties made, the waiver of the right to plead nonexhaustion of local remedies was on a reciprocal basis. Mexico's concession received emphasis, however, by reason of the fact that in the Special Claims Convention, signed two days later,[172] a like provision appeared in an arrangement for settling claims all of which were against Mexico. In this there was another specific reference to international law. The second article set forth that Mexico wished that her responsibility (to Americans who had suffered loss or damage from revolutionary acts in Mexico between Novem-

169 *For. Rel.,* 1920, III, 190.

170 *Proceedings of the United States–Mexican Commission Convened in Mexico City May 14, 1923* (1925), p. 39 (italics inserted).

171 *Ibid.,* p. 40 (italics inserted). See also *For. Rel.,* 1923, II, 536–548.

172 43 *Stat.* 1722.

ber 20, 1910, and May 31, 1920) should "not be fixed according to the generally accepted rules and principles of international law," and that Mexico, "ex gratia," felt "morally bound to make full indemnification." [173]

Similar provisions appeared in conventions concerning special claims (for damages growing out of revolutionary disturbances) which Mexico made with major states in Europe.[174] The cumulative effect has apparently accounted at least in part for some criticism which has been directed at the plan of assessing liability for damages on bases other than those of international law.[175] It is well known that the Special Claims Convention which Mexico made with the United States did not in its actual application lead to final settlement of all the claims, and that a later arrangement superseded it.[176]

In the leading case before it which involved a Calvo clause (a device by which a government seeks to restrict foreigners contracting with it to local remedies), the Mexican-American General Claims Commission did not allow the waiver of the right to plead nonexhaustion of local remedies to become a matter of any great seriousness for the respondent state. A majority of the commissioners who considered the claim of the *North American Dredging Company* against Mexico concluded that they could give the benefits under the provision for waiver (in article V of the convention) only to those claims which the applicant state had *properly presented* and which would fall within the categories of claims (listed in article I of the convention) for which the commission was competent.[177] They found that the claim of the Dredging Company had not properly come to them under article I, the company not having done

[173] On this plan of compensating *ex gratia*, see Antonio Gómez Robledo, *The Bucareli Agreements and International Law* (1940), p. 126.

[174] See Appendix II.

[175] See, for example, T. Esquivel Obregón, *México y los Estados Unidos ante el Derecho Internacional* (1926), pp. 105 *et seq.*

[176] For a summary statement of the development, see *For. Pol. Assn. Reports*, XIII, 133–134 (August 15, 1937); see also *For. Rel.*, 1932, V, 734, 746; Hearings before a Subcommittee of the Committee on Foreign Relations, U.S. Senate, 77th Cong., 2d Sess., on S. 2528, June 30, July 1, 2, 6, 10, 14 (1942); Convention of April 24, 1934, 49 *Stat.* 3071.

[177] *Opinions of Commissioners*, 1927, p. 21.

anything in Mexico to secure satisfaction.[178] Some two decades later, however, when the question was before a national claims commission (created to decide upon the validity of claims against money which Mexico has paid to the United States), the commission found that claims such as that of the Dredging Company should not be barred.[179]

Three years after signing the General and Special Claims Conventions with Mexico, the United States signed the Reciprocal Claims Convention of July 28, 1926, with Panama.[180] It contained a provision concerning exhaustion of local remedies which was substantially the same as that of the General Claims Convention with Mexico. Two claims which were before the American-Panamanian commission reveal the use which arbitrators made of the parties' waiver of the right to plead non-exhaustion of local remedies. In the *Perry* claim, the commission said, of the provision in question, "This article is clear, it calls for no comment, but it may be noted that the High Contracting Parties express as the reason for this . . . their desire of effecting an equitable settlement of the claims of their respective citizens, a desire which may be considered significant as to the general trend of the intention of the Parties." The American agent thought this use of the article concerning the waiver, in relation to that concerning equity as a basis for awards, afforded a possible explanation of the commission's advocacy of "broad conceptions" rather than "narrow interpretations."[181]

A more direct application of the waiver clause was that in connection with the claim which the United States presented on

[178] The opinion of Fred K. Nielsen, who, as agent, disagreed with the commissioners' view, seems more convincing than the latter; see remarks in his dissenting opinion in the International Fisheries Claim (*Opinions*, 1931, p. 225). However, the British-Mexican Claims Commission followed and applied the reasoning of the tribunal in the *Dredging Company* case, in the claim of the *Mexican Union Railway Company* (*Amer. Jour. Int. Law*, XXIV [1930], 388).

[179] *American-Mexican Claims Commission . . . Report to the Secretary of State* (Department of State Publications 2859), pp. 298–305.

[180] 47 *Stat.* 1915. Article V contains the provision concerning exhaustion of local remedies.

[181] Hunt's *Report*, p. 83. The use of equity as a basis for awards of this commission has been the subject of previous comment. See section 3, notes 132 and 133, *supra*.

behalf of Marguerite de Joly de Sablá. The cause of action grew out of a system for the disposal of real property in Panama. That state claimed that the system, as it had figured in this instance, was not "confiscatory by international standards," because the claimant had an adequate remedy and losses were attributable to her not having availed herself of that remedy at the time the land was about to be sold or licensed. The contention of the United States was that the procedure to which Panama proposed to hold the claimant (in the matter of filing opposition) was unnecessary, and that, if it were necessary, then "those laws as applied imposed so unreasonable a burden on private landowners as to fall below international standards." Although the claimant had sometimes successfully utilized the "opposition procedure" which the laws of Panama permitted, the American agent argued that the remedy as provided by the law of Panama was not an adequate one. Article V of the convention was then invoked to support the argument that it was "unnecessary to consider the question of what legal remedies were open to the claimant under the laws of Panama, *after the wrongful grants had been made by the government,* to obtain redress for the past wrongs, either against the government or against the grantees." [182] The commission awarded $75,546.25. In his dissent Horacio F. Alfaro, commissioner, observed that in this case the majority had held the claim to be established, not because the claimant had presented proof of the assertions made, but because the respondent government had presented no evidence.[183]

It has been seen that some judges in international adjudications have taken the position that mere submission of a case to arbitration amounts to a waiver of the defense that local remedies have not been exhausted.[184] There is, however, much to be said against this view. The arbitrators in the *Salem* case, between the United States and Egypt, apparently rejected it.[185] If it is not

[182] Hunt's *Report,* p. 447 (italics inserted). See also Whiteman, *Damages in International Law,* II, 1437.

[183] Hunt's *Report,* p. 454.

[184] See notes 150, 155, 156, *supra.*

[185] Department of State Arbitration Series 4 (6), 1933, p. 43. See also note 160, *supra.*

generally regarded as a valid position where states make an agreement to arbitrate a specific case, it would follow that where they contract for the arbitration of a great many claims falling within a designated period, there would be no implied waiver of the perfectly valid defense under international law. The motive for inserting a specific waiver, such as those in treaties noted above, may not always be the same. Political considerations may impel party states to assent to the relinquishment of the defense for a particular group of claims. There may be delicate issues which arise when an applicant state contends that a respondent state has been guilty of denying justice to aliens,[186] or perhaps essays to show that there has in fact been no justice to exhaust.[187] Whatever the occasion for the waiver, the rule of construing *stricto jure* any waiver of rights[188] and the usage which stresses that express terms are required in order to alter the law[189] suggest the need for definiteness where the parties wish to eliminate the common defense of nonexhaustion of local remedies. There have been but few treaty agreements in which the United States has assented to such a waiver. In the case of the General Claims Convention with Mexico, 1923, as has been seen, the mixed commission did not allow this part of the convention to nullify another part under which it held that a company which had signed a Calvo clause must have taken *some* steps to get satisfaction locally before there could properly be an international reclamation.

Recourse to local remedies may figure in another way in treaty relations. Parties may agree that they will not press certain claims against each other and may in effect remit private claimants to the local remedies available, at the same time reserving all rights under international law. On May 19, 1927, the United States and Great Britain signed an Agreement for the Disposal of

[186] As suggested by E. M. Borchard, *The Diplomatic Protection of Citizens Abroad* (1915), p. 341. If there were a more general agreement upon the meaning of denial of justice, one which would keep it from being identified with any international illegality, this might have some bearing upon the practice here under discussion.

[187] See the statement of Secretary of State Hamilton Fish to the Venezuelan minister, May 29, 1873, as quoted in Moore, *Digest*, VI, 677.

[188] *The Wanderer*, Nielsen's *Report*, pp. 459, 462.

[189] Cf. A. D. McNair, *The Law of Treaties* (1938), p. 228.

Certain Pecuniary Claims Arising Out of the Recent War.[190] By this they reciprocally cancelled purely intergovernmental claims growing out of prosecution of the First World War, and, with specific exceptions made in the second article (relating especially to users of inventions, and salvage services), agreed that they would not present diplomatically or request international arbitration in behalf of any national who had allegedly suffered loss or damage through the other government's war measures. Each of the contracting parties was to refer its nationals who claimed to have suffered such loss or damage to the appropriate judicial or administrative tribunal of the country against which the claim was alleged to lie, and the decision of such tribunal or of the appellate tribunal was to be regarded as the final settlement of the claims. By the final paragraph of the first article,

> the right of each Government to maintain in the future such position as it may deem appropriate with respect to the legality or illegality under international law of measures such as those giving rise to claims covered by the immediately preceding paragraph is fully reserved, it being specifically understood that the juridical position of neither Government is prejudiced by the present agreement.

From the strictly legal point of view, rather than from that of policy, the case against the American government's pressing the claims rested particularly upon the point that, as an associate of Great Britain in the war, the United States was estopped from pressing the claims, or should as a matter of comity drop them. The case for pressing the claims rested upon the fact that the United States had, while a neutral in the First World War, maintained that some of the British acts affecting American nationals were contrary to international law, and that it should, in order to be consistent, either demand a diplomatic or arbitral settlement, or itself assume liability to its nationals who held the claims.[191] A suggestion of the tenuous nature of the international law involved appeared in a memorandum by the Assistant Secretary of State (Robert E. Olds) one month before the formal signing of

[190] United States Treaty Series (hereafter U.S.T.S.) 756. On the nature and extent of the private American claims involved, see *For. Rel.*, 1926, II, 214–308.

[191] See E. M. Borchard, "The Neutrality Claims against Great Britain," *Amer. Jour. Int. Law*, XXI (1927), 764–768.

the 1927 agreement. After stating that the British would not concede the invalidity of their war measures or arbitrate the question, he added:

> It is extremely doubtful, even if an arbitration were feasible, whether any tribunal could settle the principles in the way in which we should like to have them determined. Most thoughtful students of international law are coming to feel that the rights of neutrals under these modern conditions must be defined, if at all, by some form of international legislation, rather than by tribunals bound by precedents laid down in circumstances which have little in common with those of the present day.
>
> . . . . .
>
> It appears from a careful examination of the specific cases recorded in the Department's files that there are a few American claims (of which probably not more than eleven involve any substantial sums) which the Government of the United States on further examination might regard as meritorious, but which might not be adequately provided for under the proposed agreement either because the claimants had already exhausted their legal remedies in the British courts, or because no legal remedy was open to them. As to these cases the Government of the United States proposes to say to the British Government that it will regard the net amount saved to it, under the main provision of the agreement . . . as intended for their satisfaction.[192]

In the formal exchange which constituted the executive agreement, the government of the United States indicated that it regarded the arrangement "not as a financial settlement but as the friendly composition of conflicting points of view which seemed to lend themselves to no other form of adjustment." [193] Subsequent to the agreement, the United States assumed liability for some of the claims which its nationals had submitted, and in which local judicial recourse had been exhausted.[194] Under such arrangement, there is in effect no denial of rights under international law, so far as the individual claimant is concerned. If it is not done, and

[192] *For. Rel.*, 1927, II, 748–749.

[193] *Ibid.*, p. 752.

[194] In 1935 Congress appropriated $78,025.83, plus interest, for the purpose (49 *Stat.* [2] 2150). An example of the arbitration of one of the claims, between the United States and the private claimant, is in Claim of *Edward J. Ryan, Trustee* v. *United States* (*Amer. Jour. Int. Law,* XXXII [1938], 593–620). See also *For. Rel.*, 1931, II, 729ff.

claimants are referred for remedies to national tribunals which have no option except to enforce the law which the legislature of their own country has passed (even if this be contrary to international law), the rule of resort to local remedies is carried farther than it is in ordinary international jurisprudence.[195] In this instance what the United States gave up was not an existing remedy (since there was under traditional international law no right to require another state to allow cases to go to arbitration, unless it had in a general or special agreement assented to this), but rather the right to *seek* a remedy through diplomatic or arbitral means. It is not unusual, under such conditions, for the state to assume liability to individuals for what it has asked them to give up in the national interest, as experience with many national or "domestic" claims commissions will illustrate.[196]

As to questions of international law which would have come up had the claims gone to arbitration, the handling of them in the executive agreement of 1927—so as not to prejudice the juridical position of the American government—left the way open for the United States to pursue as a neutral in 1940 and 1941 a course notably different from that which it had followed from 1914 to 1917.[197] After the Second World War, in their settlement of lend-lease, reciprocal aid, and intergovernmental claims, the United States and the United Kingdom included a waiver of all financial claims of one government against the other which "have arisen or may hereafter arise out of incidents or transactions occurring on or after September 3, 1939, and prior to September 2, 1945, connected with or incidental to the conduct of World War II." [198]

[195] Borchard, "The Neutrality Claims against Great Britain," especially p. 767n.

[196] See section 3, notes 139, 140, *supra*. On the absence of any "indefeasible right" of claimant to have his government take up his claim and present it diplomatically, see the memorandum by Assistant Secretary of State Olds, *For. Rel.*, 1927, II, 750.

[197] See Chapter V, section 3b, *infra*.

[198] T.I.A.S. 1770 (effective July 12, 1948).

Chapter III

COMMERCE AND NAVIGATION

In view of the slow development of international law pertaining to the economic relations of states, it would be natural to expect that, in contrast to treaties concerning pacific settlement, those concerning commerce, navigation, and related matters would make less use of the method of incorporating international law by reference. Traditionally, while agreeing upon freedom of the seas to commerce carriers in time of peace, states have claimed the right, without infringing international law, to withhold commercial advantages to foreign nationals, vessels, and goods. The granting of trading privileges and advantages has, in general, come through treaties, principally bilateral ones.[1] Navigation of "international" rivers, or even of important rivers that are not "international" in the sense in which that term has ordinarily been used, has also been the subject of treaty negotiations, in the course of which there has sometimes been invocation of already existing rights under customary law.

At the outset it is apparent that, in the commercial field, standards other than that of international law—particularly most-favored-nation treatment and national treatment—have played more important parts, and that these standards have been applied to much more than exchange of goods. With the utilization of the "commercial" treaty for agreements on the entry of alien persons, protection of their personal and property rights, their engagement in various activities, assurances against their being discriminated against in such matters as internal taxation, and the securing of their exemption from military service, broader descriptive words

[1] This does not overlook provisions in some multilateral treaties which relate to commercial rights, or commercial clauses in some other types of treaties such as peace treaties.

came to be in order.[2] Perhaps the term "general relations" would best convey the idea of the scope of subject matter to which modern commercial treaties relate. They have variously been called treaties of "friendship," "establishment," and, more recently, "investment." From the very first, so far as treaty making by the United States is concerned, navigation rights have been included in them. The frequent employment in treaties of this type, in the nineteenth century, of certain "stock" clauses has been regarded as making the latter, in a measure, "a substitute for norms of universal international law."[3] So far as the strictly commercial provisions are concerned, the coming into effect in 1948 of the General Agreement on Tariffs and Trade did not supersede the older type of bilateral instrument, although it has raised questions of harmonization of the two types of agreement in so far as they attempt to deal with the same kind of discriminatory practices.

Parallel with the commercial treaty development referred to, there has been a development of international case law relating to the responsibility of any state for the protection of admitted aliens and their property in the admitting state's territory. Thus there has come to be, at least on some subject matters commonly dealt with in commercial treaties, enough customary international law to make references to this law in bilateral treaties meaningful. Furthermore, it is apparent that in a new "era of multilateralism," with the establishment of rules in such instruments as the Articles of Agreement on the International Monetary Fund, the proposed Covenant on Human Rights, and possible agreements of the future on the subject of international freedom of information, the reach of such references may become significantly greater.[4]

The present chapter will deal, first, with some "establishment" provisions in bilateral treaties in which the international law standard has been employed, then with references to international

[2] B. Nolde, "Droit et technique des traités de commerce," *Recueil des cours*, III (1924), 298.

[3] Arthur Nussbaum, *A Concise History of the Law of Nations* (1947), p. 201.

[4] The integration of bilateral commercial treaties with basic multilateral agreements is touched upon in Robert R. Wilson, "Postwar Commercial Treaties of the United States," *Amer. Jour. Int. Law*, XLIII (1949), 262, 282.

law in certain agreements concerning river navigation, and, finally, with the part which international law played in opposition by the United States to the conclusion of certain treaties relating to the slave trade.

1. ESTABLISHMENT PROVISIONS

a. Residence and Engagement in Activities

It has been seen that rules of customary international law applicable to the treatment of ordinary nationals of foreign states have sometimes received treaty emphasis where there has been, in one of the party states, an earlier system of extraterritoriality.[5] Concern over the continuing legal effect of such an earlier system was a factor in the negotiation of the Treaty of Establishment and Sojourn which the United States signed with Turkey on October 28, 1931.[6] Both this and the manner in which the international law standard was utilized in connection with another standard (that of most-favored-nation treatment) seem to justify selection of this agreement as illustrative of a method.

The legal work pertaining to the treaty was complicated by reason of the Turkish Cabinet's desire to terminate all vestiges of the Turkish-American Treaty of May 7, 1830,[7] and the mutual desire of the parties to retain for Turkish merchants benefits under section 3 (6) of the United States Immigration Act of 1924, which permitted liberal rights of entry to and sojourn in the United States to be given to traders from countries which had "existing" commercial treaties with this country.[8] The first of these desires was reflected in the Turkish proposal to have in the preamble of the new treaty, concerning the conditions of establishment for nationals and companies of each party in the territory of the other, the words, "having in mind that there exist between

[5] Chapter I, section 4, *supra.*
[6] 47 *Stat.* (2) 2432.
[7] 8 *Stat.* 408; 18 *Stat.* (2) 583.
[8] This part of the Immigration Statute was subsequently revised (8 U.S.C. [1948] 203). See Robert R. Wilson, "'Treaty-Merchant' Clauses in Commercial Treaties of the United States," *Amer. Jour. Int. Law,* XLIV (1950), 145–149.

the two countries no provisions regulating the said conditions."[9] This was unacceptable to the Department of State, since a *modus vivendi* of February 17, 1927, between Turkey and the United States, which was still in force, did in fact contain provisions of the kind referred to; aside from this, the Department was unwilling to accept wording which might imply that the Capitulations in Turkey had been abolished as of the date (October 1, 1914) on which they were declared by the Turks to have been abolished.[10]

For the language which the Turkish negotiators had proposed, the American representatives received authorization to substitute the words, "being desirious of prescribing, in accordance with modern international law, the conditions under which the nationals and corporations of each of the High Contracting Parties may settle and carry on business in the territory of the other Party, and with a view to regulating accordingly questions relating to jurisdiction and fiscal charges."[11] Alternatively, the American ambassador was authorized to accept wording to the effect that the new treaty would supersede, as between the parties (thus excluding application to territories which had broken away from the Ottoman Empire), all treaties previously concluded between the United States and that Empire. On their part, the Turkish negotiators countered with a proposal for preambular language whereby the parties would set forth, "taking note of the fact (*constatant que*) that the conditions under which the nationals and corporations of each of the high contracting parties may settle and carry on their activities in the territory of the other party should be prescribed in accordance with modern international law and that questions relating to judicial competence and fiscal charges should manifestly be regulated by this same principle," that they had "decided to conclude a treaty to this effect and purpose."[12]

[9] *For. Rel.*, 1930, III, 864.

[10] *Ibid.*, p. 866. It was felt that such an implication might affect claims of United States nationals which had arisen since 1914.

[11] *Ibid.* The Department of State was willing to regard the phrase "in accordance with modern international law" as disposing of all Capitulatory provisions in the treaty of 1830 but as not disturbing the treaty-merchant privileges which Turkish merchants had in the United States by reason of article I of that treaty.

[12] *For. Rel.*, 1930, III, 870.

In the subsequent negotiations there was a suggestion from the Turkish government that the American ambassador might, in a letter to the Turkish minister of foreign affairs, say that the government of the United States was "fully alive to the changes that have taken place in Turkey," but without adding after these words the phrase, "since the establishment of the Turkish Republic." (The United States representatives had previously suggested the inclusion of the latter phrase, having in mind that the "changes" mentioned might, without the limiting phrase, be understood to relate to changes that had occurred since 1914.) [13] The Department of State agreed to the writing of such a letter, and to the inclusion therein of a statement that the treaty was negotiated on this basis. The preamble of the treaty, as actually signed, followed substantially the language that had been proposed concerning "modern international law," [14] but the standard of treatment specified in the body of the instrument was most-favored-nation treatment.[15]

[13] *Ibid.*, 1931, II, 1038, 1039.

[14] The preamble referred to the parties as being "desirous of prescribing, in accordance with modern international law, the conditions under which the nationals and corporations of each of the High Contracting Parties may settle and carry on business in the territory of the other Party, and with a view to regulating accordingly questions relating to jurisdiction and fiscal charges."

For statement as to the manner in which it had been proposed to refer to international law in a commercial treaty (between the United States and Turkey) which was under negotiation some years before this time (but not concluded), see *infra*, note 23.

[15] Writers on international law, as well as on international economic relations, have sometimes referred to most-favored-nation provision as parts of international law. See, for example, Richard C. Snyder, *The Most-Favored-Nation Clause* (1948), pp. 6, 9, 248. Cf. Georg Schwarzenberger, "The Most-Favoured-Nation Standard in British State Practice," *Brit. Year Book Int. Law*, XXII (1945), 96–121, at pp. 97, 119. The proposition is, of course, true in the sense that most-favored-nation treatment is a long-established standard recognized in this field of law, but not in the sense that by force of custom alone, and not by agreement, such treatment may be comprehended under the international law standard.

On at least one occasion the United States included in a treaty as "a principle of the law of nations" the rule that no privileges granted for equivalent or on account of propinquity or other special conditions should come under the stipulation regarding favored nations. The treaty was that of Amity, Commerce and Navigation with Tonga, signed October 2, 1886 (25 *Stat.* 1440). The purpose of inserting the provision is brought out in the instructions of the Secretary of State (Thomas F. Bayard) to George H. Bates,

Resourcefulness of the negotiators had surmounted a difficulty that was in part psychological as well as legal. The preambular reference to international law at least served the purpose of easing the parties over a drafting difficulty and, while avoiding sweeping provisions that might have undermined certain existing rights, of making clear that, as between the parties and for the purpose of their treaty relations, extraterritoriality was a thing of the past.

b. Property-Protection Provisions

When, shortly after the First World War, the United States began to negotiate a new series of commercial treaties (called treaties of friendship, commerce, and consular rights, since provisions concerning consular rights and functions were included until as late as 1938), there appeared in the standard draft a reference to international law in connection with protection of the persons and property of treaty aliens. In the treaty signed with Germany on December 8, 1923,[16] and in twelve other treaties signed between that date and 1938, the following paragraph appears:

> The nationals of each High Contracting Party shall receive within the territories of the other, upon submitting to conditions imposed upon its nationals, the most constant protection for their persons and property, and shall enjoy in this respect that degree of protection that is required by international law. Their property shall not be taken without due process of law and without payment of just compensation.

A slight variance in the formula occurs in the treaty with Siam, signed November 13, 1937, there being added to the first sentence,

---

Special Agent to Tonga, under date of July 23, 1886 (*Specials Missions, September 11, 1882–August 31, 1886*). A change from conditional to unconditional most-favored-nation treatment, such as the United States made in 1923, would not change preëxisting conditional most-favored-nation commitments to unconditional ones.

[16] 44 *Stat.* 2132. The twelve other treaties in which there is language identical with the paragraph quoted from the treaty with Germany are cited in Chapter I, note 75, *supra.* The background for treaties to be discussed in this section, with special references to provisions regarding compensation in the event of property expropriation in time of peace, is discussed in Robert R. Wilson, "Property-Protection Provisions in United States Commercial Treaties," *Amer. Jour. Int. Law,* XLV (1951), 83–107.

in a paragraph comparable to that quoted above, a statement that nationals of either party within the territory of the other "shall enjoy in this respect the same rights or privileges as are or may be granted to nationals of the State of residence"; this is followed by a phrase, similar to that in the other treaties, concerning submission to the conditions imposed upon nationals. Paragraph 4 of the Final Protocol accompanying the treaty with Siam records the parties' understanding "that the payment of just compensation provided for in Article I, paragraph 3, shall be determined by due process of law, without prejudice to redress, if any, according to international law." [17]

Several new commercial treaties which the United States has negotiated since the cessation of hostilities in the Second World War have contained somewhat similar, but not identical, language. Article VI of the Treaty of Friendship, Commerce and Navigation with China, signed November 4, 1946,[18] referred, as had the treaties of the interwar period, to "the most constant protection and security" to be accorded nationals of one party in the other party's territory; but for the words "that degree of protection that is required by international law" are substituted the words "the full protection and security required by international law." A separate paragraph provides for "due process of law" and the "prompt payment of just and effective compensation" in the event of property expropriation. Other language applied specifically to property the language concerning property protection and committed the parties to allow exchange withdrawal privileges to treaty aliens in the event of expropriation of the latters' property.

The treaty of friendship, commerce, and navigation which the United States signed with Italy on February 2, 1948, follows fairly closely the language used in the treaty with China concerning the international law standard of protection.[19] That with Ireland, signed January 21, 1950, provides that "property of nationals and companies of either Party shall receive the most constant protection and security within the territories of the other Party, in no case less than that required by international law." In the same paragraph there is provision for prompt payment of just and

[17] 53 *Stat.* 1731. [18] T.I.A.S. 1871. [19] T.I.A.S. 1965.

effective compensation and for exchange withdrawal privileges for expropriated treaty aliens. There is also (in article V) a provision for "equitable" treatment by each party of the capital of the nationals and companies of the other party.[20]

The treaty of friendship, commerce, and economic development, signed with Uruguay on November 23, 1949, does not contain a specific reference to the international law standard in connection with protection, but does provide for "the most constant protection and security" and specifies that "the taking of property legally acquired by the nationals and companies of either Party shall be subject to procedures and conditions no less favorable than those legally applicable in the case of the taking of property of nationals of such other Party." Any appropriation is to be made "in accordance with the applicable laws, which shall at least assure the payment of just compensation in a prompt, adequate and effective manner." There is, as in the Irish treaty, a separate provision for "equitable" treatment.[21]

The record of negotiations of certain of the commercial treaties modeled upon that signed with Germany in 1923, including some negotiations that did not result in perfected agreements, throws some light upon the purpose and intended legal effect of the wording which provides for the international law standard. In this connection, allowance should be made for the fact that the wording referred to comprised but one part of a long and detailed instrument, in connection with which the matter of relative emphasis could become, at least in a psychological sense, a matter of importance. Furthermore, to attempt to determine the significance of the use of the standard as specifically provided for in this one part of the treaty plan is not to overlook that there may be, in other parts of that plan (as, possibly, in connection with provisions on access to courts), what would amount to prescriptions of international law, but without mentions of that law *expressis verbis*. As to the wording wherein there is a direct reference to this standard, questions arise with respect to (1) consistency with constitutional arrangements of prospective parties, (2) relation to other standards, particularly that of national treatment and

[20] T.I.A.S. 2155.

[21] Text in Sen. Ex. D, 81st Cong., 2d Sess.

local law, and (3) connection between the wording under consideration and that of the immediately following sentence, which has to do with "due process" and "just compensation" in the event of expropriation of property.

Several of the countries with which the United States made commercial treaties in the third decade of the twentieth century, notably Germany, Austria, Estonia, and Latvia, had national constitutions providing that the generally recognized rules of international law should be applied as parts of the respective national laws. The effect of such constitutional provisions has received attention of able publicists [22] and will not be the subject of extended discussion here. It will suffice to point out that the effect of an "incorporative" clause in a national constitution might be to provide an instruction for municipal court judges or administrative officials, but it would not be to create a new international obligation for a state vis-à-vis other states. Constitutional provisions referring to international law do not appear to have entered into the treaty discussions as much as have those which related specifically to expropriation of property.

National treatment, or, as it was sometimes called, the principle of "parity," naturally came in for attention in various negotiations, in view of the mention, in the same sentence in which the international law standard is provided for, of submission by treaty aliens to conditions imposed upon nationals. Czechoslovakia proposed a modification of the language relating to international law, "because of the sufficient protection of property by the system of parity as stipulated in the first period of this paragraph." The Czech ministry of foreign affairs considered that the restriction of the standard to "the same degree of protection" as each party accorded to its own nationals would mean an even more efficient protection of the rights of nationals of both parties. In the

[22] See, for example, Ruth D. Masters, *International Law in National Courts* (1932); B. Mirkine-Guetzévitch, *Droit constitutionnel international* (1933); Gustav Adolf Walz, *Völkerrecht und Staatliches Recht* (1933). Discussions of some of the more recent constitutional provisions for applications of international law are in Lawrence Preuss, "Relation of International Law to Internal Law in the French Constitutional System," *Amer. Jour. Int. Law*, XLIV (1950), 641–669, and in David R. Deener, "International Law Provisions in Post-World War II Constitutions," *Cornell Law Quarterly*, XXXVI (1951), 505–533.

course of consideration of this proposed modification, it was pointed out, in a memorandum circulated in the State Department, that under Czechoslovak law nationals of that state were not entitled to compensation from their government for damages sustained to their property during the recent war, and that acceptance by the United States of such a modification would tie the hands of this country with respect to similar claims of American citizens against Czechoslovakia.[23]

A draft treaty which Latvia had proposed to the United States in 1922 did not specify either national treatment or international law as a standard, but provided that "the citizens of each of the High Contracting Parties shall, upon compliance with the laws of the country, enjoy constant and complete protection and security in regard both to themselves and their property." [24] As finally concluded, however, the treaty contained provision for the international law standard in the same words which had been used in the treaty with Germany. In the State Department's comment on this wording, as sent to chiefs of American missions in a number

[23] Department of State file 711.60f 2/26 (National Archives).

National treatment along with international usages and practice had been prescribed in a proposed treaty with Turkey in 1923. By provisions of the second article, "The nationals of each of the high contracting parties in the territories of the other shall in regard to their persons and property be received and treated in accordance with the general usages and practices of modern civilized nations. They shall enjoy the most complete and constant protection for their persons, property rights and interests and upon submitting themselves to the applicable laws and regulations of the country, they shall enjoy equality of treatment with the nationals thereof and with the nationals of the most favored nation in regard to freedom of access to the courts of justice and liberty of religious belief and worship; and the acquisition, possession and disposition of movable property." A Turkish counterdraft proposed a rule to apply to nationals of one party in the territory of the other: "They shall, under the conditions imposed upon the nationals of the country, enjoy the most constant protection and security for their property and persons, in conformity with international common law." Earlier in the negotiations, the Secretary of State, in a telegram to the American mission, said that what the United States proposed in this part of the draft did not call for "any grant in favor of an alien resident which a modern state worthy of complete recognition as a member of the family of nations should withhold" (Department of State files 711.672/70, 711.672/87, 711.672/92 [National Archives]). As is well known, the negotiations with Turkey on this occasion did not result in a perfected treaty.

[24] Department of State file 711.60 p2/1 (National Archives).

of countries, such as Norway, Honduras, El Salvador, Latvia, and Estonia, the following was included:

> It is believed that it may prove highly useful to acknowledge that the test of the propriety of the treatment due the resident alien is that accorded by international law, rather than by the standards fixed by the state of residence in dealing with its own nationals. The United States finds it constantly necessary to invoke the international law test in dealing with countries whose treatment of their own nationals is arbitrary and unjust.[25]

While the treaty with Honduras was before the National Congress of that country for approval, it was reported that certain anti-administration newspapers in Honduras had expressed objection through editorials to the idea of American citizens being guaranteed "a measure of safety and security not vouchsafed to Honduran citizens." [26]

From the American comment on the wording of the draft treaties, it would appear that, by including in the same sentence which refers to the international law standard the words, "upon submitting to conditions imposed upon its nationals," the United States government had no thought of reducing the degree of protection sought to be assured in the reference to international law. The presumption would be that the conditions imposed upon nationals of the local state would not be inconsistent with that law. A different conclusion would mean that international law would apply unless the local law (nondiscriminatory as between nationals and aliens) directed otherwise.

It remains to consider the separate sentence in the treaties which has to do with expropriation of property, particularly in relation to the provision for the international law standard, but also in relation to constitutions and statutes of the respective parties. The fact that "due process of law" and "payment of just compensation" are mentioned separately from international law would not appear to justify the conclusion that international law

[25] From the instruction which accompanied the draft for Norway, Department of State file 711.572/48a (National Archives).

[26] Despatch from the American minister to Honduras, January 21, 1928, Department of State file 711.152/13 (National Archives).

does not require a state which takes the property of resident aliens to comply with reasonable standards of procedure and to make adequate compensation. The commercial treaty negotiations of the interwar period do not seem to have gone into this point so much as into the consistency of a rule of due process and just compensation with existing national law.

A letter from the solicitor of the Department of State concerning the negotiations with Germany noted as "what was perhaps the major German proposal" one that would have changed the part of the draft treaty having to do with due process and just compensation. The German ambassador had stated that his country's constitution permitted the taking of property without the payment of just compensation, and that the treaty provision as proposed might be violative of the fundamental law. While intimating that it was unlikely that the German legislature would avail itself of its constitutional right to take property of aliens without payment of just compensation, the ambassador drew attention to a strong feeling in his country against interference with the constitution. The Department of State, in reply, pointed out that the sentence in the text did not contemplate a yielding of anything which the German constitution forbade and that it was in no sense a violation of that document; what Germany would do, if she accepted the treaty rule, would be to agree not to exercise a constitutional right; if after acceptance of the treaty the constitutional right should be exercised in relation to American citizens, it would lead to a protest.[27]

In the course of negotiations with Estonia, the representatives of that country proposed that the "just compensation" referred to in the proposed treaty should be defined in accordance with the Estonian constitutional provision (article 24) that "without the owner's consent it [private property] can be expropriated only in the common interest in accordance with the corresponding laws, and in the ways foreseen in the laws." The American negotiators' reply was that "just compensation" for private property expropriated for public use was understood in the United States to mean the market value of the property plus interest from the date of expropriation until the date of settlement with the private

[27] *For. Rel.*, 1923, II, 29.

owner and that the procedure defined in article 24 of the Estonian constitution seemed to relate to "due process of law" as understood in the United States.[28]

In the negotiations with Hungary and in those with Poland, the question was raised of the effect of the treaty language upon the claims that might be made by third states. The Hungarian minister said:

> My Government feels confident that no controversy will ever arise as to the interpretation of the term "just compensation" . . . as far as the United States and Hungary are concerned. My Government is unable, however, to view with the same assurance questions that might arise with respect to the property of nationals of other countries which might avail themselves, by virtue of the most favored nation . . . clause, of the provisions of the said paragraph. In order to forestall the possibility of this complication arising, it would be desirable to have the following interpretation embodied in the final protocol: "Whenever the property of nationals of one High Contracting Party within the territories of the other shall be expropriated after due process of law, the just amount of compensation to be paid shall be determined in accordance with the principle of equal treatment with the nationals of the latter party." [29]

As finally concluded, the treaty with Hungary contained, on the point under discussion, the wording which the United States had proposed. More than two decades later, following the political changes which occurred in Hungary after the Second World War, the treaty language in question was to be the subject of a strong protest from the United States because of the application to American-owned property of Hungary's Nationalization Law of December 28, 1949. The diplomatic note asserted the responsibility of Hungary for the payment of adequate and effective compensation to American owners affected, and drew attention to the fact that interests of the Soviet Union had been exempted from nationalization, this being a discrimination on Hungary's part in clear violation of the treaty.[30]

In the case of the commercial treaty with Poland, signed in

[28] Department of State file 711.60i 2/8 (National Archives).

[29] Department of State file 711.642/10 (National Archives).

[30] *Department of State Bulletin,* vol. XXII, no. 558 (March 13, 1950), p. 399.

1931, the negotiations extended over a long period of time. An early draft (1921) contained a sentence on due process and compensation which was said to have been an alteration and extension of Article XXII of the then existing commercial treaty with Italy.[81] After the signing of the treaty with Germany and the evolving of the formula which came to be the standard in all of the full-length commercial treaties of the United States in the interwar period, the discussions with Poland were on the basis of this formula. In conversations of February 1927, a Polish spokesman suggested that the expression "just compensation" was vague, and that this be remedied by omitting "just" and adding at the end of the sentence the words, "with the payment of compensation on equal terms as that of nationals of the country." [82] This emendation was found to be unacceptable to the United States. A memorandum of the solicitor of the Department of State, dated June 17, 1927, took the position that "just compensation" was no more indefinite than was "due process of law" in the same sentence or "that degree of protection that is required by international law" in the following sentence. In the very nature of the subject, the memorandum submitted, definiteness could not be obtained and indefiniteness was no objection; the object of the paragraph in the draft treaty was to assure to nationals of either party in the other's territory protection in the degree defined by international law. The Polish suggestion, it was felt, would substitute a national standard for an international one and would be contrary to the purpose of the article, there being no assurance that the compensation paid to Polish nationals for property taken by the Polish government would be "just" compensation. At a conference on January 29, 1929, the Polish representatives said that there was no question of American citizens' obtaining just compensation for property taken in Poland, but that what they feared was that inclusion of the indefinite word "just" might give persons of other nationalities in Poland an excuse, through invocation of the most-favored-nation clause, to question practically every case in which a court might decree the granting of compensation for property taken, on the ground that

[81] Department of State file 611.60c31/2 (National Archives).
[82] Department of State file 771.60c2/31½ (National Archives).

the compensation awarded by the court or other agency having jurisdiction was not "just." They then offered the suggestion that if the word "due" were substituted for "just," it would be acceptable.[33] As to the latter suggestion, the United States took the position that the word "due" would be less satisfactory than "just," since the latter expressed a little more definitely and precisely the meaning which it was sought to convey.[34] Eventually, Poland agreed to the language which had been proposed in the American draft.

While the complete records of commercial treaty negotiations to which the United States was a party in the latter part of the interwar period and in the subsequent period are not yet accessible, it is possible to conclude, on the basis of material already referred to, that there has been a close connection between the property-protection provisions which make direct reference to international law and the provision, in a separate sentence but in the same context, regarding "due process" and "just compensation." In this connection it would also appear to be clear that the "due process" is not that which is due by the Constitution of the United States or by that of any other state party to such a treaty provision, but the "due process" which is required by international law, since a standard as set by the basic law of one party to a treaty would not be controlling upon the other party and would not necessarily reflect international law.[35] Whereas treaties of the interwar period provided, as has been seen, for "just" compensation in the event of expropriation, three of the commercial treaties which the United States has signed (with China, Italy, and Ireland, respectively) since the cessation of hostilities in the Second World War provide for "prompt" payment of "just and effective" compensation, while that with Uruguay refers to ap-

[33] Department of State file 711.60c2/37½ (National Archives).

[34] Department of State file 711.60c2/41 (note from the Secretary of State to the Polish chargé ad interim, dated April 3, 1929; National Archives).

[35] Cf. a statement by a witness in Hearings before the Committee on Patents, House of Representatives, 71st Cong., 1st Sess., on H. J. Res. 32, 73, and 123, at pp. 59, 64, 69.

The applicability of the property-protection provisions to companies as well as natural persons is outside the scope of the present discussion; it has been dealt with briefly in Robert R. Wilson, "Property-Protection Provisions in United States Commercial Treaties."

plicable laws "which shall at least assure the payment of just compensation in a prompt, adequate and effective manner." [36] The treaty with Uruguay refers, in a national-treatment context, to "procedures and conditions" in connection with the taking of property; that with Ireland makes no specific reference to "process" or "procedures," but makes clear that in no case shall less than national and most-favored-nation treatment be accorded. In general, the treaties since the close of hostilities in the Second World War have tended to contain provisions (for example, those concerning exchange withdrawal after expropriation, national treatment in matters relating to the taking of privately owned and controlled enterprises into public ownership and under public control) responsive to new conditions and new needs in connection with investment abroad.

It remains to note the reality and the utility of the international law standard concerning compensation for expropriation of alien-owned property, as that standard is provided for in all but one of the treaties referred to in this subsection. Even without express reference to the law, it would still be true, as is in fact stated in the Irish-American commercial treaty, that "treaty commitments are to be construed in the light of international law." [37] A considerable body of opinion has developed in support of the view that there is, apart from treaties, no right of private property (in the sense of ownership, free from uncompensated expropriation, of that which has been acquired by foreigners, in accordance with existing municipal law) under international law.[38] Some publicists, in the face of the socialistic movements of recent decades, have sought to make a distinction between particular and general, or programmatic, expropriations.[39] More commonly, there has been offered the view that

[36] The treaties with Italy, Ireland, and Uruguay, respectively, specify that the provisions concerning protection of property shall apply to interests held directly or indirectly.

[37] T.I.A.S. 2155, Protocol, par. 12.

[38] Illustrative writings have been referred to in Wilson, "Property-Protection Provisions in United States Commercial Treaties."

[39] See, for example, Frederick S. Dunn, "International Law and Private Rights," *Columbia Law Review*, XXVIII (1928), 166, 180; Seymour J. Rubin, "Nationalization and Private Foreign Investment: The Role of Gov-

national treatment is the maximum which foreigners can, as of right, demand.[40]

The weight of authority still seems to support the view, however, that there is in time of peace an international legal obligation, apart from treaties or other specific agreements, binding a state to respect the property rights that aliens have acquired within its territory in accordance with existing and applicable law.[41] Nor has the view prevailed that no state can be legally held to accord to foreigners better treatment than that which its nationals receive. Instead, there has developed, particularly in recent decades, the concept of a "minimum standard of justice" to afford a guide for the legally required treatment of aliens.[42] As is well known, the United States in particular has held to

ernment," *World Politics,* II (1950), 482, 509–510. See also Oppenheim, *International Law,* 7th ed., I (1948), 318, to the effect that, where fundamental changes in the political system and economic structure of a state, or far-reaching social reforms, entail interference on a large scale with private property, neither the principle of absolute respect for alien private property nor rigid equality with dispossessed nationals offers a satisfactory solution, and that, in such cases, it is probable that partial compensation will offer a solution consistent with legal principle.

[40] See note 43, *infra.*

[41] Charles Cheney Hyde, *International Law Chiefly as Interpreted and Applied by the United States* (1945 ed.), I, 710–722; Oppenheim, *International Law,* 7th ed., I, 316, 627; Georges Kaeckenbeeck, "La Protection internationale des droits acquis," *Recueil des cours,* LIX (1937), 321–419; Alexander Fachiri, "Expropriation and International Law," *Brit. Year Book Int. Law,* VI (1925), 159–171, and "International Law and the Property of Aliens," *ibid.,* X (1929), 32–50; Freeman, *International Responsibility,* pp. 497–570. Among the instances commonly cited in illustration of the rule are the settlements in the *Sicilian Sulphur Monopoly* case (28 *Brit. and For. State Papers* 1166), the case of *Jonas King* (Moore, *Digest,* VI, 263), the *Delagoa Bay Railway Arbitration* (Moore, *International Arbitrations,* II, 1865), and such pronouncements of the Permanent Court of International Justice as those in the case concerning German interests in Upper Silesia (P.C.I.J., series A, no. 7, p. 22), and that concerning the *Chorzów Factory* (*ibid.,* no. 17, pp. 46–47). Cf. Emilio von Hofmannsthal, "Foreign Investments Risky under International Law," a paper presented to the 44th conference of the International Law Association (1950).

[42] See Nicholas R. Doman, "Postwar Nationalization of Foreign Property in Europe," *Columbia Law Review,* XLVIII (1948), 1125, 1135–1136; Andreas H. Roth, *The Minimum Standard of International Law Applied to Aliens* (1949), p. 122; Oppenheim, *International Law,* 7th ed., I, 316, 627; E. M. Borchard, "The 'Minimum Standard' of the Treatment of Aliens," *Proc. Amer. Soc. Int. Law,* 1939, pp. 51–64.

the view that the international law standard may, in a given case, mean something better than national treatment.[43]

A somewhat different question is that of the *utility* of the international law standard as applied in property-protection clauses. Its reach extends to both adjective and substantive law. Parties agreeing in advance to what international law requires retain, of course, the rights which they have under the well-established rule with respect to exhaustion of local remedies.[44] On the other hand, the concept of denial of justice does not seem to have become so limitative, and the idea that international remedies can be legally excluded through the conclusion of Calvo clauses does not seem to have become so widely accepted, that references to international law in this subject matter have become futile or ineffectual.[45] Difficulties are to be expected in applying the general principle of law in particular situations, in determining what constitutes a "taking," in determining "just" valuations, and in passing upon procedural requirements under local law. However, the danger of any state's arbitrary or unreasonable constructions

[43] See notes of July 21 and August 22, 1938, from the Secretary of State to the Mexican ambassador at Washington concerning compensation for lands in Mexico expropriated by the Mexican government (Department of State Publication 1288, Inter-American Series no. 16). At the Hague Codification Conference of 1930 the United States had been one of twenty-three states which opposed a Chinese proposal (supported by sixteen other states) for a formal limitation of state responsibility, so that no country would be obligated to accord to foreigners better treatment than that which it accorded to its own nationals (*Minutes of Third Committee,* Doc. C.351(c).M.145(c).1930). As is well known, the question of parity with nationals was later under discussion at general conferences of the American republics, particularly that at Montevideo in 1933 and that at Bogotá in 1948. In the latter instance, the United States successfully opposed, but by a close vote, the Mexican delegation's proposal, for insertion in article 25 of the draft Economic Agreement, of a statement whereby there would be prompt, adequate, and effective compensation for expropriated property "except when the constitution of any country provided otherwise" (*Report of . . . Ninth International Conference of American States,* Department of State Publication 3263, pp. 66, 67). The views of the minority found expression in reservations to the draft agreement, and the latter has not come into effect, notwithstanding later efforts of a commission of the Inter-American Economic and Social Council to bring the divergent views into agreement.

[44] See Chapter II, section 4, *supra.*

[45] On limitations upon the capacity of private persons to contract away international legal remedies, see K. Lipstein, "The Place of the Calvo Clause in International Law," *Brit. Year Book Int. Law,* XXII (1945), 130–145.

is presumably offset to some extent by the provision (to be found in each of the commercial treaties which the United States has signed in the period following World War II) whereby final, authoritative interpretations can be sought from the International Court of Justice. On the other hand, the prevailing lack of universal agreement on what the international law standard has come to require may furnish, as it appears already to have furnished, occasion for inserting, in establishment provisions of treaties, more precise rules.

2. NAVIGATION OF INTERNATIONAL RIVERS

The principle of free navigation of international waterways figured in early American diplomacy concerning navigation of the lower Mississippi River. In the course of the development, strongly sectional factors and pressing considerations of economic need, as well as questions of public law and treaties, came in for attention. Generally speaking, there was on the American side in this connection no aberration quite comparable with Jay's treaty concession to England in 1794 in the matter of "free" ships. There was, at one time, evidence of some willingness to make a concession on the principal legal point, but this was met by strong opposition from representatives of the region whose special interest lay in securing the navigation rights. For the present purpose, the extent to which the Americans placed their demands upon existing international law is to be the primary subject of inquiry.

By the peace treaty of 1763 Great Britain had obtained for her subjects the right of free navigation of the lower Mississippi River.[46] After they ceased to be British subjects, some of the inhabitants of the new republic were especially concerned about the possession of such navigation rights. Enough of them, particularly in the South, were concerned to bring about official action on the part of the central organ of government. Soon after declaring independence, the Continental Congress began to devote attention to the matter, which was related to diplomacy

[46] George F. v. Martens (ed.), *Recueil de traités d'alliance, de paix, de trêve*, 2d ed., I (1817), 104, 110–111 (article VII).

with both France and Spain. After Floridablanca came to power in the latter country on February 15, 1777, the Mississippi navigation question was linked up with the possibility of securing political recognition from the Spanish government and obtaining an alliance with that country as well as with France. It could be surmised that, with the movement of settlers toward the west, the United States would probably claim the east bank of the river, and that Americans would come into contact with and jeopardize Spain's possessions west of the river.[47]

At the beginning of the Franco-American alliance, Charles Gravier, Comte de Vergennes apparently supported claims of the Americans to free navigation of the Mississippi to the sea, but he did not rigidly adhere to this position, his concern being to bring Spain into the war and keep the allies which France already had in the war against England.[48] As for the Americans, their claims found expression in reports to Congress, in instructions by Congress, and in the work of American negotiators, particularly John Jay and Thomas Pinckney. In the beginning it was not always made clear whether the claims were to navigation of *all* of the lower river or navigation merely to the point on the river which marked the southern boundary of the United States. The fact of American settlements in the west created the possibility of a claim on the basis of something like conquest, rather than treaty right. It was natural, however, that claimants should make use of specific agreements whenever they were available.

In the eighth article of the definitive treaty of peace with Great Britain, signed at Paris September 3, 1783, it was provided that "the Navigation of the River Mississippi, from its source to the Ocean shall for ever remain free and open to the Subjects

[47] Paul Chrisler Phillips, *The West in the Diplomacy of the American Revolution* (1913), pp. 66 *et seq.*

[48] S. F. Bemis, *Pinckney's Treaty* (1926), p. 43. See also, in J. J. Meng (ed.), *Despatches and Instructions of Conrad Alexandre Gérard* (1939), a portion of Gérard's communication to Vergennes, at pp. 344–345, and Vergennes' to Gérard, at pp. 359–360. In the former the French envoy reported a feeling on the part of some persons that the control of navigation on the lower river should remain exclusively with Spain, in order to assure the dependence, of the western people concerned, upon the American republic.

of Great Britain and the Citizens of the United States." [49] Thereafter the Americans were able to add to their arguments from usage and from vital interest the contention that theirs were the rights of a successor state. The theory that the peace treaty was one of *partition*, which allowed American citizens and British subjects to *continue* in the enjoyment of rights (such as those in the northern fisheries and that of navigating the lower Mississippi in accordance with the 1763 treaty), furnished additional ground for argument. According to this, the inhabitants of the western country, as citizens of the new republic, were entitled to rights no less than those which they had had while subjects of Great Britain.[50]

Long before 1783, however, the American claim had received official formulation. That the claim rested in part upon general principle, independently of any treaties, appears from the first comprehensive report on the subject to Congress. This report, prepared by a committee which included James Madison, received Congressional approval on October 17, 1780, as the instruction to be sent to American representatives at Versailles and Madrid. After reciting that the United States had an indisputable right to the east bank of the Mississippi for a very great distance, the report continued:

> The usage of nations . . . seems in such cases to have given those holding the mouth or lower parts of a river no right against those above them, except the right of imposing a moderate toll, and that on the equitable supposition, that such toll is due for the expense and trouble the former may have been put to. "An innocent passage (says Vattel) is due to all nations with whom a state is at peace; and this duty com-

[49] Miller, *Treaties*, II, 155.

[50] John Quincy Adams, *The Duplicate Letters, the Fisheries and the Mississippi* (1822); the language of the Master of the Rolls in *Sutton* v. *Sutton* (1 Myl. & R. 675); Theodore Lyman, *Diplomacy of the United States* (2d ed., 1828), I, 117. The tribunal which made the award in the North Atlantic Coast Fisheries Arbitration did not agree to the American argument on the "partition" point. It concluded that the right to take fish, conceded in the peace treaty, was "accorded as a condition of peace to a foreign people; wherefore the British negotiators refused to place the right of British subjects on the same footing with those of American inhabitants; and further, refused to insert the words also proposed by Mr. Adams—'continue to enjoy'—in the second branch of Article III of the Treaty of 1783" (Sen. Doc. 870, 61st Cong., 3d Sess., I, 79).

prehends troops equally with individuals." If a right to a passage by land through other countries may be claimed for troops, which are employed in the destruction of mankind, how much more may a passage by water be claimed for commerce, which is beneficial to all nations.[51]

The subsequent handling of the matter illustrated the tendency to mix appeals to principle with demands motivated by economic interests. On October 13, 1779, Congress had, by a divided vote, rejected a proposal that American representatives be privately instructed to recede from their claims to free navigation below the thirty-first degree of north latitude, on condition of the granting of a free port, if the obtaining of full navigation rights should prove an insurmountable bar to the proposed treaties of amity and commerce.[52] In 1781 Congress did, by a majority vote, recede from the strong position that it had previously taken, but official notification of this action did not reach Jay in Madrid until five months later, and Spain did not accept the bases of a treaty which Jay suggested on condition of immediate acceptance of the treaty and of an alliance. On Franklin's advice, Jay left Madrid in June 1782.[53]

The next crucial phase of the effort for a treaty arrangement with Spain came toward the end of the Confederation period, after the arrival in the United States of Diego de Gardoqui, the Spanish envoy, in May 1785, a week after Jay had been elected Secretary for Foreign Affairs. Empowered to negotiate with a view to making a treaty, Jay again received positive instructions on the Mississippi question. The Secretary seemed to reflect weariness in negotiation when, reporting to Congress in August

[51] *Journals of the Continental Congress,* XVIII, 943. The report set forth that, notwithstanding the "equitable" claim to the free navigation of the Mississippi, Congress had so strong a desire to conform to the desires of His Catholic Majesty that they had agreed that such equitable regulations might be entered into as might be a requisite security against contraband, provided the *point of right* be not relinquished and a free port or ports below the thirty-first degree of north latitude and accessible to merchant ships be stipulated. These instructions were not to be "urged at all events" but were rather for the private use and information of the American representatives, with the expectation that arguments would be suited to the "temper and sentiments" of the receiving courts (*ibid.,* p. 947).

[52] *Ibid.,* XV, 1168–1169.

[53] F. E. Chadwick, *The Relations of the United States and Spain* (1909), pp. 20–25.

1786 on the progress of his conversations with Gardoqui, he said: "Courts never admit the force of any reasoning or arguments but such as apply in their favor . . . even if our right to that Navigation, or to anything else, was expressly declared in Holy Writ, we should be able to provide for the enjoyment of it no otherwise than by being in capacity to repel force by force."[54] In the same report he recommended that the United States agree to forbear, for a period of twenty-five or thirty years, to use the navigation of the Mississippi below American territories to the ocean. Members of Congress disagreed on the wisdom of such a policy. Charles Pinckney resolutely opposed modifications of the Secretary's instructions.[55] When at length delegates of a bare majority of the states favored an authorization to the negotiator to deviate from his original instructions, southerners challenged the validity of such an authorization unless it should have the support of at least nine states. They also raised the question of the competence of members of Congress to take such a step (since it involved important interests of their respective states) without some authorization from those whom they represented.[56] The effect of the whole situation upon the national constitutional plan, which was to provide a broad legislative base for treaties by requiring for their conclusion the advice and consent of two-thirds of that national legislative chamber in which the states were to have equal representation, has elsewhere received deserved attention.[57]

A reiteration of basic principle to buttress American claims to navigation rights came in the form of a resolution which delegates of North Carolina presented to Congress in September 1788. This declared that the clear, unalienable claim of the United States to this navigation was not only supported by the "express stipulation of treaties" but by the "great law of nature."[58] In language somewhat less vague, Congress resolved

[54] *Journals of the Continental Congress,* XXXI, 480.

[55] *Ibid.*, pp. 935–948.

[56] See, for example, *Journals,* XXXI, 610–612, 695–696.

[57] Charles Warren, "The Mississippi River and the Treaty Clause of the Constitution," *George Washington Law Review,* II (1934), 271–302.

[58] Bemis, *Pinckney's Treaty,* pp. 164–168. On November 17, 1782, Jay had written to Robert R. Livingston, concerning the Mississippi, that "our

that the free navigation demanded was "a clear and essential right of the United States" which should "be considered and supported as such." [59] Reporting to the President on March 18, 1792, Secretary of State Jefferson rested the American claim not merely upon the treaty of 1763 and that with Great Britain of 1783, but upon the "law of nature and nations" which was "still broader and more unquestionable" than either of the other bases. Continuing, he said:

> The ocean is free to all men, and their rivers to all their inhabitants . . . Accordingly, in all tracts of country united under the same political society, we find this natural right universally acknowledged and protected by laying the navigable rivers open to all their inhabitants. When their rivers enter the limits of another society, if the right of the upper inhabitants to descend the stream is in any case obstructed, it is an act of force by a stronger society against a weaker, condemned by the judgment of mankind. . . The Roman law, which, like other municipal laws, placed the navigation of their rivers on the footing of nature, as to their own citizens, by declaring them public . . . declared also that the right to the use of the shores was incident to that of the water.[60]

Final settlement of the question in the way the Americans desired became more probable with changed conditions in Europe which caused the Spanish court to fear an Anglo-American combination that might constitute a serious threat to Spanish interests. When negotiations were resumed in Madrid, Thomas Pinckney, envoy extraordinary for these discussions, arrived in the Spanish capital on June 28, 1795, with instructions which cautioned him against assenting to the free navigation of the Mississippi as a grant, or privilege, rather than a right.[61] His task was somewhat more delicate by reason of the fact that in the 1783 treaty with Great Britain the United States had already proceeded upon the *assumption* of the navigation rights, in specifying that they were to be free to citizens of the United States

right to its navigation was deducible from the laws of nature" (H. P. Johnston, ed., *The Correspondence and Public Papers of John Jay* [1890–1893], II, 406).

[59] *Secret Journals of Congress, Foreign Affairs,* IV, 453.

[60] *American State Papers, Foreign Relations,* I, 253, 254; quoted in Moore, *Digest,* I, 624.

[61] Bemis, *Pinckney's Treaty,* pp. 316, 317.

and subjects of Great Britain. The American minister stood out firmly for a right of deposit on the lower Mississippi, to the extent of asking for his passports when Godoy, the Spanish negotiator, was disinclined to yield.[62]

The treaty with Spain was signed October 27, 1795. By article XXII the Spanish king agreed to permit citizens of the United States for three years to deposit goods at New Orleans, with the proviso that permission would either be continued after the expiration of that time or another part of the banks of the river would be assigned for an equivalent establishment. The navigation question, which for nearly twenty years had been a major controversial item between the two countries, was the subject of the fourth article, which contained the following:

> It is likewise agreed that the Western boundary of the United States which separates them from the Spanish Colony of Louisiana, is in the middle of the channel or bed of the River Mississippi from the Northern boundary of the said States to the completion of the thirty-first degree of latitude North of the Equator; and his Catholic Majesty has likewise agreed that the navigation of the said River in its whole breadth from its source to the Ocean shall be free only to his Subjects, and the citizens of the United States, unless he should extend this privilege to the Subjects of other Powers by special convention.[63]

Criticism of the final settlement on this point has stressed that it actually gave up what had been claimed as a right and accepted a grant, that it was in contravention of the 1783 treaty of peace with Great Britain, and that it was in effect a "stultification" of the argument on which the Americans had originally based their claim to navigation of the river.[64] As to the second of these suggestions, it is clear that the United States and Spain could not legally reduce by treaty the preëxisting conventional rights of Great Britain, a third state.[65] The form of statement of the fourth article, however, would seem to put upon Spain the burden of reconciling this 1795 treaty with British treaty rights

[62] *Ibid.*, p. 322.

[63] Miller, *Treaties*, II, 321–322.

[64] Bemis, *Pinckney's Treaty*, pp. 333–335.

[65] See, on the general question of law, R. F. Roxburgh, *International Conventions and Third States* (1917), and Carl-Heinz Winkler, *Verträge zu Gunsten und zu Lasten Dritter im Völkerrecht* (1932).

acquired in 1763. One view has been that those rights constituted a servitude in favor of British subjects which was not disturbed by the 1783 peace treaty. This is hardly tenable, for, as the arbitral tribunal brought out in the *North Atlantic Coast Fisheries* case (1910), British statesmen were not familiar with the concept of international servitude even as late as 1818, and no English publicist employed the term before that date.[66] There is some doubt whether, even after the term became common, it could be properly applied to the navigation rights which the British gained in 1763.[67]

One of the American negotiators of a later (1818) settlement with Great Britain pointed out that, although the 1783 treaty gave to British subjects navigation rights on the Mississippi and provided that the northern boundary of the United States was to have followed a line running due west from the most northwestern point of the Lake of the Woods to the Mississippi, it was afterwards discovered that a line so drawn would not strike the Mississippi, as was at first supposed.[68] The headwaters of the river not being within British jurisdiction, there was a question of whether the Mississippi would fall within the definition of an "international" river, so far as the British were concerned after 1783. At the negotiation of the Treaty of Ghent, the British plenipotentiaries desired a clause stipulating their retention of the right to navigate the Mississippi, but they did not get it.

As for a clear legal basis for the American claim in relation to Spain, apart from any treaties, such a basis seems to have been lacking in the eighteenth century, notwithstanding the appeal which some prominent Americans of the time made to natural law.[69] Nor, with the subsequent development of customary international law, has there been a clear progression to the general rule which the United States then made, at least in part, the

[66] J. B. Scott, *Hague Court Reports* (1916), pp. 146, 159.

[67] See the definition of servitude in Helen D. Reid, *International Servitudes in Law and Practice* (1932), p. 25.

[68] See the memorandum of Richard Rush, quoted in Moore, *Digest*, I, 626.

[69] Jesse S. Reeves, "The Influence of the Law of Nature upon International Law in the United States," *Amer. Jour. Int. Law*, III (1909), 547, 560; Warren, "The Mississippi River and the Treaty Clause of the Constitution," p. 280.

ground for its claim. An arbitral tribunal in 1903, after reviewing authorities on the question of an upper state's right to navigation of a river where a lower state had jurisdiction over both banks of the stream, made the following statement:

> It seems difficult upon principle to support the right to the free use of rivers as a right stricti juris. While this is not expressly admitted, it is tacitly conceded by nearly all the advocates. They define this right of use as an "imperfect right." The term is an anomaly.[70]

The step taken at the Congress of Vienna (1815)—toward the internationalization of rivers as a principle to be a part of "European Public Law"—fitted in naturally with a theory of natural right of merchant ships to navigate streams which flowed through the territory of more than one state. Speaking of this, in relation to American claims to navigate the St. Lawrence, Henry Clay, when Secretary of State, said loftily that the regulations made at Vienna should "be regarded only as the spontaneous homage of man to the superior wisdom of the paramount Lawgiver of the Universe, by delivering His great works from the artificial shackles and selfish contrivances to which they have been arbitrarily and unjustly subjected." [71] Several decades later, Secretary of State William Learned Marcy invoked the principle and sought its general application in South America. In an instruction of 1853 to the American minister in Brazil concerning rights of navigation on the Amazon, he wrote:

> We claim for this continent the same privileges which nearly forty years ago were arranged by common consent and have been ever since applicable to the navigable waters of Europe. The regulations adopted by the allied sovereigns at the Congress of Vienna in 1815 on this subject were but the recognition of the law of nations in regard to the use of navigable waters passing through different realms.[72]

[70] *Faber Case,* Ralston's *Report,* German-Venezuelan Commission under agreement of February 13, 1903. For a recent authoritative statement of international law on the subject, see Hyde, *International Law,* I, 562–565.

[71] Moore, *Digest,* I, 633. See also Ed. Engelhardt, *Histoire du droit fluvial conventionnel* (1889), pp. 81–83.

[72] Moore, *Digest,* I, 643. The instruction emphasized that the right to use this natural avenue of trade was not derived from treaty stipulations but was a "natural one—as much as that to navigate the ocean—the common highway of nations." See also notes 80, 81, *infra.*

The dissent of certain foreign offices from such ideas as that which Clay and Marcy had expressed did not cause the United States to cease from effort to secure additional river-navigation rights in the Western Hemisphere. Americans attained them on the St. Lawrence on a temporary basis in 1854 (in exchange for certain commercial advantages) and on a more permanent basis in 1871 (by the Treaty of Washington, in exchange for navigation rights on the Yukon, Porcupine, and Stikine).[73] Treaties with some of the South American states shortly after the middle of the century recorded further successful effort. Some of these agreements contained references to general principle. There was, on the other hand, occasional concession to the principle of sovereignty. For example, the treaty of July 10, 1853, with Argentina, contained in its first article the following statement:

> The Argentine Confederation, in the exercise of her sovereign rights, concedes the free navigation of the Rivers Paraná and Uruguay, wherever they may belong to her, to the merchant vessels of all nations, subject only to the conditions which this treaty establishes, and to the regulations sanctioned, or which may hereafter be sanctioned, by the national authority of the Confederation.[74]

General Justo José Urquiza, Provisional Director of the Argentine Confederation, negotiated this treaty, and similar ones which he made with Great Britain and France, under conditions of civil war. The fifth article referred to the principle of free navigation of the mentioned rivers. The seventh envisaged application of the principle to those parts of the waterways on which Brazil, Bolivia, Uruguay, or Paraguay possessed fluvial rights. The American negotiator derived satisfaction from the thought that the treaty was to be perpetual in its duration, "without any limitation whatever." [75] In his instruction of April 29 of the preceding

[73] Moore, *Principles of American Diplomacy*, p. 131. The fourth article of the treaty of June 5, 1854, gave Americans the "right" of navigation on a national-treatment basis, but the British government retained the right of suspending this "privilege" on giving notice to the United States. The treaty, not being self-executing, required legislation to make it practically operative (10 *Stat.* 1089–1092; Miller, *Treaties*, VI, 671). See also C. C. Tansill, *The Canadian Reciprocity Treaty of 1854* (1922).

[74] 18 *Stat.* 15.

[75] Miller, *Treaties*, VI, 241, 249.

year (1852), Secretary of State Daniel Webster had said, concerning General Urquiza and the matter of free access to and from Paraguay by the rivers that empty into La Plata:

> As his own territories occupy both banks of some of those rivers, he would have at least a show of right for . . . refusal, as much, indeed, as Great Britain had for withholding from the United States the free navigation of the St. Lawrence.[76]

Conclusion of the 1853 treaty with the Argentine Confederation had as a sequel some correspondence with Brazil. In a statement communicated through the minister at Washington, the Brazilian minister of foreign affairs observed that the fifth, sixth, and seventh articles of the treaties which General Urquiza had made with France, Great Britain, and the United States, respectively, if not understood in a reasonable manner according to the imprescriptible rules of justice and the principles of universal public law, "may prove detrimental to the rights which Brazil possesses as a sovereign nation."[77] As to the main principle involved, the minister observed:

> The states of the River Plata and its confluents have the power to grant or to refuse the navigation of their inland rivers to non-riparian nations. It is a right that belongs to them and which they can exercise, considering only their [own] interests and circumstances. To claim the preservation of a right under a forced and non-conventional obligation, in favor of other nations, and, moreover, to threaten with a loss of territory a state which does not wish to subject itself to such obligation, would be a most intolerable abuse of power, and the Government of His Imperial Majesty is convinced that this proceeding is repugnant to those principles of sound policy which govern the acts of the Government of the United States.

To this the Secretary of State (Marcy) replied, some nine months later, that the Brazilian government might "rest satisfied that should any difference arise as to the interpretation of the Treaty, the Government of the United States will be found

[76] *Ibid.*, p. 221.

[77] W. R. Manning (ed.), *Diplomatic Correspondence of the United States, Inter-American Affairs, 1831–1860*, II (1933), 445–448; Miller, *Treaties*, VI, 261. Brazil's concern about the sixth article was that there should be no restraint upon her rights under international law to institute a belligerent blockade in the River Plata and its tributaries.

claiming such a construction only, as may comport with the principles of justice, with the rules of public law, and with those interests of Brazil which as a nation in amity with her she shall feel bound to respect." [78] This seems to have allayed the fears of the Brazilian foreign minister.

Still another state, Bolivia, had an active interest in the arrangement. The Bolivian government took steps to adhere to the American-Argentine treaty, but there is some doubt whether this adherence ever became legally effective.[79] Before there could be much more official application of principles, legalists had need of factual information concerning the waterways.

Exploratory activity over the next several years was to pave the way for further treaty arrangements concerning important rivers of South America. Lieutenant Matthew Fontaine Maury of the United States Navy set himself with great fervor to the task of impressing Americans and others with the importance of opening the Amazon to the world's commerce. His work received praise at the Southern and Western Commercial Convention at Memphis in June 1853, which was attended by no fewer than two thousand persons from all parts of the South.[80] While his memorial, which offered the suggestion that the United States proceed forcibly to the opening of the Amazon if necessary,[81] did not find official favor with the American government and aroused public opinion in Brazil, it emphasized the possibilities. There had already been some suggestion that, in consideration of the intervention by France and England in the affairs of La Plata, those powers should ask for application of the principle

[78] Miller, *Treaties*, VI, 263, quoting from 6 *Notes to the Brazilian Legation* 112–114 (November 16, 1854).

[79] Miller, *Treaties*, VI, 268.

[80] *Memphis Daily Eagle and Enquirer*, June 7, 1853. A resolution offered on the second day of the Convention submitted that "the interests of commerce, the cause of civilization, and the mandates of high heaven require the Atlantic slopes of South America to be *subdued* and *replenished*." It added that the river steamer and the free navigation of the Amazon were the principal levers by which that part of the world was to be raised up to the abode of a great, prosperous, and happy people (*ibid.*, June 8, 1853).

[81] See Percy Alvin Martin, "The Influence of the United States on the Opening of the Amazon to the World's Commerce," *Hisp. Amer. Hist. Rev.*, I (1918), 146–162. Maury's memorial is printed in House Misc. Doc. 22, 33d Cong., 1st Sess.

enunciated at the Congress of Vienna to those rivers which flowed from the frontiers of Brazil and Paraguay into the Atlantic.[82] The exploration and survey of the river La Plata and its tributaries, completed by Commander Thomas J. Page in 1856,[83] prepared the way for further negotiations on use of the waterways concerning which the Brazilian minister of foreign affairs had observed, in May 1853, that the right to their navigation had "not been settled." [84]

Throughout the period of exploration, Secretary Marcy had largely rested his position, in asking for the opening of the waterways, upon international law as he claimed it had been declared by the Congress of Vienna. By 1858, therefore, there had been considerable emphasis upon the legal argument. The United States secured from Bolivia in that year a treaty declaration that the rivers Amazon and La Plata, with their tributaries, were regarded, "in accordance with fixed principles of international law," as "highways or channels opened by nature for the commerce of all nations." [85] Of this declaration Charles W. Dana, negotiator for the United States, wrote that it was "as full as could be desired." He thought it made possible a permanent commercial and political influence in the granting country and in countries which Americans would traverse in order to reach the waters on which Bolivia had recognized the rights.[86]

With Paraguay, the United States had signed a treaty in 1852 which would have given rights of navigation on the Paraguay and Paraná Rivers, but it did not come into force.[87] The language of the commitment which the United States finally obtained from Paraguay, signed February 4, 1859, offers something of a contrast to the Bolivian-American treaty of the preceding year, and follows the general tenor of the 1853 treaty with the Argen-

[82] Said to have been made by Guizot to the French ambassador at London. Document cited in note 83, *infra*, at p. 461.

[83] The Secretary of the Navy submitted, with his report, a synoptical report of the explorations (Sen. Ex. Doc. 5, pt. 2, 34th Cong., 3d Sess., p. 430).

[84] *Ibid.*, p. 434.

[85] 12 *Stat.* 1003, art. 26.

[86] Miller, *Treaties*, VII, 776, 777.

[87] Similar treaties which Paraguay signed with France, Great Britain, and Sardinia, respectively, did come into force (Miller, *Treaties*, VI, 231–240).

tine Confederation. The second article of the treaty with Paraguay contained the following:

> The Republic of Paraguay in the exercise of the sovereign right which pertains to her, concedes to the merchant flag of the . . . United States of America the free navigation of the river Paraguay as far as the dominions of the Empire of Brazil, and of the right side of the Paraná throughout all its course belonging to the Republic, subject to police and fiscal regulations of the Supreme Government of the Republic, in conformity with its concessions to the commerce of friendly nations.[88]

It was nearly a decade later that the Amazon was entirely opened to the commerce of the world.[89] In the achievement of the general results recorded in its treaties, the United States had made considerable use of the argument that it was entitled to what it sought as a matter of legal right, although, as has been seen, there were in the treaties as they were finally made some statements emphasizing the sovereign rights of riverain states to prohibit use of waterways to outsiders.[90] There continue to be difficulties in the definition of "international rivers," as well as differences of opinion on existing rules of the *droit fluvial coutumier généralement reconnu*.[91] As compared with those in Europe, the rivers of South America, which figured in treaties of the United States, were never so carefully classified into international and national and were not so often the subject of multilateral treaties,[92] although, as has been seen from quotations

[88] 12 *Stat.* 1091. For the unusual circumstances which attended the negotiations, see Miller, *Treaties*, VIII, 229, 237, and Richardson, *Messages*, VII, 3091.

[89] Martin, "The Influence of the United States on the Opening of the Amazon . . . ," p. 161, referring to a Brazilian decree of December 7, 1866, concerning the Amazon and tributaries, and to Peru's declaration of December 17, 1868, concerning her rivers.

[90] Recognition of sovereign rights of this sort was not restricted to South American waterways. Thus, in connection with the Sino-American treaty of 1858, an American negotiator expressed the opinion that, while he would like to see the Chinese allow foreigners to go up and trade along the Chinese rivers at pleasure, the Chinese "had a perfect right to refuse" (Miller, *Treaties*, VII, 893).

[91] This will appear from discussions of the Institute of International Law. See, for example, the observations of M. B. Winiarski, in *Annuaire*, XXXVIII (1934), 176–181.

[92] Carlos Sosa-Rodriguez, *Le Droit fluvial international et les fleuves de l'Amérique latine* (1935), pp. 185–186, and the statement of Alejandro

above, there were sometimes references in the texts to legal principles applicable to the subject matter.

In the course of its diplomatic history, the United States has had occasion to take a position on the use of the water of an international river (in the sense of a stream in which more than one state has a valid interest) for purposes other than navigation. Its official position concerning the diversion of water by an upper state, in the case of a river which farther down its course becomes an international boundary, occasioned sharp criticism, based at least in part on legal considerations.[93] Arrangement of such difficulties, in the case of the two nearest neighbors of the United States, has furnished occasion for special treaties. The course followed here does not necessarily detract from American advocacy of the free use, for purposes of navigation, of waterways which have constituted natural highways of commerce.[94]

Without being a party, the United States received the benefit of such liberal clauses as those of the General Act of Berlin, 1885, in regard to the Congo and Niger River systems. Internationalization of European rivers in the nineteenth and twentieth centuries (much of which was suspended or interrupted by unilateral action of Germany under the leadership of Hitler) was accomplished without the participation of the United States as a party to the treaties. The movement in each case was in line with the position which the United States, for the protection of its own interests, had taken in the first and second decades of its inde-

---

Alvarez as quoted in *Annuaire de l'Institut de Droit International,* XXXVIII (1934), 178: "On n'y trouve pas reconnu, avec le caractère universel qu'il a en Europe, le principe de la libre navigation des fleuves internationaux, et quand il est admis en faveur d'autres États que les Etats riverains, il a plutôt le caractère d'une concession gracieuse que d'un véritable droit."

[93] See the opinion of Attorney General Judson Harmon in regard to certain uses of the waters of the Rio Grande (21 *Op. Atty. Gen.* 274) and criticism of this in H. A. Smith, *The Economic Uses of International Rivers* (1931), p. 42. On the Attorney General's opinion in the light of United States practice, see Hyde, *International Law,* I, 567–569. Bilateral treaty arrangement of questions concerning use of the waters of a river is illustrated in the treaty signed with Mexico on May 21, 1906 (34 *Stat.* 2953).

[94] Cf. Ruth Bacon, "British and American Policy and the Right of Fluvial Navigation," *Brit. Year Book Int. Law,* XIII (1932), 76–92.

pendence.[95] Even at the time of the Barcelona Convention (1921), the idea of free navigation by all states of international rivers was not so generally accepted that it could satisfactorily be left on the basis of a customary rule. For reasons of self-interest, the young American republic had in the matter of the Mississippi question sought, partly on the ground of an existing international right, a liberal rule which later came to be established in a measure, but through the force of specific-provisions treaties rather than through the mere affirmation of the international law standard.

3. FREEDOM OF THE SEAS AND CONTROL OF THE SLAVE TRADE

Somewhat in contrast to American official attitudes summarized in the preceding section of this chapter was the course which this country followed before 1862 in regard to search on the high seas of vessels that were suspected of slave trading. In this instance, humanitarianism was a factor, in addition to principles of public law, and there was a question of integrating municipal criminal law with proposed treaty rules. There was, furthermore, a major domestic policy which was reflected in relations with other governments (particularly with Great Britain) and which affected attitudes toward proposed new treaty rules impinging upon those grounded in custom and usage. Although in the treaty which climaxed the development there is no specific reference to the international law standard, there was effort to base the reform sought on law as well as morals. On the other hand, opposition to the rules finally included in the treaty made much use of the law.

Within two decades after Congress had formally prohibited further importation of slaves into the United States, the slave traffic became an important subject of judicial decision, treaty making, and diplomatic correspondence. At first the judicial decisions were principally those in national courts. At the beginning of the second decade of the nineteenth century, when pass-

[95] The general statement would apply particularly to the principles embodied in the Statute on the Regime of Navigable Waterways of International Concern, annexed to the 1921 Convention of Barcelona (7 L.N.T.S. 51).

ing upon captured American ships, British prize courts announced a doctrine whereby the duty of restitution was affected by a finding that vessels taken had been engaged in slave traffic in violation of the laws of their own country.[96] In the well-known case of *Le Louis*, however, Sir William Scott held that the "right of visitation" and seizure in time of peace could be exercised on the high seas against a vessel of a foreign state only if the ship were taken legally as a pirate or as a measure of self-defense in the course of repelling injury. The fact that laws of France as well as those of England proscribed the slave traffic gave to a British man-of-war, the court held, no right to visit and search a French ship on the ocean.[97] Eight years later, after a lower federal court had seemed to adopt the idea that slave trading was violative of international law, Chief Justice Marshall in the case of the *Antelope* denied that any nation could prescribe a rule for others. The slave trade not being piracy by the law of nations or contrary to that law, there was no right for an American public vessel to bring in ships even of countries whose statutes prohibited slave trading.[98]

There remained the possibility of handling the problem by means of conventional agreement. As early as 1810, Great Britain had begun to make bilateral treaties on the general subject.[99] By article X of the Treaty of Ghent, the United States and Great Britain, while stopping short of branding the slave traffic as contrary to the law of nations, did declare it "irreconcilable with the principles of humanity and Justice"; they recorded their desire for continued efforts toward abolition and agreed to use their "best endeavours" toward this end.[100] At the Congress of Vienna (1815) the principal maritime powers formally denounced the African slave trade as inconsistent with the principles of humanity and universal morality, but they left it to the individual

[96] *The Amedie*, 1 Acton 240 (1810); *The Fortuna*, 1 Dodson 81 (1811).

[97] 2 Dodson 210 (1817).

[98] 10 Wheaton 66 (1823). See also Ziegler, *International Law of John Marshall*, ch. XI.

[99] See, for example, article X of the treaty of friendship with Portugal, February 19, 1810, which speaks of the "injustice and impolicy" of the slave trade, also Additional Article (II) signed at Madrid, August 28, 1814, with similar language (1 *Brit. and For. State Papers* 292, 547, 555).

[100] Miller, *Treaties*, II, 581.

states to determine for themselves, or to negotiate with others concerning, the time of actual abolition.[101]

The possibility of a multilateral treaty or a system of treaties authorizing specific procedures was affected by fear on the part of some governments that British public ships would use treaty-given powers arbitrarily. The British tried to allay such fears. At the Congress of Aix-la-Chapelle (1818), for example, they pointed out in memoranda to the French that none of the three conventions (with Spain, Portugal, and Holland, respectively) by which Great Britain had gained the reciprocal right of searching suspected vessels had given this right in such a form that it could be used indiscriminately. Rather, each had confined it to vessels having express instructions and authority specified in the treaties. The French plenipotentiary had conceded, the memoranda pointed out, that the measures proposed (reciprocal right of search, to be followed by seizure if the evidence seemed to justify) could not be considered as infractions of the law of nations, and that they rather confirmed that law, since they envisaged a "new power as a Constitutional exception from the admitted principles of the general law."[102] The Congress of Vienna having declared the trade in slaves an odious crime and a disgrace of civilized nations, the British were still left without international authorizations for the practical measures they wished to take.

As set forth at the Congress of Verona (1822), the repressive measures contemplated were to be undergirded by a declaration of the assembled ministers which would renew the formal denunciation of 1815. There was to be an appeal to the maritime powers that had abolished the slave trade by municipal law, urging them to proclaim and treat the traffic as piracy, "with a view of founding upon the aggregate of such Separate Engagements between State and State, a General Law to be incorporated into the Publick Law of the Civilized World."[103] The same memorandum asserted that the "contraband trade" was generally moving under the flag of France, the only one of the great mari-

[101] 3 *Brit. and For. State Papers* 971.
[102] 6 *ibid.* 59–64, 77–85, at 81.
[103] 10 *ibid.* 99.

time powers of Europe which had not entered into treaty agreement with the British to give certain ships of each contracting party a limited power of search and capture. The British felt that their government had been left to "stand alone" in Europe on the question, and that British importunities had been "erroneously attributed to some selfish commercial interest."[104] In spite of these arguments the French were unwilling to go as far as their powerful neighbor desired. They referred to France's recognition of the freedom of the seas for all foreign flags, and the Congress made no declaration substantially in advance of what had previously been done about the slave trade. Later, the French attitude was to be related to American action.

An act of May 15, 1820, made slave trading piracy under United States law and punishable by death.[105] There was no implication, however, that any public vessels except American could proceed against American ships on the high seas. In its diplomatic relations the United States soon began to take a strong position regarding measures of enforcement against suspected traffickers in slaves if these measures might involve visit and search of American vessels by armed ships of other nations. In a note of August 15, 1821, Secretary of State John Quincy Adams related the matter to the old issue of impressment. Replying to a British proposal that the United States accede to certain regulations such as those operative under treaties which Britain had with Spain, Portugal, and the Netherlands, he wrote Stratford Canning, British minister, in part as follows:

> The United States had very recently issued from a war with Great Britain, principally waged in resistance to a practice of searching neutral . . . vessels for men in time of war, exercised by Great Britain, as the United States deem, in violation of the law of nations. A proposal involving the exercise in time of peace of this same practice of search,

[104] 10 *ibid.* 98. The same memorandum showed that, according to facts submitted by the Duke of Wellington to Canning, the slave traffic was being carried on to a greater extent than at any former period, that in seven months of 1821 no fewer than 38,000 persons had been taken from the coast of Africa, and that between July 1820 and October 1821 no fewer than 352 vessels had entered the rivers and ports of Africa north of the equator, for the purpose of purchasing slaves.

[105] 3 *Stat.* 600–601. This was held to be a valid exercise of congressional power (*United States* v. *Bates*, Fed. Cas. no. 14,544).

though for different purposes, could not be acceded to by the American Government consistently with their principles. . . . Of the right of mutual search it is clear that its efficiency depends altogether upon its universal adoption. So long as it shall be declined by any one maritime state, however inconsiderable, its adoption by all others would leave it altogether ineffectual . . . it is scarcely to be expected that any principle so liable to misapplication and abuse can obtain, as an innovation upon the law of nations, the universal concurrence of all maritime powers.[106]

The complete assimilation of slave trading to piracy under international law would have put visit and search of suspected slave ships on the basis of a legally justifiable procedure. There was some desire for this. After the House of Representatives in a resolution of February 28, 1823, had requested that the President open negotiations with maritime powers of Europe and America on the subject, American ministers at European and American capitals received instructions to propose that the African slave trade be proscribed by classing it as piracy and punishing as pirates those who engaged in it.[107] It is difficult to determine what sentiment there was in the country in support of such a move. According to Henry Wheaton, the United States at this time was ready to have the slave trade declared piracy by the law of nations and the slave traders subject to *seizure* by the law of any nation, but with such persons subject to *trial* only by tribunals of the state of the captured vessel, the seizing officer to be responsible for the visitation and everything done in connection with it.[108]

There was an effort to conclude an Anglo-American treaty on the subject in 1824. An agreement signed in London on March 8 of that year provided for reciprocal right of search in certain areas, including waters off the coast of "America." The Senate amended the instrument so as to omit mention of American waters, and the

[106] Moore, *Digest,* II, 919.

[107] President Monroe's annual message, December 2, 1823, *Journal of the House of Representatives,* 18th Cong., 1st Sess., p. 13. The President expressed the belief that the step would be the most effectual expedient that could be adopted for the purpose of suppressing the trade.

[108] Henry Wheaton, *Enquiry into the Validity of the British Claim to a Right of Visitation and Search of American Vessels Suspected to Be Engaged in the African Slave-Trade* (1842), p. 121.

British government declined to accept the treaty in this changed form.[109] Sixteen years later, when there was still no treaty between the parties authorizing specific procedures, a British and an American naval commander made an agreement for coöperation in action against slavers, but the Van Buren administration disavowed this arrangement.[110]

In contemplation of general international law, the traffic in slaves was still not illicit. Property in slaves was good property for the purpose of protection through international reclamations, notwithstanding the fact that some states of the world had abolished slavery. In the case of the *Enterprize,* which grew out of incidents occurring in 1835, that of the *Hermosa,* arising out of the freeing of American-owned slaves in British jurisdiction in 1840, and that of the *Creole,* which involved the bringing of an American vessel into the port of Nassau in 1841 after a mutiny of slaves on board, awards were made against Great Britain under the convention of February 8, 1853[111] In the first mentioned case the umpire said that while slavery was contrary to the principles of justice and humanity, it existed by law in several countries at the time the claim arose; it "could not then be contrary to the law of nations, and the Enterprize was as much entitled to protection as though her cargo consisted of any other description of property." In the *Creole,* the same arbiter felt that he "need not refer to authorities to show that slavery, however odious and contrary to the principles of justice and humanity, may be established by law in any country; and, having been so established by law in many countries, it can not be contrary to the law of nations."

In 1841 there was renewed effort for a multilateral treaty. On April 16, Andrew Stevenson, American minister in London, had written to Palmerston that the United States government, which had made the slave trade piracy under municipal law, had not by this step made piracy an offense against the law of nations, since

[109] *Amer. State Papers, For. Rel.,* V, 319–322, 361–362, 364–365. See also pp. 733–735 of the same volume.

[110] Hugh G. Soulsby, *The Right of Search and the Slave Trade in Anglo-American Relations, 1814–1862* (1933), p. 56.

[111] Sen. Exec. Doc. 103, 34th Cong., 1st Sess., pp. 187, 239–240, 242–245. See also Miller, *Treaties,* VI, 158 *et seq.*

one nation could not add to or limit offenses against the "public law."[112] On September 10 the minister wrote that, since the slave trade had not been acknowledged as piracy in international law, there was no case whatever for the exercise of a right of visit and search against the traders, and the right must therefore stand on the grounds of expediency and necessity as the only grounds of executing treaties for suppression of the trade.[113] In his annual message, December 7, 1841, President Tyler declared that the proposed concessions could not be made. The United States, he added, had the will and the ability to protect its flag from being used for purposes forbidden by American laws and obnoxious to the moral censure of the world.[114]

The attitude of the United States seems to have had some effect upon the policy of France. The latter country had finally made bilateral conventions with Great Britain for reciprocal visit and search, in 1831 and 1833.[115] The Department of State had informed the French and British ministers in 1834 that the United States could not give its "adhesion" to these conventions because of the British minister's statement, in a note of December 25, 1833, that in the act of accession it would be necessary that "the right of search should be extended to the coasts of the United States."[116] When representatives of Austria, Prussia, Russia, France, and Great Britain signed at London, on December 20, 1841, the so-called Quintuple Treaty for the authorization of visit and search,[117] Lewis Cass at the American Legation in Paris published, with the approval of his government, an anonymous pamphlet in which he argued with vigor that the right of search could not be legally exercised except by a belligerent. He pointed to dire results "when a few years more shall have consecrated the present doctrine, as an acknowledged principle of international law."[118] There has

[112] Soulsby, *The Right of Search*, p. 57.

[113] *Ibid.*, p. 62.

[114] Richardson, *Messages*, IV, 1930.

[115] Texts in 18 *Brit. and For. State Papers* 641–644, and 20 *ibid.* 286–301.

[116] G. H. Hackworth, *A Digest of International Law* (1940–1944), II, 660. Apparently the terms "adhesion" and "accession" were used interchangeably.

[117] Text in 30 *Brit. and For. State Papers* 269–300.

[118] *An Examination of the Question, Now in Discussion, between the American and British Governments, Concerning the Right of Search*, by an

been disagreement concerning the influence which the pamphlet actually had upon the growth of sentiment in France against the Quintuple Treaty and upon France's failure to ratify.[119]

Short of a multilateral treaty arrangement, there was the possibility of a considerable measure of coöperative action under bilateral agreement. The Webster-Ashburton Treaty, signed August 9, 1842, contained no declaration of newly established public law of general application, but, after repeating in the preamble the words of the tenth article of the Treaty of Ghent and expressing anew the determination that, in so far as it might be within the power of the signatory governments, the slave trade should be "effectually abolished," it provided in article VIII the following plan:

> The Parties mutually stipulate that each shall prepare, equip, and maintain in service, on the coast of Africa, a sufficient and adequate squadron, or naval force of vessels, of suitable numbers and descriptions, to carry in all not less than eighty guns, to enforce, separately and respectively, the law rights and obligations of each of the two countries, for the suppression of the Slave Trade, the said squadrons to be independent of each other, but the two Governments stipulating, nevertheless, to give such orders to the officers commanding their respective forces, as shall enable them most effectually to act in concert and coöperation, upon mutual consultation, as exigencies may arise, for the attainment of the true object of this article; copies of all such orders to be communicated by each Government to the other respectively.[120]

American (1842), p. 12. As to the law which the treaty was designed to change, Cass made the following observations: "The law of nations is but general opinion, illustrated by able jurists, and sanctified by time, and by universal acquiescence. Touch it rudely, and the whole fabric will disappear, leaving the nations of the world, in their mutual relations, as they existed in the most barbarous ages."

[119] As to the effect of the pamphlet, see Jesse S. Reeves, *American Diplomacy under Tyler and Polk* (1907), p. 36; Beckles Willson, *America's Ambassadors to France, 1777–1927* (1928), pp. 204–205. W. B. Lawrence wrote that the United States "not only themselves maintained the freedom of the seas, but by their interposition with France, prevented the propositions of England from being adopted as the common law of Europe" (*Visitation and Search* [1858], p. 81; quoted after Soulsby, *The Right of Search*, p. 117).

The British had signed a treaty on November 16, 1840, with the Republic of Texas, in which they obtained the reciprocal right of visit and search for the purpose of suppressing the slave trade. The right was limited as to areas, officers, and kinds of ships (29 *Brit. and For. State Papers* 85).

[120] Miller, *Treaties*, IV, 369.

A communication which the President sent to the Senate two days after the signing of the agreement explained that "the treaty . . . proposes no alteration, mitigation or modification of the rules of the law of nations." In his annual message on the following December 6, President Tyler said: "While . . . the United States have been standing up for the freedom of the seas, they have not thought proper to make that a pretext for avoiding a fulfillment of their treaty stipulations or a ground for giving countenance to a trade reprobated by our laws." He added that a similar arrangement by the other great powers "could not fail to sweep from the ocean the slave trade without the interpolation of any new principle into the maritime code." [121]

Of the pertinent parts of the Webster-Ashburton Treaty, Secretary of State Webster wrote to Edward Everett, minister to England, on March 28, 1843, that "Great Britain had claimed as a *right* that which this Government could not admit to be a *right*, and, in the exercise of a just and proper spirit of amity, a mode was resorted to which might render unnecessary both the assertion and the denial of such claim." [122] The American contention that, for the purpose under consideration, there was no valid distinction between visit and search, rested on essentially practical considerations. While admitting the right of *approach* to a vessel on the high seas, as it had been described in the case of the *Marianna Flora* (1826),[123] the United States continued to deny that there was a right, without specific assent of a state whose vessels might be visited and searched, to do what the Quintuple Treaty of 1841 had contemplated. Nor do the British appear to have denied this.

A harmonizing of the views of the two governments came considerably later. Nearly sixteen years after the Webster-Ashburton

[121] *Ibid.*, pp. 397, 439; Richardson, *Messages*, IV, 194–209.

As to the absence of any express prohibition of the search of American vessels by British cruisers, Webster wrote to Cass on December 20, 1842, that "inasmuch as the treaty gives no color or pretext whatever to any right of searching our ships, a declaration against such a right would have been no more suitable to this treaty than a declaration against the right of sacking our towns in time of peace, or any other outrage" (*The Works of Daniel Webster* [8th ed., 1854] VI, 388; Moore, *Digest*, II, 931).

[122] Moore, *Digest*, II, 935.

[123] 11 Wheaton 1.

Treaty came into force, Mr. Cass, then Secretary of State, in a note of April 10, 1858, denied "the right of the cruisers of any other power . . . for any purpose whatever" to enter the vessels of the United States by force in time of peace. "Search or visit," he said, "it is equally an assault upon the independence of nations." The British government, in a note of June 11 to the British minister at Washington, recognized as sound "those principles of international law which have been laid down by General Cass in his note of the 10th of April," and recognized that "nothing in their treaty of 1842 with the United States supersedes that law." [124] President Buchanan was able to report to Congress in his message of the following December 6 that "the long-pending controversy between the two Governments in relation to the question of visitation and search has been amicably adjusted." [125]

Within four years after obtaining from the principal maritime state concerned an affirmation of the principle of law for which she had contended, the United States agreed with the same maritime state to some deviation from the rule of freedom from visit and search on the high seas. The treaty of April 7, 1862, with Great Britain, permitted the reciprocal right of search and detention of suspected slave carriers within two hundred miles of the coast of Africa, and south of the thirty-second parallel of latitude, and within thirty leagues of the coast of Cuba. Punishment of those engaged in slave trading was to be according to laws of the country in which the vessel used was registered. A system of mixed courts was to function as part of the plan, the tribunals to be located at Sierra Leone, New York, and the Cape of Good Hope.[126] Some seven months prior to the signing of the treaty, the Secretary of State (William Henry Seward) had told Richard B. P. Lyons, the British minister, that he might inform his government "informally" that the "present Administration had none of the squeamishness about allowing the American vessels to be boarded and searched which had characterized their predeces-

[124] Moore, *Digest,* II, 943. In the note containing the last-quoted remarks, the British argued for a limited power of determining the nationality of vessels suspected, and for some discretion on the part of an officer resorting to this procedure.

[125] Richardson, *Messages,* VII, 3038.

[126] 12 *Stat.* 1225; 18 *ibid.* (2) 334.

sors." [127] On November 2, 1861, Seward indicated that he would like to receive from Lyons, "for his own private use," a memorandum on the subject of an arrangement such as would be acceptable to the British government.[128] The sequel to this was the signing, by the Secretary of State and the minister, of an "informal memorandum," dated November 13.[129] This, however, was not thought by the British government to afford ample basis for the issuance to commanders of British cruisers of instructions for searches and detentions.[130] The British minister, for his part, was concerned not merely with the feelings of the American people in regard to the slave trade, but with the mood in which the American people might happen to be with regard to England when an American slaver arrived in charge of a "British Prize Crew." [131] In an instruction of February 28, 1862, Earl Russell observed that "a verbal Agreement . . . might be of little avail against a popular cry, founded on the indisputable doctrine of International Law, that the Right of Search cannot be lawfully exercised in time of Peace." With this same instruction was forwarded a draft treaty,[132] the text of which followed the model which Great Britain had signed with Spain in 1835.

The outcome was the signing of the treaty on April 7, but this did not occur until Seward had made it clear, and the British had agreed, that the treaty must appear (when presented to the Senate for its approval) to have been a proposal originating with the United States.[133] The Senate gave its approval by unanimity, and the mixed courts were established, but some difficulty in the carrying out of the treaty plan was encountered from Gideon

[127] Miller, *Treaties,* VIII, 779.

[128] *Ibid.,* p. 781. In the same conversation the Secretary referred to the great change which had occurred in public opinion in the United States on the subject.

[129] Text in Miller, *Treaties,* VIII, 784.

[130] Instructions to Lyons, December 7, 1861, and February 28, 1862, quoted in Miller, *Treaties,* VIII, 786, 791.

[131] Despatch of February 11, 1862, quoted in Miller, *Treaties,* VIII, 789.

[132] Instructions of February 28, 1862 (Miller, *Treaties,* VIII, 792).

[133] Conversation of March 21, 1862, as reported in a despatch of March 25, 1862, quoted in Miller, *Treaties,* VIII, 793–795. The text of the treaty, as finally perfected, differed from the draft which the British had submitted in that there was added a ten-year duration clause, together with minor changes in Annex B, article 9, and in article 12.

Welles, American Secretary of the Navy. This officer, evincing lack of enthusiasm for the arrangement and for the part which the Secretary of State had had in its making,[134] at first declined to issue the necessary instructions to American naval commanders on the ground that the treaty bound the United States to give up, for the specific purpose set forth in the instrument, the general *belligerent* right of search in latitudes where the exercise of that right was important.[135] Correspondence on this point brought from the British government an indication that it did not "regard the Privileges granted by that Treaty as in any way derogatory from or conflicting with the Belligerents Rights of the United States Cruizers," powers conferred by the treaty being added to such belligerent rights and not substituted for them.[136] The point concerning the special rules under the treaty (in their relation to general international law on belligerent rights) having been set at rest, the necessary instructions to American naval commanders were issued in the form of a "Special Warrant." [137] There followed, however, no captures pursuant to the treaty terms, and as Welles later put it, the officers of the mixed courts "never had anything to do but draw their salaries." [138] The fact that no slaver was ever tried in these courts has been taken as evidence that the Lyons-Seward treaty achieved its object.[139]

An additional article signed the following year added to the treaty zones (wherein reciprocal search and detention were permissible) water within thirty leagues of Madagascar, within

[134] Gideon Welles, *Diary* (1911), I, 166–167. On the question of whether the treaty had been discussed with the President and the Cabinet (as Seward claimed it had been, and Welles said it had not been), see Miller, *Treaties*, VIII, 818. Welles later recorded his suspicion that the British were trying to secure immunity for their vessels, "thus opening a way for intercourse with the blockaded rebels" (*Lincoln and Seward* [1874], p. 141).

[135] Welles, *Dairy*, I, 167, and correspondence reproduced in Miller, *Treaties*, VIII, 806–809.

[136] Note of January 26, 1863, from Lyons to Seward, quoted in Miller, *Treaties*, VIII, 811–812. The view has been expressed that the treaty involved greater concessions by the United States than had ever been requested by Great Britain (A. Taylor Milne, "The Lyons-Seward Treaty of 1862," *American Historical Review*, XXXVIII (1932–33), 511–525, at p. 513).

[137] As reproduced in Miller, *Treaties*, VIII, 812–813.

[138] *Lincoln and Seward*, p. 144.

[139] Cf. Moore, *Digest*, II, 467.

thirty leagues of Puerto Rico, and within thirty leagues of San Domingo.[140] By the convention of June 3, 1870, it was agreed that the mixed courts should be discontinued as "no longer necessary" and cases arising thereafter under the treaty were to go to municipal courts.[141] The treaty, the additional article, and the additional convention were terminated (after notification by Great Britain) on April 29, 1923.[142]

The treaty development which has been traced was followed by steps looking to a wider multilateral system for suppression of the slave trade. As a party to the General Act of Brussels, July 2, 1890, the United States accepted a plan of allowing the examination of papers of suspected vessels of less than five hundred tons and in defined zones; the right of search became permissible with regard to vessels of those states which, in conventions on the subject, had given the right on a reciprocal basis. The articles of the General Act set forth the desire to ensure, by arrangements suitable to modern requirements, application of the general principles of civilization established by the Acts of Berlin and Brussels.[143] It remained for further effort looking to the suppression of slavery and traffic in slaves to be exerted in the twentieth century, after the close of the First World War. The United States was one of the parties which signed the Convention at Saint-Germain-en-Laye on September 10, 1919, "wishing," according to the preamble (which followed the language of the earlier multilateral instrument), to ensure by arrangements "suitable to modern requirements" the application of principles mentioned in the General Act of Brussels. The commitment was to endeavor to secure "the complete suppression of slavery in all its forms and of the black slave trade by land and sea."[144] The

[140] 13 *Stat.* 645; 18 *Stat.* (2) 345.

[141] 16 *Stat.* 777; 18 *Stat.* (2) 350.

[142] *For. Rel.*, 1922, II, 407–408; note 152, *infra.*

[143] 27 *Stat.* 886. In the meantime, the General Act of the Berlin Conference (which was not ratified by the United States) had indicated a basis in general principle for the rules, with the following language: "Conformément aux principes du droit des gens, tels qu'ils sont reconnus par les Puissances Signitaires, la Traite des Escalves étant interdite" (76 *Brit. and For. State Papers* 11, art. IX).

[144] 49 *Stat.* 3027 (art. XI).

Geneva Convention seven years later (September 25, 1926)[145] contained provisions envisaging another general convention that would provide for the stopping and bringing in of suspected vessels, a plan similar to that in the convention on trade in arms, which had been signed at Geneva on June 17, 1925.[146]

What the British had sought in nearly a half century of diplomacy in the matter of the slave trade was not the abandonment of the standard which was the freedom of the seas, but a *lex specialis* to permit procedures against vessels suspected of engaging in a special type of traffic. The method has subsequently been successfully employed with respect to certain other subject matters. Lacking a special arrangement which would have permitted, in one such subject matter, protective action without infringing the basic principle, the United States lost the Bering Sea Arbitration, but less than two decades later became a party with the other states principally concerned to a treaty that authorized procedure against individuals violating agreed rules.[147] An earlier multilateral achievement had to do with protection of submarine cables, in connection with which the United States proposed a draft that would have made individuals' acts in certain circumstances piratical acts.[148] That some needed limitation on the immunity of private vessels on the high seas may be accomplished by bilateral treaties is illustrated in certain agreements of the

[145] 46 *Stat.* 2183.

[146] The latter convention did not immediately come into effect for the United States (Hackworth, *Digest*, II, 672).

[147] 37 *Stat.* 1542. A summary of provisions is in Hackworth, *Digest*, I, 795–797.

[148] This draft was proposed in discussions of 1869, but was not adopted. Apparently it was concluded that such a punishment as that for piracy would be excessive if applied to willful acts of destruction of, or injury to, cables. Some states also opposed the idea of allowing jurisdiction to be exercised by tribunals of states that were nearest to the places where offenses might have been committed (Clark, *International Communications*, pp. 126, 134–135).

In 1879 the Institute of International Law adopted a resolution declaring that it would be useful for the states by concerted action to declare that destruction or damage to submarine cables was a "délit du droit des gens." It proposed that the right of seizing suspects be given to the public ships of all the nations, but that the right of trial should be reserved to national courts of the state in which a captured ship might be registered (*Annuaire*, III–IV [1], 394).

prohibition era [149] and in bilateral treaties with Canada concerning halibut and sockeye salmon.[150]

It may be true that, in the formulation of foreign policy with respect to the slave trade in the first half of the nineteenth century, the appeal to legal principle was a minor element,[151] and that considerations of interest, quite apart from concern for the general law of nations as such, were paramount.[152] This would, of course, be possible in almost any international situation, since the law is a means and not an end. In any case, resistance to international coöperative action persisted in this instance until there was in the United States a change with respect to the national problem which had affected the position taken on the international legal issue.

[149] See Chapter IV, section 2, *infra.*

[150] 50 *Stat.* 1351–52, 1355, 1359.

[151] Soulsby, *The Right of Search,* p. 62.

[152] On the technical correctness of the position of the United States toward the law involved, see Jesse Reeves, *American Diplomacy under Tyler and Polk,* p. 21; Richard W. Van Alstyne, "The British Right of Search and the African Slave Trade," *Journal of Modern History,* II (1930), 37–47.

The development treated in this section, in relation to the broad principle of the freedom of the seas, with particular attention to France's position, is treated in Gidel, *Le droit international public de la mer,* I, 389–410.

In 1922 the British government notified the states concerned that it intended to terminate bilateral treaties looking to suppression of the slave trade in certain parts of the world, "in accordance with the general policy of His Majesty's Government to abolish obsolete treaty instruments" (see, for example, 11 L.N.T.S. 466).

Chapter IV

INDEPENDENCE AND JURISDICTION OF STATES

It might be expected that treaty provisions touching upon such subjects as the existence and independence of states would furnish occasion for frequent reference to the international law standard. It is obvious that only in terms of that standard would a state's existence and the right to exercise its authority become, in the full legal sense, meaningful. However, except for multilateral or "code" statements on rights and duties,[1] there have been few treaties of the United States in which parties, when dealing with these broad subjects, have made specific mention of the standard.

Some questions of state jurisdiction have already been considered.[2] In the present chapter the concept of intervention, as it has presented questions of relation to the standard, will receive attention. Illustrations are from a bilateral treaty which is now of only historical interest, from official pronouncements of the Western Hemisphere republics, and from recent undertakings which have sought to reconcile the principle of nonintervention with that of collective action against aggression. A final section will relate to jurisdiction as it is involved in treaty commitments with respect to the limits of marginal seas.

1. INTERVENTION

Some modern writers on international law have denied the right of any state to intervene in the domestic affairs of another and

[1] See Chapter I, notes 82–86, *supra*. With the treaty declarations there referred to may be compared the formulation of rights and duties in the first report of the United Nations International Law Commission, as reproduced in *Amer. Jour. Int. Law*, XLIV, Supp. (1950), 1–21.

[2] See Chapter I, p. 22.

have asserted the duty of nonintervention. Others have claimed legal justification in exceptional circumstances for collective intervention, or for that which can be justified on humanitarian grounds, or for that which constitutes a kind of "temporary interposition" to protect nationals abroad, or for that invited by the *de jure* government of the state whose territory is involved, or even for that which seeks to prevent unlawful intervention by another state.[3] A reference in a treaty to intervention in relation to international law would presumably imply a rule of international law on the subject. In the treaty practice of the United States there has been at least one instance of advance authorization in terms of international law of protective action by one party in the territory of the other party state. In other instances there have been multilateral renunciations of intervention at least as toward the other parties to the agreements. Still more recently treaty makers have sought to reconcile the idea of a state to be free from intervention with the plan of collective action in the interest of international peace and security.

a. Bilateral Authorization: The Gadsden Treaty

Among the treaties which make direct reference to international law, that which the United States signed with Mexico on December 30, 1853, seems to merit special attention because of the nature of the reference and the personal and political factors that figured in the development. A brief summary of the latter is essential to a consideration of the possible purpose and effect of the mention of the international law standard.

The treaty refers at more than one place to the law of nations. By the first article, there was to be no variation of the boundary line agreed upon by the parties, except with the express and free consent of both of them, "given in conformity to the principles of the law of nations, and in accordance with the constitution of

[3] See, generally, H. G. Hodges, *The Doctrine of Intervention* (1915); W. E. Lingelbach, "The Doctrine and Practice of Intervention in Europe," *Annals Amer. Acad. Pol. and Soc. Sci.*, XVI (1900), 1–32; P. H. Winfield, *The Foundations and the Future of International Law* (1941), p. 32; Charles Cheney Hyde, *International Law Chiefly as Interpreted and Applied by the United States* (1945 ed.), I, 245–281.

each country respectively."[4] Article VII reaffirmed the 22nd article of the Treaty of Guadalupe Hidalgo, with its provisions concerning nationals of one party in the territory of the other in the event of war, humane treatment of prisoners of war, and its pledge that rules of the article were to be "as sacredly observed as the most acknowledged obligations under the law of nature or nations." Article VIII of the Gadsden Treaty had to do with a concession that the Mexican government had granted to a concern (in which Americans had an interest) to construct a plank-and-rail road across the Isthmus of Tehuantepec. The United States was to have the right of transit over such road for troops, munitions, persons, and merchandise. Furthermore, the fifth paragraph of the article contained the following:

> The Mexican government having agreed to protect with its whole power the prosecution, preservation and security of the work, the United States may extend its protection as it shall judge wise to it when it may feel sanctioned and warranted by the public or international law.[5]

The events bearing particularly upon this part of the treaty began with the granting by General Antonio López de Santa Anna, in 1842, of a concession to Don José Garay for the development of a communication route across the Isthmus of Tehuantepec.[6] Four years later (on November 5, 1846) a Mexican decree (of the Salas government) gave Garay two years of additional time within which he might begin his operations. Rights under the concession had, in the meantime, come into the hands of British subjects by transfer. Later, when the Treaty of Guadalupe Hidalgo was in the process of negotiation, the question of rights over the Isthmus of Tehuantepec was not included for discussion, after the Mexican commissioners had explained orally that rights which had been Garay's were now in English hands.[7] American

[4] 10 *Stat.* 1031, 1033. Six months prior to the signing of the treaty, Secretary of State Marcy had written Roscoe Conkling, minister to Mexico, that the United States had no intention of departing from international law in such agreements (J. F. Rippy, "The Boundary of New Mexico and the Gadsden Treaty," *Amer. Hist. Rev.*, IV (1921), 715, 732).

[5] 10 *Stat.* 1036–37.

[6] On the "extravagant and improvident" terms of the grant, see Miller, *Treaties*, VI, 310.

[7] Miller, *Treaties*, V, 282–283.

investors became parties in interest when, in 1849, Hargous Brothers of New York acquired the rights originally given to Garay.

Protection of what these American citizens had acquired then became a matter of some concern to their government. To Nathan Clifford, American minister to Mexico, on July 11, 1849, the Mexican foreign minister (Lacunza), wrote that Mexico would not annul the privileges merely because the holders were American citizens. At the same time he said, with respect to possible annulment for failure to fulfill conditions of the contract, that, "if the privilege should be annulled from motives of this kind, nothing could legalize the intervention of the government of the United States." Continuing, he observed that, however this "affair" be regarded,

> there cannot be the slightest doubt, according to the principles of the law of nations, that all questions concerning its validity, the compliance with its conditions, its forfeiture, etc., are to be discussed, decided and determined, according to the laws and by the constitutionally competent authorities of Mexico, to the exclusion of those of any other power.[8]

In September of the same year, Robert Perkins Letcher, the new minister to Mexico, received instructions to seek a convention with Mexico providing for protection of the rights and property of persons who desired to construct the communication.[9] The Letcher-Pedrazzo convention of June 22, 1850 resulted,[10] but it failed to provide a mutually agreeable assurance of protection. Under date of August 12, P. A. Hargous wrote to Daniel Webster, Secretary of State, that the parties interested in the privilege were aware that in ordinary cases it was not the practice of the United States government officially to interfere in behalf of

[8] Sen. Ex. Doc. 97, 32nd Cong., 1st Sess., p. 9.

[9] J. F. Rippy, "Diplomacy of the United States and Mexico regarding the Isthmus of Tehuantepec," *Miss. Vall. Hist. Rev.*, VI (1920), 503, 507–508.

[10] Text in Sen. Ex. Doc. 97, 32nd Cong., 1st Sess., pp. 20–23. Letcher explained that he had carefully excluded any guarantee of sovereignty of Mexico, and had specified "eventual interference" by the United States for protection, upon a summons from Mexico, of the route and territory adjacent. By article 12 of the draft convention, the actual holder of the concession was to give consent before the treaty should be submitted to the Senate.

American citizens who might complain of the violation of a contract which they had made with a foreign government. He went on to say that all general rules have their exceptions and that the American government and public, especially people in the West and Southwest, were "largely involved in the success of the Tehuantepec enterprise."[11]

The Secretary of State assured Hargous that the citizens concerned might "rely upon all the protection which the executive government of the United States can constitutionally and lawfully extend to them." He added that, if remonstrances through diplomatic channels should prove insufficient to secure the protection, "it cannot be doubted that in such a case, in which the interests of individuals would be obviously subordinate to those of the public, any other means which might be necessary for your protection would be authorized and employed." At the instance of the parties concerned, Webster sought, through the American minister at Mexico City, to secure more adequate provisions, pointing out that under provisions proposed Mexico would enjoy all the real benefits of sovereignty in the area and be relieved of some of the most onerous of its duties. A suggested convention left each party free to use its military or naval forces for the needed "protection." Webster stated that, "if Mexico should reject our overtures for this purpose, we will extend our protection to them alone, according to our own sense of right and duty, and as future events may require." Mexico refused assent, its government saying that such arrangements would infringe upon the national sovereignty, dignity, honor, and pride, and its foreign minister observing that entry of foreign military forces had always been held as an attack upon the sovereignty of the state entered—or at least that such entry should only be at the express request of the nation.[12]

A new draft convention, dated January 25, 1851, was not very different from that of the preceding year, except that it contained a provision for arbitration of differences between the Mexican government and the concessionaire.[13] Opposed by the clergy, the

[11] Sen. Ex. Doc. 97, 32nd Cong., 1st Sess., pp. 25, 26.

[12] *Ibid.*, pp. 26, 27, 31–32, 39.

[13] The text of the provision (article 5) was as follows: "In any difference . . . between the government of Mexico and the undertakers, either

press, the houses of Congress, and all political factions in Mexico, the treaty was rejected in the Mexican Senate by a vote of 71 to 1, although it received the unanimous approval of the United States Senate.[14] On May 22, 1851, the Mexican Senate declared the 1846 (Salas) decree, on which the American company relied, to be null and void. This meant the termination of all privileges under the Garay grant. It drew from Secretary Webster the following statement, on August 25, 1851:

> In all civilized countries instruments of this description are considered as contracts . . . conferring privileges which are not to be revoked without reasonable cause . . . not liable to be annulled at the pleasure of the executive or legislative power.[15]

The threat of filibustering expeditions, over the period from 1848 to 1853, was a considerable factor in the diplomacy.[16] On December 13, 1851, the Mexican foreign minister, José F. Ramirez, wrote the American minister that if the New Orleans Company (Judah P. Benjamin and associates), which had now become a party in interest, should make forcible attempts, Mexico would be under the inevitable necessity of treating the company's agents "with all the severity which the laws of nations authorize."[17] The

---

the present or the future, of the work, which may involve the loss of the right to the privilege, the complaining party shall draw up a statement of its pretensions and motives, and a similar statement shall be drawn up by the other party; and both statements shall be submitted to the decision of two arbiters who hold no diplomatic appointment or commission, and who reside in the Mexican territory. One of these arbiters shall be appointed by the holders of the privilege, and the other by the government of Mexico; and these two, in case of disagreement shall appoint a third, with the qualifications above required, who shall decide the controversy; and from the decision of these arbiters there shall be no appeal or recourse whatever. Of all other questions which may arise, the Mexican tribunals shall take cognizance."

[14] Sen. Ex. Doc. 97, 32nd Cong., 1st Sess., pp. 128, 136.

[15] *Ibid.*, p. 86.

[16] See J. F. Rippy, "Anglo-American Filibusters and the Gadsden Treaty," *Hisp. Amer. Hist. Rev.*, V (1922), 155–180; William O. Scroggs, *Filibusters and Financiers* (1916), ch. I.

[17] Sen. Ex. Doc. 97, 32nd Cong., 1st Sess., p. 108. The foreign minister declared that this would be no more than the application of "American public law" as it had been set forth by the President of the United States in his proclamations concerning incursions on the Rio Bravo. In the latter, dated October 22, 1851, President Fillmore had said, regarding persons who might be connected with military expeditions into Mexico, that "if they

legal tone of some of the discussion is further illustrated by Secretary Webster's letter to the minister from Mexico dated June 30, 1852. After saying that the isthmus, while a possession of Mexico, was important to the United States and to the world, he added:

> Mr. Larrainzer of course well understands that, according to the acknowledged principles of public law and the usages of nations, ancient and modern, the obligations of good neighborhood and national friendship, make it the duty of a state to allow reasonable transit over its own territories to the citizens and subjects of other friendly governments for the purposes of commerce and other peaceable communications.[18]

The strong tone which the State Department's pronouncements took at times seems to have been motivated by more than concern for the general principle that American concessionaires should be protected in the enjoyment of that which they had validly acquired from another government. It apparently reflected the fear that a rail route across the mountains to the southern Pacific would be difficult to build and difficult to operate in case it should be completed. That the alternative route across the Isthmus of Tehuantepec must be secured for the commerce of the United States was perhaps a natural conclusion of the expansionists.

The personal factor in the diplomacy was of some importance. After the death of Webster on October 24, 1852, the State Department was not so insistent as it had previously been about the Garay grant, although the matter continued to be the subject of consideration from the point of view of legal rights involved as well as from that of the expediency of a forceful policy. As late as February 2, 1853, the United States minister to Mexico (Roscoe

---

should be captured within the jurisdiction of the Mexican authorities they must expect to be tried and punished according to the laws of Mexico and will have no right to claim the interposition of this Government in their behalf" (Richardson, *Messages*, VI, 2648).

[18] Sen. Ex. Doc. 97, 32nd Cong., 1st Sess., p. 152. A direct communication from President Fillmore, of March 19, 1852, drew from President Mariano Arista of Mexico the statement, concerning the Garay grant and especially the attitude of the United States with respect to it, that, "the conclusion is irresistible that the object particularly aimed at was an occasion to bring the two countries into conflict, and that, with this intention, Mexico was required to do what it was known she could not and would not perform" (*ibid.*, p. 161).

Conkling) wrote to Edward Everett, Secretary of State, in a tone that suggests a broad view of American and world interests which the writer sought to harmonize with international law. Concerning the holders of the Garay grant, Conkling observed that

> the United States, without violating any principle of international law, might, at their option, insist on the recognition by Mexico of the rights claimed by these assignees, and in doing so, might further insist on stipulations from the Mexican Government, deemed necessary to the accomplishment of the great enterprise in view, and to its practical utility when completed; and that considering the vast importance of the work to the whole American people, it was fit and proper for their government to avail itself of the opportunity thus presented, to interpose in the manner it did.[19]

Three days after this communication was written, the Mexican government signed a contract with another American company, headed by A. G. Sloo, who seems to have been in conversation with Mexican officials as early as 1851. By the new arrangement, the concessionaire was to construct a plank road across the Isthmus of Tehuantepec within three years, and a railroad within four years. All questions that might arise were to be decided by the competent Mexican courts and according to Mexican laws. The company was to pay to Mexico $600,000; the Mexican government was to be a stockholder; one third of the company's stock was to be, for six months, at the disposal of Mexican purchasers.[20] The Sloo interests, incorporated as the Louisiana Tehuantepec Company, gave a lien on their grant to F. de P. Falconnet, a

[19] Sen. Ex. Doc. 72, 35th Cong., 1st Sess., p. 16. The minister said in the same communication that the United States was not under *obligation* to the assignees of the Garay contract to make itself party to their contract, which was naturally cognizable in Mexican courts. The Mexican position seems to have been that matters arising under the contract were exclusively cognizable in such courts.

Some months later, on May 7, 1853, one of those principally interested in the Garay grant wrote to Mr. Marcy that, while without legal proof, he was morally certain that the Mexican government, when it voided the Garay grant in 1851 on the ground that Salas had exceeded his authority in extending the time limits in 1846, had been influenced by the British minister at Mexico City (Senate Executive document cited).

[20] Text in Sen. Ex. Doc. 72, 35th Cong., 1st Sess., pp. 21–26. There were provisions concerning colonization and the introduction of armed forces.

By an act of its Congress on May 14, 1852, Mexico had invited proposals for opening interoceanic communication across the Isthmus of Tehuantepec.

British subject, in order to secure money to make the payment to Mexico. (The lien was acquired by P. A. Hargous of New York in 1856.)

On March 21, 1853, Conkling transmitted to President Pierce a proposed convention concerning the Sloo grant, but the President apparently did not submit it to the Senate. When James Gadsden arrived in Mexico City in August 1853, questions of rights under the old Garay grant, and of what the Sloo interests had acquired, were still at issue. There were also boundary matters, the problem of protection against filibustering expeditions, and Mexican complaints that the United States had failed to fulfill its legal obligations under article XI of the Treaty of Guadalupe Hidalgo (concerning Indian raids). Those interested in the Garay grant had not ceased their efforts, for as late as November 1853 one C. L. Ward, of Pennsylvania, brought to Gadsden supplementary instructions which, in their oral form, looked to the protection of the Garay concession.[21]

The actual negotiation of the Gadsden Treaty extended from December 10 to December 30. The treaty draft, as signed at Mexico City, provided that the United States should assume claims of its citizens against Mexico, "including the claim of the so called concession of Garay." Article VIII would have committed the United States to pursue with naval forces such filibustering expeditions as might elude civil and military forces and reach the high seas.[22] These parts were not in the draft as finally approved by the United States.[23] Gadsden, who had been wary of the instructions brought by Ward, seems to have been willing to include the provisions looking to assumption of the claim growing out of the Garay concession; but the concession furnishing occasion for special wording in the treaty, as it was "amended" by the United States Senate, was the Sloo concession.[24] The so-called

[21] J. F. Rippy, "The Negotiation of the Gadsden Treaty," *Southwestern Historical Quarterly*, XXVII (1923), 1, 18.

[22] Text in Manning, *Diplomatic Correspondence*, IX (1937), 691–694.

[23] Rippy, "Diplomacy of the United States and Mexico . . ." p. 527.

[24] Rippy, "The Negotiation of the Gadsden Treaty," p. 21. For Gadsden's later (1856) criticism of the policy of the Pierce administration as having "stimulated the interference of private individuals in international negotiations," see Miller, *Treaties*, VI, 431.

Sloo Amendment, which contains the clause regarding the right of the United States to "extend its protection as it shall judge wise" when it should feel "sanctioned and warranted by the public or international law," was apparently inserted when the treaty was before the United States Senate.[25] Inclusion of the provisions seems to have encountered considerable opposition but to have been finally approved after some political pressure.[26]

The Gadsden Treaty was not popular in Mexico. Those who accepted it for that country were regarded as having done something treasonable. Money received from the United States under the agreement went for current expenses of the government and not for services of the funded debt.[27] Article VIII seems to have shared the opprobrium attaching in Mexico to the treaty generally. Within a few years the article was again to become the subject of diplomatic correspondence.

It has been noted that P. A. Hargous, who had at one time been a principal party interested in the Garay grant, acquired (by lien) rights in the Sloo grant in 1856. In March of that year, Hargous' attorney informed Gadsden that Mexico had refused to honor the rights secured to Hargous by transfer. No substantial aid for the assignee came from Gadsden. The latter's successor at Mexico City, John Forsyth, seemed less inclined to assist the holders of the grant than was Lewis Cass, Secretary of State.

[25] In a despatch of June 30, 1854, Gadsden reported the treaty as being, to the Mexicans, "particularly exceptionable in the Eighth (8) article; as asserting under certain contingencies: the right of protection of a private interest and speculation, and on conditions which seem to involve the surrender of nationality in the right of eminent domain: not only to the U States, but to every other nation which under Treaty with Mexico, might claim what was granted to the most favored" (Desp. Mexico, vol. 18, no. 31, as quoted in Manning, *Diplomatic Correspondence*, IX (1937), 714).

[26] Paul N. Garber, *The Gadsden Treaty* (1923), pp. 109–145.

[27] Edgar Turlington, *Mexico and Her Foreign Creditors* (1930), p. 104. The grounds on which Santa Anna and his supporters sought to justify their action in the cession made to the United States in the Gadsden Treaty, particularly their point that the United States would have taken the territory by force if Mexico had not consented to the sale of it, do not bear particularly upon the clause concerning the Tehuantepec Isthmus. The Mexicans apparently did not regard the treaty as a definitive adjustment of the territorial question with the United States. See James M. Callahan, "The Mexican Policy of Southern Leaders under Buchanan's Administration," *Amer. Hist. Assn., Ann. Report for 1910* (1912), p. 136.

Judah P. Benjamin and Emile La Seré, president of the Louisiana Tehuantepec Company sought what official assistance was available. They secured and carried to Forsyth in Mexico City instructions looking to the making of a new treaty which would confirm, extend, and make more specific the protection to be had under the eighth article. On July 17, 1857, Cass wrote to Forsyth concerning the idea of treaty extension of the protection (provided for in article VIII of the Gadsden Treaty) to all routes of communication "which may now or hereafter exist across the Isthmus":

> If the jealousy of the Mexican Government . . . should interpose an insurmountable obstacle the concluding portion of the article might be made to read:—"but upon failure to do this for any cause whatever, the Government of the United States may" extend its protection to all or any such routes, according to the 8th article of the Treaty of the 30th December between the United States and Mexico.[28]

As to the already acquired rights, Cass observed:

> Under our treaty with the republic of Mexico, of December 30, 1853, the United States have acquired a right of transit across the Isthmus which they will never, under any circumstances, abandon.[29]

This clearly implied that the United States in its public capacity, and not merely as a protector of its nationals, had a treaty right in connection with traffic over the isthmus. Answering Mexican objections to a proposal of a new arrangement, Forsyth told the Mexican foreign minister, on September 15, 1857, that, "if the granting of a permission by Mexico to the United States for the transit of her troops and munitions across the Isthmus be equivalent to a depreciation of Mexican rights of sovereignty over the territory, then Mexico has already, *quo ad hoc*, parted with that sovereignty." [30] On September 3 of the same year a Mexican decree declared the Sloo privilege null and void, but four days later there was an announcement of a new grant to

[28] MS., Department of State, 17 Instructions, Mexico, no. 27.

[29] Sen. Ex. Doc. 72, 35th Cong., 1st Sess., p. 40.

[30] *Ibid.*, p. 53. In the same communication the minister said that the United States would under no circumstances yield a jot of the rights which it had acquired under the Gadsden Treaty, a declaration which proved to be as poor a prophecy as that of Mr. Cass, previously quoted.

the Louisiana Tehuantepec Company. The last article of the contract provided: "In case there should be any doubt or difference in the execution or interpretation of this privilege, it shall be decided by arbitrators and amicable compounders, one named by the government and the other by the company, who, before beginning their examination, shall name a third in case of disagreement. Against the decrees of these arbitrators and the umpire there shall be no appeal nor recourse whatever." [31]

Forsyth's mission in Mexico came to an end without his securing from Mexico a treaty which would have broadened the plan of the Gadsden Treaty so as to permit American protection of *all* routes across the isthmus and for *any* American company building a road there. The American minister believed that, had the matter not been complicated by reason of efforts to get territory, he could have secured for the United States a virtual protectorate with military occupation of the Tehuantepec route and the cession of a right of way across the northern part of Mexico.[32]

Effort looking to a new treaty continued. In March 1859 William M. Churchwell, special agent in Mexico, sent to Washington a memorandum in which Juárez, the Mexican leader, indicated willingness to grant to the United States perpetual rights of way across the Isthmus of Tehuantepec.[33] In June of the same year Robert M. McLane, minister to Mexico, reported his conclusion that the most practicable measure for securing American ascendancy and establishing constitutional freedom in Mexico would be a treaty whereby the United States would purchase such a right of way, with the privilege of using military forces for protection of it.[34] The minister seems to have believed that if the

[31] A text is in Sen. Ex. Doc. 72, 35th Cong., 1st Sess., pp. 55, 59.

[32] Callahan, "The Mexican Policy of Southern Leaders under Buchanan's Administration," p. 139. In his despatch of November 24, 1857, Forsyth went at length into the accusations made against him by Benjamin and La Seré. He insisted that there was nothing in his instructions to require him, in collusion with one set of claimants (Benjamin and the company he represented), to break down and destroy rights of another set of American claimants (represented by Sloo and company). He raised the question of whether the United States should not assume liability to the Falconnet creditors (MS., Department of State, 21 Despatches, Mexico, no. 57).

[33] Turlington, *Mexico and Her Foreign Creditors*, p. 121; Alberto Maria Carreño, *Mexico y los Estados Unidos de América* (1922), pp. 507, 508.

[34] Turlington, *Mexico and Her Foreign Creditors*, p. 122.

United States should decline to accept responsibility for assuring public order in Mexico there would be intervention from some other quarter. He reported that the Mexican foreign minister (Ocampo) had urged upon him the subject of a treaty of alliance between the two countries "for the support of Republican institutions in America," but "always in a spirit that evinced so little appreciation of the relative condition and power of Mexico and the United States that I have not felt myself encouraged to expect any practical result." On the intervention matter, McLane wrote:

> I have fully explained the traditional policy of the United States, in relation to interference with the domestic administration of another state, developing fully the idea that in no event would my government interfere with the internal concerns of Mexico unless for its own security or to protect and defend what was due to itself in the abstract or in virtue of treaty stipulations.[35]

Despite these assurances, Ocampo would not agree to permit American protection of transit across Tehuantepec as a normal procedure. He was willing to consider American employment of armed forces, with the previous consent of Mexico, if Mexico should fail to protect. He also said that forces sent in should submit to Mexican authorities in all matters not related to the internal government of the troops, and that they should exercise no jurisdiction over the inhabitants or passengers on Tehuantepec except in the suppression of crimes actually being committed. Secretary Cass thought the consent of Mexico should not be necessary in "cases of sudden emergency."[36] The American Senate

[35] MS., Department of State, 23 Despatches, Mexico, despatch of June 25, 1859.

[36] MS., Department of State, 17 Instructions, Mexico, instruction of July 30, 1859. Cass observed that the necessity of protection was less likely to arise if it were well understood that the assistance needed would be promptly furnished. If no force could be used without the previous consent of the Mexican government, it might fail wholly to answer the purpose expected. It was, the Secretary said, not fair to suppose that in a given case of clear necessity assent would be refused. Still, "the interference would be chiefly valuable upon the occurrence of a sudden emergency and before the Government could be consulted and inquire into the circumstances alleged, the injury might be inflicted and the force unavailing." It was agreeable to specify that previous assent be had from Mexico except in case of sudden emergency, and in all cases as soon as practicable. The interference, Cass pointed out, would doubtless be limited in practice to the landing of a

rejected the McLane-Ocampo treaty, which would have permitted intervention, and the Gadsden agreement remained the only one in force on the subject between the two republics.[37]

After the Mexican decree of 1857 annulling the Sloo concession, the Louisiana Tehuantepec Company exercised some of the rights which it had obtained, and transported mail across the isthmus in 1858. The Mexican government formally nullified the grant as of October 15, 1866.[38] With the completion of the transcontinental railroad in the United States three years later, the Tehuantepec route was no longer to occupy the place of great importance which it had previously had in the minds of the expansionists. Completion of the Panama Canal in the twentieth century and discussion of a Nicaraguan route caused the Tehuantepec matter to recede further into the background, so far as American public interest was concerned.

The Gadsden Treaty article with its apparent authorization of intervention continued in force until 1937, when a formal agreement of the two countries officially terminated it.[39] The Department of State announced that, from its point of view, "the provisions of Article VIII have never been operative, and they would seem to have been rendered obsolete by reason of the subsequent development of other established means of communication between the Atlantic and Pacific coasts of the United States." Mexico having long considered the article objectionable as an abridgment to her sovereignty, its removal was in line with the "Good Neighbor" policy.[40] Other parts of the treaty, including

---

detachment of men who would "return to their regular employments" at the earliest possible moment. As to intervention to protect transit through Mexico, the Secretary thought that the American minister might derive some aid from a provision in a treaty which Mirabeau B. Lamar had shortly before negotiated with Nicaragua.

Cass said that, without any treaty, the United States could, at the request of Mexico, enter that country to protect American citizens, and that the United States must be free to judge when this was necessary.

[37] The Senate's action was apparently affected by the sectional (slavery) issue (Turlington, *Mexico and Her Foreign Creditors;* see also William Stull Holt, *Treaties Defeated by the Senate* [1933], p. 93).

[38] Rippy, "Diplomacy of the United States and Mexico . . ." pp. 530–531.

[39] 52 *Stat.* 1457.

[40] The announcement stated that "the Government of the United States has been happy to acquiesce in the request on the part of the Government

those concerning the boundary (which, as has been seen, made reference to international law), were not affected.

Thus ended the legal effectiveness of a clause which had contained some rather high-sounding words. It does not appear from the record that the purpose of its inclusion in the treaty was principally to emphasize any elements of customary law. What does appear is that, while intervention was not provided for in the draft signed by Gadsden, the language of the treaty in its final form was understood by Gadsden and by Mexican authorities as implying a right to intervene. Even if the article in question had ever become "operative" in the sense of being made the occasion for forceful action by American authorities in Mexican territory, it is doubtful whether a rule of international law prohibiting or limiting such intervention would have conditioned the operation of the treaty provision. For the wording of the article did not specify resort to intervention when it should be justified by international law. What it gave the United States was the right to "extend its protection" as it should judge wise when it *might feel* sanctioned and warranted by that law.

b. Multilateral Proscription in the Western Hemisphere

To trace the evolution of ideas concerning the international legality of intervention is beyond the scope of the present chapter, which is limited to treaties that refer, in connection with intervention, to the international law standard. That feeling against intervention has been particularly strong and frequently expressed in the Western Hemisphere is well known. The International Court of Justice, in the course of its opinion in the asylum case between Colombia and Peru (decided in November 1950), noted that nonintervention was "one of the most firmly established traditions of Latin America." One of the means relied

---

of Mexico that it relinquish such unexercised rights as the Gadsden Treaty may have conferred upon it to send its troops and munitions across Mexican territory, and to extend its protection to a work which, although originally expected to be built by United States citizens, was actually undertaken and completed by the Government of Mexico after the concession of these citizens . . . had lapsed" (*Department of State Press Releases*, XVI, 238–239 [April 17, 1937]).

upon to establish and perpetuate this tradition has been the multilateral treaty. Treaty language employed has included some direct reference to law. Commitments made since 1928, and to which the United States has become a party, will illustrate.

As a subject for Pan American discussion, intervention was by no means new in 1928,[41] but in that year it figured importantly among the legal questions before the American republics. It furnished occasion for J. Gustavo Guerrero of El Salvador to introduce, in plenary session of the Sixth International Conference of American States, a resolution setting forth that "no state has the right to intervene in the internal affairs of another." [42] After impassioned speeches in favor of the proposed resolution, Charles Evans Hughes made a statement regarding consideration of the proposal in committee and subcommittee, and in regard to the position of the United States. He said in part:

> From time to time there arises a situation most deplorable and regrettable in which sovereignty is not at work, in which for a time in certain areas there is no government at all, in which for a time and within a limited sphere there is no possibility of performing the functions of sovereignty and independence. . . . What are we to do when government breaks down and American citizens are in danger of their lives? Are we to stand by and see them killed because a government in circumstances which it cannot control and for which it may not be responsible can no longer afford reasonable protection? I am not speaking of sporadic acts of violence, or of the rising of mobs, or of those distressing incidents which may occur in any country however well administered. I am speaking of the occasions where government itself is unable to function for a time because of difficulties which confront it and which it is impossible for it to surmount.
>
> . . . it is a principle of international law that in such a case a government is fully justified in taking action—I would call it interposition of a temporary character—for the purpose of protecting the lives and property of its nationals. I could say that that is not intervention. One

[41] See notes 55 and 72, *infra.*

[42] *Report of the Delegates of the United States to the Sixth International Conference of American States* (1928), p. 13. The Committee on Public International Law, feeling, as a subcommittee's report expressed it, that "the making of a declaration which is wanting in the accord which gives weight to international law would fail of its purpose," had recommended further study. In the plenary session, Raúl Fernandes of Brazil deplored the effort (through Guerrero's proposal) to reintroduce the subject, since the committee had considered it and had found it to require further study.

can read in text books that that is not intervention. But if I should subscribe to a formula which others thought might prevent the action which a nation is entitled to take in these circumstances, there might come later the charge of bad faith because of acceptance of a formula with one interpretation in mind while another interpretation of it is in the mind of those proposing the formula. . . . Of course the United States cannot forego its right to protect its citizens. No country should forego its right to protect its citizens. . . . we cannot codify international law and ignore the duties of states, by setting up the impossible reign of self-will without any recognition upon the part of a state of its obligation to its neighbors.

. . . . .

I cannot sacrifice the rights of my country but I will join with you in declaring the law. I will try to help you in coming to a just conclusion as to the law; but it must be the law of justice.[43]

After Mr. Hughes's remarks Mr. Guerrero withdrew his proposal and the conference approved the committee's report.

At the Seventh Pan American Conference there was a somewhat different atmosphere. The Convention on Rights and Duties of States, signed at Montevideo on December 26, 1933, contained five specific references to international law.[44] Two of them had to do with states as persons, one with rights of states according to the law, one with state existence as dependent on the law, and another with the effect of recognition as an admission by the recognizing state of the recognized entity's "rights and duties determined by international law." For the present purpose the essential parts of the convention are article VIII, which states that "no State has the right to intervene in the internal or external affairs of another," and article XI, which, while not specifically referring to "international law," contains the following:

The contracting states definitely establish as the rule of their conduct the precise obligation not to recognize territorial acquisitions or special advantages which have been obtained by force whether this consists in the employment of arms, in threatening diplomatic representations, or

[43] *Report of the Delegates*, pp. 14–15. On the distinction between "political" intervention and interposition upon behalf of citizens, see Borchard, *Diplomatic Protection*, p. 441; *Right to Protect Citizens in Foreign Countries by Landing Forces*, Memorandum by J. R. Clark, 3d ed., 1934 (Department of State Publication 538), pp. 24–38.

[44] See Chapter I, note 82, *supra*.

in any other effective coercive measure. The territory of a state is inviolable and may not be the object of military occupation nor of other measures of force imposed by another state directly or indirectly or for any motive whatever even temporarily.[45]

The subcommittee of the conference which considered the subject agreed unanimously that it was "indispensable and essential definitely to establish the principle that no State has a right to interfere in the domestic or foreign affairs of another State."[46] The formula was substantially that which the Argentine delegation had presented to the American Committee of Jurists at Rio de Janeiro in 1927.[47] The subcommittee at Montevideo thought it necessary to construct a definition, and reported the following:

Any act of a State, through diplomatic representation, by armed force, or by any other means involving effective force, with a view to making the State's will dominate the will of another State, and, in general, any maneuver, interference or interposition of any sort, employing such means, either directly or indirectly in matter of the obligations of another State, whatever its motive, shall be considered as *Intervention*, and likewise a violation of International Law.[48]

The discussion in committee furnished occasion for broad observations on the general subject, and for unfavorable comments on the disposition at the Havana Conference of the resolution on intervention. Portell Vila of Cuba described intervention as not only the "curse of America" but the "curse of curses" of his country.[49] A spokesman for Haiti referred to the imperialistic

[45] 49 *Stat.* 3097.

[46] *Seventh International Conference of American States, Minutes and Antecedents* (1933), minutes of the Second Committee, p. 165.

[47] See Chapter I, note 81, *supra*, concerning effort looking to codification in the Western Hemisphere under the convention of August 23, 1906. To the commissions of jurists which that convention envisaged, the Third International Conference of American States recommended for special attention the subjects and principles which had been agreed upon in conventions then existing, those which were then incorporated in the national laws of the American states, projects of earlier American effort, and "all other questions which give promise of juridical progress, or which tend to eliminate the causes of misunderstanding or conflicts. . . ."

[48] *Seventh International Conference*, p. 165.

[49] *Ibid.*, p. 105. Prior to this, David Castro of El Salvador had said, of what the Havana Conference had done concerning nonintervention, that the work of the International Committee of Jurisconsults had been thrown

extension of the Monroe Doctrine and to its abusive interpretation.[50] Cuadro Pasos of Nicaragua asked support for the "holy principle of nonintervention, to the end of averting the compromises of the Havana Conference," while Puig Casauranc of Mexico expressed satisfaction that the discussion was "free from the subterfuges and timidities of Havana." [51] The president of the Mexican delegation felt that the conference should reject as "sophisticated and not convincing" Mr. Hughes's "intelligent manner of explaining and justifying intervention as 'temporary interposition' "; as long as there was no "result of an agreement or reciprocal obligation," he considered the Monroe Doctrine "an annoyance and a humiliation." [52] Mr. Parra, of Ecuador, characterizing intervention as "a kind of war, disguised and wary," said that the Spanish American people had for a long time "maintained these principles agreeing with the postulates of international law." [53] Francisco de Campos, of Brazil, said that the principle maintained in article XI seemed to be a precept pacifically accepted by all the countries of the American Continent. He went on to observe that the label "Rights and Duties of States," as used in the proposed convention, was not designed to cover the whole of international law. Reiterating the view which his country's representative had previously had occasion to express in the subcommittee, he submitted that the rule concerning nonintervention might better be placed in the part of codified international law which would relate to the organization of peace.[54] Raimundo Rivas of Colombia undertook to show that article XI was the "concretion" of what had come out of a long development dating from the Declaration of Chile in 1810, and embracing the declarations of the American Congress of Lima in 1847, the Continental Pact of Santiago of 1886, the declaration of the first four general conferences of the American republics, and that which eighteen of these republics had made in Washington on August 3, 1932. The principle of nonintervention he found

aside and trampled on, "in order to be replaced by harmless findings, a declaration of correlated principles so interwoven that they might be used to defend either the positive or the negative side of intervention."

[50] *Seventh International Conference*, p. 106.

[51] *Ibid.*, p. 107.

[52] *Ibid.*, p. 111.

[53] *Ibid.*, p. 113.

[54] *Ibid.*, p. 119.

to be the "concretion not only of the American principle but of a universal principle as well." [55]

Secretary Cordell Hull, in a speech which was to comprise the reservation of the United States, pointed out that "under the Roosevelt Administration the United States Government is as much opposed as any other government to interference with the freedom, the sovereignty, or other internal affairs or processes of the government of other nations." He expressed the hope that interpretations and definitions of fundamental terms in the report might be prepared at the earliest possible date. He asserted that in all of its international associations and relationships and conduct the United States would scrupulously follow the doctrines and policies it had pursued since the preceding March 4 (which he said were embodied in the different addresses of President Roosevelt since that time, in his own peace address before the Montevideo Conference on December 15, and "in the law of nations as generally recognized and accepted").[56] Later in the course of the discussion, Cuadro Pasos of Nicaragua referred to the commitment of the United States as being possibly ephemeral, since it rested on the *policy* of a "great Party." He observed that the "trouble" might revive when these particular leaders should no longer be in power in the United States.[57]

The Convention on Rights and Duties of States finally became effective for the United States subject to the condition which Secretary Hull had expressed and which the American government included in a formal reservation. There was also a reservation (concerning article XI) by Brazil and Peru, which sets forth that these states "accept the doctrine in principle" but "do not consider it codifiable because there are some countries which have not yet signed the Anti-War Pact of Rio de Janeiro of which this doctrine is a part and therefore it does not yet constitute positive

[55] *Ibid.*, pp. 119–120. The speaker asserted that article XI was a corollary of article III (which asserted the right to defend the integrity and independence of the nation) and also of article X (which contained a commitment to pacific settlement).

[56] *Ibid.*, pp. 121–122; 49 *Stat.* (2) 3110.

[57] *Seventh International Conference of American States*, p. 124. The relative importance, in the convention, of the article concerning nonintervention is suggested by one representative's referring to "articles of intervention" in referring to the instrument as a whole.

international law suitable for codification." The Anti-War Pact (of October 10, 1933) had provided for the settlement of disputes or controversies by pacific means having the sanction of international law; it had specified that, in the case of noncompliance with obligations in the convention, parties other than the noncompliant ones should exercise the political, juridical, or economic means authorized by international law. When it became bound by this anti-war convention, the United States government stated by means of a reservation that, in adhering, it did not waive any rights under international law.[58] This would apparently cover the kind of situation which the Brazilians and Peruvians had in mind when they made their reservation to the Montevideo Convention on Rights and Duties of States.

Restriction of the American government's commitment under article XI of the Convention on Rights and Duties to the period of the Roosevelt administration might be considered declaratory of preëxisting international law by reason of Mr. Hull's reference at the conference to the "law of nations as generally recognized and accepted." [59]

The government of the United States soon gave evidence of the administration's sincerity concerning nonintervention. It abrogated the Platt Amendment with Cuba,[60] made a new treaty with Panama which released that country from some of the restrictions imposed in 1903,[61] and withdrew Marines from Haiti. By the time of the Buenos Aires Conference of 1936, the Latin American neighbors of the United States had some reason to expect an unconditional commitment on nonintervention. It became a reality in connection with the Convention for the Maintenance, Preservation and Reëstablishment of Peace. This instrument incorporated especially the idea of consultation as a means of preserving peace in the Western Hemisphere. The Additional Protocol Relative to Non-Intervention sets forth that intervention, directly or indirectly, in the internal or external affairs of any

[58] 49 *Stat.* 3363, 3374.

[59] The reservation which the United States made with respect to article IX of the same convention presumably had the effect of reserving this country's rights under international law.

[60] Treaty of May 29, 1934, 48 *Stat.* 1682.

[61] Treaty of March 2, 1936, 53 *Stat.* (3) 1807.

other party is inadmissable, and that any violation of the protocol is to give rise to consultation.[62] Making clear that intervention may constitute a threat to the peace of the continent, and providing for an orderly method of handling difficulties which previously might have led to intervention, the protocol established a kind of collective responsibility for finding peaceful solutions.[63] Furthermore, the conference included, in its Declaration of Principles of Inter-American Solidarity and Coöperation, the proposition: "Intervention by one State in the internal or external affairs of another State is condemned." [64] In an address shortly after the conclusion of the Buenos Aires Conference, Secretary Hull, after reviewing briefly the past policy of the United States in the matter, declared that he knew of no act of intervention undertaken by the United States which had accrued to the benefit of the American people, and that he was unable to find that the people of the countries in which intervention took place gained any other benefit than the temporary advantage which the imposed road construction or sanitation brought them.[65]

To allay the suspicion of the Spanish American peoples in regard to intervention was to take a step which facilitated the transformation of the Monroe Doctrine into a multipartite instrument for mutual protection.[66] Additional steps came in 1938. The Declaration of Lima in that year carried a reference to the principle previously adopted concerning nonintervention, with which the new solidarity was to be considered in harmony.[67] Neither intervention as a means of territorial expansion, nor intervention as a means of protecting commercial and financial interests, nor intervention as a sanction, was specifically excepted from the proscription which the treaty structure of the Western

[62] 51 *Stat.* 41.

[63] *Report of the Delegation of the United States to the Inter-American Conference for the Maintenance of Peace* (1937), pp. 19–20.

[64] *Ibid.*, p. 228.

[65] Address before the Academy of Political Science, April 7, 1937 (*Department of State Conference Series* 29, p. 3).

[66] C. G. Fenwick, "The Monroe Doctrine and the Declaration of Lima," *Amer. Jour. Int. Law*, XXXIII (1939), 257–268.

[67] *Octava conferencia internacional americana. Diario de sesiones* (1938), p. 1052.

Hemisphere now contained. On April 15, 1943, the Under Secretary of State said, "Today any United States administration that undertook to intervene in the internal affairs of other American countries would . . . be guilty of outright violation of . . . part of our public law."[68] In at least some quarters it was believed, however, that the new treaty commitments would not make illegal diplomatic efforts to secure reparation for injuries done to nationals, or joint protective action after the use of consultation.[69]

President Roosevelt indicated clearly in 1938 that the United States would not "stand idly by" and permit a European government to menace its safety by fomenting a revolution in Latin America.[70] The new American solidarity, which the principle of nonintervention was designed to promote, was soon tested in the face of danger from outside the hemisphere.[71]

Late in the course of World War II, and in the early postwar period, legal proscription of intervention again had a central

[68] *Department of State Bulletin,* April 17, 1943, p. 324.

[69] Willard B. Cowles, "Joint Action to Protect an American State from Axis Subversive Activity," *Amer. Jour. Int. Law,* XXXVI (1942), 242, 249, 250. See generally, on the matter of intervention as a sanction, Ellen D. Ellis, "Intervention as a Sanction of International Law," *Proc. Amer. Soc. Int. Law,* 1933, pp. 78–86.

[70] "Suppose certain foreign governments, European governments, were to do in Mexico what they did in Spain. Suppose they would organize a revolution, a Fascist revolution in Mexico. Mexico is awfully close to us. Suppose they were to send planes and officers and guns and were to equip the revolutionists and get control of the whole of Mexico and thereupon run the Mexican Government, run the Mexican Army and build it up with hundreds of planes. Do you think that the United States could stand idly by and have this European menace right on our own borders? Of course not. You could not stand for it" (Samuel I. Rosenman, ed., *The Public Papers and Addresses of Franklin D. Roosevelt,* 1938 vol. [1941], pp. 255–256).

On the German technique as it was tried in the Western Hemisphere, see Charles G. Fenwick, "Intervention by Way of Propaganda," *Amer. Jour. Int. Law,* XXXV (1941), 626–631.

[71] The Inter-American Act of July 30, 1940, referred to an emergency committee (with one member from each American republic), and provided that, "should the need for emergency action be so urgent that action by the committee cannot be awaited, any of the American Republics, individually or jointly with others, shall have the right to act in the manner which its own defense or that of the continent requires" (54 *Stat.* [2] 2493, 2504).

place in Western Hemisphere conference discussions. The Act of Chapultepec (1945), after recording that the peoples of the Americas remained "sincerely devoted to the principles of international law," set forth as one of the principles which the American states had been "incorporating in their international law, since 1890, by means of conventions, resolutions and declarations," the "condemnation of intervention by one State in the internal or external affairs of another." [72] Later, when proposals were being made for what came to be the Inter-American Treaty of Reciprocal Assistance (1947), various American republics availed themselves of the opportunity to suggest that the principle of nonintervention be mentioned in it.[73] While this was not done in so many words, the Treaty of Reciprocal Assistance secured the effect by its preambular reaffirmation of the parties' "adherence to the principles of inter-American solidarity and coöperation, and especially to those set forth in the preamble and declarations of the Act of Chapultepec, all of which should be understood to be accepted as standards of their mutual relations and as the juridical basis of the Inter-American System."

At the Ninth International Conference of American States, in 1948, intervention again came under discussion. The essential problem was to reconcile the principle of nonintervention, as previously declared, with the American community's techniques for the maintenance of peace. At the same time there was a desire to proscribe intervention on the part of more than one state and to broaden the concept apparently inspired by observation of the type of "indirect aggression" that had occurred in Eastern Europe.[74] Articles 15 through 19 of the Charter of the Organization of American States record the result. By article 15,

> No State or group of States has the right to intervene, directly or indirectly, for any reason whatever, in the internal or external affairs

[72] 60 *Stat.* 1837.

[73] For examples, see the proposals of Colombia, Panama, Bolivia, and Ecuador, respectively, *Report of the Delegation of the United States to the Inter-American Conference for the Maintenance of Continental Peace and Security*, Department of State Publication 3016 (1948), pp. 69, 73, 77, 78.

[74] *Report of the Delegation of the United States to the Ninth International Conference of American States*, Department of State Publication 3263 (1948), p. 38.

of any other State. The foregoing principle prohibits not only armed force, but also any other form of interference or attempted threat against the personality of the State or against its political, economic and cultural elements.

While article 16 proscribes the use by any state of "coercive measures of an economic or political character" in order to force the sovereign will of another state and obtain from it advantages of any kind, article 17 relates to the inviolability of territory, and in article 18 the "American States bind themselves in their international relations not to have recourse to the use of force, except in the case of self-defense in accordance with existing treaties or in fulfillment thereof." Article 19 seeks to keep these commitments within the treaty framework of collective security. It states that "measures adopted for the maintenance of peace and security in accordance with existing treaties do not constitute a violation of the principle set forth in Articles 15 and 17."[75]

The coming into force of the Bogotá Charter would not, therefore, be a move in the direction of narrowing the concept, but would simply establish, for the parties, an exception for action taken under other multilateral treaties for the maintenance of peace and security.

c. Collective Action against Aggression

Even if viewed merely as an exception to the prevailing rule of nonintervention, treaty acceptance of the legality of collective action against aggression seems likely to affect profoundly the development of the interna onal law standard. For the present purpose (i.e., that of seeing how it has affected the independence of states and their freedom from intervention), consideration may be limited to the nature and scope of aggression, the manner of determining that it has occurred, and the effect of such determination upon the legal situation of a particular state in relation to the aggressor.

No comprehensive, all-inclusive definition of aggression has evolved. It is well known that, some years before the outbreak

[75] *Ibid.*, pp. 169–170.

of hostilities in World War II, there was private effort in the United States toward projecting rules applicable in the event of aggression.[76] Official action, in the form of intergovernmental instruments to which the United States was a party, was to follow. Declaration XV of the Second Meeting of the Ministers of Foreign Affairs, at Havana, in 1940, was to the effect that any attempt on the part of a non-American state against the integrity or inviolability of the territory, the sovereignty, or the political independence of an American republic would be considered an act of aggression against *all* the American republics.[77] The Act of Chapultepec contained a statement to the same general effect, and, anticipating the establishment of a more general international organization than that in the Western Hemisphere, sought to relate the principle stated to the purposes and principles of the former.[78] In the same year (1945), the San Francisco Conference provided occasion for fuller discussion of the concept of aggression. Some delegations favored rather specific definition of aggression or, in any case, the listing in the Charter of certain acts which would be considered within that description.[79] At one point in the discussions it was suggested that the use as a standard of an inexplicit word such as "aggression," instead of something explicit, such as "force," would give an opportunity to a state to engage in an act of aggression while calling it by another name.[80] Some of the states represented at San Francisco were, however, already parties to treaties which designated cer-

[76] See Chapter V, section 3a, *infra*.

[77] On the part taken by the United States at the meeting, see *Postwar Foreign Policy Preparation, 1939–1945* (1950), Department of State Publication 3580, General Foreign Policy Series 15, pp. 35, 36.

[78] 60 *Stat.* 1837.

[79] In Commission I, for example, a Belgian spokesman suggested that the Commission should not be disturbed by the difficulty of defining aggression. It was submitted that the League of Nations had been able to define it when it had occurred, and the term itself had been found acceptable for use in the Charter (United Nations Conference on International Organization [hereafter cited as UNCIO], *Documents*, VI, 345). A group of states led by Bolivia took the position that it should be known beforehand what acts would constitute aggression, and, consequently, what acts would be subject to sanctions; in Commission III, Bolivia's motion relating to this question was defeated by a vote of 22 to 12 (*ibid.*, XII, 341, 349).

[80] Remarks of the United Kingdom representative in Commission I (UNCIO, *Documents*, VI, 356).

tain kinds of activity as "aggression," and they thought it feasible and desirable to have similar provisions in the Charter.[81] Several delegations were in favor of inserting clauses concerning territorial integrity and independence, while others, particularly Latin American ones, proposed that the Charter should set forth actions from which states should refrain in their relations with other states, such as direct or indirect intervention.[82] A majority of Commission III, however, felt that a preliminary definition of aggression went beyond the possibilities of the Conference and the purpose of the Charter, progress in the technique of modern warfare making it difficult to define so as to cover all cases that might arise.[83] The United States delegation, opposing the idea of listing in the Charter acts that would constitute aggression, submitted that to enumerate all such acts would be impossible; it was further suggested that refusal of a state to comply with a decision of an international court had been improperly included (in a proposal of Bolivia) as aggression. In the American delegation's view there was no one kind of act that had been sug-

[81] See the statement concerning treaties to which Czechoslovakia was a party (UNCIO, *Documents*, III, 468–469). See also the Philippine proposal of a fourfold category of acts, the first state to engage in any of which would be considered as "threatening the peace" or as an aggressor (*ibid.*, p. 538).

[82] UNCIO, *Documents*, VI, 304, 558–559, 562. The Brazilian proposal included a mention of "excessively foreign influence."

Since the word "intervene" appears in article II, paragraph 7, of the Charter, it is pertinent to the present discussion to note, not only that there has been no complete agreement on its meaning in that context, but also that the United States and three other major states (rather than the small states) proposed that the paragraph, with somewhat changed wording, be placed not in the chapter on pacific settlement (as it had been placed in the Dumbarton Oaks proposals) but in the chapter on Principles of the United Nations. Thus placed, such restricting force as the paragraph has would reach to all parts of the Charter (UNCIO Doc. 2, G/29, May 5, 1945, p. 2).

The question of whether the United Nations decision leading to the action taken in relation to Spain in 1946 amounted to a move "to intervene" in that country was discussed in the first session of the General Assembly. See *Official Records of the Second Part of the First Session of the General Assembly*, First Committee, Summary Report of Meetings, 2 November–13 December 1946, pp. 229, 230, 232, 233, 238; Plenary Meetings, 23 October–16 December 1946, pp. 1174, 1180, 1182. See also Hans Kelsen, *The Law of the United Nations* (1950), pp. 769–791, especially pp. 770, 785n.

[83] UNCIO, *Documents*, XI, 17.

gested for inclusion as aggression which, in conceivable circumstances, might not be a legitimate act of self-defense; even in the event of invasion by armed force, it might be difficult to determine the aggressor, if there had been provocation on one side which forced action on the other.[84]

The Conference decision not to list acts that would be considered as aggression left the manner of determining aggression to designated United Nations agencies, and did not follow the proposal that the doing of certain things by one or more states would automatically impose obligations upon other members. The taking of action constituting a threat to the peace would, therefore, not change *ipso facto* the legal relation between the state taking the action and other states in the organization. The retention of the right of self-defense on a single state or a regional basis was to become important to the United States in relation to the North Atlantic Pact and the Inter-American Treaty of Reciprocal Assistance. In the meantime, however, the proceedings in connection with the Nuremberg trials furnished further occasion to consider the possible definition of aggression.

In the negotiations which produced the Agreement for the Prosecution and Punishment of the Major War Criminals, and the Charter of the International Military Tribunal, the question of defining aggression arose in somewhat different circumstances. Past acts, not future ones, were primarily under discussion. The representative of the United States apparently did not at first think it necessary to define aggression, but eventually concluded that it would be necessary for the formulators of the agreement, or for the tribunal, to define the concept on which it was proposed to predicate a charge of crime. Supported in this by the representative of the British government, he was opposed by those of both the Soviet Union and France, who were prepared to condemn the Nazi leaders as bandits rather than as criminals under international law. The Soviet spokesman thought it de-

[84] UNCIO, *Documents*, XII, 342. Senator Arthur H. Vandenberg seemed to anticipate later events when, at another point in the Conference proceedings, he said, "We here recognize the inherent right of self defense, whether individual or collective, which permits any sovereign state among us or any qualified regional group of states to ward off attack pending adequate action by the parent body (*ibid.*, XI, 53).

sirable to rely on definitions in previous documents or leave the defining to the United Nations. "Aggression," he said, had become a kind of formula in itself. The French negotiator thought that there were sufficient documents in international law defining aggression and that a definition in the Nuremberg Agreement and Charter might not agree with what might ultimately be worked out by the United Nations.[85] The result of the disagreement was the inclusion in article 6(a) of the Nuremberg Charter of a reference to "a war of aggression," but the omission from the instrument of a definition of the concept.

A comprehensive definition was not supplied by the tribunal at Nuremberg. At the trial of the major war criminals, the chief prosecutor for the United States suggested that, while it was perhaps a weakness of the tribunal's charter that it failed to define a war of aggression, an aggressor was generally held to be that state which should be the first to commit any of four listed actions.[86] He submitted that by this test each of the series of wars begun by the Nazi leaders under indictment was "unambiguously aggressive." The chief prosecutor for the United Kingdom, in turn, after referring to some past moves toward defining the concept, said that there was "no definition of aggression, general or particular, which does not cover and cover abundantly and irresistibly in every detail, the premeditated onslaught by Germany on the territorial integrity and political independence of so many sovereign states."[87] The tribunal itself, holding that its charter was "not an arbitrary exercise of power

[85] *Report of Robert H. Jackson* (1949), pp. 293, 294, 295, 296, 304–306, 308, 309, 317, 328.

[86] These were: (1) declaration of war upon another state; (2) invasion by its armed forces, with or without a declaration of war, of the territory of another state; (3) attack by its land, naval, or air forces, with or without a declaration of war, on the territory, vessels, or aircraft of another state; and (4) provision of support to armed bands formed in the territory of another state, or refusal notwithstanding the request of the invaded state, to take in its own territory, all the measures in its power to deprive those bands of all assistance or protection. The prosecutor added that "exercise of the right of legitimate self-defense, that is to say, resistance to an act of aggression, or action to assist a state which has been subjected to aggression, shall not constitute a war of aggression" (*Trial of the Major War Criminals before the International Military Tribunal*, II [1947], 148).

[87] *Ibid.*, III (1947), 108.

on the part of the victorious Nations, but . . . the expression of international law existing at the time of its creation" and, "to that extent, a contribution to international law," declared that to initiate a war of aggression was not only an international crime but the supreme international crime. Of preventive action in foreign territory, such as the Germans claimed to have taken in Norway, it said that "whether action taken under the claim of self-defense was in fact aggressive or defensive must ultimately be subject to investigation and adjudication if international law is ever to be enforced." War for the solution of international controversies undertaken as an instrument of national policy was found to include a war of aggression.[88]

The failure to adopt any hard and fast definition of aggression did not detract from the far-reaching effect of the Nuremberg decisions. That the idea of legal action against aggression was to be a central element in the treaty law of the United States was demonstrated in the signing of the Inter-American Treaty of Reciprocal Assistance in 1947, which came into effect on December 3, 1948. Like the Act of Chapultepec, this treaty provides for meeting aggression from within or from without the Western Hemisphere, and declares the principle that an armed attack by any state against an American state shall be considered an attack against all the American states. It distinguishes between an aggression which is not an armed attack and other aggressions. While aggression is not defined, article 9 provides:

> In addition to other acts which the Organ of Consultation may characterize as aggression, the following shall be considered as such:
> a. Unprovoked armed attack by a State against the territory, the people, or the land, sea, or air forces of another State;
> b. Invasion, by the armed forces of a State, of the territory of an American State, through the trespassing of boundaries demarcated in accordance with a treaty, judicial decision, or arbitral award, or, in the absence of frontiers thus demarcated, invasion affecting a region which is under the effective jurisdiction of another State.[89]

Both the Rio de Janeiro Pact and the Atlantic Pact incorporate the idea that an attack against one is an attack against all, and

[88] *Ibid.*, I (1947), 186, 208, 218, 220.

[89] *Report of the Delegation of the United States to the Inter-American Conference*, p. 62.

provide for consultation in the event of a situation that threatens the security of the parties. The Rio Pact goes further, in that it has provisions concerning voting in the organ of consultation, specifies the measures which that organ may agree upon, and has some provisions on procedures to be followed in the event of conflict between the parties themselves.[90]

Events beginning in Korea late in June 1950 were to afford convincing evidence that aggression is more than a mere concept. The United Nations Security Council's finding of aggression on the part of North Korea, and, after the adoption late in 1950 of the Uniting for Peace Resolution, the finding by the Assembly in 1951 of aggression on the part of Communist China, provided occasion for a reëxamination of the principle of nonintervention in relation to commitments for collective security. The problem of reconciling the two was before the ministers of foreign affairs of the American states at their meeting at Washington in March and April 1951. The preamble of the Declaration of Washington set forth that the conference had been called because of the need for prompt action "against the aggressive activities of international communism," activities that were declared to be "in disregard of the principle of non-intervention, which is deeply rooted in the Americas." The foreign ministers declared, *inter alia,* that the world situation required positive support by the American republics for coöperation "to prevent and suppress aggression in other parts of the world." At the same time, they looked to collective defense within the hemisphere which would not involve a departure from the traditional attitude toward nonintervention.[91]

[90] *The North Atlantic Pact,* Department of State Publication 3462 (1949), pp. 6–7. See also Edward G. Miller, Jr., "Non-Intervention and Collective Responsibility in the Americas," *Department of State Bulletin,* XXII, 768–770 (May 15, 1950).

On the successful operation of the Treaty of Reciprocal Assistance in a controversy between Costa Rica and Nicaragua, see Paul C. Daniels, "Influence of Inter-American Relations on U.S. Foreign Policy," *Department of State Bulletin,* XX, 460–461 (April 10, 1949). On action taken under the treaty in a later case (between Haiti and the Dominican Republic), see the *Bulletin,* XXII, 771–774 (May 15, 1950).

[91] Final Act of the meeting, as reproduced in *Department of State Bulletin,* XXIV, 606 (April 16, 1951).

It would be highly unrealistic to consider today the standard which is international law without taking into account what the law has at length come to contain concerning aggression. After the United Nations General Assembly had directed the International Law Commission to formulate the "principles of international law" recognized in the charter of the Nuremberg tribunal and in the judgment, the Commission proceeded upon its task of formulation after concluding that the Assembly had affirmed the Nuremberg principles and that the task entrusted to the Commission was that of formulating, not of expressing "any appreciation of these principles as principles of international law." [92]

2. TERRITORIAL WATERS: THE THREE-MILE LIMIT

When they occur in connection with the extension, beyond ordinary limits, of the right to use state control over foreign merchant ships, jurisdictional arrangements may require adaptation to the preëxisting law which sets the normal limits. In the third decade of the twentieth century the United States made a group of sixteen treaties in which it gave up the right to enforce to the limit, with respect to merchant vessels under flags of certain other countries, a municipal statute. The statute in question was pursuant to an express constitutional provision. The United States Supreme Court had said that the legislation was applicable to foreign vessels coming into American waters. In return for what it gave up in these treaties, the United States gained rights (of visit and search out to an hour's sailing distance from low-water mark) which it did not clearly have by customary international law. As is well known, these so-called "liquor" treaties, the first being that with Great Britain, signed January 23, 1924,[93] grew out of difficulties encountered in the enforcement of national prohibition. Some of the questions of international law involved had given rise to pronouncements early in the nation's history concerning the nature and degree of control which a state

[92] Report of the Commission concerning its second (1950) session, as reproduced in *Amer. Jour. Int. Law*, XLIV, Supp. (1950), 105, 125–126.
[93] 43 *Stat.* 1761.

may exercise in the waters off its coasts. Within a few years after conclusion of the "liquor" treaties, similar questions were to be the subject of discussion at a conference of states seeking to codify international law relating to territorial waters. Still later, the international law standard was to figure in discussions regarding waters over the continental shelf.

The rule concerning the three-mile limit antedates the establishment of the United States as a nation.[94] Acceptance of the general rule did not set at rest all the questions which were to arise, and there soon came to be assertions of rights in a wider area of coastal waters. Attorney General Edmund Jennings Randolph in 1793 observed that "the *necessary* or *natural* law of nations . . . will, perhaps, when combined with the treaty of Paris of 1783, justify us in attaching to our coast an extent into the sea beyond the reach of cannon-shot." [95] In 1804 Chief Justice John Marshall in the case of *Church* v. *Hubbart* offered a justification for a state's claiming a right to control to such distance from its shore as might be necessary for its protection, including the enforcement of such municipal laws as those against smug-

[94] At the Hague Codification Conference in 1930, Sir Maurice Gwyer, British delegate, said: "I am not prepared to argue that the rule of three miles has existed from the beginning of all things, even though its existence was not revealed to the human race until a comparatively recent date . . . I do say that it is a rule now of very respectable antiquity. I think it can be traced back . . . at least three hundred years . . . How a limit of three miles came to be suggested in the first instance I do not know. I very much doubt whether it was selected as the extreme range of cannon-shot at that time. I should doubt myself whether, in the middle of the seventeenth century, the effective range of cannon-shot was three miles or anything like it; and I am much more disposed to think that three miles was selected more or less by chance, and that the jurists afterwards invented reasons for it and, among other reasons, the range of cannon-shot theory.

"I think that theory is first found in the pages of Bynkershoek in the early years of the eighteenth century; but, whatever its origin may be, the rule itself has now been before the world for nearly three hundred years, and it has received growing support from the great majority of maritime nations" (*Minutes of the Second Committee: Territorial Waters,* League of Nations Doc. C.351(b).M.145(b).1930. V, p. 140). See also W. L. Walker, "Territorial Waters: The Cannon Shot Rule," *Brit. Year Book Int. Law,* XXII (1945), 210–231.

[95] 1 *Op. Atty. Gen.* 34. An even earlier statement on the point, occasioned by consideration of fisheries interests, is in Robert R. Livingston's letter of January 7, 1782, to Benjamin Franklin (S. F. Bemis, ed., *The American Secretaries of State and Their Diplomacy* [1927–1929], I, 42).

gling.[96] As one writer has put it, the rule of *Church* v. *Hubbart* has been approved rather than applied, probably because there were more convenient bases or doctrines at hand which municipal courts might utilize when passing upon the legality of protective activity beyond the three-mile limit.[97]

It has been seen that the United States emphasized the principle of freedom of the seas when its official view was that plans for reciprocal visit and search of vessels suspected of engaging in the slave trade would jeopardize the principle.[98] In the Bering Sea arbitration in the last decade of the nineteenth century, the tribunal held to a rigid rule, which it applied against the United States, asserting liability for forceful action against vessels of a foreign state outside territorial waters.[99]

In 1923 the United States Supreme Court in the case of *Cunard Steamship Company* v. *Mellon* held that the Eighteenth Amendment and the Volstead Act were, by direction of Congress, applicable to ships under foreign flags in American waters, since these waters comprised "territory" within the meaning of the municipal law.[100] In the preceding year Congress had passed (and was to reënact in 1930) legislation authorizing protective activity against suspected smugglers within twelve miles of the American coast.[101] Protests from foreign governments did not bring about a change of American policy. After receipt of one of these protests—that from Mexico—Secretary of State Hughes sent the following directive to the American diplomatic representative in Mexico City:

> You are instructed informally to state to the appropriate authorities of the administration now functioning in Mexico that this Government cannot undertake to discuss the legality, in an international sense, of the operation of an Act of Congress, the scope of which, within the territorial limits of the United States, has been authoritatively determined by the Supreme Court of the United States.[102]

[96] 2 Cranch 187.
[97] Edwin D. Dickinson, "Jurisdiction at the Maritime Frontier," *Harv. Law Rev.*, XL (1926), 1–29.
[98] See Chapter III, section 3, *supra.*
[99] Moore, *International Arbitrations,* I, 755.
[100] 262 U.S. 100.
[101] 42 *Stat.* 858, 979; 46 *ibid.* 590, 747.
[102] *For. Rel.,* 1923, I, 162.

The sixteen treaties which soon followed contained provisions looking to the arbitration of questions, if any of the states which had contracted with the United States should claim that this country's rights under the treaties had been overstepped. Each of them also contained the provision that, "in the event that either of the High Contracting Parties shall be prevented either by judicial decision or legislative action from giving full effect to the provisions of the present Treaty, the said Treaty shall automatically lapse, and . . . whenever this Treaty shall cease to be in force, each High Contracting Party shall enjoy all the rights which it would have possessed had this Treaty not been concluded." [103]

Six of the treaties in this group make use of the international law standard by committing the parties to a recognition of the three-mile limit as the established one,[104] while each of the others makes clear that the conclusion of the agreement does not commit the parties to this or any other precise limit. In view of the fact that universal agreement has so far been practically achieved only on the proposition that the three-mile limit marks the minimal extent of territorial waters, it cannot be said that the law on this subject is settled, especially when it has bearing upon important interests, such as fisheries.[105] Even with a minimal width of the coastal sea agreed upon,[106] there are, admittedly, limits to

[103] There was a further provision whereby either party might, three months before the expiration of any year of the duration of the treaty, give notice of a desire to propose modifications; if such modifications should not be agreed upon before the expiration of the year referred to, the treaty was to lapse.

[104] These were, in addition to the British treaty already mentioned, those with Germany (43 *Stat.* 1815), Panama (43 *ibid.* 1875), the Netherlands (44 *ibid.* 2013), Cuba (44 *ibid.* 2395), and Japan (46 *ibid.* 2446), respectively. On the significance of the treaty statements concerning the three-mile limit, see Gilbert Gidel, "La Mer territoriale et la zone contiguë," *Recueil des cours,* XLVIII (1934), 133–278, at 182.

[105] See Joseph W. Bingham, *Report on the International Law of Pacific Coastal Fisheries* (1938); Philip C. Jessup, "The Pacific Coast Fisheries," *Amer. Jour. Int. Law,* XXXIII (1939), 129–138; *Proc. Amer. Soc. Int. Law,* 1940, pp. 54–71.

[106] See the statement of Jesse S. Reeves, "The Codification of the Law of Territorial Waters," *Amer. Jour. Int. Law,* XXIV (1930), 491. Professor Reeves also asserted, in this connection, that, "the legal status of the territorial sea does not actually depend upon any universal or cast-iron agree-

what a state may lawfully do to merchant vessels under the flags of other states passing through its jurisdictional waters.[107] The authority which any coastal state has over such vessels is, however, rather extensive. The relaxation of a particular part of it may represent a concession which is not required by international law. The delegate of the United States in the Second Committee of the Hague Codification Conference in 1930 expressed this idea when he said:

> I wish . . . to point out that the necessity for the enforcement of the law of the coastal State is obvious, and that the situation of various countries in this respect—the situation of the United States of America, in particular—has led us to conclude certain treaties which are well known to you all and which have given us some opportunity to suppress, or at least to limit, the evil activities of would-be criminals whose position can have no merit in any sense or in any view. It is the opinion of the Government of the United States of America that this ancient and well-established policy might be recognized in a general rule. . . .[108]

It has been claimed for the so-called "liquor" treaties that they have the merit of recognizing the separability of full jurisdiction (in the sense of complete control and responsibility to others for what happens) and protective control, which may be conceded with a particular object or with respect to a particular interest.[109] Discussion at the Hague Codification Conference revealed a strong sentiment for a "contiguous" zone, beyond the legal limits of the territorial waters, in which there could rightfully be protective measures by the shore state in the sense suggested. It did not prove possible, however, to reach agreement upon the principle of such a zone. Some of the difficulties are set

---

ment, or unanimous expression, as to its width, and the modern practices of states certainly rest upon this idea" (*ibid.*, p. 496).

Contrast the statement of Stefan-Albrecht Reisenfeld that, "if you look at the problem of the territorial sea as a whole, then it is simply not so that the three-mile zone is anywhere established" (*Proc. Amer. Soc. Int. Law*, 1940, p. 70).

107 The part of the Report on Territorial Waters (produced at The Hague in 1930) on "innocent passage" will illustrate.

108 Remarks of David Hunter Miller, *Minutes of the Second Committee: Territorial Waters*, p. 18.

109 Cf. remarks of Athern P. Daggett, *Proc. Amer. Soc. Int. Law*, 1940, p. 67.

forth in the report that the Second Committee adopted on April 10, 1930, which is, in part as follows:

> The first question to be considered was the nature of the rights which would belong to the coastal States in such a zone. The supporters of the proposal contemplated that, first of all, the coastal State should be able to enforce its Customs regulations over a belt of sea extending twelve miles out from the coast. It need scarcely be said that States would still be free to make treaties with one another conferring special or general rights in a wider zone—for instance, to prevent pollution of the sea. Other States, however, were of opinion that, in Customs matters, bilateral or regional agreements would be preferable to the making of collective Conventions, in view of the special circumstances which would apply in each case. These States were opposed to granting the coastal State any right of exercising Customs or other control on the high seas outside the territorial sea, unless the right in question arose under a special Convention concluded for the purpose. The opposition of these States to the establishment of such a zone was further strengthened by the possibility that, if such rights were accorded, they would eventually lead to the creation of a belt of territorial sea which included the whole contiguous zone.
>
> Other States declared that they were ready to accept, if necessary, a contiguous zone for the exercise of Customs rights, but they refused to recognize the possession by the coastal State of any rights of *control* with a view to preventing interference with its *security*. The recognition of a special right in the matter of legitimate defence against attack would, in the opinion of these States, be superfluous, since that right already existed under the general principles of international law; if, however, it was proposed to give the coastal State still wider powers in this matter, the freedom of navigation would thereby be seriously endangered, without, on the other hand, affording any effective guarantee to the coastal State. But other States regarded the granting of powers of this nature in the contiguous zone as being a matter of primary importance. The opinion was expressed that the coastal State should be able to exercise in the air above the contiguous zone rights corresponding to those it might be in a position to claim over the contiguous zone itself. The denial of such rights over the contiguous zone both of sea and air would therefore, they stated, influence the attitude of the States in question with regard to the breadth of the territorial sea.[110]

Whatever right coastal states may have, under general international law, in the zone beyond their territorial waters has been aptly described as something fragmentary and specialized, rather

[110] *Minutes of the Second Committee: Territorial Waters,* p. 210.

than a full, general jurisdiction.[111] By consenting to have the United States authorities visit and search suspected vessels under their respective flags out to a distance beyond the traditional limit of territorial waters, the other contracting parties at least waived the right to challenge such protective activity as illegal (provided it is done in the manner which the treaties contemplated).

The treaties as a whole represented a practical handling of a situation which was complicated by reason of the lack of complete agreement upon the points of law involved and which, at the same time, called for action that would protect the national interests of each state concerned.[112] That the instruments represented no permanent or very serious relinquishment of rights under general international law is suggested by the provisions concerning termination. There seems to have been less of an extension of the authority of the United States into the open sea than, for example, that under the 1935 Anti-Smuggling Act passed by Congress.[113] Limited as is the plan of the treaties to coastal waters and a relatively narrow extent of waters immediately contiguous thereto, the instruments do not record any more far-reaching departure from accepted rules of international law than did the Convention of July 7, 1911, on Pelagic Sealing[114] or the more recent agreements with Canada concerning halibut and sockeye-salmon fishing.[115] There is evidence that American courts have, in interpreting and applying them, shown careful consideration for the other party states and their interests.[116] The

[111] Gidel, *Le Droit international public de la mer,* III, 364.

[112] For an account of the development, see Robert L. Jones, *The Eighteenth Amendment and Our Foreign Relations* (1933). See also E. D. Dickinson, "The Effect of Prohibition Repeal upon the Liquor Treaties," *Amer. Jour. Int. Law,* XXVIII (1934), 101–104.

[113] See Philip C. Jessup, "The Anti-Smuggling Act of 1935," *Amer. Jour. Int. Law,* XXXI (1937), 101.

[114] 37 *Stat.* 1542.

[115] 50 *Stat.* 1351–52, 1355, 1359.

[116] See, for example, *The Marjorie E. Bachman,* 4 Fed. (2nd) 405 (1925); *Cook* v. *United States,* 288 U.S. 102 (1933). Cf. the Canadian government's view, expressed in connection with the *I'm Alone* claim, that it was essential for the effective operation of the 1924 convention that its terms should be strictly observed (*For. Rel.,* 1929, II, 32).

international arbitration of the *I'm Alone* case,[117] which came up under the first of these treaties, provided no authoritative, clarifying pronouncement upon the subject of "hot pursuit" from territorial waters onto the high seas, and resulted in no contribution of substantial importance to the body of international law against the background of which the parties contracted in those treaties.

Such relinquishment of rights as the parties made in the treaties involved no serious concessions. Bilateral in form, unrelated to international organization, and easily terminable, the treaties assume no such significance because of supposed waiver of "sovereign" rights as do existing multilateral arrangements concerning traffic in narcotic drugs.[118] Experience under the treaties affords little if any assistance toward an answer to the very fundamental question of how far states may go in waiving rights under international law.[119] Since the treaties were concluded there has been substantial progress toward an effective world organization which may, ultimately, itself determine the limits within which states may waive their normal rights. That organization has a stake in protecting from impairment the members of the international community. It could reasonably concern itself, for example, with whether mergers of states or transfers of territory are with the free consent of the peoples concerned, whatever appearance of consent through treaties there may be.

That the international law standard still has an important place in the policy of the United States in the subject matter to which the "liquor" treaties principally relate is indicated by its denial that conservatory measures with respect to the continental shelf can have the legal effect of extending the limits of territorial waters or bringing the air space over the open sea under the

[117] Department of State Arbitration Series, no. 2.

[118] The statement would seem to apply especially to the 1931 treaty, 48 *Stat.* (2) 1543.

[119] See Georg Schwarzenberger, *A Manual of International Law* (1947), pp. 12, 63, to the effect that states are still free to replace, in their relations *inter se*, any rule of customary law by other rules, and that it would be premature to overemphasize the desirability of developing principles which might limit this process. The same writer refers, however, to the likelihood of such development in an international society more highly integrated than is the present interstate system.

exclusive control of any national state.[120] That what the standard requires is still the subject of some disagreement would seem to be reflected in a provision of the Northwest Atlantic Fisheries Convention (effective July 3, 1950). This convention contains the provision that nothing in it "shall be deemed to affect adversely (prejudice) the claims of any Contracting Government in regard to the limits of territorial waters or to the jurisdiction of a coastal state over fisheries." [121]

[120] See, for example, the note from the United States government to that of El Salvador concerning definition of territorial sovereignty, *Department of State Bulletin,* January 1, 1951, p. 24. The note had reference to the application of certain provisions in the 1950 Constitution of El Salvador.

[121] T.I.A.S. 2089 (art. I, par. 2). There were ten signatories in addition to the United States.

Chapter V

WAR AND NEUTRALITY

Many provisions of United States treaties have related to war or neutrality, but not all of them have made express reference to the international law standard. Furthermore, where there has been a policy of seeking adoption of a specific rule by the nations generally, the treaty makers have not usually sought their objective by proceeding upon the assumption that the desired rule was already a part of established international law. Thus the rule of "free ships, free goods," incorporated in the first commercial treaty of the United States,[1] and marking a departure from what had been laid down in the *Consolato del Mare* some three centuries earlier,[2] was proposed and secured in relation to individual foreign countries long before it secured anything like universal acceptance.[3]

It has sometimes been stated officially, of certain treaties which

[1] Miller, *Treaties,* II, 21, article 25 (23) of the commercial treaty with France. On the respective positions of the French and the Americans on what the treaty should contain, see Vernon G. Setser, *The Commercial Reciprocity Policy of the United States, 1774–1829* (1937), pp. 15–22.

[2] Ernest Moliné y Brasés (ed.), *Llibre del consolat de mar* (1914), ch. 276, pp. 154–156.

[3] See the comment, and classification of American treaties in which the rule of "free ships, free goods" found expression, in Moore, *Digest,* VII, 435–436.

A tracing of the well-known development is beyond the scope of the present chapter. It may be noted in passing, concerning the second article of the Declaration of Paris, that a Secretary of State (Cass) in 1859 took the position that it was not necessary for a neutral state to adhere in order for its vessels to be entitled to the immunity (Hyde, *International Law,* III, 2044n.). On the point that, prior to the Declaration of Paris, treaty clauses on the subject merely bound the parties thereto in relation to each other and did not change the generally accepted law, see Carlton Savage, *Policy of the United States toward Maritime Commerce in War* (1934), I, 114–115. Cf. Robert Lansing's instruction of December 1, 1916, to Walter H. Page in London, as quoted in Hackworth, *Digest,* I, 18–19.

do not in terms refer to customary international law, that they are "but declaratory of the law of nations."[4] On the other hand, as has been seen, the treaties have often referred to the international law standard without trying to set forth the law existing on the particular points.[5]

The present chapter will consider adaptations to the standard (1) in provisions concerning the conduct of hostilities, and particularly in connection with the effort to regulate uses of submarines in war, (2) in provisions on neutral duties as they provided occasion for what is perhaps the most celebrated arbitration in United States history, and (3) in certain statutory and treaty provisions that reflect a changing concept of neutrality.

1. REGULATION OF CONDUCT OF HOSTILITIES

a. Development in General

The justification for effort to secure conventional agreement upon rules governing the conduct of hostilities has received much attention. According to one view, international jurists have in the past been too much concerned with such effort, and too little aware that as long as war was recognized as legal, it was futile to try to frame rules for its conduct.[6] An opposing view has urged that the law does not bring about human activities but merely recognizes and attempts to regulate them, and that it is humane and desirable to keep the operations within the bounds of some rules in order that war may not become indiscriminate ruthlessness.[7] In general, foreign offices seem to have proceeded upon

[4] 7 *Op. Atty. Gen.* 386 (1855). The occasion was a discussion of foreign enlistments in the United States, with particular reference to a convention of 1815, as continued by conventions of 1818 and 1827. Prior to this, an Attorney General had "conceived to be declaratory of the usage of nations" the twenty-third article of the Jay Treaty concerning hospitality in ports for ships of war (1 *ibid.* 89 [1799]).

[5] Chapter I, section 3, *supra.*

[6] See, for example, Salvador de Madariaga, *The World's Design* (1938), p. 116.

[7] J. B. Moore, "An Appeal to Reason," *For. Affrs.*, XI (July 1933), 547, 558, 560. On the point that it is desirable to provide rules for the regulation of force, even when there is a collective security system in operation, see

the assumption that there could be useful and desirable regulation. Schemes for collective security would seem to imply ordered operations rather than unregulated procedures against peacebreakers or aggressors. At the same time, many of the technical rules which in the nineteenth and early twentieth centuries came to apply as between belligerents and neutrals would presumably need to be brought into conformity with the idea of differential treatment of belligerents. Principles of collective security have not meant the abolition of rules intended to secure humane treatment for combatants taken prisoners, of prohibitions upon the general confiscation of private property in occupied territory, or of restrictions upon the slaughter of persons who are not combatants.[8]

If it is admitted that some rules are desirable, the form which they shall take becomes a practical question. It has sometimes been suggested that customary rules are more desirable than conventional ones, for the reasons that no particular and solemn forms are needed, that custom is more satisfactory because it is variable and malleable, that custom is more adaptable and more complete, and that it cannot lose its force, as conventions would, with the termination of the instruments.[9] The formulation of treaty rules on the conduct of hostilities may leave the impression that these alone are operative, and that if they prove insufficient or technically not binding in a given situation no other restrictions are legally applicable. The situation becomes more involved with the invention of new weapons or new uses of old ones, since it is but natural that legality should be claimed for defenses used

---

Josef L. Kunz, "The Chaotic Status of the Laws of War and the Urgent Necessity for Their Revision," *Amer. Jour. Int. Law*, XLV (1951), 37–61.

[8] On the adaptation of the law of military occupation to the fact of the authority of the United Nations, see Charles Fairman, "Military Occupation and the Development of International Law," *Proc. Amer. Soc. Int. Law*, 1947, pp. 131–141. Experience especially with the occupation of Germany since 1945 has led to some tendency to distinguish between "military" government (as under the provisions of Hague Convention IV of 1907) and "civil" government.

[9] Jean Brucy, *Les Traités et la réglementation du droit de la guerre* (1917), pp. 225–226, and general discussion at pp. 223–237. Contrast the views of Germain Watrin, *Le Pacte de la Société des Nations et la constitution française* (1932), p. 309.

against unanticipated methods of an enemy.[10] There is, in addition, the inevitable strain upon all such rules which develops with the exigencies of the contending parties.

In order to avoid the conclusion that all the rules on a subject are comprehended in any particular convention on it, treaty makers have sometimes related the instruments in terms to what is already established and what may come to be established (through custom) in the future. Mentions of general international law in the Hague Conventions attest the background of custom against which the agreements were intended to be constructed.[11] The reference may be to "laws of war" rather than to international law generally, as in article VII of Hague Convention X of 1907.[12] On such subjects as contraband of war, it has been difficult to assure that specific enumeration of articles would be limitative so as to restrict the parties more than would preëxisting rules and usages.[13]

[10] Cf. the reference by the Secretary of State (Stimson) on August 5, 1932, to "new agencies of destruction turned loose under the sanction of international law" (*For. Rel.*, 1932, I, 577).

[11] Illustrated in the preamble of Hague Convention XIII of 1907 (36 *Stat.* 2415). Hague Convention IV of 1907 (36 *Stat.* 2277, 2280), with its reference in the preamble to principles of the law of nations as they result from usages established among civilized nations, laws of humanity, and the exigencies of the public conscience, was thought sufficient to make illegal such acts during the First World War as German deportation of French and Belgians for forced labor (Jules Basdevant, *Les Déportations du nord de la France et de la Belgique en vue de travail forcé et le droit international* [1917]; J. W. Garner, *International Law and the World War* [1920], II, 184; see also Chapter I, note 61, *supra*, and note 23, *infra*).

[12] 36 *Stat.* 2371.

[13] Cf. the statement of Attorney General Philander Chase Knox in 1902: "Each new case that arises seems to present new difficulties, and because it is new the nation interested in carrying on the commerce argues from that part of international law which is based upon express treaties and distinct precedents, and affirms that it cannot be shown by the actual practice of nations and by treaties that all nations have recognized that such a transaction as is in question is prohibited by the common consent of nations" (24 *Op. Atty. Gen.* 19). With this may be compared an observation of a dissenting commissioner (Aldis) in the case of *Jules Le More* v. *United States*, which was brought under the Franco-American treaty of January 15, 1880: "The doctrine and policy of nations as to what is and what is not contraband advance and recede according to their necessities as belligerents or their interests; but the doctrines of international law must stand upon principle to command the assent and respect of mankind" (Moore, *International Arbitrations*, IV, 3313n.).

There is much treaty material concerning contraband.[14] The sum of the treaties concluded and of the precedents accumulated up to 1939, apparently did not seem to the American State Department such as would justify arbitrary extension of contraband lists by belligerents in World War II.[15]

In connection with regulation of the conduct of hostilities on land, the role of the United States in helping to establish upon a treaty basis the substance of Francis Lieber's *Instructions*, approved by President Lincoln in 1863 as General Order No. 100, is too well known to require extended comment. This codification "apparently excited efforts on a larger scale in Europe."[16] The first of the significant efforts in Europe, in which twenty-three states had part through conferences at Geneva in 1864 and 1868, was directed toward humane treatment of the wounded and to rules concerning agencies of mercy. The Declaration of St. Petersburg (December 11, 1868) was the work of representatives of seventeen states; its limitation (as between the parties) upon the use of projectiles affords a striking contrast to some later practices.[17] At the Conference of Brussels, 1874, something more comprehensive in the form of a code was before the representatives of thirty-two states, and a declaration was produced. The British apparently decided against participating in any

[14] See the statement of Attorney General James C. McReynolds that "all of our treaties which deal with contraband at all have endeavored to limit the scope of the term to those articles which are manufactured and used primarily for warfare." He gave as examples article 18 of the 1831 treaty with Mexico and article 14 of the 1832 treaty with Chile (30 *Op. Atty. Gen.* 213).

[15] As late as June 1941, after the sinking of the American steamer *Robin Moor*, the Under Secretary of State in a note to Germany insisted upon the right of an American vessel, under international law, to carry noncontraband material to either of the contending parties and noted that the United States had never acquiesced in the British or German lists of what was claimed to be contraband (*New York Times*, June 14, 1941, 3:2). For a discussion of law involved, see James W. Ryan, *Freedom of the Seas and International Law* (1941).

[16] Theodore D. Woolsey, *Introduction to the Study of International Law* (5th ed., 1878), p. 235. See also George B. Davis, "Doctor Francis Lieber's Instructions for the Government of Armies in the Field," *Amer. Jour. Int. Law*, I (1907), 13–25.

[17] An English translation of the draft declaration concerning the laws and customs of war, as adopted by the Conference of Brussels, August 27, 1874, is in A. Pearce Higgins, *The Hague Peace Conferences* (1909), pp. 273–280.

discussions which seemed to bear upon principles of international law not already generally accepted.[18] The Institute of International Law, which soon after this gave detailed consideration to the rules and approved a revision of the declaration, expressed the opinion that, as compared with the code of Lieber, it contained new requirements at once practical, humane and progressive.[19] Illustrative of the skepticism of the time, concerning the principles against the background of which this declaration stood, was a statement in a pamphlet published in the same year. The writer of this pamphlet seemed to think there was "no generally recognized international law, in spite of the nonsense talked . . . about the danger of altering what does not exist." [20]

Although the United States did not sign all of the Hague Conventions of 1907, this country had an important part in the general effort.[21] The rules of Hague Convention V received application through municipal courts,[22] although that convention, like others signed at The Hague, by its terms did not apply "except between contracting powers, and then only if all the belligerents are parties to the convention." Nearly four decades later the Nuremberg tribunal was to find, after it had noted that Hague Convention IV had expressly stated that it was an attempt "to revise the general laws and customs of war" which it recognized to be then existing, that "by 1939 these rules laid down in the Convention were recognized by all civilized nations, and were regarded as being declaratory of the laws and customs of war which

[18] *For. Rel.*, 1874, p. 565.

[19] *Annuaire*, I (1877), 134.

[20] Elihu Rich, *The Brussels Conference and the Universal Alliance* (1874), p. 9n.

[21] See the opinion of S. O. Levinson that the United States "contributed more to the success and progress of the two Hague Conferences than any other nation," and E. M. Borchard's views on the large extent to which the Hague rules were observed in the First World War (House Committee on Foreign Affairs, *Hearings on . . . a Conference for Codification of International Law,* 69th Cong., 1st Sess. [1926], pp. 71, 87).

[22] See, for example, *Ex parte Toscano et al.* (208 Fed. 938 [1913]), in which the court held that Hague Convention V was self-executing and should be applied by American courts; *L'Affaire Krug* (*Journal du droit international* [Clunet], 1919, p. 1108), holding that a French executive decree would not transcend the limitative definition of spies in the annex to Hague Convention IV of 1907. Numerous prize-court decisions attest the vitality of rules in the Hague Conventions on the conduct of maritime war.

are referred to in Article 6(b) of the [Nuremberg] Charter."[23]

As is well known, many questions were left unsettled by the Hague Convention rules, and, on some of these, precedent and usage afforded no very satisfactory guidance. Rules to regulate the conduct of maritime war, for example, remained sadly deficient. The Declaration of London (February 26, 1909) was partly the work of American jurists, and in the First World War the United States sought assurances from the principal belligerents that the rules of that unratified instrument would be observed. While not regarded as wholly operative, the rules were copied in part in the prize law of some major states. It continued to be true, however, as stated in the preamble of the declaration, that "the general principles of international law are often in their practical application the subject of divergent procedure."

A subcommittee of the Washington Conference on Limitation of Armament (1921–22) reported that rules on the conduct of hostilities were in many cases nonexistent or inadequate; the committee reviewed the types of measures which had been tried and did not minimize the difficulties of enforcement. It leaned, however, to the view that enforcement through the means of international judicial processes would be more satisfactory than any other available.[24]

In 1929 the United States participated in the drawing up of rules, some of which were apparently declaratory and others new, on the subject of prisoners of war. Parties to the Convention of July 27, 1929, on that subject were "desirous of developing the principles which inspired the international conventions of The Hague."[25] In prohibiting reprisals against prisoners, the treaty makers took a step in advance of what had previously been accomplished, and in avoiding the possibility of technical inapplicability because not all of the belligerents in a particular war were parties, the states participating closed a gap which had existed under the plan of the Hague Conventions.[26] Thus, more

[23] *Trial of the Major War Criminals,* I (1947), 253–254.

[24] *Conference on the Limitation of Armament November 12, 1921–February 6, 1922* [Proceedings of] Subcommittees (1922), pp. 332–346.

[25] Preamble, 47 *Stat.* 2021.

[26] The substantive contents of the code are dealt with by Gustav Rasmussen, *Code des prisonniers de guerre* (1931), by William E. S. Flory,

than fifteen years before the Nuremberg trials, was laid a firmer legal basis for "war crimes" growing out of acts contrary to "legislative" conventions restricting methods of conducting hostilities. It has been seen that, in the revision of 1949, the rules regarding prisoners of war were related to preëxisting conventional and customary law.[27]

Discussion of the 1925 Protocol on Poison Gas and Bacteriological Warfare evoked the opinion that while the undertaking in article I to abstain from the use of poison gases could normally be observed only subject to reciprocity, the undertaking to abstain from the use of bacteriological warfare should be absolute. "The use of such methods would, in any case, constitute a crime against international law." [28]

One field of law on which practically no conventional rules had evolved prior to the beginning of the European war in 1939 was that relating to aircraft and their use in war. There was able American representation on the commission of jurists which, after the Washington Conference of 1921–22, examined this subject (and that of radio in war). The commission prepared draft rules which did not find adoption,[29] although the United States regarded the jurists' report as "a satisfactory basis for elaboration" and by 1932 had made "several efforts to persuade other nations to conclude a convention" which would put the rules into effect.[30]

Prisoners of War (1942), and by Auguste-Raynald Werner, *La Croix-Rouge et les conventions de Genève* (1943), especially pp. 269–279. See also *For. Rel.*, 1929, I, 320, and Robert R. Wilson, "Standards of Humanitarianism in War," *Amer. Jour. Int. Law*, XXXIV (1940), 320–324.

[27] Chapter I, note 63, *supra*. For commentaries on the Geneva Conventions of 1949, see *Department of State Bulletin*, May 28, 1951, pp. 866, 868–879.

[28] See Appendix II, p 268. On the necessity of unanimity in banning the use of poison gas and bacteriological warfare, and on the question of a general renunciation or prohibition as against a reciprocal agreement, see *For. Rel.*, 1932, I, 334, 355, 368, 402.

[29] *Naval War College Publications*, 1924, pp. 96–154; *Amer. Jour. Int. Law*, XXXII, Supp., 1–56. Part I of the commission's report sets forth that the regulation of radio in time of war is not a new subject, and lists other conventions which have some bearing. The new rules were prepared with the object of "completing and coördinating existing texts."

[30] *For. Rel.*, 1932, I, 152. On the point that there was, by the time of the Second World War, some customary law which applied to air warfare, see

b. Use of Submarines

The foregoing brief statement concerning effort to make international rules on the conduct of hostilities, and concerning participation by the United States in such effort, affords some background for a more detailed consideration of attempts at law making on a particular subject, that is, the submarine and its use as a destroyer of commerce. In this connection the United States participated in an effort to project rules of law and to obtain for them universal acceptance.

At the Washington Conference on the Limitation of Armament, 1921–22, the British, who had suffered grievously from the use of the submarine in the First World War, denounced the weapon as one "of murder and piracy, involving the drowning of noncombatants." The device was "certain to be abused" and not "consistent with civilization." [31] The so-called Root treaty,[32] which was defective in its drafting, failed to obtain ratification, and the matter was left for the London Naval Conference of 1930.[33] In part IV of the three-power treaty of that year, the parties contracted that "in their action with regard to merchant ships, submarines must conform to the rules of International Law to which surface vessels are subject"; in a separate paragraph they pledged themselves to invite all other powers to express their assent to the agreed rules.[34] The question of the abolition of the sub-

---

Georg Röhrig, *Die Ziele selbständiger Luftangriffe* (1938), pp. 50, 79, 87, 92. Cf. Philip C. Jessup, "International Law and Totalitarian War," *Amer. Jour. Int. Law*, XXXV (1941), 329–331.

[31] *Conference on Limitation of Armament, 1921–1922*, Sen. Doc. 126, 67th Cong., 2d Sess., pp. 269, 288, 297.

[32] This treaty provided for the trial of a person violating any of its rules "as if for an act of piracy." On comparison of this with the rules drafted at London in 1930, see *For. Rel.*, 1930, I, 51–54.

[33] In the decade following the Washington Conference, the United States appears to have officially advocated abolition of submarines. See *For. Rel.*, 1929, I, 162; 1932, I, 22, 24, 73, 182, 264, 532.

[34] 46 *Stat.* 2858, article XXII, pars. 1 and 3.

On the evolution of what came to be part IV of the London Naval Treaty, see *For. Rel.*, 1930, I, 33–130. From the beginning, the French were apparently not agreeable to the complete prohibition of the use of submarines as commerce destroyers, but representatives of all five powers in the First Committee adopted unanimously, on April 9, the form of the proposed declaration of international law concerning protection of crews and passengers of vessels attacked by submarines (*ibid.*, pp. 34, 104).

marine had been before the conference at its fourth plenary session. Spokesmen for the British Commonwealth and the United States supported this drastic move, but France and Japan opposed, on the ground that the submarine was a legitimate defensive weapon and especially valuable for states with small navies. Italy, not taking a strong stand for any particular disposition of the question, intimated that abolition would be much more favorably considered if the abolition of capital ships were also agreed upon. The effort to secure agreement on abolition having failed, the heads of delegations instructed the first commission of the conference to draw up rules intended to "humanize" the submarine. The resulting rules, which had the unanimous support of the experts, were accepted without dissent by the First Committee as *established* rules of international law.[35]

The extent of the commitment under the treaty as a whole occasioned more discussion in the United States than did the part concerning submarines. Secretary of State Stimson wrote to Senator William E. Borah that "the question of whether this treaty is or is not in the interest of the United States . . . must in the last event be determined from the language of the document itself and not from extraneous matter."[36] The Senate, however, gave its advice and consent with the understanding that there were no agreements, secret or otherwise, express or implied, between any parties, concerning the construction that should thereafter be given to any of the statements or provisions.

[35] *Report of the Canadian Delegate to the Conference on the Limitation of Naval Armament held at London, January 21, 1930, to April 22, 1930* (1930), pp. 14, 78.

The rules were as follows:

1. In their action with regard to merchant ships, submarines must conform to the rules of international law to which surface vessels are subject.

2. In particular, except in the case of persistent refusal to stop on being duly summoned, or of active resistance to visit or search, a warship, whether surface vessel or submarine, may not sink or render incapable of navigation a merchant vessel without having first placed passengers, crew, and ship's papers in a place of safety. For this purpose the ship's boats are not regarded as a place of safety unless the safety of the passengers and crew is assured, in the existing sea and weather conditions, by the proximity of land or the presence of another vessel which is in a position to take them on board.

[36] Letter of June 6, 1930, in *Limitation and Reduction of Armament, Minority Views*, Sen. Rep. 1080, pt. 2, 71st Cong., 2d Sess., p. 26.

Hearings before the Senate Committee on Naval Affairs elicited various opinions from naval men concerning the treaty's part IV. Calling article 22 "the work of the legal men," Admiral William V. Pratt said that it was "just trying to move along certain lines" by saving as much of the unratified Root treaty as the French would assent to; the admiral's opinion was that the negotiators would not have reached an agreement on anything if they had tried to go beyond the first two articles of the former instrument.[37] Another opinion was that the provisions concerning submarines were "hopelessly indefinite" and that the first paragraph of article XXII would have been complete in itself and would have taken care of the situation as well as it could be done.[38] The question of arming merchant ships naturally came in for attention; Admiral Ridley McLean, who would have favored a "world abolition" of the submarine, although he said he realized that this would have been impracticable, thought the most effective step toward humanizing the use of submarines in war would have been a prohibition of the arming of merchant vessels on peaceful missions; he was afraid of the treaty because it did not go far enough.[39]

For the minority which opposed the treaty, Senator Hiram W. Johnson of the Committee on Foreign Relations said:

> The much-heralded accomplishment at London, by which future submarine warfare was to be humanized, struck a responsive chord with all of us. A reading of the provisions of the treaty, however, from which we expected so much and obtained so little, leaves us quite as disillusioned as to accomplishment as we have been left by many other provisions of the treaty.
>
> There is no objection . . . to the particular article relating to submarine warfare. In substance these provisions merely amount to a reaffirmation of many existing humanizing rules in international law applicable to all forms of warfare on the sea. It will be recalled that during the World War it was a violation of international law by submarines

[37] *Hearings on London Naval Treaty of 1930*, Senate Committee on Naval Affairs, 71st Cong., 2d Sess., May 14, 15, 16, 19, 21, 22, 23, 26, 27, 28, 29, 1930 (1930), at pp. 85–87.

[38] *Ibid.*, p. 343 (testimony of Admiral George C. Day).

[39] *Ibid.*, pp. 392–395. Admirals Henry A. Wiley and Louis McCoy Nulton also favored abolition of submarines, "providing all nations agree" (*London Naval Treaty of 1930*, Sen. Doc. 197, 71st Cong., 2d Sess., p. 43).

operating against commerce which formed the basis of the repeated American protests. Such laws then existed, still exist, and the framers of the London treaty have done no more than rather ambiguously to state them, and the uncertain statement affords no special reason for the ratification of the treaty.[40]

At the Naval Conference of 1935 in London, there was endorsement of the idea of "humanizing" submarine warfare in the manner followed in article IV of the 1930 treaty. However, the conclusion reached was that rules on this subject should not be placed in the general treaty, as they had been in 1930.[41] When the treaties for limitation of naval armament ceased to be in force (after denunciation by Japan in accordance with the treaty terms), the particular rules of article XXII survived this termination and were incorporated in a separate protocol of 1936. The three signatories of the 1930 treaty became parties, as did also France, the British Dominions, and Italy, with the idea, as reported in the press at the time, "that the rules will eventually become embodied in international law as universally accepted and binding in perpetuity."[42] The protocol recites that, by the terms of the old article XXII, the contracting parties invited all other powers to express assent to the rules, and continues:

Whereas all the signatories of the said Treaty desire that as great a number of Powers as possible should accept the rules contained in the said Part IV as established rules of international law; The Undersigned, representatives of their respective Governments, bearing in

[40] *Limitation and Reduction of Armament, Minority Views*, Sen. Rep. 1080, pt. 2, 71st Cong., 2d Sess., pp. 17–18.

[41] *The London Naval Conference, 1935, Report of the Delegates of the United States*, Department of State Publication 896, Conference Series 24 (1936), pp. 58, 59, 64, 73, 80, 295. See also *Memorandum on the London Naval Conference, December 9, 1935, to March 25, 1936*, Cmd. 5137, *Parl. Pap.*, Miscellaneous no. 2 (1936), wherein it is explained (in paragraph 21) that, since part IV of the 1930 treaty had not become binding upon Italy and France, those states having signed but not having ratified, it was not possible for the British government to communicate the rules to countries in respect of which the treaty had not been signed; France and Italy having accepted the rules by 1936, a separate protocol was to be the method of authorizing communication of the rules (as a "continuing obligation and not one for a short time only") to all other maritime countries, with an invitation to them to accede without limit of time.

[42] *New York Times*, October 15, 1936, p. 4.

mind the said Article 22 of the Treaty, hereby request the Government of the United Kingdom of Great Britain and Northern Ireland forthwith to communicate the said rules as annexed hereto, to the Governments of all the Powers which are not signatories of the said Treaty, with an invitation to accede thereto definitely and without limit of time.[43]

The original treaty plan for securing general acceptance of the rules was carried out. At least thirty-five states besides the original signers, including all of the principal maritime powers, gave assent. There was no serious question of divergent interpretation to delay the projection of the protocol provisions. There remained, however, the serious question of what utility the rules would have in the absence of agreement on the subject of armed merchant ships.

The problem was not a new one in 1936. Two decades earlier, the United States, as a neutral, had felt impelled to take some official position concerning the status of armed merchantmen, the development of the submarine having brought complications.[44] Robert Lansing as Secretary of State apparently relinquished the opinion originally set forth in his statement of January 18, 1916, to the effect that merchant ships of belligerent countries should be prohibited from carrying armament,[45] and President Wilson's policy of arming American merchantmen involved an attempt at a difficult distinction between arming for offense and for defense.[46] The status of armed merchant ships remained in doubt during the First World War. Inevitably the question arose of whether such a vessel as the *Lusitania* was armed, and, if so, the effect of this upon the legality of her being sunk by the German submarine.[47]

[43] *Rules of Submarine Warfare,* Cmd. 5302, *Parl. Pap.,* Treaty Series 29 (1936).

[44] See, generally, Adolphe Laurens, *Le Blocus et la guerre sous-marine 1914–1918* (1924), and "La Guerre sous-marine et les neutres," *Revue d'histoire de la guerre mondiale,* IX (1931), 337–368; Joseph Trévily, *Essai sur l'histoire et la situation du sous-marin en droit international* (1931); Jean Vidaud, *Les Navires de commerce armés pour leur défense* (1936).

[45] *For. Rel.,* 1916, Supp., p. 147.

[46] Edwin M. Borchard, "Armed Merchantmen," *Amer. Jour. Int. Law,* XXXIV (1940), 107–112.

[47] See T. A. Bailey, "The Sinking of the Lusitania," *Amer. Hist. Rev.,* XLI (1935), 54–73.

When becoming a party to the Havana Convention of 1928 on Maritime Neutrality, the United States did not accept that part of the convention which provided that armed merchantmen of belligerent countries which might come into neutral ports and territorial waters should be assimilated to warships and treated accordingly.[48] As already seen, the subject did not come up for actual settlement at the conferences on limitation of naval armament in 1921–22, 1930, or 1935. The period of the civil strife in Spain (1936–1938) furnished occasion for pronouncements concerning submarines. In the Nyon Arrangement between nine states, adopted September 14, 1937, submarine attacks upon merchant vessels were branded as "acts contrary to the most elementary dictates of humanity, which should be justly treated as acts of piracy."[49]

The old idea of a defensive armament's being permissible and making no difference in the status of a commercial vessel appears again in a clause of the Declaration of Panama, October 3, 1939, by which the parties agreed not to

> assimilate to warships belligerent armed merchant vessels if they do not carry more than four six-inch guns mounted on the stern, and their lateral decks are not reinforced, and if, in the judgment of the local authorities, there do not exist other circumstances which reveal that the merchant vessels can be used for offensive purposes.[50]

It was inevitable that, with the outbreak of the Second World War, employment of submarines should lead to differences regarding its legality. In the opening months of the war the German government announced that it had the right to sink on sight all armed merchantmen of the enemy nationality,[51] and early in

[48] 47 *Stat.* 1989, art. 12, par. 3, and United States reservations.

[49] *Amer. Jour. Int. Law,* XXXI, Supp. (1937), 179; G. G. Wilson, "The Submarine and Place of Safety," *ibid.,* XXXV (1941), 496–497.

[50] *Amer. Jour. Int. Law,* XXXIV, Supp. (1940), 11–12. The American republics in a separate resolution urged the belligerents to abstain from sinking merchant ships without having first placed the passengers, crews, and ship's papers in a place of safety (*ibid.,* p. 13).

[51] On the government's position early in the war, see the *Völkischer Beobachter* for October 18, 1939, p. 1, and for November 14, 1939, p. 5. The Germans also announced that they would sink on sight *all* armed ships which were considered parts of the British navy (*New York Times,* October 1, 1939, 1:8). As to the privileged status which the Germans accorded to

1940 it began to establish "operation areas" in which neutral ships were to be sunk without warning. This did not deter the British from following their policy of arming merchantmen, in many cases convoying them, and giving them orders to send position reports upon sighting submarines. The British Admiralty announced (on October 1, 1939) that British merchant ships had been ordered to ram U-boats if possible, and some armed merchantmen apparently became raiders. At least one American publicist took the position that the 1936 agreement "cannot be deemed to have extended these immunities to *armed* merchant vessels," [52] but this would seem to be arguable in view of the disagreement which had previously existed and the absence of specific reservations on the point.

While American neutrality legislation sought to keep United States merchant ships out of danger zones in the early part of the Second World War, charges of illegal uses of the submarine were eventually forthcoming from the United States. In a message to the Congress of the United States, President Roosevelt charged that a German submarine on May 21, 1941, sank the *Robin Moor* without showing its flag or announcing its nationality, and without making provision for the safety of passengers and crew. "The total disregard shown for the most elementary principles of international law and of humanity," said the President, "brands the sinking of the *Robin Moor* as the act of an international outlaw." Viewed in the light of the circumstances, the sinking was considered a "disclosure of policy as well as an example of method." [53] In the same message the President told Congress that the Amer-

---

passenger steamers in the early part of the war, see Kurt Assman, "Why U-boat Warfare Failed," *For. Affrs.*, XXVIII (1949–50), 659–670.

[52] Borchard, "Armed Merchantmen." In its draft on Rights and Duties of Neutral States in Naval and Aerial War (*Amer. Jour. Int. Law*, XXXIII, Supp. [1939], 169–817), formulated on the eve of the Second World War, the Harvard Research in International Law proposed (pp. 432, 435):

"Art. 27. A neutral State may exclude belligerent submarine vessels from its territory, or admit such vessels on condition that they conform to such regulations as may be prescribed . . .

"Art. 28. A neutral State shall either exclude belligerent armed merchant vessels from its territory or admit such vessels on the same conditions on which it admits belligerent warships."

[53] *Department of State Bulletin*, June 21, 1941, pp. 741–742.

ican government believed that "freedom from cruelty and inhuman treatment is a natural right." [54]

The rules that had been projected in 1930 and 1936 did not avert sinkings without warning. The legality, under international law, of acts of the German leaders who had directed their country's submarines was before the Nuremberg tribunal in the case of Doenitz and in that of Raeder. The former testified that the German navy remained at all times within the confines of international law and of the 1936 protocol, that the German Prize Ordinance of the beginning of the war was taken almost literally from the protocol, that he had ordered U-boats to attack all merchant ships in convoy and all that refused to stop or used their radios upon sighting a submarine, and that when his reports indicated that British merchant ships were being armed and were attacking submarines on sight, he ordered his submarines (on October 17, 1939) to attack all enemy merchant ships without warning, on the ground that resistance was to be expected.[55] Evidence brought out that the British Admiralty armed its merchant ships, in many cases convoyed them, and gave orders to merchantmen to send position reports upon sighting submarines. As to the operational zones and the German sinking of merchant vessels therein, the tribunal found that, since the protocol of 1936 made no exception for such zones, Doenitz's orders constituted a violation of the protocol. It reached a similar conclusion regarding the admiral's orders that rescue provisions should not be carried out by submarines. It did not find the evidence to establish, with the certainty required, that Doenitz had deliberately ordered the killing of shipwrecked survivors. As to the charges in general, the tribunal said:

> In view of all the facts proved and in particular of an order of the British Admiralty announced on 8 May 1940, according to which all vessels should be sunk at night in the Skagerrak, and the answers to

[54] *Ibid.* In the later discussion growing out of the torpedoing of the *Pink Star*, an American-owned freighter flying the flag of Panama, the United States government took a strong position against the Germans, although the ship was reported to have been under Canadian convoy and armed at least against aircraft.

[55] *Trial of the Major War Criminals*, I (1947), 311. See also Kurt Assman, "Why U-boat Warfare Failed."

interrogatories by Admiral Nimitz stating that unrestricted submarine warfare was carried on in the Pacific Ocean by the United States from the first day that Nation entered the war, the sentence of Doenitz is not assessed on the ground of his breaches of the international law of submarine warfare.[56]

Thus the effort of 1930 and 1936 toward subjecting submarines to the "rules of international law to which surface vessels are subject" fell far short of its objective. A simple explanation of why it did so would be that the specific rules that were stated as being included in the standard were incomplete. A more basic explanation would be that force overshadowed the law. In any case, the Nuremberg tribunal emphasized that the standard still existed, whatever circumstances seemed to it to justify the nonapplication of penalties upon individual violators.

2. THE "RULES" OF THE *Alabama* AWARD

One of the most celebrated instances in which the United States participated in an effort to apply the international law standard and to project rules for general acceptance was that in connection with the *Alabama* claims settlement. In contrast to the development recounted in the previous subsection, there was in this case a successful application of the rules in the claims adjudication, but a failure to secure immediate adoption of them by other states.

The history of the Treaty of Washington, 1871, is well known. It has been the subject of so much discussion and critical analysis that it is not easy to focus attention upon but one aspect of the treaty, that is, the references therein to general international law in its relation to the "rules" of the treaty. In this particular case of utilizing the standard, it might be misleading to undertake even a brief summary of the development without giving some attention to personal and political factors which affected the final outcome, although, for the present purposes, these factors are of secondary importance when compared with remarks by public officers concerning the nature of international

[56] *Trial of the Major War Criminals*, I, 313. The tribunal made a similar finding in the case of Admiral Raeder on the charge of carrying out unrestricted submarine warfare and violating the 1936 protocol.

law as a whole and the effect, upon that law, of this treaty as interpreted and applied.[57] It will be convenient to consider separately for this purpose the period from 1865 to the negotiation of the treaty, the actual negotiation and ratifications in 1871, the period of the arbitration itself, the sequel to the arbitration (including the conversations on wider projection of the rules), and action ultimately taken at the Second Hague Peace Conference. Of special importance, for the present purpose, are the distinctions between international law and municipal law (and the relation between the two in the jurisprudence of the respondent state), and between rules of international law admittedly preëxisting and some whose prior existence was in controversy.

The whole question of British responsibility for allowing the ships later used by the Confederates to be built or supplied in British ports was tied in, through the discussions, with other legal questions, such as the alleged prematurity of British recognition of the belligerency of the Confederates, and the legality of negotiations conducted indirectly with the representatives of Jefferson Davis (looking to Confederate adherence to the Declaration of Paris). As to the question of fitting out ships, the representative of the Confederate government who concluded the contract for construction of the *Alabama* had previously procured legal counsel in England and advice that the transactions were legal under British law.[58] In a case in the Exchequer Court involving the *Alexandra*,[59] there had been, in Lord Chief Baron Pollock's charge to the jury, an apparently clear holding that the activities were not violative of the Foreign Enlistment Act. In May of the

[57] Since there is danger in evaluating statements apart from their respective contexts—as the Americans said of British use of passages from the American case in the Geneva arbitration—it has been thought necessary to include, in this section, considerable quotation and many references in a relatively small number of pages.

[58] James D. Bulloch, *The Secret Service of the Confederate States in Europe* (1884), I, 65–68, 295–375. That Captain Bulloch had no exalted idea of international law is suggested by his statement that it "has never received the willing or unanimous consent of all nations, but bears upon its face the impress of having been forced by the stronger upon the weaker" (I, 74), and by his later reference to "the very complex and elastic code commonly called international law" (II, 409).

[59] *The Attorney General* v. *Sillem, et al.* (1863), 2 Hurlstone and Coltman 431; 159 English Reprints (Full Reprint) 178.

same year (1863), Richard Cobden had lamented the failure of the American government to make a clear distinction between the selling of ordinary contraband and the equipping of "privateers"; he thought that if a "plain, simple, short and dignified reclamation" had been made at the first because of the fittings out, the British government could not have resisted it.[60] Other Englishmen were of a different opinion concerning neutral duties under international, as distinguished from municipal, law. Illustrative is Lord Robert Cecil's statement in Parliament on May 13, 1864, that "it is quite as much within the International Law to sell ships of war to another nation as it is to sell any munitions of war."[61] In his notes to Charles Francis Adams, the American minister, Earl Russell sometimes referred to the law, "municipal and international," sometimes merely to the law.[62]

If it be true that the period from May 1865 to May 1871 (the date of signing of the Treaty of Washington) comprised "years of rapid education toward a new code of international law,"[63] the effects of such education were not to be immediately apparent. Lord Clarendon, who became Secretary for Foreign Affairs in

[60] See Cobden, *Speeches on Questions of Public Policy* (1870), II, 84–85. See also letter of May 22, 1863, quoted in *Amer. Hist. Rev.*, II (1896), 310–311.

[61] Hansard, *Parliamentary Debates*, 3d ser., vol. 175, p. 509. Captain Bulloch, in his attempted justification, under international law, of the furnishing to Confederates, quoted Palmerston, Prime Minister, to the effect that there was no difference in principle between supplying a belligerent with rifles or with ships, and that on the mere ground of international law it was quite permissible to supply either of two belligerents not only with arms and cannon but with ships destined for warlike purposes (*The Secret Service*, I, 447). Before the tribunal at Geneva the British were to rely upon an article in the *American Law Review* for January 1871 (V, 371) on the point that ships are ordinary articles of commerce (*Papers Relating to the Treaty of Washington* [1872–1874], II, 402). Two other distinctions were later stressed for the United States (by counsel, in argument before the tribunal at Geneva in 1872), namely, (1) that between acts public and private, and (2) that between those acts which a neutral state's government was under *obligation* (in 1861–1865) to prevent, so far as it was able, and acts as to which the government owed only a negative duty—that of not protecting persons from penal consequences "which the law of nations attaches to them" (*Treaty of Washington Papers*, III, 265).

[62] Charles Francis Adams, *Lee at Appomattox and Other Papers* (1902), p. 56.

[63] *Ibid*, p. 79.

the autumn of 1865, said in an interview with Adams that there were many things in what was called international law that were then in a vague and unsatisfactory condition and inquired if the American minister thought that British-American consultation might be favorably regarded by the United States.[64] Shortly afterward the British government was to pursue the subject further. "England and the United States," an official communication observed, ". . . had each become aware of the defects that existed in international law, and . . . it would greatly redound to the honor of the two principal maritime nations of the world to attempt the improvements in that code which had been proved to be necessary." Although war wounds were still too recent and ill will toward England still too rife to render such an undertaking practicable at that time, it was a thing to be kept in mind and earnestly desired by Her Majesty's Government, a work which would be "worthy of the civilization of our age, and which would entitle the governments which achieved it to the gratitude of mankind." [65]

To the Earl of Clarendon's suggestion of a concurrent revision of the statute law of the two countries on the subject of neutrality, Adams replied on November 18, 1865, challenging the assumption that the legislation of the two states was equally efficacious. Seward (for President Johnson) approved the minister's views.[66] After a Conservative government had replaced a Liberal one in England in 1866, Lord Stanley, as Secretary for Foreign Affairs, negotiated with Reverdy Johnson, Adams' successor, in regard to an Anglo-American treaty, but the draft instrument was not referred to the American Senate. With the fall of the Conservative government, Johnson's negotiations with Lord Clarendon, foreign secretary in Gladstone's Cabinet, did produce a convention, which was disapproved by the Senate in 1869. In the meantime, the British had taken steps toward revising their Foreign Enlistment Act of 1819. The government appointed, on January 31, 1867, a commission "to inquire into and report

[64] *Ibid.*, p. 88.

[65] *Parl. Pap., North America,* no. 1 (1866), Correspondence respecting the "Shenandoah" [3581], p. 164 (Sessional Papers, 1866, vol. 75).

[66] *Treaty of Washington Papers,* III, 246–247.

whether any and what changes ought to be made in such laws for the purpose of giving to them increased efficiency, and bringing them into full conformity with our international obligations." In its report which led to the passage of the Act of August 9, 1870,[67] the commission said:

> In making the foregoing recommendations we have not felt ourselves bound to consider whether we were exceeding what could be actually required by International Law, but we are of opinion that if those recommendations should be adopted, the municipal law of this realm available for the enforcement of neutrality will derive increased efficiency and will, so far as we can see, have been brought into conformity with your Majesty's international obligations.[68]

In the minds of Seward and Adams, the American complaint of premature British recognition of the Confederates' belligerency had been an important element of grievance. This complaint was to come up again with Senate action on the Johnson-Clarendon convention (signed January 14, 1869), and in connection with instructions to J. Lothrop Motley, the new American minister to England and close friend of Senator Charles Sumner, chairman

[67] 33 and 34 Vict., ch. 90.

[68] *Treaty of Washington Papers,* II, 212; III, 226. The House of Representatives in 1866 had passed a bill which would have revised the neutrality act of 1818 and which contained the following section: "*Be it further enacted,* That nothing in this act shall be so construed as to prohibit citizens of the United States from selling vessels, ships, or steamers built within the limits thereof, or materials or munitions, the growth or product of the same, to inhabitants of other countries or Governments not at war with the United States: *Provided,* That the operation of this act shall be suspended whenever the United States shall be engaged in war."

A spokesman for the minority of the Foreign Affairs Committee (Henry J. Raymond, of New York) said in part, in opposition to the bill: "It is proposed in this bill . . . to base our laws of neutrality, not upon the principles which we ourselves have always held on this subject, but upon the laws and practices of a foreign Power. Now, sir, I submit that that is not a wise basis for our action. I concur fully in the sentiment that members cherish here concerning the action of certain foreign Powers on the subject of neutrality during our recent civil war. But do we not owe it to our own dignity and honor to continue to do hereafter what we have always done hitherto—base public laws of this kind upon the public principles which have come to be known as the American principles on the subject of international law? I shall with great reluctance consent to a departure from that which is our traditional policy, and which I believe to be the policy most consistent with the dominion and greatness of our nation" (*Congressional Globe,* 1865–1866, pt. V, pp. 4194, 4195, 4197).

of the Senate Foreign Relations Committee. Apparently the Johnson-Clarendon instrument did not find favor with either the President-elect (Grant) or with the leaders of the Senate.[69] In his uncompromising speech in the Senate on April 13, 1869, Sumner scored the proposed treaty because of its following as a model the Anglo-American claims convention of 1853 (which had provided for settlement of claims of nationals, not of the governments themselves), because of its provision for choice of an arbitrator by lot, because of its ignoring the national public grievance as compared with individuals' claims, and because it recognized no rule of international duty applicable to such cases. Developing the case against Great Britain, the Senator proceeded, from the point concerning the unjustified recognition by Britain of belligerency of the Confederates, to a claim of British responsibility for "the additional expenditure to which our country was doomed" because of the prolongation of the war. This prolongation, he submitted, was due to assistance which the Confederates had obtained through the fitting out of the *Alabama* and other cruisers, hospitality to these "pirates" in British ports, and their destruction of shipping under the American flag. The intimation was that damages would run to billions of dollars.[70] The Senate, by a vote of 54 to 1, rejected the treaty. To Francis Lieber, Sumner wrote on May 30, "How the case shall be settled, whether by money more or less, by territorial compensation, by apology, or by an *amendment of the law of nations*, is still an open question; all may be combined." [71]

[69] Edward L. Pierce, in his *Memoir and Letters of Charles Sumner* (1893), supports his statement that the instrument was "a dead treaty as soon as it was signed" (IV, 384) by the fact that Grant had expressed himself freely (in conversation) against the treaty, and that all members of the Foreign Relations Committee, which considered the treaty in February, had opposed its ratification.

[70] A text of the speech is in *Charles Sumner: His Complete Works,* XVII, 53–93. On the question of damages, Sumner said that the rule of Roman law was the rule of international law and that it was broader than that of the common law (*ibid.,* p. 87). On the effect of the speech in England, see William Salter, *The Life of James W. Grimes* (1876), p. 371.

[71] Pierce, *Memoir and Letters,* IV, 388 (italics inserted). On June 15, Sumner wrote to Motley: "I do not despair seeing the debate end—(1) In the withdrawal of England from this hemisphere; (2) In remodelling maritime international law" (*ibid.,* p. 410).

At Sumner's suggestion and apparently with the assent of Secretary Fish, Motley was allowed to prepare a "memoir" on the instructions he was to receive. Sumner, who was consulted about the contents of the instructions, disapproved Fish's idea of abandoning the position which he (Sumner) had stressed in his Senate speech concerning recognition of belligerency. Caleb Cushing helped toward an adjustment. As finally formulated, the instructions conveyed to the American minister the President's desire to "simplify" the American case; the British declaration concerning the Confederates' belligerency was to be regarded "as a part of the case only so far as it shows the beginning and the animus of that course of conduct which resulted so disastrously to the United States." The American envoy was to place the cause of grievance not so much upon Great Britain's recognition of belligerency, "but upon her conduct under, and subsequent to, such recognition." Another part of Motley's instructions, relating to possible negotiations looking to agreement upon the respective rights and duties of either party when the other should be a belligerent, was as follows:

> The absence of some agreement or definition on this subject was among the causes leading to the rejection of the recent convention, under which, had it been adopted by the two countries, none of the grave questions which have arisen would have been passed upon by a tribunal whose decision either party (much less other nations) would regard as authority, so as to prevent repetition or retaliation. . .
>
> If . . . the two great leading maritime commercial nations of the world establish a rule to govern themselves, each with respect to the other, they may reasonably hope that their conclusion will be accepted by the other powers, and will become for the future recognized as a part of the public law of the civilized world.[72]

In his conversation of June 10, 1869, with Lord Clarendon, Motley—as the Secretary of State later claimed—missed the intended emphasis regarding recognition of belligerency, and said what seemed to the President to reflect more the views of Senator Sumner than those of Grant and Fish. The American minister referred to the recognition, and, while saying that the President desired the latter to be used only as showing animus, he de-

[72] The instructions are printed in Sen. Ex. Doc. 11, 41st Cong., 3d Sess., at pp. 2–5.

scribed it as being "the fountain head of the disasters which had been caused to the American people, both individually and collectively, by the hands of Englishmen." [73] A year and a half later Fish wrote, after Motley's recall, that in this interview the minister had spoken in direct opposition to the "temper and spirit" of his instructions. Motley, in answer to Lord Clarendon's suggestion (concerning the choice of an arbiter by lot, as proposed in the Johnson-Clarendon convention) that the throwing of dice or the drawing of lots was "not a new invention" but a "not uncommon method in arbitrations," had observed that "such an aleatory process seemed an unworthy method for disposing of questions hinging on great principles of law and involving the welfare of nations and the contingencies of war and peace." Fish in his communication of December 30, 1870, to Benjamin Moran at the American Legation in London, pointed out that Motley's suggestive words, "aleatory process," had previously been used in a speech made in the Senate on the ratification of the treaty.[74]

On the question of agreement upon some general principles of law pertinent to the matters involved in the *Alabama* claims, Motley reported, concerning his interview with Lord Clarendon:

> I observed further, that the President hoped, when negotiations on these grave matters should be renewed, for the establishment of general and fundamental principles, binding upon both nations, in full view of

[73] *Ibid.*, p. 9. Apparently Grant was inclined to recall Motley soon after this, but he did not actually do so until more than a year later. Some historians have attributed Grant's displeasure over Motley's use of his instructions to the fact that the President favored recognition of the Cuban insurgents in 1869 and did not like Motley's emphasis upon the illegality of the British proclamation of 1861 (Adams, *Lee at Appomattox*, p. 119 and Appendix E; C. C. Tansill, *The United States and Santo Domingo, 1798–1873* [1938], pp. 423, 423n.). The views of Sumner on the Cuban question are well known. On July 10, 1869, the Senator wrote to Caleb Cushing: "My desire is to act so that our example may give new force to international law and help future peace . . . It is plain that there is nothing to justify this great concession to insurgent Cubans, unless you discard all rules and follow simply your own passions or desires. They have not reached that point of reasonable certainty for the present and future which alone can justify such a step on our part, unless we accept the hazard of war with Spain" (Pierce, *Memoirs and Letters*, IV, 402–403).

The controversy relating to Motley's recall, being quite incidental to the present study, has been touched upon but briefly.

[74] Sen. Ex. Doc. 11, 41st Cong., 3d Sess., pp. 9, 31.

the fact that what should, after this long international debate, be adopted by the two leading naval and commercial powers of the world, as the amended public law for their own guidance, would probably be considered as the *norma agendi* for the civilized world. His lordship heartily concurred in this view of the case, saying that it was what he had always earnestly desired.[75]

The possible projection of new rules on neutrality was again the subject of a reference in an instruction of September 25, 1869, to the American minister in London. This note related mainly to the nature of the American grievances and said that it did not fall within the scope of the communication "to discuss the important changes in the rules of public law, the desirableness of which has been demonstrated by . . . incidents of the last few years, now under consideration, and which, in view of the maritime prominence of Great Britain and the United States, it would benefit them to mature and propose to the other states of Christendom." [76]

The subsequent discussions of importance were to be conducted, not through Motley in London, but in Washington. The temporary interruption of conversations looking to a settlement seems to have caused some concern to the British government. In the latter part of 1869, Sir Edward Thornton several times referred to the matter in conversations with the Secretary of State, and desired to know what kind of settlement would be acceptable to the United States.[77]

In his first annual message, on December 6, 1869, after stating to Congress that the rejected Johnson-Clarendon Convention was "misconceived in its scope and inadequate in its provisions" (since it treated the injuries which had resulted to the United States simply as "ordinary claims"), President Grant expressed the hope that the two governments could approach the solution "with the determination not only to remove the causes of complaint in the past, but to lay the foundation of a broad principle of public law which will prevent future differences and tend to firm and continued peace and friendship." [78] That the possibility of a settle-

[75] *Ibid.*, p. 8.
[76] *For. Rel.*, 1873–74, III, 336.
[77] Pierce, *Memoirs and Letters*, IV, 414–415.
[78] Richardson, *Messages*, VIII, 3988.

ment which would be more than a mere disposal of particular claims was never lost sight of is also suggested by Secretary Fish's mention, in a letter to a correspondent in September 1869, of a possible definition of "what *shall* be Maritime International Law in the future." [79]

Sir John Rose, member of the ministry in Canada and British commissioner to settle the claims of the Hudson's Bay Company and of the Puget Sound Company against the United States, had an important part in the conversations which soon followed. He was an unofficial envoy for the purpose. Not only the labor of this Anglo-American for a peaceful solution, but the seriousness (for Great Britain) of the current developments in Europe, and the firmness of the President on the subject of the claims against Great Britain,[80] seem to have figured in the outcome.

The actual negotiation of the Treaty of Washington came about after an accord in four diplomatic notes, which the Secretary of State called "the official particulars of twenty months' secret diplomacy." [81] To a proposal by the British that a joint high commission of the two countries treat on outstanding questions of fisheries and other matters affecting the relation of the United States to the British possessions in North America, the United States assented, on condition that the *Alabama* claims should also be referred to this commission.[82] There was a preliminary under-

[79] Adams, *Lee at Appomattox*, p. 126.

[80] In Grant's annual message to Congress, December 5, 1870, there was a recommendation of appointment of a commission to take proof of the claims and of the ownership thereof (Richardson, *Messages*, IX, 4056).

[81] The notes are quoted in Moore, *International Arbitrations*, I, 532–535.

On January 17, 1871, Senator Sumner, while still chairman of the Foreign Relations Committee, had submitted to Fish the memorandum in which the Senator made his suggestion of a hemispheric flag-withdrawal by the British, which he said could not "be abandoned as a condition or preliminary of such a settlement as is now proposed." No proposition for a joint commission, he wrote, could be accepted unless the terms of submission were such as to leave no reasonable doubt of a favorable result (text in Moore, *International Arbitrations*, I, 525–526).

On the relative importance of the Sumner position and its connection with other matters of policy of the Grant administration, see J. C. Bancroft Davis, *Mr. Fish and the Alabama Claims* (1893), pp. 22, 145; Tansill, *United States and Santo Domingo*, pp. 340–341.

[82] According to the biographer of the chief British commissioner, Lord Tenterden offered to the British Cabinet the ingenious suggestion for bring-

standing that there should be, in the final treaty, an expression of regret, not inconsistent with the dignity of England, for the fact of escape of and depradations by the *Alabama*, but no advance admission of legal liability on these claims. The British foreign secretary was willing to negotiate with regard to the future rules of maritime neutrality.[83]

Coming together for organization on February 27, 1871, the commissioners subsequently had thirty-seven sittings. The British members, headed by the Earl de Grey and Ripon, had instructions which authorized their expressing regret for the escape of the *Alabama* and the consequent injury to the commerce of the United States, in terms agreeable to the United States and not inconsistent with the previously maintained position of the British government regarding the international obligations of neutral nations. The instructions also set forth that it would be desirable "to take this opportunity to consider whether it might not be the interest of Great Britain and the United States to lay down certain rules of international comity in regard to the obligations of maritime neutrality, not only to be acknowledged for observance in their future relations, but to be recommended for adoption to the other Maritime Powers." [84] As to the *Alabama* claims, the British commissioners had instructions to propose unrestricted arbitration.

In a statement read to the commission on March 8, Secretary Fish declared that Great Britain was liable for her failure to exercise neutral duties toward the United States upon "principles of International Law" which the Americans would submit. As presented, these principles were to govern consideration of the claims, whether this be by the commissioners or by a separate tribunal. For the British, Ripon assented to discussion of the principles outlined, as rules which might be accepted for the future, but at first reserved the question of their use in the proposed arbitration.[85]

---

ing about the actual negotiations (Lucien Wolf, *Life of the First Marquess of Ripon* [1921], I, 239).

[83] Moore, *International Arbitrations*, I, 531.

[84] *Parl. Pap., North America*, no. 3 (1871), C. 346, p. 4.

[85] Wolf, *Life of . . . Ripon*, I, 244, 245. The rules as quoted by this author (pp. 243–244) differ somewhat from the ones finally agreed upon.

The American Secretary of State, having proposed the bases of negotiation or arbitration, discussed the nature and extent of claims for direct damages to property. As to indirect losses, the Secretary said that, in the hope of an amicable settlement, he presented no estimate, "but without prejudice to the right to indemnification on their account." [86]

The "three rules" of what came to be the Treaty of Washington had their origin in a proposal by the American commissioners, on March 14, 1871, of four rules, one of which (relating to treatment of vessels which had departed from the jurisdiction of a neutral government in violation of the neutrality of the latter and which were afterward found within the jurisdiction of the same neutral government) was later dropped. A cabled request for authorization brought to the British commissioners instructions to assent to the rules, not as a statement of principles of international law which were in force at the time the *Alabama* claims arose, but as applicable to these claims, and as rules to apply in the future. On this basis, the rules, as redrafted by the British so as to include some slight amendments but no essential changes, were ready for incorporation in the treaty.[87] As that instrument recites, "Her Majesty's Government in order to evince its desire of strengthening the friendly relations between the two countries and of making satisfactory provisions for the future, agrees that in deciding the questions between the two countries arising out of those claims, the Arbitrators should assume that Her Majesty's Government had undertaken to act upon the principles set forth in the rules." The arbitrators were to be governed by these rules, "and by such principles of international law not inconsistent there-

[86] Allan Nevins, *Hamilton Fish: The Inner History of the Grant Administration* (1936), p. 481. This writer says that Englishmen were still almost unanimous in holding that their country had not violated international law.

[87] Texts of the four rules as proposed by American commissioners and of the three rules in the form accepted are in Moore, *International Arbitrations*, I, 542–544, and in the Protocols of Conference between Commissioners (*Treaty of Washington Papers*).

The biographer of Hamilton Fish records that, according to entries in the diary of the Secretary of State, when the "rules" were read at a Cabinet meeting on March 31, the President and the Secretary of the Treasury seemed to think that the articles were possibly more stringent than the United States would like to have them in the future (Nevins, *Hamilton Fish*, p. 486).

with as the arbitrators shall determine to have been applicable to the case." For the present purpose, the most significant part of the treaty was the last paragraph of article VI, by which the parties agreed "to observe these rules as between themselves in future, and to bring them to the knowledge of other maritime powers, and to invite them to accede to them." [88]

The failure of the commissioners to reach any specific agreement upon the national, or, as they had begun to be called, the "indirect," claims of the United States was to cause much subsequent discussion. However, this shortcoming was apparently not anticipated in 1871, and in its final form the treaty did not encounter serious opposition. The Senate majority for approval included Senator Sumner. Although Earl Russell called the agreement a British yielding and offered a motion for refusal to ratify any convention for the settlement of the *Alabama* claims by anything except the rules of international law and of British municipal law in force at the time the events occurred,[89] the plan was approved in London. Earl Granville contended that the three rules were completely covered by the 1870 Act of Parliament, and Sir Roundell Palmer argued that the "substance of the obliga-

[88] 17 *Stat.* 863. Sir Roundell Palmer, who was called in for advice to members of the British government when it was considering assent to the American proposals, afterward wrote: "The risk . . . before the arbitrators, would be caused by translating retrospectively into the form of a hypothetical international Convention, which did not exist when the events happened, a duty which we had recognised as incumbent upon us under our own laws, and which we had always professed and endeavoured to perform with as much diligence as was reasonably practicable in affairs of domestic government: and this, so far as national honour was concerned, seemed to me to have some advantages, even over a perfectly open arbitration, before arbitrators who might possibly be influenced by the teachers and advocates of new ideas concerning international law" (*Memorials, Part II: Personal and Political* [1898], I, 214–215). Palmer wrote to Lord Russell that he did not believe the treaty intended to make any assumption or admission whatever as to the obligations incumbent upon England by general international law (*ibid.*, p. 217). He thought the rules "were so loosely expressed, as to leave some points uncertain"; he feared the result might be to "unsettle the whole fabric of international law for the future" (since the rules were to be communicated to other powers); he thought the second rule furnished no "safe, certain, and convenient standard of practical obligation for the future" (*ibid.*, pp. 221, 222, letter to Granville).

[89] Hansard, *Parl. Deb.*, 3d ser., vol. 206, p. 1838 (House of Lords, 12 June 1871).

tion" which Great Britain was accepting in the three rules, as distinct from its "foundation and origin," did not differ materially from that in the municipal law of England as interpreted and actually understood by the government and as the government at the time undertook to execute it.[90] In the House of Commons on August 4, 1871, Gladstone, defending the treaty, expressed the hope that the basis of understanding between the two countries would "harden and widen into an International Law for the benefit of the world."[91] With the appointment of arbitrators and their meeting for organization at Geneva, Switzerland, on the following December 15, the way was prepared for attempted interpretations of the rules in relation to national statutes and to preëxisting international law.

Described by one public man in England (who represented the minority view) as "loaded dice,"[92] and by a leading periodical as "so hopelessly vague that they would cover almost any view of international law ever propounded,"[93] the "rules" as stated did not preclude the possibility of American presentation of the "indirect" claims at Geneva.[94] Inclusion of these claims in the

[90] *Ibid.*, vol. 208, pp. 894, 895.

[91] *Ibid.*, p. 916. In the course of the same speech, Gladstone took the position that "the principle embodied in the rules in the Treaty of Washington are the very principles for which the Executive Government of this country contended in the Courts of this country, and which, therefore, it was not too much for the American Government to expect we should be prepared to act on in coming to an ultimate settlement." At another place he said that the "treaty has laid the foundation of future advantage in the administration and action of International Law" (*ibid.*, pp. 915, 917).

[92] Letter of August 7, 1871, as quoted by Sir Roundell Palmer, *Memorials, Part II*, I, 225.

[93] Excerpt from *Fraser's Magazine* for June 1872, as quoted in *Treaty of Washington Papers*, IV, 555.

[94] This possibility is evident in the text of the rules, which is as follows:

"A neutral government is bound—

"First, to use due diligence to prevent the fitting out, arming or equipping, within its jurisdiction, of any vessel which it has reasonable ground to believe is intended to cruise or to carry on war against a Power with which it is at peace; and also to use like diligence to prevent the departure from its jurisdiction of any vessel intended to cruise or carry on war as above, such vessel having been specially adapted, in whole or in part, within its jurisdiction, to warlike use.

"Secondly, not to permit or suffer either belligerent to make use of its ports or waters as the base of naval operations against the other, or for the

Case of the United States as prepared by Bancroft Davis and presented to the tribunal caused a storm which evoked further public statement as to the meaning of the agreement and led to negotiation looking to some arrangement of the issue. The official British view had been that through the work of the high commissioners at Washington the matter had been set at rest, and in the House of Commons, on February 6, Gladstone said that the British construction of the treaty could be shown to be "the true and unambiguous meaning of the words" and therefore the "only meaning admissible, whether tried by grammar, by reason, by policy, or by any other standard."[95] Secretary of State Fish seems to have had the indirect claims included in the American Case not because he thought damages on them would or should be allowed by the arbitrators, but because he was concerned about the attitude of the Senate;[96] while unwilling to regard these claims as excluded because of the soundness of the British position on what had been done by the high commissioners at Washington, he was apparently not expecting a pecuniary award on these bases.[97] To Minister Robert Cumming Schenck in London he

---

purpose of the renewal or augmentation of military supplies or arms, or the recruitment of men.

"Thirdly, to exercise due diligence in its own ports and waters, and, as to all persons within its jurisdiction, to prevent any violation of the foregoing obligations and duties."

The sequel to the discussions of the high commissioners seems to show that the British members were honestly of the opinion that the indirect claims would not be brought under the treaty, and that the American members believed they had yielded nothing on this point. The Marquis of Ripon (Lord de Grey), head of the British commissioners who negotiated the treaty, admitted (according to Morley) his awareness of the possibility that the indirect claims might be brought on the basis of the treaty; he believed that if he had insisted that a formal repudiation be written in, it would not have been possible to get any treaty at all (John Morley, *Life of William Gladstone* [1903], II, 408; Robert B. Mowat, *The Diplomatic Relations of Great Britain and the United States* [1925], p. 217).

[95] Hansard, *Parl. Deb.*, 3d ser., vol. 209, pp. 85, 86. The Queen's speech contained the statement that "in the Case . . . submitted on behalf of the United States large claims have been included which are understood on my part not to be within the province of the Arbitrators."

[96] Nevins, *Hamilton Fish*, pp. 520–521, 533–534, 537–538, 562.

[97] As Fish wrote to Schenck on April 23, 1872 (*Treaty of Washington Papers*, II, 475).

wrote, on February 29, that "the meaning of the Treaty is within its four corners." [98]

The British government's position was that the indirect claims must be entirely excluded. The whole arbitration proceedings seemed likely to be discontinued. On March 20 Earl Granville wrote to Schenck, drawing attention to the fact that the parties to the Treaty of Washington

> have . . . bound themselves to bring these Rules to the knowledge of other maritime Powers, and to invite them to accede to them. Could it have been expected that those Powers would accept a proposal which might entail upon a neutral such an unlimited liability, and, in some instances, might involve the ruin of a whole country?
>
> Her Majesty's Government cannot for themselves accept such a liability, nor recommend the acceptance of it to other nations.[99]

The British government had now taken the position that the indirect claims were wholly beyond the reasonable scope of *any treaty* of arbitration, and that their submission would be damaging to the interests of all nations and to the future peace of the world.[100] Sir Roundell Palmer, counsel for his country in the arbitration at Geneva, thought the submission would have made it possible for the arbitrators to "mulct this country in more than the whole expenses of the war" and that war would have been a preferable alternative; in a letter to the Lord Chancellor and to Gladstone he pictured the American Case as "an attempt to evade and enlarge the limits within which the subject-matter of the reference to the arbitrators was intended to be confined by the Treaty of Washington, and to found enormous and intolerable claims upon the enlargement of those limits." [101]

Friends of the treaty and advocates of the arbitral method of

[98] Nevins, *Hamilton Fish,* p. 532. Fish wrote to Schenck in June that the government of the United States hoped, as it had reason to believe, that the treaty would be "its own interpreter" (*Treaty of Washington Papers,* II, 548). This was directed to the meanings of the words in article I of the treaty, reading, "All claims, growing out of acts committed by the aforesaid vessels, and generically known as the 'Alabama Claims,' shall be referred."

[99] *Treaty of Washington Papers,* II, 439.

[100] Statement of Granville, as quoted by Schenck, *Treaty of Washington Papers,* II, 539.

[101] Palmer, *Memorials, Part II,* I, 231, 233.

settling even serious disputes between nations used their efforts to save the situation.[102] After prolonged discussion, largely by telegraph, regarding the form in which the two governments might agree to withdrawal of the objectionable claims, the effort still seemed likely to fail. Grant's Cabinet appears to have agreed on April 19 that, while the indirect claims could not be withdrawn, it was to the interest of the United States that there be an arbitral pronouncement against a pecuniary award on the claims. Adams, the American arbitrator, who was about to leave for Europe, was told of the decision and was willing to communicate the view to the British government.[103] After abandonment of the idea of an exchange of notes, Granville handed to Schenck on May 10 a proposed supplemental article. By the latter, each nation would have bound itself not to prefer in future any claims against the other for consequential damages, and in consideration of this promise the United States would drop the "indirect" claims which had been presented at Geneva. A preambular statement inserted by the Senate was thought by the British to broaden the article unduly.[104] As is well known, the final arrangement came by action of the tribunal itself, through the judicial statesmanship of Adams. On June 19, in a *declaration*, not a decision—a matter of form which seemed important to American counsel—the arbitrators announced that they had arrived, "individually and collectively, at the conclusion that these claims do not constitute, upon the principles of international law applicable to such cases, good foundation for an award of compensation or computation of damages between nations; and should, upon such principles, be wholly excluded from the consideration of the Tribunal in making its award, *even if there were no disagreement between the two Governments as to the competency of the Tribunal to decide thereon.*"[105] A telegram of three days later to Minister

[102] T. Wemyss Reid, *Life of the Right Honourable William Edward Forster* (1888), II, 30, 32.
[103] Nevins, *Hamilton Fish*, p. 538.
[104] *Ibid.*, pp. 544, 549.
[105] *Treaty of Washington Papers*, II, 578 (italics inserted). This declaration was regarded not as an exercise of jurisdiction but as a statement of what the arbitrators would have felt impelled to do if they had clearly had jurisdiction.

Schenck conveyed Grant's acceptance of the arbitrators' declaration upon the question of public law.[106]

The amount of attention which the arbitrators gave, in the actual arbitration, to relation of the "three rules" to general international law has been the subject of some disagreement. The secretary to Caleb Cushing, senior American counsel, had the impression that the arbitrators, with the exception of Sir Alexander Cockburn, the British member, paid no attention to whether the "rules" were new or merely stated principles of preëxisting international law.[107] Count Frederic Sclopis of Italy, the presiding arbitrator, did not entirely clarify his own position when, in the course of his individual opinion, he said:

> Even if precedents could be quoted contrary to the opinion I maintain, I should reply that the letter and spirit of the three rules laid down in the sixth article of the treaty of Washington do not allow us to follow the old ruling.
>
> It must be steadily borne in mind that it is a new law, full of equity and foresight, which we are now to follow. . . .
>
> The powers which signed the treaty of Washington express . . . the desire and hope that the three rules which they have there laid down will be adopted by the other maritime powers. It must then be inferred that the signing powers considered these rules as clear, precise, and applicable to the various cases which are therein contemplated. If, on the contrary, it is to be supposed that the intention of the contracting parties . . . was to admit explanations and reservations of these same rules in the sense "of not largely transcending the views of international maritime law and policy which would be likely to commend themselves to the general interests and intelligence of that portion of mankind," the advantage of the example given would be entirely lost. The uncertainty of its interpretation would always endanger the stability of the rule.[108]

Nor did the Italian member make it perfectly clear whether he was thinking primarily of international customary law or of treaty law when, in discussion of the effect as *res judicata* of the decision of the admiralty court of the Bahamas regarding

[106] *Ibid.,* pp. 578–579. Apparently Fish was not pleased at the complacency with which the British government announced to Parliament that the indirect claims had been excluded from consideration.

[107] Frank W. Hackett, *Reminiscences of the Geneva Tribunal of Arbitration, 1872* (1911), p. 297n.

[108] *Treaty of Washington Papers,* IV, 71, 73–74.

the *Florida,* he said that it was a case of "the responsibility which results from the principles of international law, and the moral conviction at which we have arrived in consequence of the acts imputed to the Florida." He thought it was for the arbitrators to "repair the effects" produced, "no longer taking as our point of departure the provisions of a municipal law, but the principles of international law, and the rules laid down in Article VI of the treaty."[109]

Viscount d'Itajubá, Brazilian arbitrator, in his opinion, did not mention general international law in terms, but referred carefully to the three rules. Justice Jacques Staempfli, the Swiss member, alluded to the law behind the treaty and the arbitration when he spoke, with respect to the *Alabama,* of what was allowable by "the first rule, and according to the natural interpretation of the obligations of the law of nations," and, regarding the *Shenandoah,* of what was correct "according to international law." He elsewhere referred to the "maintenance of a real and effective neutrality." In a general description of the law of the tribunal, after observing that the rules took precedence "of the principles which might be drawn from historical international law and from science," he said:

> Historical international law, or the practice of the law of nations, as well as science and scientific authorities, may be considered as subsidiary law, in so far as the principles to be applied are generally recognized . . . nor at variance with the three rules. . . . If one or other of these conditions fail, it is for the tribunal to supply what is wanting by interpreting and applying the three rules to the best of its power and in all conscientiousness.[110]

In his opinion, Adams referred to British denial that the measure of diligence due to the United States from Great Britain was as great under the law of nations as it had been made, with her consent, by the terms of the treaty. He further noted that, in either case, the British government claimed to be the exclusive judge of the fulfillment of the duty, and held that it was for the tribunal to determine the "debt" which might have been contracted by the use of the "terms" (rules). Throughout, Adams

[109] *Ibid.,* pp. 92, 96.

[110] *Ibid.,* p. 104. The earlier quotations from Staempfli's opinion are in the same volume at pp. 124, 133, and 137.

was careful to find liability or lack of it under "terms of the Treaty of Washington." [111]

Sir Alexander Cockburn, who at one point in his separate opinion referred to himself as "in some sense the representative of Great Britain" on the tribunal, contended that the United States virtually admitted that the "rules" had not previously been international law, "for it 'agrees to observe the rules as between itself and Great Britain in future, and to bring them to the knowledge of other maritime powers, and to invite them to accede to them'—all of which would plainly be superfluous and vain if these rules already formed part of the existing law recognized as obtaining among nations." He regretted that the whole subject matter was not left open to be decided by the arbitrators according to the "true" principles of international law in force when the alleged causes of complaint were said to have arisen. He dealt with a point relating to the theory of incorporating international into municipal law when, after attempting to refute the point that the commissioners who framed the Foreign Enlistment Act of 1870 meant the municipal law to come up to international obligations, he declared equally unfounded "the assertion that the provisions of the foreign enlistment act are only a statutory declaration of the common law of England," since the "enactment of that statute could only be declaratory of the common law, if co-extensive with the obligations of international law; whereas, in fact, it went far beyond them." [112] He expressed doubt that the rules, interpreted (as they were by the majority) to place so extensive a liability upon a neutral, would find favor with other nations, and thought it strange "if regulations, more stringent than the rules of international law, framed by a neutral sovereign for the very purpose of insuring the observance of neutrality, can be made to create an antecedent liability which never would have existed without them." [113] Cockburn was

[111] *Ibid.*, pp. 145, 230.

[112] *Ibid.*, p. 258. Cockburn expressed his wish that if the "rules" had to be made, "due diligence" might have been more precisely defined, and that the "principles of international law not inconsistent with them" might have been set forth (*ibid.*, p. 232).

[113] *Ibid.*, p. 512. Earlier in the course of his very lengthy opinion he had attempted to show, on a comparative view of the laws of leading maritime countries, that there was none in which the equipping or arming of vessels

most vigorous in his reference to his colleague Staempfli, to whom he attributed the idea that there was no such thing as international law and that the tribunal was creating it for the first time.[114] At an earlier point in his opinion he had said:

> I cannot concur with Mr. Staempfli that, because the practice of nations has at times undergone great changes, and the views of jurists on points of international law have often been and still are conflicting, therefore there is no such thing as international law, and that, consequently, we are to proceed independently of any such law—for such is the effect of his reasoning, if I understand it rightly—according to some intuitive perception of right and wrong, or speculative notions of what the rules as to the duties of neutrals ought to be.[115]

The sharpness of Cockburn's criticisms did not detract from the importance of a successful adjudication. For the present purpose it is not necessary to reconstruct the arguments which were presented. The whole proceeding illustrated the manner in which, when the international law standard was to be applied, custom and precedent might be invoked, writings of publicists adapted, use made of such municipal court decisions as that concerning the *Santissima Trinidad*[116] and that concerning the *Gran Para,*[117] and attention drawn to official statements made

---

was (prior to the outbreak of the American Civil War) prohibited except under circumstances which would make it a violation of neutrality according to international law (*ibid.*, p. 278). Some laws had been changed after the outbreak of the war to put them on the same basis as those of England and the United States.

Cockburn (*ibid.*, pp. 248–255) challenged the authority by which J. K. Bluntschli had attempted a distinction (*Das moderne Völkerrecht,* § 765) between the selling of ordinary contraband and the selling of warships.

[114] *Treaty of Washington Papers,* IV, 497.

[115] *Ibid.*, p. 233. Caleb Cushing wrote that no such statement as that quoted appears in any of the printed opinions of Staempfli and that no such declaration was ever made by him orally at any of the conferences. Cushing thought this a sample of Cockburn's "rashness and inaccuracy" (*The Treaty of Washington* [1873], p. 142).

[116] 7 Wheaton 283 (1822).

[117] 7 Wheaton 471 (1822). By emphasizing this decision, which was given by Chief Justice Marshall, counsel for the United States attempted to offset any "apparently broad or ill-considered statements" in the opinion on the *Santissima,* which had been written by Justice Joseph Story. "There can be no doubt," the American Case submitted, "that they were considered together in the consultation room" (*Treaty of Washington Papers,* I, 82–84; see also, IV, 252).

previously from the complainant state (such as the ruling of a United States Attorney General in 1841),[118] in an effort to convince arbitrators of what had been existing international law and what would be a reasonable interpretation of the "rules" as affecting that law. As has been seen, much discussion related to "municipal laws in excess of antecedent international obligation." Actual practice of states, as revealed in what the United States had done with regard to the revolting colonies of Spain, as well as what had been done in international wars, also received detailed attention. The tribunal found that the international duties of a neutral are quite distinct from its own municipal laws on the subject, which may fall quite short of the obligatory international standard. The arbitrators further laid down that the meaning of an elastic phrase such as "due diligence" may be properly given in relation to the particular circumstances, and that damages for failure to use such diligence may be proportioned to the loss thereby sustained by the offended belligerent.[119]

Acceptance of the award by both parties marked the conclusion of the particular controversy but did not end discussion of the points involved in the arbitration or of its general significance. The effect of the adjudication upon the substantive content of the future law of nations elicited expressions of opinion from both officials and publicists. The view seems tenable that at the time the *Alabama* claims arose, international customary law relating to neutral duty in the matter of ships fitting out in a state's ports for the use of belligerents was at least evolving toward a

[118] 3 *Op. Atty. Gen.* 738, 741. This was a ruling that the prohibition in United States law against the sale of completed warships was not required by international law. See, in this connection, Minister Schenck's reported statement to Granville in January 1872 that "in morality and in the view of neutral obligation it was, perhaps, as essentially wrong to furnish a gun to be used against a friendly power as it was to fit out a ship, only the rule had, of necessity, to be modified, because of the greater practical difficulty of applying or enforcing it in one case than in the other" (Sen. Ex. Doc. 26, 45th Cong., 3d Sess., 1879, p. 22).

[119] There were other legal questions which figured in the proceedings which do not require to be considered in the present study. One was the legality of a British-built boat's being converted into a war vessel on the high seas. See Bulloch, *The Secret Service,* II, 373; *Treaty of Washington Papers,* I, 386. Another was the question of interest.

rule of prohibition.[120] Whether the Americans were right that the "rules" of the treaty were expressive of what already existed, or whether the British view that new obligations were retroactively imposed by the treaty was sound, the treaty provisions and the effect given to them by the arbitrators were bound to have influence upon the development. In a letter of October 22, 1872, to J. C. Bancroft Davis, Secretary Fish observed:

> It needs but the most cursory glance at the mass of correspondence and of other documentary matter submitted to the tribunal of arbitration to see how thoroughly the remonstrances and protestations of the Government of the United States against the conduct of Great Britain have quickened and stimulated the European, and above all the British, mind into more careful examination and more complete perception of the rights and obligations of neutral powers, for the question of rights is inseparable from that of obligations.[121]

[120] Cf. Egidio Reale, *L'Arbitrage international: Le Règlement judiciaire du conflit de l'Alabama* (1929), p. 106. Cf. J. K. Bluntschli, "Opinion impartiale sur la question de l'Alabama et sur la manière de la résoudre," *Revue de droit international et de législation comparée*, II, no. 3 (1870), 452–485.

[121] *Treaty of Washington Papers*, IV, 548. The Institute of International Law, at its session in 1874, received the report of a commission which included as members Calvo, Hautefeuille, Lorimer, Rolin, and Woolsey. The commission, with Bluntschli as reporter, found in substance that the three "rules" were but the application of recognized legal principles, but that, with a view to avoiding controversies regarding their interpretation, revision of their text was desirable. This finding was favorably received. Four new members were added to the commission, and a seven-point redaction presented at the session at The Hague in 1875 was approved by a majority of the Institute members present (*Annuaire*, I, 108–114). Lorimer, Bernard, and Twiss opposed the adoption. Lorimer had criticized the rules at the 1874 session, asserting that neutrality itself was by no means a constant duty, but rather circumstantial; he also opposed the idea of making the intention with reference to the use of a ship, rather than the actual character of the latter, the criterion for determining the effect upon neutrality. The text adopted by the majority in 1875 was in part as follows (*Annuaire*, I, 139–140):

"II. . . . L'État neutre ne peut mettre, d'une manière quelconque, à la disposition d'aucun des États belligérants, ni leur vendre ses vaisseaux de guerre ou vaisseaux de transport militaire, non plus que le matériel de ses arsenaux ou de ses magasins militaires . . . en vue de l'aider à poursuivre la guerre. En outre l'État neutre est tenu de veiller à ce que d'autres personnes ne mettent des vaisseaux de guerre à la disposition d'aucun des Etats belligérants dans ses ports ou dans les parties de mer qui dépendent de sa juridiction.

"III. Lorsque l'Etat neutre a connaissance d'enterprises ou d'actes de ce genre, incompatibles avec la neutralité, il est tenu de prendre les mesures

There remained the matter of carrying out the agreement of the parties to communicate the "rules" to other maritime states and invite accession. The chief apparent difficulty grew out of the fact that the second rule had from the first been unclear and that, after the arbitration, the British government was not desirous of proposing the rules to other states *with the interpretation of them* which the tribunal had given. Immediately after the treaty was made, there was concern in England lest the second rule prevent the sale of arms and other military supplies, by a neutral or in a neutral country, in the ordinary course of commerce. Fish telegraphed to Schenck on June 10, 1871, that the President understood the rule did not prevent the open sale of arms or military supplies in the ordinary course of commerce; the Secretary of State added that the United States, in bringing the rules to the knowledge of other powers and asking their assent to them, as the contracting powers had agreed to do, would insist that such was their proper meaning.[122] From the side of England there was an effort to secure adoption by the United States Senate, at the time it approved the Treaty of Washington, of a resolution interpreting the rules so as to prohibit aid to or through vessels, but making clear that the sale of arms or military supplies in the ordinary course of commerce was not covered.[123] The resolution was tabled. Schenck, anticipating serious objections to ratification in England unless the second rule should be interpreted in the way suggested, received assurance that President Grant would authorize a statement of the sort when bringing the treaty rules to the attention of other states. On the day ratifications were exchanged in London, Earl Granville sent to Sir Edward Thornton in Washington a proposed draft of a note to be used in presenting the rules to the other powers.[124]

nécessaires pour les empêcher, et de poursuivre comme responsables les individus qui violent les devoirs de la neutralité.

"IV. De même l'État neutre ne doit ni permettre ni souffrir que l'un des belligérants fasse de ses ports ou de ses eaux, la base d'opérations navales contre l'autre, ou que les vaisseaux de transport militaire se servent de ses ports ou de ses eaux, pour renouveler ou augmenter leurs approvisionnements militaires ou leurs armes, ou pour recruter des hommes."

[122] Moore, *International Arbitrations,* I, 554.

[123] 65 *Brit. and For. State Papers* 393–399.

[124] *Ibid.,* pp. 399–400; *Revue de droit international et de législation comparée,* VI, 59, 62. The draft (a text of which is in Sen. Ex. Doc. 26, 45th

After the actual arbitration the treaty apparently became more unpopular in England, and agreement upon a formulation for presentation to other powers became less likely. Already intimations of some unfavorable reactions to the projected "rules" of international law had come from outside states. Bismarck's reported position was one unfavorable to the rules because they did not go far enough, the intimation being that the supply of arms and other munitions of war from a neutral country should be forbidden. Schenck in a despatch of October 7, 1872, sent word of the statement by the German ambassador (Albrecht von Bernstorff) to Granville that the German government would probably oppose the rules when they were presented for acceptance.[125] Count Friedrich F. von Beust, Austrian ambassador at London, had objected to the rules as narrowing the rights of neutrals unduly and giving undue advantage to belligerents; he was opposed to any modifications in the law of nations not existent in the "natural development of international right." [126] More specifically, he had expressed apprehension lest England, through her possession of naval stations in all parts of the world, secure great advantage over other states which did not have comparable facilities at their command.[127] Granville himself seems to have believed, or to have caused the Americans to think he believed, that the rules would be rejected by some other maritime states.[128]

Various views of the treaty rules found expression in a debate in the House of Commons on March 21, 1873. There was a motion that, "having regard to the oppressive and impracticable character of the obligations, hitherto unknown to International Law, which would be imposed on neutral nations through the

---

Cong., 3d Sess., pp. 15–16) set forth that the parties "thought it to be their duty, in the interest of the common harmony of nations" to bring the rules to the knowledge of the other maritime powers and invite them to accede.

[125] *For. Rel.*, 1873–74, I, 301–302.

[126] The material appeared in the *Austrian Red Book*, extracts from which are given in a despatch of October 11, 1872, from Delaplaine, secretary of the American legation at Vienna, to Fish (*For. Rel.*, 1873–74, I, 59–62).

[127] Sen. Ex. Doc. 26, 45th Cong., 3d Sess., p. 23; Cushing, *The Treaty of Washington*, pp. 180–181.

[128] Nevins, *Hamilton Fish*, p. 867; Sen. Ex. Doc. 26, 45th Cong., 3d Sess., p. 63.

interpretation placed by the Tribunal of Geneva upon the three Rules . . . and upon the principles of International Law," the government should transmit to other powers, with the rules, its dissent from the interpretation of them by the arbitrators.[129] Its maker pointed with alarm to certain *dicta* of the arbitrators. He urged that the rules were not self-interpreting, and that anyone reading them for himself "would put upon them an interpretation much more moderate than that of the Award." [130] For the government, W. E. Forster expressed belief that it had been very much owing to the ambiguity of British municipal law that "any *Alabama*" escaped; he endeavored to show that such a motion would be a kind of censure of the arbitrators, and offered reasons why Her Majesty's Government did not think there was any need for hurrying into a joint communication to foreign powers —for example, the desirability of first fulfilling other engagements of the treaty, the advisability of allowing any heat which might have been engendered in England because of the indirect claims to cool, and of allowing the Americans to reflect that in a future war they might return to their traditional role of neutrality.[131]

For the opposition, Vernon Harcourt supplied observations on international law, which he described as "constructed out of the precedents furnished by great transactions," and later defined as a "law of public opinion of states." [132] He suggested that the arbitration had shown the "imprudence of attempting to settle the law of nations by the electric telegraph." [133] The three rules he described as "leaky," as "not worth mending," as a "piece of careless juridical slipslop." [134] He thought the "tendency of these

[129] Hansard, *Parl. Deb.*, 3d ser., vol. 214, pp. 1963–64.

[130] *Ibid.*, pp. 1965, 1979.

[131] *Ibid.*, pp. 1984–1991. Later in the course of the debate a member urged that it would be "madness to throw away an interpretation of international law which, though for the moment against us, seemed contrived for our special benefit in the long run" (*ibid.*, p. 2013). Another observed that, "in drawing up the Rules, which were to be at once the Rules for permanently settling the international law and the Rules to settle our temporary difference with the United States, both sets of Commissioners were placed in a very difficult position, because they had in a manner to look both forwards and backwards at the same time" (*ibid.*, p. 2025).

[132] *Ibid.*, pp. 1993–1995.

[133] *Ibid.*, p. 1997. [134] *Ibid.*, p. 2006.

Rules of the Treaty of Washington was to reverse the whole stream of civilization" by putting neutrals into a position where the "conditions of neutrality" were intolerable.[135] The Attorney General spoke of the arbitrators' interpretations as "glosses," and thought that the "Rules" themselves were only new to this extent, that, the character of wars and the relations between states having altered since the last great war, circumstances had necessitated *"a new statement of principles which were as old as the relations of civilized nations."*[136] Disraeli expressed the conviction that "unless we arrive at some precise meaning as to the engagements into which we have entered by the intended introduction of the Three New Rules into the international law of Europe, we shall find ourselves involved in great difficulties." Observing that "the greater portion of the law of nations does not depend upon Treaties," he pointed out that the treaty did not clearly bind the parties to *joint* communication to the powers.[137]

Gladstone, who apologized for his earlier erroneous statement to the House that the government had already communicated the new rules to the powers of Europe, expressed the government's view that, whether the state was bound or not, he would anticipate very little advantage from a separate communication; a joint communication was evidently contemplated by the treaty, and would alone afford reasonable promise of attaining the objects of the treaty. There would be little chance of getting others to accept the rules if the two powers originally accepting them were unable to agree in submitting them. For this reason the government did not contemplate immediate pressure upon the United States to resume the correspondence, in view of the disagreement on interpretation. The Prime Minister indicated that Britain's recommendation of the three rules would not carry with it the recitals of the arbitrators as being "of any authority in the matter."[138] The motion was then withdrawn.

Subsequent attempts to reach agreement and transmit the rules to other powers for their acceptance were unsuccessful. The United States had proposed the insertion of the word "open"

[135] *Ibid.*

[136] *Ibid.*, pp. 2035, 2041 (italics inserted).

[137] *Ibid.*, pp. 2043–44, 2046.

[138] *Ibid.*, pp. 2048, 2049, 2054–55.

before "sale" in the proposed explanatory note making clear that the second rule did not contemplate any prohibition upon the sale of arms and other military supplies in the ordinary course of commerce. In a communication of December 22, 1871, Granville objected that this insertion would have the effect of leaving the two governments responsible to third powers for the clandestine dealings of their citizens and subjects.[139] In June 1873, Fish told the British minister (Thornton) that since the two governments had given it out to the world that they would invite the other maritime powers to accede to the rules, it appeared "undignified that they should abstain any longer from doing so." He observed that both Gladstone and Sir Stafford Northcote had in the recent debate on the *Alabama* indemnity declared that the three rules were not *ex post facto* but actually represented international law at the time of the origin of the claims. It therefore appeared to Fish that the two governments were now even more in accord concerning the rules than they had been when the treaty was signed; in any case, the American Secretary of State thought it "high time" Her Majesty's Government should either refuse or consent to join with the United States in addressing the invitation to the maritime powers.[140]

In October of the same year Granville made known that "Her Majesty's Government would think it necessary to accompany such a submission with a comment, and they could not in such comment adopt all the principles laid down by the Tribunal of Geneva."[141] In a memorandum to Schenck, dated November 1, Granville suggested that "consequences are involved in the rules which they [the British government] have never intended."[142] Furthermore,

> It also appeared desirable, with regard to the maritime Powers, to state, in submitting the three rules for their acceptance, that the Rules

[139] Sen. Ex. Doc. 26, 45th Cong., 3d Sess., p. 74.

[140] *Correspondence with the Government of the United States respecting the communication to other Governments of the Rules of the Treaty of Washington*, C. 1012, *Parl. Pap., North America*, no. 1 (1874), p. 16.

[141] *Idem*, p. 19. Secretary Fish later suggested that the financial crisis late in 1873 might have diverted attention from this question.

[142] Sen. Ex. Doc. 26, 45th Cong., 3d Sess., p. 64. Granville had previously suggested, in view of the probability that not all of the maritime powers

embody what, according to recent American statements of the view entertained in the United States, was international law before they were made, and that, although Great Britain did not accede to this proposition, yet we held them to express what we had thought fit to carry into effect through the action of that law, at a time when the Rules did not exist. It would remain for inference, that they do not constitute the innovation which some other Powers might think there was to be found in them.[143]

Mere verbalisms brought the foreign offices no closer to joint action. On May 9, 1874, Benjamin Moran reported a growing public opinion in England against bringing the three rules to the attention of the other maritime powers.[144] To Secretary Fish's inquiry of June 24, 1875, Thornton replied that he thought it possible Her Majesty's Government was "unwilling to make an application to other Governments which might be refused."[145] To an inquiry of October 28, 1875, Thornton replied that he hoped the United States would not press the question, and that no harm could come from postponement. Fish reminded him that they had consumed four years on the question.[146] Replying to another inquiry, that of February 17, 1876, Thornton remarked the "disinclination" which Her Majesty's Government had to proceed in the matter and suggested delay until some occasion presented a necessity for doing something. The American Secretary of State pointed out that this would be just the moment when it might be impossible to proceed, and that the rules were intended to guard against that contingency.[147] On the following

---

would accept the three rules, that a refusal would lose much of its importance if the two governments could agree on the mode in which they could "with most dignity as regarded themselves, and with the greatest advantage for the future, make the submission" (*ibid.*, p. 63).

143 *Correspondence . . . respecting the communication to other Governments of the Rules of the Treaty of Washington*, C. 1012, p. 21.

144 Sen. Ex. Doc. 26, 45th Cong., 3d Sess., p. 67.

145 *Correspondence . . . respecting the communication to other Governments of the Rules of the Treaty of Washington*, C. 8393, *Parl. Pap., United States*, no. 2 (1897), p. 9 (referred to in Fish's note of September 18, 1876).

146 *Idem.* See also the account of the interview in Nevins, *Hamilton Fish*, pp. 867, 868. To the British minister's suggestion that the treaty was very unpopular with the English public and that the government shrank from bringing it into further notice, Fish is said to have suggested that the British either abrogate the rules or urge them upon other powers.

147 Sen. Ex. Doc. 26, 45th Cong., 3d Sess., p. 87.

March 9, Thornton intimated that if the rules were submitted, Great Britain might desire to make some disclaimers. Fish held to the position that the matter should be disposed of, and declared that the United States was willing to submit the rules as agreed, "or to do whatever could properly be done toward meeting any wishes which Her Majesty's Government may entertain, and to co-operate in guarding against any unpleasant or injurious consequence which might arise, or be apprehended from their submission." He expressed the opinion that injury was more likely to occur through delay until serious events should precipitate a discussion of a practical application of the rules and the two governments be called upon to consider the extent of their obligation under this part of the treaty.[148] Toward the end of the long-drawn-out conversations, Fish suggested that the same clause by which the contracting parties agreed to observe the rules between themselves in the future required that they bring them to the knowledge of other maritime powers and invite accession; he said that the stipulation was regarded by the United States as indivisible, so that a failure to comply with one part might, and probably would, be held to carry with it the "avoidance and nullity" of the other.[149] But even this did not lead to an arrangement, and the last clause in the sixth article of the treaty remained unfulfilled.[150]

[148] *Ibid.*, pp. 87, 88. [149] *Ibid.*, p. 88.

[150] The method of prescribing, for an arbitral settlement, one or more specific rules and international law "not inconsistent therewith," for which the Treaty of Washington provisions concerning the *Alabama* claims furnished a precedent, found application two and a half decades later in the treaty of February 2, 1897, which the United States was able to arrange, after the Anglo-American crisis of 1895–96, between Great Britain and Venezuela in the boundary dispute between those two powers. It has been said that Secretary Olney "made" the treaty (Henry James, *Richard Olney and His Public Service* [1923], p. 134).

The major rule to be applied by the arbitrators in the settlement of the boundary dispute was: "Adverse holding or prescription during a period of fifty years shall make good title." The arbitrators were also directed to apply "such principles of international law not inconsistent" with the stipulated rules as they might determine to be applicable; by the treaty terms, the arbitrators were permitted some latitude in determining the boundary line (article IV, a text of which is in *Parl. Pap.*, Treaty Series no. 5, 1897, C. 8439).

As to the fifty-year rule, the British ambassador in Washington, Sir

As elements of law to be recognized in the future, the rules of the treaty thus had an inauspicious beginning. Before the end of the century some doubt arose of whether the rules continued to bind the two countries which originally contracted to observe them, and the opinion was expressed that instead of settling disputed points, the rules had raised new difficulties.[151] At the Second Hague Conference in 1907, Louis Renault, in his report on a project of a convention concerning the rights and duties of states in maritime war, referred to the expression "due diligence" in the Treaty of Washington as having become celebrated by its obscurity since it had been solemnly interpreted.[152] A regulation on the general subject with which Great Britain and the United States had attempted to deal through the rules of 1871 was at length incorporated in Hague Convention XIII of 1907. The phrasing was changed, however, so as to omit a reference to "due diligence" and to include references to the neutral's duty to use "the means at its disposal." Article 8 of the convention provided:

> A neutral Government is bound to employ the means at its disposal to prevent the fitting out or arming of any vessel within its jurisdiction which it has reason to believe is intended to cruise, or engage in hostile operations, against a Power with which that Government is at peace. It is also bound to display the same vigilance to prevent the departure from its jurisdiction of any vessel intended to cruise, or engage in hostile operations, which had been adapted entirely or partly within the said jurisdiction for use in war.[153]

Julian Pauncefote, seems to have contended that thirty years' settlement should be sufficient to secure title by prescription. The American government would not agree to less than fifty years (James Louis Garvin, *The Life of Joseph Chamberlain* [1932–1934], III, 164).

[151] Thomas J. Lawrence, *Principles of International Law* (1895), p. 554; Reale, *L'Arbitrage international,* p. 107n.

[152] *Deuxième Conférence international de la paix, actes et documents* (1907), I, 302. For other criticisms of the principal rules of the Treaty of Washington at the same conference, see the remarks of Ruy Barbosa, who invoked the opinion of Hall, Lawrence, Wheaton, and others, and pointed to practice during the Russo-Japanese war, in the effort to show that the furnishing of warships from neutral countries was not contrary to established, customary international law (*ibid.,* III, 468–474).

[153] 36 *Stat.* 2415. The preamble made a general reference to the international law standard in relation to the divergent views still held on the relations between neutral powers and belligerent powers, and to the diffi-

The preceding article stated specifically that a neutral power was not bound to prevent the export or transit, for the use of either belligerent, of arms, ammunitions, or, in general, of anything which could be of use to an army or fleet.

When, early in the period of the First World War, the question was raised of preventing American vessels from furnishing coal and supplies to belligerent warships at sea, the Attorney General of the United States suggested that "no neutral nation is called upon to interfere with the commercial activities of its citizens further than may be required by the *doctrines* and *precedents* of international law." [154] In the course of World War II, there was some preventive action by neutrals.[155] The applicability of Hague Convention XIII in 1940, when the United States supplied overage destroyers to be used by the British in return for bases in the Western Hemisphere, and consistency (with the convention) of the policy which the United States followed from the passage of the Lend-Lease Act of 1941 to the date when the United States became a belligerent, will receive separate attention.[156]

Acceptance of the substance of the three rules as customary or conventional international law did not set at rest all questions concerning legal responsibility for raiding of commerce at sea. Charles Francis Adams thought it safe to predict that the *Florida*, the *Alabama*, and the *Shenandoah* would go down in history, not as pirates, "but as the last lineal survivors of the black-flagged banditti of the olden time." [157] As Confederate leaders

culties to which such divergence might give rise; in cases not covered by the convention, the parties agreed that it was "expedient to take into consideration the general principles of the law of nations." By article 18, belligerent warships were forbidden to "make use of neutral ports, roadsteads, or territorial waters for replenishing or increasing their supplies of war material or their armament, or for completing their crews." By article 25, a neutral power was to be "bound to exercise such surveillance as the means at its disposal allow to prevent any violation of the provisions of the above Articles occurring in its ports or roadsteads or in its waters."

[154] 30 *Op. Atty. Gen.* 316 (italics inserted).

[155] See, for example, the statement by Cemil Bilsel regarding justification of Turkey's action in preventing the departure of two Roumanian vessels from Istanbul harbor (*Amer. Jour. Int. Law*, XXXVIII [1944], pp. 546, 554).

[156] See section 3, *infra*.

[157] Charles Francis Adams, *Before and After the Treaty of Washington* (1902), p. 141.

pointed out, however, the named vessels were under responsible commanders operating for a government whose belligerency was recognized. Neutrality rules applicable not only under such circumstances but under conditions of international war were to come in for critical reëxamination, as the following section will endeavor to show.

3. CHANGING CONCEPTS OF NEUTRAL DUTIES

a. Developments Prior to the Second World War

Provisions in treaties of the United States relating to neutrality go farther back than the date of formulation by President Washington and his Cabinet of international law principles asserting neutral rights and obligations as "crystallized from . . . European treaties and practice." [158] Many clauses in early treaties related to contraband of war. Those with France (1778), the Netherlands (1782), Sweden (1783), Prussia (1785 and 1799), Great Britain (1794), and Spain (1795) contained contraband lists. The first of these instruments referred in the preamble to the parties' willingness to "fix" in an equitable and permanent manner the rules "which ought to be followed." It also referred to "just Rules of free Intercourse" and to "reciprocal Utility," but not directly to preëxisting law.[159] The treaty with Sweden made reference to what "ought" to be followed. Those with the Netherlands and Prussia, respectively, specified what was to be followed, and emphasized equality and reciprocity as basic principles.

In bilateral agreements of the nineteenth century, particularly those with Latin American republics, the United States commonly included lists of contraband articles.[160] The question in-

[158] Bemis, *The American Secretaries of State*, II, 296.

[159] Treaty of Amity and Commerce (Miller, *Treaties*, II, 3, 4). With this preamble may be compared language in the treaty of alliance with France, signed at the same time, with its recital of what the parties proposed to do in the event of Great Britain's hindering French commerce "in a manner contrary to the Rights of Nations."

See the useful list of treaty provisions relating to neutral rights and duties for the period from 1778 to 1936, in Sen. Doc. 24, 75th Cong., 1st Sess. (1937).

[160] See the comparative presentation in the document cited at the end of the preceding note.

evitably arose of whether international customary law set limits to what could be classified as contraband. In actual practice the claim that each state could define contraband for its own purpose, except in so far as it had limited itself by treaties (and then only in relation to the other signatories), seems not to have been effectively denied.[161] When belligerents in the First World War greatly extended contraband lists, the Department of State in a circular of August 15, 1914, invoked "well-recognized principles of international law" in support of a neutral's right to trade with belligerents, but added, regarding contraband:

> What is contraband of war is to be determined by international law and usage, influenced in some degree by the positions assumed by the belligerents. As there is no final tribunal for the definite determination of these international questions, they are not as determinable as questions of domestic law. There are no general treaties amongst the nations of the world determinative of contraband of war.[162]

Such a "general treaty" was the objective in the framing of the Declaration of London, the signatories to which "agreed that the rules . . . correspond *in substance* with the generally recognized principles of international law." [163] The declaration was not ratified, and the problem of defining contraband remained without a multilateral settlement.[164] Some of the bilateral treaties which had sought to meet the problem had also been designed to assure that judicial procedure in the captor state against alleged contraband carriers would be "according to law," a phrasing which would presumably be broad enough to include international law relating to prize.[165]

[161] The statement to the contrary in the *Prometheus* case (2 Hong Kong Law Reports 207 (1906–07), does not seem to express what was the prevailing rule of law. See the statement of Attorney General Knox (section 1, note 13, *supra*).

[162] *For. Rel.*, 1914, Supp., p. 275. On the general development, see Geoffrey Butler and Simon Maccoby, *The Development of International Law* (1928), pp. 292–330, and, on American policy, Carlton Savage, *Policy of the United States toward Maritime Commerce in War*, vol. I.

[163] Preliminary provision; text in *For. Rel.*, 1909, p. 318 (italics inserted).

[164] See section 1, notes 13 and 15, *supra*.

[165] Treaties with the Central American Federation, 1825, 8 *Stat.* 322 (art. XVIII); Peru-Bolivian Confederation, 1836, 8 *Stat.* 487 (art. XV); Venezuela, 1836, 8 *Stat.* 466 (art. XIX); Ecuador, 1839, 8 *Stat.* 534 (art. XIX); New Granada, 1846, 9 *Stat.* 881 (art. XIX); Guatemala, 1849, 10

Legal controversies about neutral duties under treaties have, of course, involved more than definition of contraband and procedure in prize courts. At the time of the Crimean War, for example, there was a question of foreign enlistments in the United States, with particular reference to the Anglo-American Convention of July 3, 1815, as continued by conventions of 1818 and 1827. The Attorney General at the time found that some treaty provisions which did not refer to the general law at all were "but declaratory of the law of nations."[166] At the beginning of the First World War there were serious questions that were not settled, although the "doctrine" and "precedents" of international law might be acknowledged.[167] It seems clear that not all of the Hague Conventions of 1907 were declaratory of existing international law, a good example being article 23 of Convention XIII.[168]

Stat. 873 (art. XVIII); El Salvador, 1850, 10 *Stat.* 891 (art. XIX). The treaties of amity, commerce, and navigation which the United States made with Latin American countries up to about the middle of the century followed, to a large extent, the same general form. The treaty with Costa Rica signed July 10, 1851 (10 *Stat.* 916), marked a departure from the use of this model (Miller, *Treaties,* V, 1003–1004).

For an interpretation of one article of a treaty with a Latin American state which provided for "perfect neutrality," see 11 *Op. Atty. Gen.* 67, 391.

As is well known, the principal controversies about procedure in dealing with alleged contraband carriers have come not with Latin American states but with principal maritime states in Europe. Illustrative of the United States government's critical attitude is the statement made concerning the British black-listing device in the First World War, that it condemned "without notice, without hearing, and in advance" (*For. Rel.,* 1916, Supp., p. 422).

[166] 7 *Op. Atty. Gen.* 367 (1855).

[167] 30 *Op. Atty. Gen.* 316.

[168] The preamble recited that in cases not covered by the convention it was convenient to take into consideration the general principles of the law of nations, but stated that the "common rules" which the parties agreed to observe could not "modify provisions laid down in existing general Treaties."

Article 23, relating to prizes in neutral ports and roadsteads, was not accepted by the United States, which by reservation excluded it. The article was the subject of judicial consideration in the case of the *Appam* (243 U.S. 124), decided in 1917. It also came into the discussion which followed the capture by the Germans of the American steamer *City of Flint* in 1940 and the taking of the vessel into a neutral port. On the points (1) that the article in question was considered an addition to customary rules, and (2) that the United States reservation to it, while not formally acknowledged or accepted by other contracting parties, was printed with the official text of the convention in the German *Reichsgesetzblatt,* see C. C. Hyde, "The City of Flint," *Amer. Jour. Int. Law,* XXXIV (1940), 89–95.

In the period between the First and Second World Wars, multilateral treaty making in the Western Hemisphere sometimes involved references to international law relating to neutrality, but without complete clarification of substantive rules. In the same year that the Kellogg-Briand Pact became a part of the law of the United States, this country had a part in consolidating through treaties some of the codification work of the Commission of Jurists which served the Conference of American States. The United States delegation to the Sixth Conference was instructed that, "in many cases the Commission . . . has set forth what it apparently has considered International Law should be." Of the projects submitted at this conference, the instructions noted: "Most of them contain subjects which are either outside the realm of International Law or on which the practice of Nations has not been sufficiently uniform as to warrant the conclusion that it has crystallized into International Law." [169] However, the Convention regarding Maritime Neutrality, which was one of the products of the conference, seems to have been considered by the American government as in line with the basic assumptions underlying the Hague Conventions of 1907 concerning neutrality. In the preamble of the 1928 agreement, the parties acknowledged that neutrality "creates rights and imposes obligations of impartiality," and the first article referred to cargo "prohibited" by international law.[170]

[169] *For. Rel.*, 1928, I, 543.

[170] See Chapter I, note 64, *supra*.

Referring to the United States as a "Power which is very much interested in the laws of neutrality," Secretary Hughes, before the fifth session of the Second Committee of the Conference on February 1, commented on Project No. 9 (Maritime Neutrality). In regard to one article, he raised the question of whether it was in accordance with international law and, concerning another, the question of whether it was more specific than a corresponding article of Hague Convention XIII of 1907. A draft submitted by a subcommittee to the Committee on Public International Law on February 14 contained the expression "prohibited transport." On the same day, in a session of the committee, Dr. J. B. Scott defended the American delegate's proposal to substitute for "contraband," as it had appeared in an early draft, some expression of more general import, since (1) experience had emphasized the difficulty or impossibility of defining "contraband," and (2) the latter word was not large enough to cover the transportation of some things that should be covered. In the course of his remarks he said that "we are here to codify" existing law (MS, Sixth Annual Conference of American States, 1928: Minutes and Reports of Committees, part I).

Five years later the Anti-War Treaty contemplated the adoption by the parties of a solidary attitude in the event of a conflict and made mention of the means authorized by international law, but did not specify those means.[171] The Buenos Aires Convention of December 23, 1936, for Coördination, Extension and Fulfillment of Existing Treaties, was signed without prejudice to the "universal principles of neutrality" in the event of war outside the Western Hemisphere. Colombia's reservation expressed the view that the treaty words, "in their character as neutrals," implied "a new concept of international law which allows a distinction to be drawn between the aggressor and the attacked, and to treat them differently," but the United States ratified the convention subject to the declaration that reservations were not amendments to the text and not intended to be controlling upon the United States.[172]

In certain bilateral commitments of the period, the United States included exceptions clauses referring more or less specifically to neutrality,[173] but in view of the Congressional joint

---

The draft convention had originally contained provisions intended, in the interest of neutrals, to change existing practice, but there was objection to variations from general usage, and the subcommittee took account of desires that there should be general conformity to the practice of nations. The convention as finally approved followed largely Hague Convention XIII of 1907, with some changes to take into account measures that neutrals had taken to preserve their rights during the First World War. It was considered "indispensable that the practice of nations should be strictly observed, as it would be undesirable on the part of the American states to attempt to change the general rights of all neutrals by a special agreement of their own" (*Report of the Delegates of the United States of America to the Sixth International Conference of American States* [1928], pp. 18–19).

[171] See Chapter II, section 1, *supra.*

[172] "The United States of America holds that the reservations . . . do not constitute an amendment to the text, but that such reservations, interpretations, and definitions by separate governments are solely for the benefit of such respective governments and are not intended to be controlling upon the United States of America" (51 *Stat.* 116, at 122; see also 151).

[173] This is illustrated in the field of commercial treaties and agreements. Exceptions clauses commonly referred to obligations under treaties as well as to neutrality in more general terms. See, for example, article XVI, 1(f) of the trade agreements with Great Britain, signed November 17, 1938 (54 *Stat.* [2] 1904), by which the agreement was not to interfere with rights or obligations under any treaty or other international instrument in force between the parties, and article IV, paragraph 1, of the Treaty of Commerce and Navigation with Iraq, signed December 3, 1938 (54 *Stat.* [2] 1790),

resolution of August 31, 1935, as amended February 9, 1936, and the Neutrality Act of May 1, 1937, it would seem that some of these clauses contemplated measures that were parts of municipal law or authorized thereby, even if the latter went beyond what international law required.[174]

More significant than some of the technical provisions in bilateral treaties was the developing idea that states resorting to war should not thereby acquire rights. The use made in this connection of the Kellogg-Briand Pact, even before the Second World War, has already been noted.[175] About the middle of the interwar period, a British government memorandum had declared that "as between Members of the League, there can be no neutral rights, because there can be no neutrals."[176] While four South American states declared their neutrality in the Chaco War in 1933, the Commission of Neutrals in the Chaco

---

by which the provisions were not to interfere with rights or obligations arising under the Covenant of the League of Nations.

[174] As is well known, the United States neutrality legislation of 1935 and 1936, as applied to embargoes upon arms and munitions destined for Italy, was questioned by certain of its critics as possibly in violation of an existing commercial treaty with Italy. On the other hand, there was serious questioning of isolationist views that were written into legislation. Illustrative are the following remarks of Senator Tom Connally on August 24, 1935 (79 *Cong. Rec.* 14433):

"I cannot . . . subscribe to the doctrine that we should in advance by statute put ourselves in a plaster cast internationally, and give up whatever international influence America may possess toward peace and toward the pacification of disputes throughout all the world. I cannot subscribe to the doctrine that no matter where the contest, no matter what the issue, America in advance promises that she will exert no influence, will do no act either to bring about peace or to prevent the outrage of the weak and the defenseless by the powerful and by the aggressor."

On so-called "neutrality" laws that are purely domestic legislation, see Charles G. Fenwick, *International Law* (3d ed., 1948), pp. 651–652.

One trade agreement of the period, that with Venezuela (54 *Stat.* [2] 2375), which contained the usual exception clause to the effect that the engagement would not be construed to prevent the adoption or enforcement of measures relating to neutrality, was signed two days after passage of the Act of November 4, 1939, which lifted the embargo on arms and munitions of war. Differences concerning interpretation or execution of the agreement were to be decided by the pacific means recognizd by international law "in conformity with treaties and conventions in force between the Parties."

[175] See Chapter II, section 1, *supra*.

[176] *Parl. Pap.*, Miscellaneous no. 12 (1929), Cmd. 3452.

Dispute seemed to emphasize the transitional state of fundamental rules when it referred to a "re-examination of many formerly existing precepts of international law," and observed: "An effective rule of international procedure does not always come into being fully grown, but arrives at its greatest prestige through a period of growth starting often from the mere sowing of an idea which acquires force and vigor through its appeal to the imagination of the peoples . . . of the world." [177]

In the early years of the nation's history the United States had sometimes derived commercial advantage from its neutrality,[178] and in the First World War there was a near doubling of export trade from 1914 to 1916 and, in nearly three years of neutrality, an increase in the excess of exports over imports from approximately four hundred seventy millions to over two billions of dollars.[179] However, with the development of new devices for business controls in wartime, for commerce destruction, and for the isolation of countries through new-style "blockades," there had come to be less opportunity for neutral traders to profit. The idea of neutrality as a hostilities-limiting device, which draws lines within which the battles may go on, in a sense treats war as a disease, and denies that any war is a direct concern of every state,[180] was offset by the growing feeling that an attitude of indifference to war-making was not a moral one.

Five years before the outbreak of World War II, a group of private jurists concluded that if one party to the Kellogg-Briand

[177] Translation in *For. Rel.*, 1932, V, 211.

[178] On the importance of commercial interests in the neutrality of Washington's administration, see C. S. Hyneman, *The First American Neutrality* (1934), and C. M. Thomas, *American Neutrality in 1793* (1931). See also, in this general connection, the much-quoted statement of Jefferson that he hoped the new world would "fatten on the follies of the old" (*Writings*, Ford ed., V, 197).

[179] Ethel C. Phillips, "American Participation in Belligerent Commercial Controls, 1914–1917," *Amer. Jour. Int. Law,* XXVII (1933), 675.

For an example of foreign criticism of the "vaunted neutrality" of the United States in the early part of the First World War, see *Papers Relating to the Foreign Relations of the United States: The Lansing Papers, 1914–1920,* I, 761.

[180] Cf. E. M. Borchard, "International Law," *Encyclopedia of the Social Sciences* (1937), VII, 167–173.

Pact should resort to war in violation of it, other parties in their relations with the violator might rightfully decline to observe the duties prescribed by international law, apart from the Pact, for a neutral in relation to a belligerent.[181] On the eve of the Second World War, a group of American jurists set forth, in the final article of a draft convention on Rights and Duties of Neutral States in Naval and Aerial War, published for the Harvard Research in International Law, that "every neutral State has a direct interest in the observance by belligerents of the law defining neutral rights, and a violation . . . of a neutral right of one neutral State constitutes a violation of a neutral right of all neutral States." [182] At the same time certain of these jurists produced a set of draft rules which seemed to reflect changing concepts of neutral duties, since their authors looked to new relationships between aggressors and outside states as well as between the victims of aggression and outside states. In the draft appeared such terms as "defending states," co-defending states" and "supporting states," as well as the term "aggressor." [183]

In his speech of October 5, 1937, President Roosevelt vigorously proclaimed the intention to quarantine aggressors. Warning that the "landmarks and traditions which have marked the progress of civilization toward a condition of law, order and justice" were "being wiped away," he declared that "the peace-loving nations must make a concerted effort in opposition to those violations of treaties and those ignorings of humane instincts which today are creating a state of international anarchy and instability from which there is no escape through mere isolation." On the unsoundness of a policy of indifference to foreign wars, he declared that "there is a solidarity and interdependence about the modern world, both technically and morally, which makes it impossible for any nation completely to isolate itself from

[181] " 'Budapest' Articles of Interpretation of the Pact for the Renunciation of War," adopted at Budapest, *International Law Association: Report of the 38th Conference* (1934), p. 66.

[182] *Amer. Jour. Int. Law,* XXXIII, Supp. (1939), 788. On the general subject of a more adequate multilateral treaty base for neutrality and possible interneutral coöperation for enforcing neutral rights, see Philip C. Jessup, *Neutrality,* vol. IV, *Today and Tomorrow,* published in 1936.

[183] *Amer. Jour. Int. Law,* XXXIII, Supp. (1939).

economic and political upheavals in the rest of the world," and that "the 90 per cent who want to live in peace under the law and in accordance with moral standards that have received almost universal acceptance through the centuries, can and must find some way to make their will prevail." As to the nature of the standards which he had in mind, the President said, "The questions involved relate not merely to violations of specific provisions of particular treaties; they are questions of war and of peace, of international law, and especially of principles of humanity. It is true that they involve definite violations of agreements, and especially of the . . . Nine Power Treaty. But they also involve problems of world economy, world security, and world humanity." [184]

The emerging problem of reconciling traditional concepts of neutrality with the kind of quarantining of aggressors which the President advocated, or with some effective form of collective security,[185] inevitably involved a rethinking of the whole concept of war in relation to the law. The hostilities which began in September 1939 provided an element of urgency.

b. Developments During and Subsequent to the Second World War

As applied in the Second World War, neutrality practice was in some instances affected by preëxisting treaties.[186] There still existed, by common acceptance, a body of rights and duties identifiable with the status of a neutral. The principal European belligerents evinced distrust, however, of their opponents' respect for this law. The official organ of Nazi Germany declared that

[184] *Department of State Press Releases,* October 9, 1937, pp. 275–279.

[185] For the view that it is possible to reconcile a kind of neutrality, and the use of reprisals, with collective security, see H. Lauterpacht, "Neutrality and Collective Security," *Politica,* II (1936), 133–155. For an argument that there was, even under traditional neutrality, no neutral duty to act impartially, see Clyde Eagleton, "The Duty of Impartiality on the Part of a Neutral," *Amer. Jour. Int. Law,* XXXIV (1940), 99–104.

[186] The situation of Egypt in relation to Great Britain is particularly illustrative. See Robert R. Wilson, " 'Non-Belligerency' in Relation to the Terminology of Neutrality," *Amer. Jour. Int. Law,* XXXV (1941), 121–123, and "Some Current Questions Relating to Neutrality," *ibid.,* XXXVII (1943), 651–656.

the neutrals were, to England, only a means to an end.[187] After the German invasion of Belgium, the Netherlands, Norway, and Denmark, a British editorial opinion viewed neutrality, in the situation which had developed, as an "anachronism," and regarded the Nazi war on neutrals not as a mere incident dictated by military exigencies but as an essential part of the plans of the German leaders.[188]

In the United States, public opinion moved but slowly toward the principles which President Roosevelt had enunciated in his speech of October 5, 1937. As late as September 21, 1939, the President, at the time of his asking Congress to repeal the embargo upon arms, spoke of putting the country "back on the solid footing of real and traditional neutrality." [189]

The making of the Hull-Lothian agreement of September 2, 1940, marked a definite veering away, by the executive, from old-style neutrality. The Attorney General's opinion relating to the agreement was directed to a technical analysis of municipal law provisions [190] and did not touch upon the questions of international law involved. An authority on American constitutional law expressed the view that the executive had invaded the field of Congressional power to declare war (by departing from the country's duty as a neutral and thus drawing the nation closer to war).[191] It seemed difficult to reconcile the new position of the United States with its obligations under Hague Convention XIII, or, if this were technically inapplicable because of the general-participation clause, those under customary in-

[187] *Völkischer Beobachter,* January 17, 1940, p. 4. In a statement reported from the Berlin press after the outbreak of hostilities between Italy and Greece in 1940, there was the assertion that "in the decisive battles for the new European order, no nation adhering to the party of the enemies of the new order may hope to remain unrecognized as such by retiring into the semi-darkness of 'neutrality'" (*New York Times,* October 30, 1940, 4:1).

[188] *The Times* (London), September 2, 1940, p. 5; September 4, 1940, p. 5. The same paper had previously said (August 30, 1940, p. 5), "One moral which seems clearly to emerge from the experience of the war is the qualification which will have to be applied to the concept of neutrality . . . The smaller countries of Europe will rightly and naturally want to paddle their own canoes. But . . . they will have henceforth to do so in convoy."

[189] *Department of State Bulletin,* I, 278 (September 23, 1939).

[190] 39 *Op. Atty. Gen.* 484–496 (1940).

[191] E. S. Corwin, in *New York Times,* October 13, 1940, E6, 7.

ternational law.[192] By the month following the Hull-Lothian agreement it was being concluded by some legalists that the United States was not a neutral in relation to the European hostilities.[193]

That the Axis states were making propaganda uses of international law was suggested by the Secretary of State in an address of October 26, 1940, to the Press Club of Washington. Cordell Hull said, of the nations "vaguely describing themselves as the 'have nots'":

> They cynically disregard every right of neutral nations, and, having occupied several such countries, they then proceed to warn all peaceful nations that they must remain strictly neutral until an invading force is actually crossing their borders.[194]

Even under the League of Nations plan for collective security, there was no clear acceptance by all member states of the notion that, if neutrality were no longer to mean the acceptance of duties in relation to an aggressor, each state must take sides, in a military way or otherwise. In the early part of World War II there evolved a new descriptive term, "nonbelligerency," whose connotation was difficult to determine, unless, indeed, by reasoning simply that neutral duties were being violated.[195] The tendency to distinguish a status somewhere between a perfect neutrality, in the "old" (i.e., nineteenth and early twentieth century) sense of the term, and outright belligerency, suggests the tenacity with which the old concept held on and was associated

[192] See Herbert W. Briggs, "Neglected Aspects of the Destroyer Deal," *Amer. Jour. Int. Law,* XXXIV (1940), 569–587. On other developing questions relating to neutral rights and duties, see Lester H. Woolsey, "Government Traffic in Contraband," *ibid.,* pp. 498–503, and "The Taking of Foreign Ships in American Ports," *ibid.,* XXXV (1941), 497–506.

[193] See statement of Quincy Wright in "The Transfer of Destroyers to Great Britain," *Amer. Jour. Int. Law,* XXXIV (1940), 685, 689; and Charles G. Fenwick's statement in "Neutrality on the Defensive," *ibid.,* p. 699: "The United States is clearly no longer neutral in the normal, technical sense of the term." See also the latter author's *American Neutrality: Trial and Failure* (1940), *passim.*

[194] *New York Times,* October 27, 1940, p. 34.

[195] As suggested by Briggs, "Neglected Aspects of the Destroyer Deal," p. 569n. See also Josef Kunz, "Neutrality and the European War, 1939–1940," *Mich. Law Rev.,* XXXIX (1941), 719–754.

with some kind of peace.[196] In the United States, in such a period as that from June 1940 to December 1941, advocacy of neutrality in the traditional sense tended to be widely branded as an isolationist, escapist device which might lull into unpreparedness and cover a retreat from a moral choice.

The occasion for a full discussion of the law of neutrality was provided by the introduction of the Lend-Lease bill. The Secretary of State and administration leaders in Congress relied upon the principle of self-defense as a basic right of all nations and one which, it was urged, must take precedence over anything in the Hague Conventions or in customary international law.[197] There was the further argument that a fundamental rule of international, as of domestic, law was that parties must obey the rules on a basis of mutuality, and that if one country violated basic rules it could not, with unclean hands, claim that another country should strictly adhere in relations with it to *less* basic laws, at the risk of destruction.[198] The majority of the Senate Foreign Relations Committee appeared to endorse the Budapest (International Law Association) Articles of Interpretation of the Kellogg-Briand Pact when it said, in reporting the Lend-Lease bill:

> The Kellogg-Briand Pact is recognized by eminent scholars of international law to give any signatory the power, where the pact's provi-

[196] See Robert R. Wilson, "'Non-Belligerency' in Relation to the Terminology of Neutrality," pp. 121–123.

[197] The Secretary said in part: "It may be urged that the provisions of the U.S. Code and the quoted provisions of the Hague Convention are declaratory of international law on the subjects mentioned and that to do the things contemplated by the proposed act would render us unneutral. This would be largely true under ordinary circumstances but we are not here dealing with an ordinary war situation. Rather, we are confronted with a situation that is extraordinary in character." The full statement is reproduced in *Department of State Bulletin*, January 18, 1941, at p. 90.

[198] See the remarks (in a radio address) of Senator Walter F. George, 87 *Cong. Rec.* (10) A281, January 29, 1941; also the statement in the majority report of the Foreign Relations Committee (cited in note 199) that mutuality is a doctrine that prevails in international law, as in equity.

Senator Connally argued that when Germany and Italy became parties to the Kellogg-Briand Pact they agreed that if they should attack any other nation in violation of the Pact, any other nation which was a signatory to the Pact might supply arms and munitions to the nation attacked or invaded (87 *Cong. Rec.* [2] 1158, February 19, 1941).

sions are violated by another nation, to cease to abide by the neutrality laws which govern in normal times, and to "Supply the State attacked with financial or material assistance, including munitions of war." [199]

In the course of discussion on the bill, Secretary of War Stimson expressed the view that the nations accepting the Pact had "adopted really a new legal view of the word 'war' in the relations and the obligations and the duties that come under it as between each other." [200] In the Senate debate Senator Warren R. Austin endeavored to show that the "rules of the game" had been changed—that international law had been changed not only by treaty but by custom.[201]

Arguments which the opponents of the bill drew from the law of nations varied from simple statements that the measure violated "every principle of neutrality and international law" [202] and would "violate American treaties, laws, traditions, and what remains of international law," [203] to the accusation that the bill would be a "legislative condonation of acts of war." [204] The Budapest Articles of Interpretation, the opposition urged, would "violate everything the people of the United States ever stood for"; "under no circumstances whatever, under international law as commonly interpreted and enforced today," it was argued, could the United States "justify the particular course sought for under this bill." [205] On the general subject of continued ap-

[199] *To Promote the Defense of the United States* (H.R. 1776), Sen. Rep. 45, 77th Cong., 1st Sess., p. 4.

[200] Senate Committee on Foreign Relations, 77th Cong., 1st Sess., *Hearings on S.275* (superseded by H.R. 1776), pt. 1 (January 27–February 3, 1941), p. 123.

[201] 87 *Cong. Rec.* (1) 1050, February 17, 1941. Senator Austin applied this in an endeavor to show that the United States, in opening ports to the British navy, was acting realistically in its own defense.

[202] *Ibid.*, p. 563, February 4, 1941 (remarks of Representative George A. Dondero in the House).

[203] *Ibid.*, p. 797, February 8, 1941 (remarks of Representative Hamilton Fish in the House). Representative George H. Tinkham submitted that acts under the bill would be "violations of a vital principle of international law of long standing" (*ibid.*, p. 627).

[204] *Ibid.* (2) 1244, February 21, 1941 (remarks of Dr. Edmund A. Walsh, S.J., printed in the *Record* at the request of Senator Gillette).

[205] *Ibid.*, p. 1325, February 24, 1941 (remarks of Senator John A. Danaher). Senator Burton K. Wheeler said: "I have no idea who are the eminent scholars of international law, referred to by the committee, who supplied

plicability of rules fixing neutral rights and duties, Senator Guy M. Gillette secured Senate approval for printing in the *Record* a statement by Dr. Edmund A. Walsh, S.J., which contained the following:

> For every panel of distinguished authorities appearing in support of the contention that no international law is violated an equally imposing aggregation of experienced jurists is available ruling that it is flagrant violation of international law, at least of the law of nations, which the Government of the United States has so frequently invoked. The Kellogg Pact did not suspend these obligations, since several important reservations made by signatories respecting special circumstances and regional interests practically nullified the high purpose of that agreement and left each signatory free to act exactly as he deemed advisable for his national defense.[206]

Opponents of Lend-Lease in the House of Representatives failed to get favorable action on the Dworshak amendment, which would have inserted in the bill the statement that "Nothing in this act shall be construed as authorizing or permitting the authorization of any violation of international law." [207] Some cynical suggestions concerning international law came in the course of the debate, such as the observation that the law was "practically non-existent," [208] that it had gone "by the board" so far as Hitler and the Axis Powers were concerned,[209] that the law is "what victorious nations say it is," and that it is "written by the sword . . . and interpreted solely by victorious conquerors." [210] One member of the House suggested that

> international law is only a set of rules by which nations can get together after their troubles are over and see how much they owe each

---

so convenient an interpretation of our rights and duties with respect to other nations, but I may be pardoned for hoping that the United States will not sink to their moral and ethical level. Their thesis is the negation of all law except self-interest" (*ibid.*, p. 1588, March 1, 1941).

206 *Ibid.*, p. 1244, February 21, 1941.

207 *Ibid.* (1) 814, February 8, 1941.

208 *Ibid.*, p. 586, February 5, 1941 (remarks of Representative John Kee).

209 *Ibid.*, p. 798, February 8, 1941 (remarks of Representative Charles L. Gifford). The same speaker expressed the view that "international law has not gone entirely by the board as far as Guatemala and other friendly nations are concerned."

210 *Ibid.* (2) 1256, February 21, 1941 (remarks of Senator William J. Bulow).

other. That is all its effect is, even though some say that international law may prevent our doing some things that are to our interest to do. In the present-day world Hitler, Mussolini, and every other ruler abroad ignores international law and the rules and regulations drawn up in accordance with those general basic principles . . . at any time it pleases them so to do.[211]

Hearings on the proposed legislation elicited various opinions on the nature of treaties in general, particularly multilateral ones. One idea was that if Germany had breached the Kellogg-Briand Pact, she had not done so *with regard to the United States,* and therefore the United States could not depart from preëxisting rules of international law merely because of what Germany had done—a kind of segregated bilaterality within the multilateral treaty structure being suggested.[212] One supporter of the administration bill in the Senate urged the contractual basis of international law in an effort to support his argument that the United States owed no obligations under that law to international outlaws.[213]

With the passage of the bill the United States became committed to a positive program not consistent with notions of neutral obligations under traditional rules but ably and realistically urged as thoroughly consistent with the new conception of aggressive war and its legal consequences for the aggressor. It was, of course, possible to make a case for United States policy by positing that the conventional rules regarding neutrality, specifically those in the Hague Conventions of 1907, were tech-

[211] *Ibid.* (1) 576, February 5, 1941 (remarks of Representative Edouard V. Izac).

[212] Senate Committee on Foreign Relations, 77th Cong., 1st Sess., *Hearings on S.275,* pt. 2 (February 4–10, 1941), p. 463 (remarks of Professor Herbert Wright). For discussion of a similar point before the American Society of International Law some five years earlier (in connection with Italy's resort to force against Ethiopia), see *Proceedings* of the Society for 1936, at pp. 154, 155.

[213] 87 *Cong. Rec.* (2) 1162, February 19, 1941 (remarks of Senator Josiah W. Bailey). The Senator said, in part: "International law is not derived from sovereignty; it has no sanction. International law is not laid down; international law is derived from contract, which makes all the difference in the world, because a contract rests upon mutuality." At a later point in the debate, Senator Bailey said that "international law is based on the obligations of contracts, and not the sanctions of treaties, and there is a great difference" (*ibid.,* p. 1590, March 1, 1941).

nically inapplicable or that, if they were applicable, the aggressor states had forfeited any right which might have existed under them to demand the traditional abstention and impartiality of states not engaged in hostilities. Such a position would not necessarily have implied the end of neutrality as a body of rules of international law.[214] Spokesman for the new point of view in American foreign policy seemed, however, to anticipate something more than escape from traditional neutral duties through interpretation of particular treaties. In his Havana address of March 27, 1941, Attorney General Robert H. Jackson took the position that the League of Nations Covenant had begun the modification of the old concept that all wars were just and legal, and submitted that the Pact of Paris and the Argentine Anti-War Treaty had completed the outlawry of war. While claiming that the applicability of traditional neutrality rules had thus been superseded (although he thought some scholarship had "not caught up" with the century), and that as a result third parties had a right (although not a duty) of discriminating against an aggressor, he said that the new multilateral treaties which he mentioned, "by altering fundamentally the place of war in international law," had "effected a parallel change in the law and status of neutrality." The United States, he added, claimed "the wider rights which that change imparts." [215]

As a separate ground to provide legal justification for the new American policy, the Attorney General invoked the fundamental international law principle of self-defense. This he found to supply an adequate basis for what the United States had set

[214] The status of "non-belligerency" was apparently regarded, during World War II, as an alternative to neutrality or belligerency.

[215] Text in *Amer. Jour. Int. Law,* XXXV (1941), 348–359. The Attorney General's statement that a "state which has gone to war in violation of its obligations acquires no right to equality of treatment from other states, unless treaty obligations require different handling of affairs," would leave no room for an argument that if such an agreement as Hague Convention XIII of 1907 were technically inapplicable, its rules could nevertheless be regarded as assertive of independently existing (that is, customary) international law. The Attorney General did not in this address discuss the Pact of Paris as a treaty of superior obligation for its parties. See, however, the address of Justice Jackson some six months later (October 2, 1941), before the American Bar Association, on the developing legal significance of the Pact (Chapter II, note 20, *supra*).

out to do, notwithstanding the fact that in certain quarters the government was charged with "ignoring or violating the less fundamental rules of neutrality" which, the Attorney General submitted, were "both in fact and in law, irrelevant to the existing situations."[216]

The extent of departure, so far as the United States was concerned, from a "perfect" neutrality was apparent from the fact that some of the sinkings which it denounced in 1941 were of ships that were actually in belligerent-convoyed groups. The strong moral position of the United States and its military and industrial strength were such that they could be a major factor in effecting the transition from the traditional concept of neutrality to a new one. The solution did not lie in the mere creation of a more adequate multilateral treaty base for neutrality, with interneutral coöperation for enforcing action under it.[217] Retention of the concept of neutrality through such an arrangement, even with recognition of the rule of some discrimination against law-breakers as a matter of legal right (and not simply a matter of practice), would have fallen short of what the architects of the United Nations Charter eventually devised.

The transition to a world-wide collective security system could not be suddenly accomplished. It was perhaps inevitable that in

[216] Havana address referred to in preceding note. Such moves prior to Pearl Harbor as (1) those for Western Hemisphere solidarity, emphasized in a memorandum of Under Secretary Sumner Welles, July 1, 1941, in support of a Uruguayan proposal to have a new content and definition of inter-American solidarity (*Department of State Bulletin,* July 5, 1941, pp. 8–9), (2) the agreement on integrating the defense production of the country with that of Canada, a belligerent (55 *Stat.* 1444), and (3) protective action taken by the United States concerning Iceland and Greenland, could doubtless have been legally justified on the ground of self-defense.

In 1946 Mr. Welles testified, with respect to the meeting between President Roosevelt and Prime Minister Churchill which resulted in the Atlantic Charter: "The President had during preceding weeks told me of his thought that in view of the increasingly serious world situation, in view of the spread of the war in Europe, that nothing would be more valuable from the standpoint of keeping alive in a . . . darkening world some principles of international law, some principles of moral and human decency, than for him to make some kind of a public statement of the objectives in international relations in which the Government of the United States believed" (*Hearings before the Joint Committee on the Investigation of the Pearl Harbor Attack* [1946], 79th Cong., 1st Sess., pt. 2, p. 537).

[217] See note 182, *supra*.

the early stages of the process the central importance of the principle of legality, as distinct from power, should not receive primary emphasis.[218] Because of the very unevenness in the international community, some states must naturally accept more responsibilities than others for the maintenance of international peace and security, and some of those not taking primary roles of enforcement in the suppression of aggression may be nominally committed but relatively inactive. The coming into use, in journalistic discussions in 1951 of possible alignments in a large-scale controversy, of such an expression as "neutralism," indicates that, however far-reaching has been the change in the legal conception of neutrality, some of the practical problems remain.

Among the legal questions which arise in connection with the application of the international law standard under conditions of the new collective security, two may be noted here because of their bearing upon treaty relationships. The first has to do with references in treaties made subsequent to the establishment of the United Nations Organization, to "neutrality" or some comparable expression. Thus it is somewhat striking to find, in the Geneva Conventions of August 12, 1949, for the protection of war victims, numerous references in such bodies of rules as those on the treatment of prisoners of war and on the protection of civilian persons in time of war, to "neutral state," "neutral power," and "neutral country." [219] The significance of these mentions of neutral states, powers, or territories, in multilateral formulations which also contain rather frequent references to international law, can only be surmised. It seems possible that, under the rule of article 103 of the United Nations Charter,

[218] Cf. Clyde Eagleton, "International Law and the Charter of the United Nations," *Amer. Jour. Int. Law*, XXXIX (1945), 751–754.

[219] The first of these expressions occurs twice in the Convention Relative to the Treatment of Prisoners of War and four times in the Convention Relative to the Protection of Civilian Persons in Time of War. "Neutral Power" is used six times in the convention on prisoners of war and three times in that on protecton of civilian persons. There are twelve references to "neutral country" in the convention on prisoners of war and four in that on the protection of civilian persons. At four places in the convention on prisoners of war the reference to "neutral Power" is to such power "or non-belligerent" (article 4B [2] and article 122). Texts in *Geneva Conventions of August 12, 1949, for Protection of War Victims*, Department of State Publication 3938, General Foreign Policy Series 34 (1950).

meaning would be found not inconsistent with the new collective security system. That system is not directly referred to in Resolution 10 of the Geneva Conference, according to which, "The Conference considers that the conditions under which a Party to a conflict can be recognized as a belligerent by Powers not taking part in this conflict, are governed by the general rules of international law on the subject and are in no way modified by the Geneva Conventions."

The second question is the more fundamental one of whether the elements of law on aggression and the duty to maintain international peace and security have now come to be based not merely upon the Charter of the United Nations and such other multilateral instruments as those now in force in the Western Hemisphere, but have come to be parts of international common law. It is, of course, true that not all members of the community of nations are parties to the basic treaty arrangements referred to.[220] It would appear, however, that only the most ardent of positivists would contend that such a provision as article II, paragraph 6, of the United Nations Charter represents nothing more than a device looking to the imposition, in violation of international law rights, of obligations upon non-member states. Constitutional development within the framework of the United Nations has been flexible enough to permit assumptions of power, by the General Assembly, such as that under the Uniting for Peace Resolution of 1950, where the purpose is the central one of preserving international peace and security. It would appear that obligations in relation to the latter might well become the most central element of the new international law.

[220] One of the new Geneva Conventions called forth, from a non-member of the United Nations, a reservation which may have bearing upon the general question. Article 99 of the Convention Relative to the Treatment of Prisoners of War contains a reference to "an act . . . forbidden . . . by international law, in force." Spain's signature of the convention was subject to the reservation that "under 'International Law in force' (article 99) Spain understands she only accepts that which arises from contractual sources or which has been previously elaborated by organizations in which she participates."

Chapter VI

SUMMARY AND CONCLUSION

States making treaties against a background of already existing law may by specific wording in their agreements take cognizance of that law as it is found in custom and prior treaties. They may reaffirm and reacknowledge in a very general way, or may indicate some special application to be made of, established rules.[1] They may, of course, project new rules designed for general or universal acceptance. Or they may contract that certain of the generally recognized rules shall not apply in the normal way in the relations of the signatories *inter se*. In any of these situations the effect of a treaty reference to international law may present a question of interpretation, and the latter may be complicated by reason of factors other than legal ones which have affected the making of the agreement.[2]

The treaty practice of the United States reveals much integration of conventional rules with customary ones. To only a limited extent has this been a process of transmuting law from customary to written form and thus securing greater definiteness. In large measure it has been a matter of attesting or confirming in a general way what is admitted as binding the parties at the time the treaties come into effect—or what may come to bind them at some

[1] On the common "lay error" of drawing a "sharp distinction between treaties and international law in general," see Philip C. Jessup, *A Modern Law of Nations* (1948), pp. 124–125. Some distinction, however, has frequently been made by treaty makers themselves, as will appear from the foregoing chapters.

[2] Cf. Lauterpacht's statement that, "unlike the case of contracts in the sphere of municipal law, treaties, or some of their provisions, are often a political substitute for rather than a legal expression of the agreement of the parties" ("Restrictive Interpretation and the Principle of Effectiveness in the Interpretation of Treaties," *Brit. Year Book Int. Law*, XXVI [1949], 82).

future time when there is occasion to apply the treaties.[3] Particular stipulations, unaccompanied by indication of how they are meant to apply in relation to what is already in force, are the rule rather than the exception. Clearly, the inclusion of such stipulations does not justify the inference that as a matter of customary international law the *reverse* of these rules would constitute the law, any more than the occurrence of a rule in a considerable number of treaties would necessarily prove the existence of universally established law to the same effect.[4] This conclusion does not overlook the importance of usage as a guide to treaty construction.[5] When, in exceptional cases, treaties make mention of the body of international law behind the particular agreements, they may do so for various purposes. These purposes can be conveniently considered under broad classifications according to substantive contents.

In United States treaties there have been numerous references to the law of nations in agreements concerning pacific settlement. These references have sometimes occurred in commitments to use peaceful means, but often in contexts which present more technical questions. As to the former, the United States has in its international agreements stopped short of unqualified commitments to refer disputes of every conceivable kind to specific judicial agencies such as the International Court of Justice; on the other hand, it has gone very far, through certain multilateral and bilateral instruments made in recent years, in the direction of obligatory jurisdiction. The strong position which the United States representatives took in the course of the framing of the Nuremberg Charter and at the time of the trials has helped to establish that,

[3] See the suggestion of Philip Marshall Brown that positivists tend to put treaty law ahead of custom, and his view that "with very rare exceptions . . . treaties do not create international law, but confirm and register established usage. Treaty-made law necessarily represents diplomatic compromise and frequently reveals gross inconsistencies with accepted usage" ("The Renovation of International Law," *Amer. Jour. Int. Law,* XXXVI [1942], 634).

[4] McNair, *The Law of Treaties,* pp. 255, 256.

[5] *Ibid.,* pp. 196, 252, 253, and cases there cited. It has been seen that in certain subject matters the very term "usage" has commonly occurred in American treaties, as, for example, in conventions relating to consular privileges and immunities, although not usually in provisions concerning diplomatic privileges and immunities, regarding which the international law standard has frequently been specified.

except for defensive measures, none but peaceful means resorted to in national policy will be consistent with the international law standard.

At a more technical level, the law has been specified in provisions of arbitration treaties setting criteria for distinguishing juridical questions. The designation of disputes "susceptible of settlement" by application of the principles of law presupposes that there can be disputes not within that description. To this position the United States has consistently held, despite a strong view (although still a minority one, it would appear) among publicists and governments that the concept of nonjusticiable disputes is unsound. The limiting effect of holding to a concept of nonjusticiable questions, in an international legal system which has traditionally imposed upon states no obligation to submit to any jurisdiction to which they have not assented, should presumably decrease with the progressive development of international law.

As the principal basis for awards in international adjudications, the international law standard has found frequent application in United States treaties. Such application is consistent with the Anglo-American view that arbitration, as well as what is specifically called "judicial settlement," is essentially a judicial procedure. Even when *ad hoc* bases for settlement have received approval, their application has sometimes been provided for along with that of the principles of international law not inconsistent therewith. Furthermore, assent to the application of "equity" as well as the law has, in general, not led to serious departures from legal principles. Nor has an authorization to apply "public" law brought about such a departure. Even in passing upon claims for which the United States has assumed liability (as, for example, where a foreign government has been discharged, by international agreement, from liability), members of domestic claims commissions of the United States have ordinarily taken the common statutory formula of "justice, equity and the law of nations" as instruction to apply the basic standard.

In a few of its agreements for international claims adjudications, the United States has referred to international law in provisions for waiving a respondent state's right to use, in a plea to the jurisdiction, the defense that local remedies have not been exhausted. In one such arrangement (in the terms of submission under the claims arbitral agreement of 1910 with Great Britain) the waiver was not a complete one. In a leading adjudication under another, in which a Calvo clause figured, a Mexican-American tribunal in the *North American Dredging Company* case interpreted a separate article of the convention so as to find, in spite of the article dealing with nonexhaustion of local remedies, that it did not have jurisdiction—a ruling which a domestic claims commission that later considered the same claim did not follow. The setting aside of this particular basic rule of law by specific agreement of the parties is still an exceptional rather than a normal procedure.

Although the very limited employment of waivers in connection with state responsibility here referred to (and also in connection with jurisdictional questions such as those touched upon in Chapter IV, section 2) would not justify broad conclusions in regard to the process, questions naturally arise concerning the limitations within which arrangements of the kind can legally be made. In a sense, any treaty provision authorizing what international law does not authorize might be regarded as at least a temporary relinquishment of a right or rights under that law. While positing certain fundamental rights, such as those of existence and independence, the prevailing concept of international law has in the past permitted states to go very far in the direction of doing, by contract, what would otherwise be inconsistent with the generally applicable law. In the absence of a principle that a threat of force (except, traditionally, force used upon the persons of negotiators) would invalidate a treaty thus secured, there was even the possibility of a valid treaty arrangement for the absorption of one state into another, with the reality or the fiction of consent by the former. Although there has been little progress toward marking them out with clarity, the idea of the supremacy of law presupposes some limits upon the right to waive by contract. For example, the attempted legalization of a regional tyranny under the label of a "new order" might conceivably transgress these limits, and the resulting hegemony might be found inconsistent with the essential purposes in a system of law.[6] A finding to this effect, which would be regardful not merely of the rights and interests of individual third states but of the collectivity of them, would presumably be a proper function for a community agency. In so far as treaties are found to affect international peace and security, there is an existing agency with competence to consider them, but there has come to be no routine censorship in connection with treaty-registration procedure. Much leeway remains within which states may relinquish rights in their relations *inter se*, and without some such leeway for experimentation, an important means of promoting the growth of the law might be lacking. The problem of keeping the uses of the method within reasonable bounds, in order to safeguard community interests, is obviously one in international organization and not merely in international law.

In the field of commerce and navigation, treaty provisions concerning the international law standard have not been very numerous. Other standards, such as those of most-favored-nation treatment and national treatment, have had greater utility in view of the fact that the basic law stops short of obligating a state to admit aliens or to trade with other states. Under certain circumstances, particularly in its agreements with states in which its nationals have previously had extraterritorial privileges, the United States has made reference to "modern" international law in arrangements for initiation of normal relations. Such provisions have sometimes, as in the Turkish-American establishment treaty of 1931, provided the general framework within which other standards might be applied.

Among the establishment matters commonly dealt with in general commercial treaties, the protection of alien-owned property furnished occasion for direct references to international law in fifteen agreements between 1923 and 1950. The meaningfulness of the provisions depends particularly upon the body of case law that has established the right of the alien owner to be free from uncompensated expropriation of that which he has acquired in ac-

[6] See Eric Voegelin, "Some Problems of German Hegemony," *Journal of Politics*, III (1941), 154–168; Quincy Wright, "International Law and the Totalitarian States," *Amer. Pol. Sci. Rev.*, XXXV (1941), 738–743; Charles Kruszewski, "Hegemony and International Law," *ibid.*, pp. 1127–1144.

cordance with the law in force at the time of acquisition. The United States has at times insisted upon the inclusion of a reference to the international law standard, along with a "due process" clause, even when other states concerned have claimed that, under their respective constitutions, uncompensated takings were in certain circumstances legal. Also encountered in this connection has been the idea that national treatment is the maximum which foreigners should be given as a matter of policy, and even the notion that national treatment is the maximum which foreigners can demand as of right under international law. Nationalization programs in various countries and new devices employed particularly since the beginning of the 1930's, including prohibition of exchange withdrawals and methods of rendering foreigners' investments unproductive and therefore unprofitable even without formal "takings," have led to complications. Difficulties of deciding what constitutes a "taking," and of evaluating for the purpose of determining what is "just" compensation, seem likely to continue. In view of the prevailing lack of complete agreement on what the international law standard now requires, there has seemed to be, from the point of view of United States policy, justification for supplementation with more precise rules. When such a term as "just" appears in provisions on compensation, there will presumably be, even without specific mention of international law, authorization for interpreters to apply the international law standard as a floor. Since each of the more recent bilateral commercial treaties which the United States has signed since the end of hostilities in the Second World War contains a compromissary clause whereby questions of interpretation and application not satisfactorily adjusted by diplomacy are, unless the parties shall agree to settlement by some other pacific means, to be submitted to the International Court of Justice, such questions as that of what compensation is just, adequate, or effective need not, in the last analysis, be left for decision by each interested party for itself.

The record of United States treaty making on the subject of river navigation reveals much invocation of international law in the diplomacy which led up to some of the agreements and, exceptionally, actual treaty specification of the standard. The rivers involved were in the Western Hemisphere, where there have been no such regional arrangements as have been made for some international rivers outside this hemisphere. In the most celebrated case in its early diplomatic history concerning river navigation, the United States secured navigation privileges not as a matter of recognizing what preëstablished law already gave, but as a grant from the riparian state.

Frequent acknowledgment of the international law principle concerning freedom of the seas marked the Anglo-American diplomacy of the nineteenth century relating to the slave trade, but the treaty of 1862 which marked the culmination of this diplomacy contained no direct reference to the standard. The British-led effort for multilateral arrangements to accomplish a humanitarian reform encountered American opposition based at least in part upon legal considerations, although the latter may not have been major factors in policy. Domestic political forces delayed full American coöperation through treaty until, with the rearrangement of these forces, the objective which had been sought through humanitarian effort could be attained. It was attained, not through a new rule of universal law, but through relinquishment in a bilateral treaty of the parties' right for their respective vessels to be free from visit and search if the vessels were suspected of carrying slaves on the high seas.

In general, the independence of states has not occasioned treaty references to international law except in connection with formulations on the rights and duties of states. The subject of intervention has provided occasion for a relatively small number of references, but the proscription of intervention by the American republics and the reconciliation of the principle of nonintervention with states' commitments under the collective-security systems of the United Nations and the Western Hemisphere have had much attention from treaty makers. In one bilateral treaty, that signed with Mexico on December 30, 1853, there was in the text as revised while it was before the United States Senate a direct mention of the law of nations, with the implication that that law authorized intervention under some circumstances. The unused provision did nothing to clarify the law concerning intervention or to settle the difference of opinion among publicists as to whether intervention could be legally justified. The long-continued effort under Latin-American leadership to secure treaty renunciation of intervention was unsuccessful in 1928, so far as getting a provision in a Pan American convention was concerned, but proponents of this move achieved their objective in 1933 through the Convention on Rights and Duties of States, to which the United States assented with the reservation (regarding this point) that it would apply during the Roosevelt administration. The limiting reservation was not carried over when the United States joined with other American republics in 1936 in condemning intervention by one state in the internal or external affairs of another. At the San Francisco Conference in 1945 the United States was one of four major states to propose that a paragraph on domestic jurisdiction be placed, not in a context which would make it applicable only to the pacific settlement of international disputes, but in a chapter on the principles of the United Nations. The effect was to extend the possible reach of the restriction, the interpretation and application of which have become of central importance in the law of the United Nations.

Subsequent efforts, in which the United States has participated, have looked to preventing the rule of nonintervention from paralyzing collective-security procedures on a regional or wider basis. The development of the concept of aggression has played a part. Although opposing, at the San Francisco Conference, a move to list in a definitive way acts that would be considered as constituting aggression, the United States through its representative at the London conversations on the Nuremberg Charter endeavored without success to secure agreement on the term. Nevertheless, there has at least been authorization for specific international organs to decide that there has been aggression and significant use of this authorization. Regional defensive arrangements have supplied a basis of treaty law for forceful action (even within a state) to oppose Communist expansionism. Such principle of nonintervention as now receives the support of the United States is apparently to be understood not as outside, but as inside, the system for safeguarding international peace and security.

A jurisdictional question which occasioned declaratory treaty references to international law during the period of national prohibition in the United States related to territorial waters. In six instances the United States accepted the three-mile limit as marking the legal extent of such waters. There being no universal agreement on the extent of marginal seas except on the point that the three-mile limit marks their *minimal* extent, the effect of the six treaties is at least to commit the parties to the three-mile rule as something more than a *lex specialis* binding the signatories. In the other "liquor" treaties, the parties agree upon measures that may be taken without prejudice to the views which they may hold concerning the legal extent of the marginal sea. In so far as these measures permit action that is not permitted by preexisting international law, the easily terminable arrangements have authorized practical procedures that do not involve for the parties any serious relinquishment of legal rights.

The great number of provisions in American treaties which relate to war and neutrality have included some that refer specifically to the law of nations. Early treaties contained rules designed to limit what belligerents might do in relation to nonparticipants in a war, with the admission—at least with respect to some of the provisions—that these rules "should" be the law. The treatment of prisoners of war came to be a subject of some bilateral, as well as multilateral, conventions which make mention of the law. Hague Convention IV of 1907 refers to the law in such a way as to leave possible the application of other rules (for example, those grounded in custom) in addition to those written out in the convention and its annexes. The 1949 revision follows a similar plan, but with the reference to such other rules being usefully placed in the article which pertains to denunciation of the convention rather than in the preamble.

A striking example of effort through conventional agreement to "make" international law concerning the conduct of hostilities was that concerning the use of submarines. Part IV of the London Naval Treaty of 1930, as carried over into the protocol of 1936, set forth rules that were accepted by many states after their projection as existing international law by the original signatories. From their inception, however, the utility of the rules was in doubt, because of their failure to cover certain points as well as because of the strain resulting from the development of new methods of hostilities and the blurring of some preëxisting distinctions, such as that between warships and merchant vessels which might be assimilated in some measure to units in naval forces. The incompleteness of the rules apparently played a part in their failure to accomplish what was sought through them, although the possibility that there would have been full enforcement, even if they had been more adequate in the sense of being technically more complete, seems very doubtful. They were, in any case, found by the Nuremberg tribunal in the trial of the major Nazi leaders to be in force as law, although, in view of all the circumstances, punishment under them was not meted out.

Neutral duties received much attention at the time of the *Alabama* claims settlement, when the United States participated in a bilateral treaty effort to secure specific assent to rules as a part of the applicable body of law. Although the signatories were committed to invite acceptance by states not parties to the original treaty, the sequel did not impressively demonstrate the utility of the method. The parties disagreed over whether the "three rules" were expressive of already existing law. There was further disagreement between them concerning whether certain municipal enactments of the British covered only obligations under international law or went further with controls than that law required. Intelligence and diplomacy averted a breakdown of the effort for arbitral settlement of the "direct" claims, but the widely acclaimed award by the majority left open questions regarding the relative weight which the arbitrators had given to the preëxisting law of nations and to what the British agreed to as *ad hoc* rules. The British government's objection to the tribunal's interpretation of the second of the three rules was a stated reason for British lack of enthusiasm for inviting adherence by other maritime states to what the two countries had used as a basis for the settlement. Intimations of objections on the part of certain outside states to the Anglo-American formulation perhaps had some deterring effect. In the final outcome, the parties to the Treaty of Washington did not formally invite acceptance by other states, as they had agreed to do. Difficulty in assigning a satisfactory meaning to the words "due diligence," as used in the treaty rules, was not resolved in later discussion, as the proceedings of the Second Hague Peace

Conference attest. In article VIII of Hague Convention XIII of 1907 a revised formula on neutral duties was accepted.

More fundamental than that looking to the revision of the law on particular neutral duties has been the effort toward a revision of the concept of neutrality itself. Unsettled questions concerning the law of neutrality provided some impetus. Limitations upon what belligerents could do concerning contraband of war, for example, have been sought through many treaties in the past, but there has been no universal acceptance of a rule preventing a belligerent from extending contraband lists as he pleased. Hague Conventions V and XIII of 1907 contained some provisions purporting to be declaratory of preëxisting general law, while others, in the view of the American government, did not.

A greater impetus came from growing belief that there should be a proscription of war and a denial of rights that had traditionally accrued to a state resorting to war. When, in the third and fourth decades of the twentieth century, the United States became a party to multilateral commitments designed to limit the purposes for which states might legally resort to armed force against other states, the legal implications of the commitments and their effect upon the traditional law of neutrality were not immediately apparent. The concept of aggression was difficult to reconcile with the idea that a state by resorting to force might thereby acquire rights against outside states. Customary as well as conventional rules concerning neutrality were affected. The development which came started largely as a matter of practice under new conditions of the 1930's and early 1940's, rather than as an inevitable consequence of the Kellogg-Briand Pact, although the latter figured much in discussions. Even after the Pact was in force, certain Western Hemisphere agreements to which the United States was a party seemed to envisage continued application of neutrality rules in something like the traditional sense, but they did not noticeably impede the larger development. At the time of the Lend-Lease debate in 1941, the executive and the majority of Congress seemed to proceed upon the idea that the Kellogg-Briand Pact had superseded even declaratory provisions of the Hague Conventions to the extent at least of creating a right, if not imposing a duty, upon the United States in the particular situation in which it found itself to distinguish between the belligerents and to depart from the kind of impartiality that traditional neutrality implied. Alternatively, it was possible to make a strong case for the steps that were taken as legally justified measures of self-defense.

In this instance the practical interpretations which the United States put upon its treaty and other commitments figured more constructively for law development than have the provisions of many treaties which have made express references to international law. Debate on the Lend-Lease Bill elicited various views concerning the nature of that law, but also some realistic observations on the role of a state such as the United States under conditions in which the breaking of the peace was recognized as the central problem with which the law of nations must attempt to deal.

In the course which it has followed since the Second World War the United States has, through treaties and otherwise, affirmed its views on aggression and emphasized responsibility of states to take cognizance of it when it is found to exist. It is of no great practical importance that the law establishing this responsibility is, in a technical sense, "general" rather than "universal." For, although the principal collective-security organization rests upon a treaty base which not all the states of the world have even nominally accepted, and although the word "neutral" has not completely fallen into disuse even in treaty provisions, it would be idle to view the United Nations Charter as simply another treaty and not the basic device of the still very imperfectly organized community of states. In 1949 the International Law Commission of the United Nations submitted, as the final article of its draft declaration on the rights and duties of states, that "every State has the duty to conduct its relations with other states in accordance with international law and with the principle that the sovereignty of each State is subject to the supremacy of international law." For substantially all, if not quite all, of the nations of the world, a central element of that law has come to be the part which looks to what shall be done concerning aggression upon a finding that it exists by community organs empowered to authorize procedure against it.

Perhaps the most general impression to be had from a study

of the manner in which—in such widely differing situations as those that have been examined in the foregoing chapters—the international law standard has been the subject of specific provisions of treaties is that the principle of legality may be underlined and strengthened through treaty acknowledgment of a pre-existing body of law. Far from being a substitute for constructive effort for the law's development, such acknowledgment may actually stimulate, or in any case parallel, effort to that end. It may be questioned whether mention of the law in a general, declaratory way has not at times been a substitute for commitments to something more specific. It is easier to agree that the law of nations will continue to apply (or that the law will have full application and will replace special arrangements which have existed between the parties) than it is to say what the law is. In fields wherein sharp controversies develop between states or between groups of states concerning what the standard means or has come to mean, as in connection with certain rights of resident foreigners, treaty makers may feel impelled to specify other standards or to specify treatment that is not on a contingent or qualified basis. Nevertheless, a formal recording of the parties' intention to adhere to the standard, or of their deferring to it when for special purposes over a temporary period they agree to apply special treaty rules, frequently has represented more than high-sounding phraseology. Even when the parties disagree over what the law is on particular matters and perhaps "reserve all rights" in connection with it, the method leaves open the possibility of their later agreement, when occasion arises for application of the treaty clauses. It is obvious that references of the kind under discussion will become more meaningful when special compromissary clauses or more general undertakings commit the parties to obligatory adjudication of disputes concerning interpretation and application.

A policy of constructive adherence to law, not as an end in itself, but as a means to moral ends, has frequently figured in the conduct of American foreign relations in the past. The United States has not, in the techniques and formulas used, followed a unique course in its integration of particular treaty commitments with other international rules that are binding upon it.[7] In the years since the Second World War, however, the process as illustrated in this country's practice has become more significant with the increase of the nation's responsibility for maintaining an ordered world. A part of that responsibility is to promote respect for, and to be concerned for the justness and viability of, the law of nations.

[7] See Appendix II.

APPENDICES
BIBLIOGRAPHY

Appendix I

TABLE OF UNITED STATES TREATIES

1778, Feb. 6	France	Alliance	8:6[a]
1778, Feb. 6	France	Amity and Commerce	8:12
1782, Oct. 8	Netherlands	Amity and Commerce	8:32
1783, April 3	Sweden	Amity and Commerce	8:60
1783, Sept. 3	Great Britain	Peace	8:80
1785, Sept. 10	Prussia	Amity and Commerce	8:84
1794, Nov. 19	Great Britain	Jay Treaty	8:116
1795, Oct. 27	Spain	Pinckney Treaty	8:138
1799, July 11	Prussia	Amity and Commerce	8:162
1800, Sept. 30	France	Convention	8:178
1802, Aug. 11	Spain	Indemnification	8:198
1805, June 4	Tripoli	Peace and Amity	8:214
1814, Dec. 24	Great Britain	Peace (Ghent)	8:218
1815, July 3	Great Britain	Commerce	8:228
1818, Oct. 20	Great Britain	Convention	8:248
1819, Feb. 22	Spain	Settlement and Limits	8:252
1825, Dec. 5	Central America	Commerce and Navigation	8:322
1826, Dec. 23	Hawaii	Arrangement	3 Miller[b] 269
1827, Aug. 6	Great Britain	Continuing Convention of July 3, 1815	8:361
1830, May 7	Turkey	Commerce and Navigation	8:408
1831, April 5	Mexico	Commerce and Navigation	8:410
1831, July 4	France	Claims and Duties	8:430
1832, May 16	Chile	Commerce and Navigation	8:434
1836, Jan. 20	Venezuela	Commerce and Navigation	8:466
1836, Nov. 30	Peru-Bolivia	Commerce and Navigation	8:487
1839, April 11	Mexico	Claims	8:526
1839, June 13	Ecuador	Commerce and Navigation	8:534
1842, Aug. 9	Great Britain	Webster-Ashburton Treaty	8:572
1846, Dec. 12	New Granada	Commerce and Navigation	9:881
1848, Feb. 2	Mexico	Treaty of Guadalupe Hidalgo	9:922
1849, March 3	Guatemala	Commerce and Navigation	10:873
1850, Jan. 2	El Salvador	Commerce and Navigation	10:891
1851, July 10	Costa Rica	Commerce and Navigation	10:916
1853, Feb. 8	Great Britain	Claims	10:988

[a] Citations are to the volume and page of the *United States Statutes at Large*, unless otherwise noted.

[b] David Hunter Miller, ed., *Treaties and Other International Acts of the United States of America.*

1853, Feb. 23	France	Consuls	10:992
1853, July 10	Argentina	Navigation of Rivers	10:1001
1853, Dec. 30	Mexico	Gadsden Treaty	10:1031
1854, June 5	Great Britain	Canadian Reciprocity	10:1089
1858, May 13	Bolivia	Commerce and Navigation	12:1003
1858, July 29	Japan	Commerce and Navigation	12:1051
1859, Feb. 4	Paraguay	Commerce and Navigation	12:1091
1862, April 7	Great Britain	Slave Trade	12:1225
1863, Feb. 17	Great Britain	Slave Trade	13:645
1868, July 4	Mexico	Claims	15:679
1870, June 3	Great Britain	Slave Trade	16:777
1870, Dec. 6	El Salvador	Commerce and Consuls	18(3):725
1871, Feb. 26	Italy	Commerce and Navigation	17:845
1871, May 8	Great Britain	Treaty of Washington	17:863
1880, Jan. 15	France	Claims	21:673
1884, March 14	Multilateral	Submarine Cables	24:989
1886, Oct. 2	Tonga	Commerce and Navigation	25:1440
1890, July 2	Multilateral	Slave Trade	27:886
1898, Dec. 10	Spain	Peace	30:1754
1899, July 29	Multilateral	Pacific Settlement (Hague)	32:1779
1900, May 14	Switzerland	Extradition	31:1928
1903, Feb. 17	Venezuela	Claims	U.S.T.S.[c] 420
1903, Oct. 8	China	Commerce	33:2208
1906, May 21	Mexico	Waters of the Rio Grande	34:2953
1906, Aug. 23	Multilateral	International Law Commission	37:1554
1907, Oct. 18	Multilateral	Pacific Settlement (Hague I)	36:2199
1907, Oct. 18	Multilateral	Laws and Customs of War on Land (Hague IV)	36:2277
1907, Oct. 18	Multilateral	Neutrality in case of War on Land (Hague V)	36:2310
1907, Oct. 18	Multilateral	Maritime Warfare (Hague X)	36:2371
1907, Oct. 18	Multilateral	Maritime Neutrality (Hague XIII)	36:2415
1908, April 11	Great Britain	Canadian Boundary	35:2003
1910, Aug. 18	Great Britain	Claims	37:1625
1911, July 7	Multilateral	Fur Seals	37:1542
1913, March 26	Paraguay	Extradition	38:1754
1919, June 28	Multilateral	International Labor Organization	49:2712
1919, Sept. 10	Multilateral	Slave Trade	49:3027
1921, June 30	Norway	Claims	42:1925
1921, Aug. 25	Germany	Peace	42:1939
1923, Aug. 6	Turkey	Extradition	49:2692
1923, Sept. 8	Mexico	Claims	43:1730
1923, Sept. 10	Mexico	Claims	43:1722
1923, Dec. 8	Germany	Commerce and Consuls	44:2132
1924, Jan. 23	Great Britain	Liquor	43:1761
1924, May 19	Germany	Liquor	43:1815

[c] United States Treaty Series.

1924, June 6	Panama	Liquor	43:1875
1924, June 12	Dominican Rep.	Evacuation	44:2193
1924, Aug. 21	Netherlands	Liquor	44:2013
1925, Jan. 23	Netherlands	Arbitration, Palmas Is.	44:2007
1925, June 24	Hungary	Commerce and Consuls	44:2441
1925, Dec. 23	Estonia	Commerce and Consuls	44:2379
1926, Feb. 22	El Salvador	Commerce and Consuls	46:2817
1926, March 4	Cuba	Liquor	44:2395
1926, July 28	Panama	Claims	47:1915
1926, Sept. 25	Multilateral	Slave Trade	46:2183
1927, May 19	Great Britain	Claims	U.S.T.S. 756
1927, Dec. 7	Honduras	Commerce and Consuls	45:2618
1928, Feb. 6	France	Arbitration	46:2269
1928, Feb. 20	Multilateral	Pan American, Maritime Neutrality	47:1989
1928, April 20	Latvia	Commerce and Consuls	45:2641
1928, May 14	Persia	Commercial Relations	E.A.S.[a] 19
1928, May 31	Japan	Liquor	46:2446
1928, June 5	Norway	Commerce and Consuls	47:2135
1928, June 19	Austria	Commerce and Consuls	47:1876
1928, Aug. 27	Multilateral	Renunciation of War	46:2343
1929, Jan. 5	Multilateral	Inter-American Arbitration	49:3153
1929, May 31	Multilateral	Safety of Life at Sea	50:1122
1929, July 27	Multilateral	Red Cross	47:2074
1930, April 22	Multilateral	Naval Armament	46:2858
1930, May 26	Canada	Fisheries	50:1355
1931, June 15	Poland	Commerce and Consuls	48:1507
1931, July 13	Multilateral	Narcotics	48:1543
1931, Oct. 28	Turkey	Establishment	47:2432
1932, Dec. 17	Panama	Claims	48:1485
1933, Oct. 10	Multilateral	Pan American, Anti-War Treaty	49:3363
1933, Nov. 7	Saudi Arabia	Commerce and Navigation	48:1826
1933, Dec. 26	Multilateral	Pan American, Rights and Duties of States	49:3097
1934, Feb. 13	Finland	Commerce and Consuls	49:2659
1934, March 9	Danzig	Commerce	48:1680
1934, April 24	Mexico	Claims	49:3071
1934, May 29	Cuba	Relations	48:1682
1935, April 15	Canada	Trail Smelter Arbitration	49:3245
1936, March 2	Panama	Coöperation	53:1807
1936, March 25	Multilateral	Naval Armament	50:1363
1936, March 26	Afghanistan	Friendship	49:3873
1936, Dec. 23	Multilateral	Pan American, Non-Intervention	51:41
1936, Dec. 23	Multilateral	Pan American, Coördinating Convention	51:116
1937, Jan. 29	Canada	Fisheries	50:1351
1937, April 13	Mexico	Terminating Art. VIII of Gadsden Treaty	52:1457

[a] United States Executive Agreement Series.

1937, May 8	Multilateral	Capitulations in Egypt	53:1645
1937, Nov. 13	Siam	Commerce and Navigation	53:1731
1937, Dec. 13	Multilateral	Inter-American Radio Communication	53:1593
1938, March 18	Netherlands	Arbitration	53:1564
1938, Aug. 8	Liberia	Commerce and Navigation	54:1739
1938, Nov. 17	Great Britain	Reciprocal Trade	54:1897
1938, Dec. 3	Iraq	Commerce	54:1790
1939, Feb. 20	Canada	Radio: Civil Aeronautics	53:2157
1939, Nov. 6	Venezuela	Reciprocal Trade	54:2375
1940, July 30	Multilateral	Inter-American Act (Havana)	54:2493
1940, Sept. 2	Great Britain	Destroyers-for-Bases Exchange	54:2405
1941, March 17	Canada	Economic Coöperation	55:1444
1942, Jan. 1	Multilateral	Declaration of United Nations and Atlantic Charter	55:1600
1943, Jan. 11	China	Relinquishment of Extraterritoriality	57:767
1944, Dec. 7	Multilateral	Civil Aviation	61:1180
1945, March 8	Multilateral	Act of Chapultepec	60:1831
1945, June 26	Multilateral	United Nations Charter	59:1031
1945, Aug. 8	Multilateral	Trial of Major War Criminals	59:1544
1946, May 4	Yemen	Commerce	T.I.A.S.[e] 1535
1946, July 4	Philippines	General Relations	61:1174
1946, Aug. 14		Optional Clause of Statute of International Court of Justice	61:1218
1946, Nov. 4	China	Commerce and Navigation	T.I.A.S. 1871
1947, Feb. 10	Multilateral	Peace, Italy	61:1245
1947, Feb. 10	Multilateral	Peace, Roumania	61:1757
1947, March 14	Philippines	Consuls	T.I.A.S. 1741
1947, April 25	Nepal	Commerce	61:2566
1947, Sept. 2	Multilateral	Inter-American Assistance	T.I.A.S. 1838
1948, Jan. 12	Costa Rica	Consuls	T.I.A.S. 2045
1948, Feb. 2	Italy	Commerce	T.I.A.S. 1965
1948, April 30	Multilateral	Organization of American States	T.I.A.S. 2361
1948, July 12	Great Britain	Lend Lease, etc.	T.I.A.S. 1770
1949, Feb. 8	Multilateral	Northwest Atlantic Fisheries	T.I.A.S. 2089
1949, Aug. 12	Multilateral	Geneva Conventions	Dept. of State publication 3938
1949, Nov. 23	Uruguay	Commerce	Sen. Ex. D, 81st Cong., 2d Sess.
1950, Jan. 21	Eire	Commerce	T.I.A.S. 2155
1950, Jan. 26	Panama	Claims	T.I.A.S. 2129

[e] United States Treaties and Other International Acts Series.

Appendix II

PRACTICE OF OTHER SELECTED STATES

An examination of the practice of other major states may assist toward viewing in better perspective the treaty practice of the United States. In general, only perfected international agreements of Great Britain, France, Germany, Russia, Japan, and Italy concluded within the period from 1900 to the outbreak of the Second World War have been considered.[1]

1. GREAT BRITAIN

British treaties of the selected period reveal a variety of clauses carrying some reference to general international law. Some, such as those in certain of the Hague Conventions of 1907 and the Montreux Convention with Egypt,[2] duplicate matters already discussed, since the United States was a party. In the peace treaties after the First World War there were some specific mentions of international law, both in the Covenant of the League of Nations[3] and in the articles by which the Central Powers admitted the right of the victors to institute trials for war crimes.[4] Also in the peace treaties, however,

[1] The arbitrary selection of this period has seemed justifiable partly by reason of the fact that the United States, whose treaty practice has already been examined, has been a party to the principal multilateral treaties since 1939 which have particular importance for the present study.

[2] The same would apply to the Geneva (Red Cross) Convention, to the 1929 Convention concerning Prisoners of War, and to the 1936 protocol concerning submarines. It has been thought unnecessary to mention in this chapter certain bilateral agreements with the United States.

[3] Among these are the references to "firm establishment of the understandings of international law" in the preamble, to arbitrability in article 13, paragraph 2, and (in article 15, paragraph 8) to "a matter which by international law is solely within the domestic jurisdiction."

At Paris in 1919, President Wilson, in a discussion concerning submarine cables, observed that the Allied and Associated Governments had "taken certain liberties with international law in the Peace Treaty" (*For. Rel., The Paris Peace Conference, 1919,* IV [1943], 496–497).

[4] Article 228, Treaty of Versailles: "The German Government recognizes the right of the Allied and Associated Powers to bring before military tri-

were such clauses as those setting forth that the Reparation Commission should not be bound by any particular code or rules of law or by any particular rule of evidence or of procedure, but should be guided by "justice, equity and good faith." [5]

Aside from the peace treaties, it was in keeping with the prevailing Anglo-American conception of arbitration that Great Britain should specify international law in her treaty provisions concerning bases for awards of international tribunals.[6] The claims convention with Costa Rica, signed January 12, 1922, directed that the arbitrator should take into consideration "the principles of public and international Law." [7] An unratified commercial treaty with Turkey contained, in an interpretation of a compromissory clause, a mention of international law as marking the proper limits of arbitration.[8] Two treaties with Portugal provided that the awards should be made *ex aequo et bono;* [9] by the instruction of another, the arbitrator was to be governed by such principles of international law as he should deem applicable to the case.[10] In at least one other the decisions were to be in conformity

---

bunals persons accused of having committed acts in violation of the laws and customs of war." There was a corresponding provision in article 173 of the Treaty of St. Germain, in article 118 of the Treaty of Neuilly, and in article 157 of the Treaty of Trianon.

[5] Part VIII, Annex II, par. 11, Treaty of Versailles, Cmd. 153 (1919). Similar provisions were in the Treaties of St. Germain and Trianon.

[6] Thus the agreement of October 25, 1910, with France for reference of the *Savarkar* case provided: "An Arbitral Tribunal . . . shall undertake to decide the following question:—Should Vinayak Damodar Savarkar, in conformity with the rules of international law, be restored or not be restored by His Britannic Majesty's Government to the Government of the French Republic?" (Cd. 5294 of 1910).

See reference to "international law and of equity" in 1910 agreement with the United States (Chapter II, note 125, *supra*).

[7] 116 *Brit. and For. State Papers* 438, 439.

[8] Cmd. 3536 of 1930, Protocol, article 10, relating to article 35: "It is understood that, in accordance with the usage of international law, no matter which falls within the domain of sovereignty or the exclusive competence of the State can become the subject of arbitration."

[9] Article 56 of Agreement of November 17, 1934, revising the Convention of September 11, 1928, relating to Native Labour from Mozambique, Railway Matters and Commercial Intercourse (Cmd. 5085 of 1936); article 8 of Agreement of May 11, 1938, regulating Commercial Relations between Swaziland, Basutoland and Bechuanaland Protectorate, and the Portuguese colony of Mazambique (Cmd. 5807 of 1938). The awards were to be made *ex aequo et bono* and "in accordance with the terms of submission to be agreed upon in each particular case."

[10] Treaty and Declaration of November 6, 1901, with Brazil, concerning reference to arbitration of the question of the boundary between Brazil and British Guiana (94 *Brit. and For. State Papers* 23, 25).

with "the principles of international law or considerations of equity." [11]

Some of the mentions of the law in Great Britain's treaties of the period are obviously intended to be declaratory. At least seven extradition engagements contained the clause, familiar in United States treaties, in regard to piracy by the law of nations.[12] Treaties with states in the Near East contained clauses specifying "international usage" or "international practice" as the standard which was to govern treatment of officials or nationals of the parties, or to be used in fixing compensation for damages, or (in the case of private international law) to govern the application of foreign law in national courts when cases should involve certain commercial matters.[13] There have sometimes been references to international law in relation to what major powers might do with regard to Near Eastern states. Thus in the joint note addressed to the Persian government on September 11, 1907, British and Russian representatives mutually engaged their governments "in the case of irregularities in the amortisation of or in the payment of interest on the above-mentioned loans, to enter on a friendly exchange of views in order to determine by common agreement the measures which, *in conformity with the law of nations,* it would be necessary to take in order to safeguard the interests of the creditors." [14] More than three decades later, after abolition of the Capitulations in Persia in 1928, it was provided that the "rules and practices of international law" should govern the admission and treatment of British subjects, on a most-favored-nation basis. Special attributions of consular officers (in matters of personal status) "in accordance with international law" were not to be affected by what was agreed upon with respect to personal status of British nationals.[15]

[11] Convention between Great Britain, Germany, and the United States, November 7, 1899, concerning settlement of certain claims arising in Samoa (91 *Brit. and For. State Papers* 78, 79).

[12] Illustrated in the treaty of October 29, 1901/December 6, 1901, with Belgium (94 *Brit. and For. State Papers* 7, 10).

[13] See, for example, an agreement with Iraq, March 25, 1924, article 4: "In matters relating to the personal status of foreigners or in other matter of a civil and commercial nature in which it is customary by international usage to apply the law of another country, such law shall be applied in [a] manner to be prescribed by law" (119 *Brit. and For. State Papers* 416, 418–419).

The Treaty of Friendship and Mutual Cooperation between the United Kingdom and the Kingdom of Yemen, February 11, 1934, contained the following in article 4: "After the coming into force of the present treaty, the high contracting parties shall, by mutual agreement and concord, enter into such agreements as shall be necessary for the regulation of commercial and economic affairs, based on the principles of general international practice" (Cmd. 4630 of 1934).

[14] Cd. 6077 of 1912 (italics inserted).

[15] Cmd. 3606 of 1930.

The Treaty of Peace and other instruments signed with Turkey at Lausanne on July 24, 1923, furnished occasion for the confirmation of standards set by international law. By the Treaty of Peace (article I) official relations were to be resumed and diplomatic and consular representatives were to receive treatment in accordance with the general principles of that law. The Convention relating to the Regime of the Straits referred (in paragraph 1c of the annex to article II) to the rights of Turkey to apply to enemy vessels the measures allowed by international law. The Convention concerning Conditions of Residence and Business and Jurisdiction recorded in its preamble the parties' desire to prescribe bases in conformity with modern international law. By the second article Turkey was to receive and treat nationals of the other contracting parties, with respect to their persons and property, in accordance with international common law. Questions of jurisdiction were, by article 15, to be decided in accordance with the same standard, and article 17 emphasized that the Turkish courts would assure (to foreigners and their goods) protection in accordance with international law (as well as principles and methods generally followed in the other countries). The preamble of the Commercial Convention signed at Lausanne contained a recital similar to that in the Convention concerning Conditions of Residence and Business and Jurisdiction.[16]

Other provisions apparently designed to be declaratory had to do with principles of maritime law,[17] exercise of jurisdiction or attempted enforcement of a judgment against a person entitled to immunity therefrom,[18] and immunity for the official correspondence of the Brit-

[16] 117 *Brit. and For. State Papers* 545, 594, 605, 607, 610, 611, 612.

[17] These provisions were in conventions on air navigation. That with Austria, signed July 16, 1932/January 14, 1933 (Cmd. 4263), provided (article 18) that with regard to the salvage of aircraft wrecked at sea, "the principles of maritime law resulting from the international agreements in force shall apply." On the same subject matter, the convention of March 22, 1937, with Hungary (Cmd. 5535) provided (article 17) that "the principles of maritime law resulting from the international agreements in force *or otherwise* shall apply" (italics inserted).

[18] These provisions were in agreements with France and Belgium, respectively, for reciprocal enforcement of judgments in civil and commercial matters. A judgment was not required to be recognized if it were against a defendant who "under the rules of public international law" was entitled to immunity from the jurisdiction of the court applied to (Cmd. 4618, art. 3f [1934] and Cmd. 4717, art. 3c [1934]).

In view of certain litigation in England concerning jurisdictional immunity of Russian agents sent to England after the conclusion of the trade agreement by which Britain extended *de facto* recognition to the Soviet government (for example, the case of *Fenton Textile Company* v. *Krassin* [1921], 38 Times Law Reports 259), it was perhaps to be expected that, in the official correspondence concerning resumption of relations between the

ish forces in Egypt and of their couriers.[19] There was in a convention with Finland a declaration of intention to uphold the principle that three marine miles from low-water mark constituted the "proper" territorial waters; [20] but, consistently with their disagreement over whether the law was fixed on this subject matter,[21] Great Britain and the Soviet Union, in a fisheries agreement, set forth that nothing therein was to prejudice the views of either regarding the limits, in international law, of territorial waters.[22] Characterized in an annex to a *compromis* with Finland as "a question of public international law only" was the matter of whether claimants' failure to exhaust "means of recourse" in British courts would prevent their government's claiming from the British in their behalf.[23]

It was natural that Great Britain, in diplomatic correspondence with such countries as the Netherlands concerning neutral losses in the World War of 1914–1918, should make reference to obligations under international law, but in such instances, unless formal treaties or agreements resulted—such as that with the United States, signed May 19, 1927 [24]—the references made to international law would not fall within the purview of the present study.

In addition to accepting some of the conventions constructed at the Second Hague Conference, Great Britain in the period after the First World War became a party to such multilateral treaties as the Geneva Conventions of 1929 and the Protocol of 1936 concerning submarines, which have received attention as instruments to which the United States is also a party. The British government was a principal party to the Protocol of June 17, 1925, for Prohibition of Use in War of

---

two countries, there should be a British statement of an understanding that "the reciprocal rights and duties which international law recognizes as incumbent on States in their relations with one another subsist between this country and the Union of Soviet Socialist Republics" (Cmd. 3418 of 1929).

[19] Convention concerning the Immunities and Privileges to Be Enjoyed by the British Forces in Egypt, signed August 26, 1936 (Cmd. 5360 of 1937), at the same time as the Treaty of Alliance between the two countries. The immunity was to be the same as that "enjoyed in International Law by the Diplomatic representatives of foreign States" (art. 6j).

[20] Convention of October 13, 1933, regarding the suppression of illicit importation of alcoholic liquors into Finland (Cmd. 4436 of 1933, art. I, par. 1a); see also proposals for agreement with Norway concerning territorial waters and fisheries off the Norwegian coast (Cmd. 3121 of 1928).

[21] See Chapter I, note 16, *supra*.

[22] Temporary Fisheries Agreement signed at London, May 22, 1930 (Cmd. 3583 of 1930).

[23] Agreement for the submission to arbitration of a question connected with a claim in respect of certain Finnish vessels used during the war, September 30, 1932 (Cmd. 4179 of 1932, Annex I6).

[24] Cmd. 2877 of 1927. See Chapter II, section 4, *supra*.

Poisonous Gases and Bacteriological Warfare, which was made to the end that "this prohibition shall be universally accepted as a part of International Law, binding alike the conscience and the practice of nations." [25]

In some commitments falling within the selected period, the parties made it clear that the arrangements were not (or not necessarily) on the basis of customary international law. A British-Siamese boundary agreement recorded a deviation from "international practice." [26] In two special claims conventions with Great Britain, Mexico assented to the proposition that its responsibility for damage to British subjects during revolutionary disturbances in Mexico was not to be measured by rules of international law, the responsibility accepted being somewhat wider.[27]

In certain multilateral conventions other than those already noted, Great Britain as a party accepted treaty provisions concerning the relation of rules to preëxisting general law. The Hague Convention of 1930 on Certain Questions relating to the Conflict of Nationality Laws makes it clear that while the parties agree to apply the principles

[25] Cmd. 3604 of 1930. The Report of the Preparatory Commission for the Disarmament Conference made the point, in respect to this convention, that while the commitment in the first article to abstain from using gases could normally be observed only subject to reciprocity, the undertaking to abstain from the use of bacteriological methods should be absolute. "The use of such methods would, in any case, constitute a crime against international law" (Cmd. 3757 of 1931, p. 47). The Draft Disarmament Convention submitted to the Disarmament Conference at Geneva on March 16, 1933, by Ramsay MacDonald, proposed that the following provisions be accepted as "an established rule of International Law" (Cmd. 4279 of 1933, p. 21):

"The use of chemical, incendiary and bacterial weapons, as against any State, whether or not a party to the present Convention, and in any war, whatever its character, is prohibited.

"This provision does not, however, deprive any party which has been the victim of the illegal use of chemical or incendiary weapons, of the right to retaliate, subject to such conditions as may hereafter be agreed."

[26] Agreement and Exchange of notes concerning boundary between Burma and Siam, August 27, 1931/March 14, 1932. The rule related to the method of fixing a boundary line in a river (Cmd. 4112).

[27] By article VI of the Convention of November 19, 1926, with Great Britain (Cmd. 2876 of 1927), the "Government of Mexico being desirous of reaching an equitable agreement in regard to the claims . . . and of granting to the claimants just compensation for the losses or damages they may have sustained, it is agreed that the Commission shall not set aside or reject any claim on the grounds that all legal remedies have not been exhausted prior to the presentation of such claim." Article 2 of the Supplementary Convention of December 5, 1930 (Cmd. 3768 of 1931) sets forth "the desire of Mexico *ex gratia* fully to compensate the injured parties, and not that her responsibility should be established in conformity with the general principles of International Law."

and rules of the convention, inclusion of principles and rules shall in no way be deemed to prejudice the question whether they do or do not already form part of international law, and that in so far as any point is not covered by the articles, the existing principles and rules of international law are to remain in force.[28] The 1923 Convention concerning Development of Hydraulic Power Affecting More than One State is, by its terms, not to affect the right of each party, "within the limits of international law," to carry out operations for the development of hydraulic power on its own territory.[29] The International Convention and Statute Establishing an International Relief Union, July 12, 1927, to which Great Britain acceded on January 9, 1929, contained a preambular statement of the purpose, among others, to "further the progress of international law in this field." [30]

2. FRANCE

Some fifty references to general international law in treaties which France concluded during the twentieth century and before the Second World War revealed practice similar to that of the British.[31] Perhaps the most common cases of treaty references to the rules of international law are in instruments concerning justiciable questions and in those setting standards to govern the treatment of nationals, diplomatic agents, or consular officers. Illustrative of the former are clauses obliging the parties to submit to arbitration or judicial settlement questions of international law.[32] Even before the League of Nations came into being, France had made some commitments in which she recognized that the fact of a dispute in regard to international law would confer the right to have the question arbitrated.[33] About the time of the appearance of the General Act for the Pacific Settlement of International Disputes evolved by the League of Nations, French treaties on the subject of pacific settlement began to reflect the spirit of apparent optimism concerning obligatory adjudication. Thus in a convention signed with the Netherlands on March 10, 1928, France recorded (in a preambular statement of purpose) the desire to make arrangements

[28] Article 18 (Cmd. 4347 of 1933).

[29] 36 L.N.T.S. 77, 81.

[30] Cmd. 4243 of 1933.

[31] This and the following sections do not include, among the treaties used in illustration, those instruments already discussed to which Great Britain or the United States is also a party.

[32] These references were either in the form of general agreements, such as the protocol of signature of the Statute of the Permanent Court of International Justice, or in compromissory clauses whose effect was restricted to the particular instruments.

[33] See the first and second articles of the arbitration convention of July 3, 1914, with Argentina (*Journal Officiel de la République Française*, December 27, 1916, p. 11112).

which would, "conformément aux progrès du Droit des gens," thenceforth assure peaceful settlement.[34] A conciliation convention with the Soviet Union four years later authorized a commission to study "questions litigieuses" and to recommend such interpretation as it should judge to be "fondée en droit." [35] Employing a formula not peculiar to French treaties but occurring quite commonly in modern arbitration agreements, several instruments provided that arbitrators should determine the nature and extent of reparation to be made if they should find that a decision in a court of one of the parties had been contrary to international law.[36]

Especially in her treaties with states in the Near East, France made reference to the general law as providing the standard of treatment of nationals or of official representatives. In a 1929 treaty of amity with Persia, there were three distinct provisions of the kind, covering, respectively, the treatment of diplomatic agents, consular officers, and nationals. An earlier agreement with the same country had recorded that diplomatic representatives should, subject to reciprocity, enjoy privileges and immunities recognized by "le droit commun international." [37] The 1929 instrument, which contained wording on this point somewhat similar to provisions in treaties concluded with Yemen, set, as a standard, most-favored-nation treatment under international law.[38]

[34] 102 L.N.T.S. 109. A treaty of conciliation and obligatory arbitration signed with Sweden on March 3, 1928, omitted mention of the progress of the law, but expressed the parties' desire to provide for settlement "conformément au droit des gens moderne" (95 L.N.T.S. 89).

[35] Convention signed November 29, 1932 (157 L.N.T.S. 421, 425).

[36] There is some variation in the language of such clauses. See article 22 of the arbitration treaty of July 10, 1929, with Spain, in which a condition is inserted that the constitutional law of the country concerned does not permit, or only imperfectly permits, the overcoming of the decision by "voie administrative" (148 L.N.T.S. 369, 381). See also part IV, article 22, of the treaty signed with Finland, April 28, 1930 (*Journal Officiel,* June 27, 1933, p. 6640). In a claims convention with Venezuela in 1913, France obtained the right to bring a claim by reason of any "sentence Vénézuellienne contra laquelle il croirait devoir élever des objections fondées sur le droit et l'équité" (*Journal Officiel,* June 17, 1913, p. 5198).

[37] 82 L.N.T.S. 43, 45 (provisional agreement signed May 11, 1928).

[38] 150 L.N.T.S. 329, 330, 331 (treaty of amity, May 10, 1929, with Persia). The treaty of amity signed with Yemen, April 25, 1936, specified for diplomatic agents and consular officers, under condition of reciprocity, rights and prerogatives consecrated by international usages and treatment accorded to representatives of the most favored nation (140 *Brit. and For. State Papers* 516). The treaty of amity which France signed on November 10, 1931, with the kingdoms of Hejaz, Nejd and Dependencies, had specified, for diplomatic and consular representatives, treatment conforming to rules and usages of public international law (134 *Brit. and For. State Papers* 823, 824).

A clause occurring in certain consular conventions which France made with middle European states during the period set forth that consular officers might defend rights and interests of nationals in accordance with international law and usage.[39] International usage was set up as a standard (for treatment of property and premises in France serving exclusively for the exercise of the diplomatic and political rights of the Soviet government) in a provisional commercial agreement of 1934 with the Soviet Union.[40] It has been seen that, when the Allies made peace with Turkey in 1923, a number of provisions concerning international law were in the Lausanne agreements. A section of a treaty which seems to have envisaged that conventional law in the form of bilateral arrangements might not keep pace with customary rules is in a Franco-Swedish convention of 1936. The provisions of this instrument were not to affect the right of diplomatic or consular officers to benefit "by any more extensive exemptions already accorded to such officials under the general rules of international law, or which may hereafter be accorded under any other rules that may be made."[41]

There are some references to international law as defining questions within the "sovereignty" of the respective parties.[42] An extradition commitment which France signed in 1930 contained an exception clause to cover cases which, in accordance with international usage, do not give rise to extradition.[43] As did some of the other major states, France secured a treaty commitment from Mexico by which that country consented to the adjudication of claims growing out of revolutionary disturbances in Mexico, without limiting the liability to that which would be due under international law.[44] An

[39] Illustrated in consular convention of June 3, 1927, with Czechoslovakia (131 L.N.T.S. 177, art. 10, par. 1) and in that of June 19, 1936, with Latvia (169 L.N.T.S. 125, art. 9, par. 1).

[40] 167 L.N.T.S. 349 (art. 7, par. 2).

[41] Convention for the Avoidance of Double Taxation and for the Establishment of Rules for Reciprocal Administrative Assistance in the Case of Direct Taxes, signed December 24, 1936 (184 L.N.T.S. 35, 55, Protocol, art. XV).

[42] The Four-Power Treaty signed at Washington, December 13, 1921, concerning possessions in the Pacific, refers in the accompanying Declaration to questions which, according to principles of international law, lie exclusively within the domestic jurisdiction (*souveraineté*) of the respective powers (25 L.N.T.S. 183). A Treaty of Amity and Good Neighborship between Turkey on the one side and France on behalf of Syria and Lebanon on the other, signed at Angora, May 31, 1926, contained in article 14, paragraph 4, the following: "Les parties contractantes reservent leur liberté en ce qui concerne les questions de souveraineté telles qu'elles sont définies par les règles du droit international" (54 L.N.T.S. 195).

[43] Article 9 of convention regulating relations between France and China with respect to French Indo-China, signed May 16, 1930 (162 L.N.T.S. 99).

[44] The special claims convention with Mexico, signed September 25,

unusual provision, which would seem to have importance for private law rather than public, was that in the condominium arrangement made with Great Britain concerning the New Hebrides, by which it was agreed that the Joint Court should judge according to substantial justice respecting, as far as possible, native customs and the "general principles of law." [45] Indirect references to international law can probably be assumed from mentions of "principes fondamentaux" [46] or advantages had "par Traité, Convention ou autrement." [47] Rights under the general law during conditions of war are mentioned in a number of multilateral conventions to which France became a party.[48]

3. RUSSIA

In the treaties which Russia made during the same period there are some variants from the forms of reference to international law which marked the treaty making of other major states already noted. Outside of multilateral agreements such as those of the Hague Peace Conference of 1907 which Czarist Russia accepted, nearly all of the treaty clauses listed postdate the First World War.[49] Fairly numerous are those which set forth that the law will provide the standards by which diplomatic protection will be accorded or consular officers will function in the safeguarding of rights of nationals.[50] These references commonly occur in consular conventions or treaties of commerce. Protection specified for nationals of one party in the territory of the other may be national or most-favored-nation treatment in conformity

---

1924, article 2 of which sets forth the extent of Mexico's accepted liability (122 *Brit. and For. State Papers* 590, 591).

[45] Convention signed October 20, 1906, art. 21, par. 3 (99 *Brit. and For. State Papers* 229, 237).

[46] Article 11 of a treaty between France and Belgium respecting immigrant workers, signed December 24, 1924. Arbitrators were to decide questions according to fundamental principles and the spirit of the treaty (122 *Brit. and For. State Papers* 119, 121).

[47] The reference (in a protocol signed July 1, 1905, with Ecuador, concerning literary and artistic property) is to rights which may be conceded by either party in the subject matter (98 *Brit. and For. State Papers* 456).

[48] See, for example, article 2 of the Red Cross Convention of July 6, 1906 (*Journal Officiel*, September 9, 1913, p. 8046).

[49] An exception is the fisheries convention of 1907 with Japan, referred to in note 65, *infra*.

[50] Illustrative of such provisions are the consular treaty of October 12, 1925, with Germany (53 L.N.T.S. 163, art. 16) and the consular convention of November 16, 1935, with Czechoslovakia. By the English translation of article XII of the Czechoslovak treaty, "Consuls shall be entitled to protect nationals of the State which has appointed them and to defend, in accordance with international law . . ." (159 L.N.T.S. 143, 151).

with international law,[51] or there may be simple specification that nationals and national vessels are to be treated in accordance with international law.[52] Even a provision for appointing additional consuls and consular officials in towns and ports, in the treaty of commerce and navigation signed with Norway on December 15, 1925, contained the statement that the right accorded was to be subject to the general stipulations of international law.[53] The consular treaty of the same year with Germany made it clear that consular officers, in the exercise of their official duties, would "be entitled to apply to the judicial and administrative authorities in their consular district and to make representations to them . . . in case of violations of the general principles of international law." Another article provided that mentioned parts of the treaty would "also apply to officials who . . . are entrusted with the exercise of consular duties, without prejudice to the privileges already enjoyed by these officials in accordance with the principles of international law." [54] In the period when the Soviet government had been recognized by some states as a *de facto* but not as a *de jure* regime, it is understandable that the government should seek commitments by which "official delegations" should be entitled to rights under international law.[55]

Further evidence of the effort to assure the Soviet Union a legally obligatory standard of treatment occurs in articles concerning state property in the territory of the other party.[56] In at least one of these instruments there is mention of property protection in accordance with

[51] See article IV, par. 1 of the commercial treaty of May 17, 1929, with Estonia (94 L.N.T.S. 323); article X, par. 1 of agreement of October 12, 1925, with Germany (53 L.N.T.S. 7).

[52] See article VIII, par. 1, and article IX, par. 1, of the agreement regarding relations and trade between Russia, Austria, and the Ukraine, December 7, 1921 (20 L.N.T.S. 150); article X, par. 1, of a temporary agreement signed with Germany, May 6, 1921 (6 L.N.T.S. 267); article III, par. 1, of agreement supplementary to the Agreement of Rapallo, November 5, 1922 (26 L.N.T.S. 387).

[53] 47 L.N.T.S. 9 (art. I, par. 1).

[54] Articles XVI (par. 2) and XXX (53 L.N.T.S. 163).

[55] See, for example, article II, par. 2, of the preliminary agreement with Norway, signed September 2, 1921. By article IV, par. 2, of the same agreement, property of the Russian government in Norway was to enjoy the immunity extended to property of friendly governments under international law (7 L.N.T.S. 293).

[56] See, for example, article III, par. 4, of the preliminary agreement which Russia signed with Denmark, April 23, 1923 (18 L.N.T.S. 15); article XI, par. 5, of the Treaty of Establishment, Commerce and Navigation with Iran, August 27, 1935 (176 L.N.T.S. 299); article XV, par. 2, of a provisional commercial convention with Belgium and Luxembourg, September 5, 1935 (173 L.N.T.S. 169). According to the treaty with Iran, "Distraint in execution of judicial decisions which have become legally enforceable shall not

international law.[57] The descriptive phrasing varies; in some instances the property to be protected is that which gives effect to "sovereign rights." Somewhat related to this is the Soviet government's reservation to the multilateral convention of August 19, 1925, for the suppression of contraband traffic in alcoholic liquors. By this, "the Government of the Union of Socialist Soviet Republics, in approving the provisions of the . . . Convention, in no way intends to prejudice its position as regards the status in international law of vessels which are the property of the State." [58]

Another reservation to a multilateral treaty, in which the Soviet government sought to avoid prejudice to its particular view, was that made at the time of signing the International Convention concerning the Use of Broadcasting in the Cause of Peace, September 23, 1936. This reservation stated:

> The Delegation of the Union of Soviet Socialist Republics declares that, pending the conclusion of the procedure contemplated in Article 7 of the Convention, it considers that the right to apply reciprocal measures to a country carrying out improper transmissions [*des émissions abusives*] against it, in so far as such a right exists under the general rules of international law and with the Conventions in force, is in no way affected by the Convention.[59]

The peace arrangements which Russia made with neighboring states at the end of the First World War contained various references to the general law. In addition to the short-lived Treaty of Brest-Litovsk there was a treaty which provided for indemnity to cover damage caused to consular officials and buildings during the war in violation of international law, and for damages inflicted on citizens in violation of the law.[60] Treating with Finland in 1922 on measures to be taken in order to secure peace at the frontier, the Russian government became party to a commitment whereby "the two Contracting countries undertake, in the event of armed risings occurring in the territory of the other

---

be levied on the property of the Trade Delegation, if such property is intended to give effect to the sovereign rights of the State, in accordance with the general rules of international law."

[57] Article XIII of temporary agreement signed with Germany, May 6, 1921 (6 L.N.T.S. 267, art. 13).

[58] 42 L.N.T.S. 73, 87. The Soviet Union became a party to the multilateral Convention for the Suppression of Counterfeiting Currency, April 20, 1929, by article XVII of which "the participation of a High Contracting Party . . . shall not be interpreted as affecting that Party's attitude on the general question of criminal jurisdiction as a question of international law" (112 L.N.T.S. 371).

[59] 186 L.N.T.S. 301, 317.

[60] 10 N.R.G. (3d ser.) 797, 799, 804 (arts. 2, 14).

State, to observe the precepts laid down by international law." [61] Some of the peace treaties provided for the settlement by mixed commissions of public-law questions (between citizens of the contracting parties).[62]

In a conciliation treaty with France, signed in 1932, the Soviet government assented to a clause whereby conciliation commissioners were to study disputes and recommend interpretations considered "fondée en droit" or deemed equitable.[63] In other treaties on the same subject matter, there are references to equitable arrangements without mention of law.[64]

In fisheries arrangements with Japan, one made by the Czarist government in 1907 and the other by the Soviet government in 1928, references to international law occur in rather unusual form. In the earlier of these, Czarist Russia assented to the fixing of limits between rivers and sea in accordance with the principles and usages of international law.[65] In the 1928 undertaking, the Soviet Union and Japan agreed that "in matters concerning the boundaries of rivers in relation to the sea, the two Governments shall follow the principles and usages of the law of nations." [66]

The effect, upon legal relations, of forceful action by states against other states is anticipated in such commitments as Russia made to Afghanistan, Lithuania, and Roumania, in conventions for the definition of aggression. In annexes to the respective conventions, the parties "agree to recognize that the present Convention can never legitimate any violations of international law that may be implied in the circumstances comprised in the above list." [67] In her peace treaties

[61] Convention signed June 1, 1922 (16 L.N.T.S. 317, art. VI, par. 2). An additional protocol explains (in par. 7): "In . . . elucidation of article 6, it is hereby decreed that the two States bind themselves to take immediate measures to suppress organizations taking part in the preparation and execution of attacks, or guilty [of] assisting in attacks in foreign territory or against such territory."

[62] See, for example, the treaty of peace with Estonia, February 2, 1920 (11 L.N.T.S. 51, art. 14).

[63] Cited in note 35, *supra*.

[64] See, for example, those with Finland, Latvia, Poland, Estonia, and Germany, respectively (157 L.N.T.S. 401; 148 *ibid.* 129; 136 *ibid.* 55; 131 *ibid.* 309; 90 *ibid.* 219). The last-cited convention contains in the German text a reference to "eine gerechte . . . Loesung."

[65] 101 *Brit. and For. State Papers* 453, 457 (Protocol, art. II).

[66] 80 L.N.T.S. 341, Protocol (A), art. 2.

[67] 147 L.N.T.S. 67; 148 *ibid.* 79; 148 *ibid.* 211. In each case the interpretive statement is an annex to the third article of the convention. The second article defines aggression, while the third sets forth that neither political, military, economic, nor other considerations could justify aggression. The annex is in the nature of an elaboration of the third article; it deals with international conditions of a party state, and, separately, with international conduct.

with some of the new states carved out of Russian territory, the Soviet government included provisions whereby the parties were to prohibit the navigation in their respective territorial waters of the naval vessels of any power at war with or about to attack the other contracting party, except in cases provided for by international law.[68] In a collective arrangement supplementary to the Nyon Arrangement, September 17, 1937, Russia along with the other parties assented to the application of the Nyon instrument to an attack at sea "accompanied by a violation of the humanitarian principles embodied in the rules of international law with regard to warfare at sea" referred to in part IV of the London Naval Treaty of 1930 and confirmed in the Protocol of 1936.[69]

In at least one exchange of notes (that of June 18, 1924, with Denmark), it was recorded that, pursuant to the *de jure* recognition of the Soviet government by Denmark, a preliminary commercial agreement should be modified in accordance with general principles of the law of nations.[70] It was in the same year that the Soviet government made with China an Agreement on General Principles, proclaiming that equality, reciprocity, and justice were to form the basis for new agreements between the two countries, as distinguished from old principles which the Czarist government had followed.[71] The principle of self-determination received formal endorsement in treaty relations with the Ukraine, with Poland, and with Finland in 1920 and 1921.[72] In various Russian treaties of the period there are references to custom, to international commercial usage, or to the established practice of commercial nations.[73]

[68] See, for example, the treaty of peace with Estonia, February 2, 1920 (11 L.N.T.S. 51, art. VII, par. 4), and that with Latvia, August 11, 1920 (2 L.N.T.S. 195, art. IV, par. 4).

[69] 181 L.N.T.S. 149. See Chapter V, section 1b, *supra*.

[70] The language referred to is in the Danish note of the given date (27 L.N.T.S. 150).

[71] 37 L.N.T.S. 175, arts. III, VIII, XIII. See, on the general nature of this treaty policy, T. A. Taracouzio, *The Soviet Union and International Law* (1935). On the relative emphasis which the Soviet Union places upon treaties as a source of law, see John N. Hazard, "The Soviet Union and International Law," *Ill. Law Rev.*, XLIII (1948), 591, 594–595.

[72] See the Treaty of Peace, Russia-Ukraine-Poland, March 18, 1921 (6 L.N.T.S. 51, arts. II, par. 1, and VII, par. 1). The last-mentioned portion of the treaty refers to the principle of the equality of peoples. See also the Treaty of Peace with Finland, October 14, 1920 (3 L.N.T.S. 5, art. XXXV, par. 4).

[73] See articles VI and XII of the convention with Finland of July 28, 1923, regarding the maintenance of order in the parts of the Gulf of Finland situated outside territorial waters (32 L.N.T.S. 101). Vessels were to be allowed to seek refuge in territorial waters of the other state and to put into port there in accordance with international custom. In case of accidents

A realistic evaluation of such references as have been examined in this section would, of course, have to take into account Soviet views on the function of law in national societies and in the international community.

4. GERMANY

The treaties containing reference to international law which Germany made between the opening of the twentieth century and the outbreak of the Second World War fall mainly in the period after 1920. There were some instances in the period before 1914, such as an exchange of notes between Germany and Panama in 1903, which mentioned the general principles of the law of nations as relating to the applicability to Panama of treaties and agreements that had been previously in force between Germany and Colombia.[74] In a commercial treaty which Germany signed on July 22, 1908, with Bolivia, it was agreed that diplomatic representatives were not to intervene in behalf of private individuals, in case of violation of the rules of public and private international law universally recognized by civilized nations, except where all judicial recourse had been exhausted.[75] An agreement between Prussia and Basel-Stadt, signed December 20, 1910/January 28, 1911, for the prevention of double taxation, contained an article making it inapplicable to persons exempt from taxation under international law.[76] There were some references to matters to which rules of international law pertain in commercial agreements. Thus a German-Portuguese commercial treaty of November 30, 1908, provided that in case of sequestrations or appropriations of property for public purposes compensation was to be accorded on

---

at sea or in territorial waters, the vessels or lifesaving stations of each party were to afford to persons in distress assistance in accordance with international custom. International commercial usage is prescribed in a convention with Latvia, October 10, 1927, regarding arbitration in commercial and civil matters (84 L.N.T.S. 47, art. XI), as also in an agreement of October 12, 1925, with Germany (53 L.N.T.S. 7, art. XII of Agreement VI). There is a reference to the "established practice of commercial nations" as a standard to be followed in the treatment by each party of the ships of the other, in a preliminary agreement of September 2, 1921, with Norway (7 L.N.T.S. 293, art. IX, par. 1), and in the agreement of similar type with Denmark signed April 23, 1923 (18 L.N.T.S. 15, art. VII). In a 1922 convention with Finland regarding fishing regulations in the Gulf of Finland, it was agreed that "bag-nets" must be provided during hours of darkness with signal lights in conformity with "international navigation instructions" (19 L.N.T.S. 143, art. IV, par. 4).

[74] 4 N.R.G. (3d ser.) 796.

[75] 101 *Brit. and For. State Papers* 911, 913.

[76] 7 N.R.G. (3d ser.) 845; *Deutscher Reichsanzeiger*, 1911, no. 77.

just and equitable bases.[77] Rules based on custom or usage were sometimes referred to in multilateral conventions to which the Empire was a party.[78]

During the First World War there were occasional mentions of the general law in Germany's treaties. One which was signed in 1917 provided that consular relations between the two parties should be governed by general international law.[79] Some agreements drawn up late in the war with principal Allied and Associated Powers referred to preëxisting rules concerning the treatment of prisoners of war. The agreement with France of April 26, 1918, provided that retaliation contrary to international law in existing accords should not be resorted to until one month after due notice had been served on the competent diplomatic agent and on the Swiss government.[80] The terms of peace treaties which Germany prepared early in 1918, in relation to entities that had formerly been parts of Czarist Russia, looked to indemnities for damage done to consular officials and buildings during the war, and for that which civilians had sustained, in violation of international law.[81] A trade treaty with Finland, signed March 7, 1918, stated that protection of industrial property and copyright was to be granted in harmony with principles of law recognized in international relations.[82]

Clauses in the Treaty of Versailles which make direct reference

[77] 101 *Brit. and For. State Papers* 924, 925.

[78] In the agreement of November 4, 1911, relating to French Equatorial Africa, there is provision for the application of the assurances of commercial liberty and liberty of navigation as laid down in the Berlin Act, 1885, but without more direct mention of established customary law (104 *Brit. and For. State Papers* 956, 959).

[79] Consular Convention of January 11, 1917, with Turkey, and extension of this convention so as to make it applicable to German protectorates (9 N.R.G. [3d ser.] 691, 707, Preamble, par. 2). Article 14 of the first-mentioned convention provided that consular representations should be admissible in case of violations of general principles of international law.

[80] 111 *Brit. and For. State Papers* 713, 721 (art. XLII, par. 1). In an annexed agreement bearing the same date there is a reference to international law in connection with work of civilians in occupied territory (*ibid.* 721, 724, art. XVII, par. 3b).

[81] See the treaty of March 7, 1918, with Finland, articles III, XV (par. 1), and XVII (par. 2), and Additional Protocol of the same date with Finland, par. 2 (10 N.R.G. [3d ser.] 835). By the first of these instruments a mixed commission was to decide upon damages inflicted upon citizens in violation of international law and was to set forth the principles which should govern its decision.

See also the Additional Treaty of Peace drawn up with the Ukraine, February 9, 1918, articles II, XIII (par. 1), and XIV (par. 4) (10 N.R.G. [3d ser.] 763). The last-mentioned part of this treaty provided for the mutual cancellation of expenses incurred on account of war prisoners in accordance with principles of international law.

[82] 10 N.R.G. (3d ser.) 844 (art. XIII).

to international law have been noted in a previous section.[83] Perhaps the most conspicuous references to the general law in treaties which republican Germany made were in bilateral instruments providing for arbitration and conciliation. Of these, that with Switzerland, signed December 3, 1921, became the model for some later agreements. It provided for submission to arbitration of any point of international law arising between the two signatory countries, for the application (along with custom and conventions) of the general principles of law recognized by civilized nations, and for further powers of the arbitrators which were described as follows:

> If, in a particular case, the legal bases mentioned above are inadequate, the Tribunal shall give an award in accordance with the principles of law which, in its opinion, should govern international law. For this purpose it shall be guided by decisions sanctioned by legal authorities and by jurisprudence.[84]

Other bilateral arbitration agreements, without entrusting such wide powers to arbitrators, made questions of international law arbitrable.[85] In the Swiss treaty and in the treaty of arbitration and conciliation with Italy, December 29, 1926, there is the familiar provision looking to equitable satisfaction in the event an international tribunal should

[83] Section 1, this Appendix, notes 3–5.

[84] Art. V, 12 L.N.T.S. 271. The same provision appears in the 1924 convention of arbitration and conciliation with Sweden (42 L.N.T.S. 111), also in similar conventions made in 1925 with Finland and Estonia, respectively (43 *ibid.* 347; 63 *ibid.* 111). By a final protocol subjoined to the treaty with Sweden, there is inserted the same rule which was to be followed with Switzerland, namely: "The Contracting Parties are agreed that in doubtful cases the stipulation of the present Convention shall be interpreted in favour of the application of the principle of settlement of disputes by arbitration."

This general form of arbitration commitment was followed only in part in other instruments. See, for example, the treaty of May 16, 1929, with Turkey (109 L.N.T.S. 451). A variant from the formula of the Swiss-German treaty concerning the power of the arbitrators occurs in the convention which Germany signed with the Netherlands, May 20, 1926, and with Denmark, June 2, 1926 (66 L.N.T.S. 103; 61 *ibid.* 325). Instead of an authorization to arbitrators to decide according to rules which, in their opinion, should be rules of international law, there was an enumeration, in line with the general plan of the 38th article of the Statute of the Permanent Court of International Justice, of permissible bases for awards. In the Netherlands convention (article IV) the fourth of the bases listed consisted of "precedents laid down in recognized doctrine and legal practice as an auxiliary factor in the establishment of rules of law," while in the Danish agreement were specified (in article IV) "the results of recognized doctrine and legal practice as aids in the establishment of rules of law."

[85] See, for example, the 1928 treaties with the United States and Lithuania, respectively (90 L.N.T.S. 177, 233).

find that a decision of a court of law or other authority of one of the parties was wholly or partly at variance with international law and where the constitutional law of that party did not allow the cancellation of such decision.[86] By its terms, the treaty was not to apply to "disputes which, under the terms of Treaties in force between the two Parties, and according to international law, fall within the jurisdiction of either Party." [87] Equity (*Billigkeit*) is, by some treaties of this type, made a normal basis for tribunals' decisions; under others, it may be the basis if the parties specifically agree to it.[88] When becoming a party to certain multilateral agreements during the period, Germany subscribed to the principle, set forth in compromissary clauses, that questions of international law were arbitrable or justiciable.[89]

Perhaps the most common references to international law, for the

[86] Article III of the German-Italian treaty (78 L.N.T.S. 383).

[87] Article XIII.

[88] The former plan is illustrated in the convention of April 21, 1921, between Germany, Poland, and Danzig, concerning freedom of transit between East Prussia and the other parts of Germany (12 L.N.T.S. 61, art. XI, par. 2), and in the German-Polish treaty of June 11, 1931, regarding social insurance (141 L.N.T.S. 91, art. XLVII, par. 2). Illustrative of the latter is the treaty of arbitration and conciliation with Luxembourg, September 11, 1929 (118 L.N.T.S. 97). The latter contains in article V the authorization to tribunals similar to that quoted above from the Swiss treaty, but adds the statement, "If both parties agree, the Tribunal may, instead of basing its decisions on legal principles, give an award in accordance with considerations of equity."

In its claims arrangement of March 16, 1925, with Mexico, the German government provided in the second article for decision in conformity with the principles of equity, and in the third article the following: "The German Reich appreciates the friendly attitude adopted by . . . Mexico in consenting to its responsibility being fixed for the purposes of the present Arrangement only, in accordance with the principles of equity, and in refraining from basing a dismissal of these claims on Article XVIII of the Treaty of Friendship, Commerce and Navigation now in force between the two countries" (52 L.N.T.S. 93). The effect of such an authorization for application of equity was considered by the commission established under this agreement, which referred in one of its awards (relating to damages for the loss of crops in the field) to equity as authorizing the consideration of damages not according to fixed law. The German commissioner in a dissenting opinion thought that the cost of harvesting, labor, and expenses (elements for the estimation of which had not been furnished by the claimant) "must be calculated in equity" (Whiteman, *Damages in International Law,* II, 1453).

[89] See, for example, the Convention and Statute on the International Regime of Railways, December 9, 1923, art. XXXVI, par. 4 (47 L.N.T.S. 55); the Convention and Statute on the International Regime of Maritime Ports, of the same date, art. XXII, par. 4 (58 L.N.T.S. 285).

apparent purpose of declaring adherence to already established rules, occur in clauses relating to consular and diplomatic relations. Thus consular officers may be given the right to make representations for violations of the law [90] or existing rules made the standard for the obligatory concession of diplomatic or consular immunities.[91] Germany, like other principal states of Western Europe, in its treaties with Near Eastern states agreed to the application of rules of the law of nations as governing the treatment of diplomatic agents, consular officers, and nationals.[92] Prior to making these treaties, Germany had, in her agreement with China regarding the restoration of the state of peace, May 20, 1921, agreed that the two states' respective diplomatic agents should enjoy privileges and immunities accorded by international law.[93] By an exchange of notes at the time of the conclusion of

[90] Illustrated in consular conventions with Estonia (March 13, 1925), Lithuania (October 30, 1928), and Bulgaria (June 4, 1929), respectively (51 L.N.T.S. 263; 90 *ibid.* 255; 106 *ibid.* 49). Each of these conventions contains a clause whereby mentioned provisions are to apply to diplomatic representatives entrusted with consular duties, "without prejudice to the privileges already enjoyed by these officials in accordance with the principles of international law."

[91] Illustrated in certain agreements concerning double taxation, such as that with Hungary, November 6, 1923 (45 L.N.T.S. 253), that with Italy, October 31, 1925 (53 *ibid.* 245), those with Sweden, April 25, 1928, and May 14, 1935 (81 *ibid.* 281; 163 *ibid.* 459), and that of September 25, 1935, with Finland (172 *ibid.* 359). The typical statement, found in a final protocol in each case, is: "The present Convention shall not affect the immunities which are or may hereafter be granted to diplomatic or consular officials in virtue of the general rules of international law."

[92] See article II, par. 1, of the Treaty of Friendship with Afghanistan, March 3, 1926 (62 L.N.T.S. 115); articles II and III of the Treaty of Friendship with Turkey, March 3, 1924 (41 *ibid.* 237); article II of the Convention of January 12, 1927, with Turkey, concerning conditions of residence and business (73 *ibid.* 187); articles II and III of the Treaty of Friendship with Hejaz, Nejd and Dependencies, April 26, 1929 (115 *ibid.* 265); articles I, II, and III of the Convention of February 17, 1929, with Persia, regarding conditions of residence (111 *ibid.* 241). See also the earlier (May 15, 1928) exchange of notes with Persia, whereby, as from May 10, 1928, the diplomatic representatives of the Reich on Persian territory were to enjoy, subject to full reciprocity, the privileges and immunities established by "ordinary international law," and the consular representatives of the Reich on Persian territory were to enjoy the honorary privileges and personal immunities from jurisdiction and taxation established by "ordinary international law," subject to full reciprocity.

By article XXIX of the German-Turkish consular treaty of May 28, 1929 (133 L.N.T.S. 257), "the Constracting States agree that in cases for which no provision is made in the present Treaty they shall not act in a manner contrary to the principles of international law."

[93] 9 L.N.T.S. 271 (art. I).

this agreement, China promised that it would not again confiscate German property in China save in accordance with the recognized principles of international law (or its national law) and subject to reciprocity.[94]

Other declaratory references have to do with penal proceedings,[95] asylum,[96] territorial waters,[97] expulsion of foreigners from state territory,[98] police or military measures to be taken in a frontier region,[99] and to belligerent and neutral rights and duties.[100] Some elements of

[94] 9 L.N.T.S. 288 (par. 4a).

[95] Treaty of July 25, 1931, between Germany and Czechoslovakia, regulating the conditions of railway traffic across the frontier between the two countries: "In the matter of penal proceedings, execution of sentence or surrender affecting a person brought before the authorities in virtue of paragraph 3 of Article 21 for offences other than infringement of the Customs and Passport regulations, Article 12 of the Germano-Czechoslovak Extradition Convention of May 8, 1922 . . . shall apply. Failing an agreement, the rules of international law generally recognized as governing the particular principles involved shall be applicable" (187 L.N.T.S. 269, 369, final protocol, Ad Arts. 21 and 22, no. II).

[96] In the German-Polish agreement of June 16, 1926, regarding customs and passport formalities and railway traffic at Korzeniow (Kurzabrack), there is in the final protocol (Ad Art. II, b) a reservation on the granting of the right of asylum in accordance with the general principles of law (65 L.N.T.S. 379).

[97] In an agreement with Great Britain, March 11, 1913, Germany had assented to the rule that a boundary should extend as far as the three-mile limit of territorial jurisdiction (106 *Brit. and For. State Papers* 782, 785; art. XXI). In the convention of May 19, 1924, with the United States, she accepted the three-mile limit as marking the "proper" limits of territorial waters (41 L.N.T.S. 271, art. I). In the treaty of April 10, 1922, concerning transfer of North Schleswig, Germany and Denmark reserved the right to stop and search vessels within territorial waters in accordance with generally recognized rules of international law (10 L.N.T.S. 73, 251, art. IV, par. 1).

[98] A protocol supplementing certain parts of a commercial agreement between Germany and France, signed August 17, 1927, contains the following: "Subject to the right of expulsion which each of the High Contracting Parties may exercise in conformity with its laws and police regulations and with international law, each of the High Contracting Parties shall not restrict or limit the establishment or activities of the nationals of the other Party at present residing in its territory" (76 L.N.T.S. 5, 491, Ad Arts. 25 and 26, par. 3).

[99] See the reference, in an additional agreement to article 20 of the Commercial Treaty of June 1, 1923, with Lithuania, to measures to be taken over and above those which the Lithuanian government was bound to afford under international law (85 L.N.T.S. 357, art. XI, par. 8, no. 5).

[100] See, for example, article XVIII of the multilateral Convention and Statute on the International Regime of Maritime Ports, December 9, 1923 (58 L.N.T.S. 285). Rights and duties of belligerents and neutrals were

international law may be incorporated by broad references to general international practice, general rules of law, customary rules and usages, public law, existing practice, or usages in force. The rule concerning reciprocal freedom of commerce and navigation, which Germany and Japan had agreed upon in their commercial treaty of June 24, 1911,[101] was referred to in a German-Turkish treaty of commerce and navigation of January 12, 1927, which also mentioned "international principles" in an exceptions clause.[102] In a number of bilateral conventions and agreements regarding air navigation, made in the third and fourth decades of the twentieth century, the German government accepted the rule that the salvage of aircraft in distress at sea should, in the absence of arrangements to the contrary, be governed by the principles or rules of maritime law as embodied in existing international agreements.[103] An unusual provision, listed not because of its incorporation of international law, but because of the invocation of a set of rules outside the law of the parties, was included in the German-Polish convention of March 15, 1922, regarding Upper Silesia. In this the signatories agreed to arrange for the exchange of priests between two parts of the plebiscited territory in accordance with prescriptions of canon law.[104] In regulations which Germany and Denmark accepted for the common fisheries in Flensburg Fiord, technical rules were adopted pursuant to international agreement.[105]

So far as the mere language of the treaties is concerned, the period beginning with the coming to power of the National Socialists in Germany in 1933 does not reveal any sharp divergences from earlier treaty usage in the matter of incorporation by reference of parts or all of

---

not to be affected by the statute. By article VIII of the multilateral Convention of May 24, 1934, for the Unification of Certain Rules relating to the Immunity of State-Owned Vessels, nothing in the instrument was to affect the rights of the contracting states to take any measures that the rights and duties of neutrality might demand (176 L.N.T.S. 199).

[101] 105 *Brit. and For. State Papers* 646, 647 (art. III, par. 1).

[102] 73 L.N.T.S. 133 (art. IV, par. 2, clause 3).

[103] See the agreement with Great Britain and Northern Ireland (71 L.N.T.S. 165, art. XVIII, par. 2), the convention with Italy (79 *ibid.* 179, art. XVIII, par. 2), that with Spain (79 *ibid.* 203, art. XX, par. 2), that with Czechoslovakia (89 *ibid.* 231, art. XX, par. 2), that with Norway (93 *ibid.* 197, art. XIX, par. 2), that with Belgium (127 *ibid.* 149, art. XVIII, par. 2), that with Poland (146 *ibid.* 333, art. XX, par. 2), that with Greece (182 *ibid.* 9, art. XVIII, par. 2), that with Estonia (189 *ibid.* 333, art. XX, par. 2), and that with Roumania (190 *ibid.* 369, art. XX, par. 2). In all except the agreement with the United Kingdom and the convention with Poland, it was provided that, in the absence of conventions, salvage would be subject to the law of the salvors' state. The Polish-German convention refers merely to the principles of maritime law.

[104] 118 *Brit. and For. State Papers* 365, 399 (art. XCIV, 2).

[105] Regulations adopted January 25, 1926; text in 44 L.N.T.S. 389.

general international law. National Socialist doctrines regarding the relative value and force of international agreements would, of course, need to be considered in estimating the possible significance of these clauses or any others in treaties of the Third Reich.

5. ITALY

It has been seen that in various Hague Conventions of 1907 there were references to the general law. To a number of these Italy became a party.[106] Another instance, in the period before 1914, in which the Italian government subscribed to customary international law was in the treaty of peace, commerce, navigation, emigration, and arbitration signed with Cuba on December 29, 1903. The parties agreed that, "as regards the claims or complaints of private individuals in matters of civil, criminal, or administrative nature," their diplomatic agents would not intervene except "in cases of . . . express violation . . . of the precepts of international law, public or private, generally admitted by civilized nations." [107] A convention signed with Guatemala on November 13, 1905, relative to the position of the consuls and subjects of the two countries, provided that "in case of defect or insufficiency in the dispositions of the present Convention, recourse will be had to the general principles of international law and of international law and custom, the strictest reciprocity being observed in all cases." [108] Italy went further than did some of the other major states, in the period before 1914, toward acceptance of obligatory arbitration in bilateral commitments. It was consistent with this tendency to provide in treaties that questions relative to the interpretation and application of a principle of international law should be arbitrable [109] or that an arbiter must decide according to the principles of law, unless the parties by a special agreement should direct otherwise.[110] In the treaty of peace at the end of the Italo-Turkish War in 1912, Italy promised support to the Sublime Porte in negotiations looking to the replacement of the system of Capitulations with "le régime du droit international." [111]

Of the later treaties falling within the classification, those relating to consular matters are perhaps most conspicuous. With countries

[106] The same general statement would apply to the Red Cross Convention of July 6, 1906, which contained at least four references to more general law (99 *Brit. and For. State Papers* 968, at pp. 972 and 974, arts. II, par. 1; XV, par. 1; XVI; XVII, par. 2).

[107] 96 *Brit. and For. State Papers* 370, at 374 (art. XII, par. 2).

[108] 100 *Brit. and For. State Papers* 1061, at 1070 (art. XXIV).

[109] As in article II, par. 2, of the arbitration convention of September 22, 1911, with Brazil (104 *Brit. and For. State Papers* 833).

[110] As in article IX of the general treaty of arbitration with Peru, April 18, 1905 (101 *Brit. and For. State Papers* 374, at 376).

[111] 106 *Brit. and For. State Papers* 1100, at 1102.

where extraterritoriality had once existed, Italy made the same general type of agreement that other major European states made. Thus in the treaty of friendship, commerce, and navigation with Siam, signed May 9, 1926, there was a provision that consular officers should exercise all the powers and functions, and enjoy all the "honours," privileges, exemptions and immunities which are generally accorded by international law." [112] With Persia, in the treaty of friendship signed September 5, 1929, it was agreed that the parties should continue their diplomatic and consular relations "in conformity with the principles and practice of common international law," and that diplomatic and consular representatives of each should receive, in the territory of the other, the treatment recognized by such principles and practice.[113] The Italo-Turkish consular convention of September 9, 1929, stated in the preamble the parties' desire to establish consular relations between themselves "on the basis of general international law and the principle of reciprocity," and provided that consular officers might apply to the administrative authorities within their respective consular districts and make claims for breach of treaties or of "the general principles of international law." [114] The treaty of friendship with Hejaz, Nejd and Dependencies, signed February 10, 1932, set forth that the diplomatic and consular representatives of each party should enjoy in the territory of the other the treatment established by the principles of international law, and separately recorded the understanding that "the principles of international law in force between independent Governments shall be respected." [115]

Conventions with other states contained references to the general law in connection with consular functions, duties, and immunities. With Panama, in 1929, Italy contracted that consuls should enjoy in the discharge of their duties and with regard to their persons "the same honours, privileges, immunities and exemptions as are generally admitted by international law." [116] Conventions of 1924 with Czechoslovakia and Yugoslavia, respectively, gave to consular officers the right to protect their nationals and defend their rights and interests "within the limits of international law and custom." [117] In certain treaties of commerce and navigation, Italy agreed that obstacles to trade would not be imposed except for sanitary protection and reasons of public health, in conformity with "international usage in this matter" or "international principles in this respect." [118]

[112] 124 *Brit. and For. State Papers* 1000, at 1007 (art. 23, par. 3).
[113] 141 L.N.T.S. 185, at 187 (art. 2).
[114] 129 L.N.T.S. 195, 197, 205 (preamble and art. 16).
[115] 135 *Brit. and For. State Papers* 572, 573 (arts. 2, 5).
[116] 138 L.N.T.S. 355, at 389 (art. 20).
[117] 34 L.N.T.S. 56, at 63 (art. 11); 82 *ibid.* 445, at 459 (art. 19, par. 1).
[118] Commercial treaties with Yugoslavia (1924), Greece (1926), and Lithuania (1927) will illustrate (82 L.N.T.S. 257, at 265, art. 7, sec. 5; 63

Agreements for pacific settlement of international disputes contained references to international law, for example, the statement that a question of international law was adjudicable,[119] or that there should be equitable satisfaction where a measure of a court or other national authority of one of the parties should be found contrary to international law and the constitutional law of that party should not permit a remedy through administrative procedure.[120] In their treaty of neutrality, conciliation, and judicial settlement, signed in 1928, Italy and Turkey reserved questions relating to sovereignty "according to international law," [121] and in agreements with certain other states there were reservations of questions falling within domestic jurisdiction.[122] In a number of treaties providing for judicial settlement, Italy agreed to the rule that if, in the opinion of the Permanent Court of International Justice, a particular dispute were not of a legal nature, it should be decided *ex aequo et bono*.[123] In a convention with Mexico for the settlement of Italian claims arising out of revolutionary disturbances in Mexico, Italy secured a provision similar to that which appeared in the special claims conventions which Mexico made with the United States, Great Britain, France, and Germany, respectively.[124]

Certain of Italy's treaties referred incidentally to the international

---

ibid. 51, at 61, art. 10, sec. 5; 73 *ibid.* 9, at 17, art. 7, sec. 5). Variants of the same provision occur in at least seven other treaties of commerce and navigation listed, the typical statement being that the parties will not apply trade restrictions save in those cases where measures taken are in the interest of public health and are in conformity with the international principles adopted on this subject.

[119] See, for example, the multilateral Opium Convention of February 19, 1925, art. 32, par. 7 (81 L.N.T.S. 317, at 347), and the Italian-Siamese treaty of December 3, 1937 (189 L.N.T.S. 255, at 262), article 7 of which provided for the application of the Convention and Statute on the International Regime of Maritime Ports, December 9, 1923 (58 L.N.T.S. 285).

[120] Eleven such treaties of Italy have been listed, all of them being with European states except the agreement with Chile. See, for example, the treaty between Italy and Germany (78 L.N.T.S. 383, at 397, art. 3).

[121] 95 L.N.T.S. 183, at 187 (art. 3). The same article provided that arbitral awards should be rendered according to the principles of international law.

[122] See the treaty of December 29, 1926, with Germany (cited in note 120), and that of February 6, 1930, with Austria (105 L.N.T.S. 97, at 115). The former was not to apply to disputes which "according to international law" fell within the jurisdiction of either party; the latter excepted questions which, "in virtue of treaties in force between the two Parties or of international law" should come within the jurisdiction of either party.

[123] Illustrated in treaties with Lithuania (72 L.N.T.S. 439, at 447); Yugoslavia (18 *ibid.* 461, at 508); Chile (69 *ibid.* 277); Spain (67 *ibid.* 365, at 379); and Finland (129 *Brit. and For. State Papers* 510, at 513).

[124] 127 *Brit. and For. State Papers* 780, 781 (art. 2).

law of war. For example, conventions with her near neighbors on the subject of railway communication and transit made it clear that the instruments did not prescribe rights and duties of belligerents or neutrals, and that the conventions were to continue in force in time of war so long as belligerent rights and duties should permit.[125] As one of the parties to the Convention on the Regime of the Straits, 1923, Italy assented to the provision that the rights of Turkey as a belligerent (specifically, the right to apply to enemy vessels the measures allowed by international law) were not affected by the convention.[126] With the other states which signed the Convention on the Non-Fortification of the Aaland Islands, October 20, 1921, Italy agreed that, despite the convention, the right of innocent passage would continue to be governed by "the international rules and usages in force." [127]

Of all the treaties which Italy made during the selected period, that of February 11, 1929, with the Holy See, in which the Italian government recognized the Vatican State, contains the greatest number of references to customary international law. By article 7, "in conformity with the rules of international law, the flight of aircraft of any kind whatever over Vatican territory is prohibited." By article 9, "in accordance with the rules of international law all persons having permanent residence within the Vatican City shall be subject to the sovereignty of the Holy See." In article 12, Italy recognized the right of the Holy See to active and passive legation "in accordance with the general rules of international law"; envoys of foreign governments were to enjoy the privileges and immunities appertaining to diplomatic agents "in virtue of international law"; their headquarters could remain in Italian territory and there enjoy the immunities due them in accordance with international law; diplomatic agents of the Holy See were to enjoy in Italy the treatment due diplomatic agents of foreign governments in accordance with rules of the law. Property of the Holy See in Italian territory was, by article 15, to have immunities recognized by international law as appertaining to the headquarters of foreign diplomats. Finally, article 23 provided that the rules of international law were to apply as regards the execution in Italy of judgments of the courts of the Vatican City.[128]

The evidence seems to support two general observations concern-

[125] See the convention of July 14, 1924, with Yugoslavia, art. 14 (82 L.N.T.S. 327, at 337); that with Yugoslavia, Austria, and Hungary, March 29, 1923, art. 7 (23 *ibid.* 255, at 416); multilateral convention on International Regime of Railways, December 9, 1923, statute, art. 32 (47 *ibid.* 56, at 85). A similar provision is in the convention on International Regime of Maritime Ports, December 9, 1923, statute, art. 18 (58 *ibid.* 285, at 307).

[126] 28 L.N.T.S. 116, at 121 (art. II, annex 1, c). Other references to belligerent rights, in the same convention, are at pp. 123, 131.

[127] 9 L.N.T.S., 211, at 219 (art. 5).

[128] A text of the treaty is in 130 *Brit. and For. State Papers* at 791.

ing Italian treaties of the period. Those concluded after 1922 do not in terms reveal any distinctive theory of international law identifiable with fascism. Aside from provisions that arbitrators may decide questions *ex aequo et bono,* there seems to have been little tendency to specify, in connection with mentions of the law, standards to be derived from equity, custom, or usage.[129]

6. JAPAN

In contrast to the treaty practice of the other major states, that of Japan from the beginning of the twentieth century to the outbreak of the Second World War shows that very little use was made of the technique of incorporating the rules of general international law by reference in texts. It has been seen that in at least two instances (fisheries agreements with Russia, in 1907 and 1928), the law was specified as the standard to determine the limits of rivers in relation to the sea.[130] Diplomatic relations furnished occasion for some references to general rules. For example, the Japanese-Mexican commercial treaty of October 8, 1924, set forth that diplomatic agents should not intervene (in behalf of their respective nationals) unless all legal methods should have failed and in the case of an express violation of the "rules of International Law both public and private as generally recognized by civilised nations." [131] Under Japan's treaty of friendship and commerce with Albania, signed in 1930, diplomatic representatives of each party were to receive, in the territory of the other, the treatment established by the principles of international law.[132] In the same year Japan and Afghanistan provided in a treaty of friendship that the head and members of a diplomatic mission, being of the nationality of the country represented, should enjoy all the rights, privileges, exemptions, and immunities which were then or might thereafter be recognized in international law.[133]

A treaty of judicial settlement, arbitration, and conciliation which Japan signed with the Netherlands on April 19, 1933, referred, in connection with the bases for arbitral awards, to "international custom regarded as the expression of general practice accepted as law" and

[129] In the preliminary treaty of amity and commerce with China, signed November 27, 1928, the principles of absolute equality and nondiscrimination in the parties' commercial relations, and of mutual respect for sovereignty, are emphasized (93 L.N.T.S. 173, at 177). The principle of equal treatment (with third states) is specified in a convention respecting commercial travelers, which Italy signed with Turkey in 1927 (127 *Brit. and For. State Papers* 795, at 797).

[130] See notes 65 and 66, *supra.*

[131] 36 L.N.T.S. 259, at 281 (art. XXV).

[132] 123 *ibid.* 295, at 297 (art. II).

[133] 121 *ibid.* 237, at 239 (art. 1).

to "general principles of law recognized by civilised nations."[134] An exceptions clause in a commercial treaty (with Poland, 1922) referred to the "special laws of protection of the national commercial vessels according to the international custom."[135] Rights and duties of belligerents and neutrals are the subjects of references in certain conventions to which Japan became a party, such as the Barcelona Convention and Statute on Freedom of Transit, 1923.[136]

While the Japanese Empire in the early part of the period under review appears to have made some use of the method of treaty reference to the law relating to consular relations, its later policy was apparently to avoid specific mentions in the treaties of those consular functions which clearly rest upon international usage,[137] and merely to indicate in treaties the right of consular officers to exercise functions permitted to like agents of the most favored nation. On matters such as the administration of estates of deceased nationals, there was apparently thought to be more need for precision in treaties, but not necessarily for mention of the general rules of international law, since those rules did not afford specific guidance on the points.[138]

[134] 163 *ibid.* 351, at 357 (art. 8).

[135] 120 *Brit. and For. State Papers* 724, at 729 (art. 18).

[136] 7 L.N.T.S. 11, at 29 (art. 8).

[137] On the point that some consular functions are based on customary international law, while others are not, see Oppenheim, *International Law* (3d ed., 1920), I, 599.

[138] See K. Matsudaïra, *Le Droit conventionnel international du Japon* (1931), p. 147. The same writer suggests (p. 67) that the development of law concerning a state's responsibility for the protection of foreigners within its jurisdiction probably makes it less necessary than it was in the seventeenth and eighteenth centuries to cover in great detail in treaty texts the different phases of protection.

On subjects other than those mentioned in this section, there are in the treaties of Japan some indirect references to international law. See, for example, the affirmation in a Japanese–Russian treaty of the parties' desire to respect scrupulously the "droit incontestable" of a state to organize its internal life within the limits of its own jurisdiction (referred to by Matsudaïra, pp. 15–16).

BIBLIOGRAPHY

OFFICIAL DOCUMENTS

American and British Claims Arbitration, under special agreement concluded between the United States and Great Britain, August 18, 1910; Report of Fred K. Nielsen. Washington: Government Printing Office, 1926.

American-Mexican Claims Commission under Act of Congress approved December 18, 1942; Report to the Secretary of State. Department of State Publication 2859. 1948.

American and Panamanian General Claims Arbitration, under conventions between the United States and Panama of July 28, 1926, and December 17, 1932; Report of Bert L. Hunt, Agent for the United States. Department of State, Arbitration Series 6. 1934.

American State Papers: Foreign Affairs.

Annual Message of the President to Congress. Senate Document 1, 28th Congress, 1st Session. 1843.

Boutwell's *Report.* See *French-American Claims Commission.*

British and Foreign State Papers. Great Britain, Foreign Office. London: H. M. Stationery Office, 1841–1950.

Clark, J. Reuben. *Right to Protect Citizens in Foreign Countries by Landing Forces; Memorandum of the Solicitor for the Department of State, October 5, 1912.* Department of State Publication 538. 3d rev. ed., 1934.

Commission Franco-Mexicaine. *La Réparation des dommages causes aux étrangers par les mouvements révolutionnaires: Jurisprudence de la commission franco-mexicaine des réclamations* (*1924–1932*). Paris: A. Pedone, 1933.

Compensation for American-owned lands expropriated in Mexico; full text of official notes, July 21–November 12, 1938. Department of State Publication 1288. 1939.

Conference on Limitation of Armament, 1921–1922. Senate Document 126, 67th Congress, 2d Session. 1922.

Conference on the Limitation of Armament, November 12, 1921–February 6, 1922: [*Proceedings of*] *Subcommittees.* 1922.

Congressional Globe. December 2, 1833–March 3, 1873.

Congressional Record.

Correspondence regarding the resumption of relations with the Government of the Union of Soviet Socialist Republics. Cmd. 3418. *Parliamentary Papers.* 1929.

Correspondence with the Government of the United States respecting communication to other Governments of the Rules of the Treaty of Washington. No. 1: C. 1012 (1874); No. 2: C. 8393 (1897). *Parliamentary Papers.* 1874 and 1897.
Department of State Bulletin.
Department of State Press Releases.
Despatch from Viscount Cecil of Chelwood inclosing the report of the Preparatory Commission for the Disarmament Conference and the Draft Disarmament Convention. Cmd. 3757. *Parliamentary Papers.* 1931.
Deutscher Reichsanzeiger. Publication of the German Reichsministerium des Innern.
Deuxieme Conférence internationale de la paix, actes et documents. 3 vols. La Haye: Imprimerie national, 1907.
Diplomatic Correspondence of the United States of America from September 10, 1783, to March 4, 1789. 1833.
Draft Disarmament Convention submitted to the Disarmament Conference at Geneva on March 16, 1933, by the Right Honourable J. Ramsay MacDonald. Cmd. 4279. *Parliamentary Papers.* 1933.
Executive Agreement Series. United States Department of State.
Fourth International Conference of American States, 1910. Senate Document 744, 61st Congress, 3d Session. 1911.
French-American Claims Commission; Report by George S. Boutwell. House Executive Document 235, 48th Congress, 2d Session. 1884.
Geneva Conventions of August 12, 1949, for Protection of War Victims. Department of State Publication 3938, General Foreign Policy Series 34. 1950.
Hackworth, Green Haywood. *A Digest of International Law.* 8 vols. Washington: Government Printing Office, 1940–1944.
Hague Conference for the Codification of International Law, 1930. *Minutes of the Third Committee: Responsibility of States for Damage Caused to the Person or Property of Foreigners.* League of Nations Document C.351(c).M.145(c).1930.V.
Hague Conference for the Codification of International Law, 1930. *Minutes of the Second Committee: Territorial Waters.* League of Nations Document C.351(b).M.145(b).1930.V.
Hansard. *Parliamentary Debates.*
Hearings before the Joint Committee on the Investigation of the Pearl Harbor Attack. 79th Congress, 1st Session. 1946.
Hearings before a Subcommittee of the Committee on Foreign Relations, United States Senate, 80th Congress, 2nd Session, on a Treaty of Friendship, Commerce and Navigation between the United States of America and the Republic of China, Together with a Protocol thereto Signed at Nanking, November 4, 1946. 80th Congress, 2d Session. 1948.

Hearings on H.J. Res. 32, 73, 123 (International reciprocity in patents and payments and protection). House of Representatives, Committee on Patents, 77th Congress, 1st Session. 1941.

Hearings on H.J. Res. 221 requesting the President to Propose Calling of a Third Hague Conference for Codification of International Law. House of Representatives, Committee on Foreign Affairs, 69th Congress, 1st Session. 1926.

Hearings on H.R. 1776 (Lend-Lease bill). House of Representatives, Committee on Foreign Affairs, 77th Congress, 1st Session. 1941.

Hearings on S. 275 (superseded by H.R. 1776, Lend-Lease bill). Senate, Committee on Foreign Relations. 77th Congress, 1st Session. 1941.

Hearings on London Naval Treaty of 1930. Senate, Committee on Naval Affairs, 71st Congress, 2d Session. 1930.

Hearings on S. 2528 (claims of American nationals against the Mexican government). Senate, Committee on Foreign Relations, 77th Congress, 2d Session. 1942.

House of Representatives. *Journal.*

Hunt's *Report.* See *American and Panamanian General Claims Arbitration.*

"I'm Alone" Case. Department of State, Arbitration Series 2.

International Law Commission: Report Covering Its First Session, April 12–June 9, 1949. United Nations, General Assembly, *Official Records,* 4th Session, Supplement 10 (A/925), June 24, 1949. Also in *American Journal of International Law,* XLIV, Supplement (1950), 1–21.

International Law Commission: Report Covering Its Second Session, June 5–July 29, 1950. United Nations, General Assembly, *Official Records,* 5th Session, Supplement 12 (A/1316). Also in *American Journal of International Law,* XLIV, Supplement (1950), 105–148.

International Law Documents. United States Naval War College. Before 1940 this series was called *International Law Situations.*

International Technical Consulting Committee on Radio Communication. Department of State Publication 320. 1932.

Journal Officiel de la République Française.

Journals of the Continental Congress, 1774–1789. Edited by W. C. Ford, G. Hunt, J. C. Fitzpatrick, R. R. Hill. 34 vols. Washington: Government Printing Office, 1904–1937.

Continental Congress: Secret Journals of Congress, Foreign Affairs.

League of Nations Treaty Series (L.N.T.S.).

Limitation and Reduction of Armament; Minority Views. Senate Report 1080, part 2, 71st Congress, 2d Session. 1930.

London Naval Treaty of 1930. Senate Document 197, 71st Congress, 2d Session. 1930.

London Naval Conference, 1935; Report of the Delegates of the United States. Department of State Publication 896, Conference Series 24. 1936.

Memorandum on the London Naval Conference, December 9, 1935, to March 25, 1936. Cmd. 5137. *Parliamentary Papers,* Miscellaneous no. 2. 1936.

Memorandum on the signature by His Majesty's Government in the United Kingdom of the Optional Clause of the Statute of the Permanent Court of International Justice. Cmd. 3452. *Parliamentary Papers.* 1929.

Memorial on Navigation of the Amazon. House of Representatives, Miscellaneous Document 22, 33d Congress, 1st Session. 1854.

Message of the President on the Right of Way across the Isthmus of Tehuantepec. Senate Executive Document 97, 32d Congress, 1st Session. 1852.

Message on Correspondence with Mr. J. L. Motley. Senate Executive Document 11, 41st Congress, 3d Session. 1871.

Message on Neutrality Rules (Treaty of Washington). Senate Executive Document 26, 45th Congress, 3d Session. 1879.

Message on Railroad across the Isthmus of Tehuantepec. Senate Executive Document 72, 35th Congress, 1st Session. 1858.

Miller, David Hunter (ed.). *Treaties and Other International Acts of the United States of America.* 8 vols. to date. Washington: Government Printing Office, 1931–1948.

Moore, John Bassett. *A Digest of International Law.* 8 vols. Washington: Government Printing Office, 1906.

Nielsen's *Report.* See *American and British Claims Arbitration.*

The North Atlantic Pact. Department of State Publication 3462. 1949.

Octava conferencia internacional americana. Diario de sesiones (Versiones Taquigraficas). Lima, Peru: Imprenta Torres Aguirre, 1938.

Official Opinions of the Attorneys General of the United States. Department of Justice. 1852 to present.

Papers Relating to the Foreign Relations of the United States.

Papers Relating to the Foreign Relations of the United States: The Lansing Papers, 1914–1920. 2 vols. Washington: Government Printing Office, 1939–1940.

Papers Relating to the Foreign Relations of the United States: The Paris Peace Conference, 1919. 13 vols. Washington: Government Printing Office, 1942–1947.

Papers Relating to the Treaty of Washington. 5 vols. Washington: Government Printing Office, 1872–1874.

Parliamentary Papers: North America, no. 1. 1866.

Parliamentary Papers: North America, no. 3. 1871. c. 346.

Permanent Court of International Justice. Series A: *Judgments.* Series A/B: *Combined Opinions.* Leyden: A. J. Sithoff.

Postwar Foreign Policy Preparation, 1939–1945. Department of State Publication 3580. 1950.

Proceedings of the Commission for the Adjustment of Claims under the Convention with Great Britain of February 8, 1853. Senate Executive Document 103, 34th Congress, 1st Session. 1856.

Proceedings of the International Civil Aviation Conference, Chicago, Illinois, November 1–December 7, 1944. 2 vols. Department of State Publication 2820. 1948, 1949.

Proceedings of the United States–Mexican Commission Convened in Mexico City, May 14, 1923. 1925.

Proposals for agreements between His Majesty's Government in Great Britain and the Norwegian Government regarding territorial waters and fisheries off the Norwegian coast. Cmd. 3121. *Parliamentary Papers.* 1929.

Ralston's *Report.* See *Venezuelan Arbitrations of 1903.*

Reply of Soviet Government to His Majesty's Government on the relations between the two Governments. Cmd. 1874. *Parliamentary Papers.* 1923.

Report of Robert H. Jackson, United States Representative to the International Conference on Military Trials, London, 1945. Department of State Publication 3080. 1949.

Report of the Canadian Delegate to the Conference on the Limitation of Naval Armament held at London, January 21, 1930, to April 22, 1930. Canada, Sessional Paper 47. 1930.

Report of the Delegates of the United States of America to the Sixth International Conference of American States. Washington: Government Printing Office, 1928.

Report of the Delegation of the United States to the Ninth International Conference of American States, with Related Documents. Department of State Publication 3263. 1948.

Report of the Delegation of the United States to the Inter-American Conference for the Maintenance of Peace, Buenos Aires, December 1–23, 1936. Department of State Publication 1088, Conference Series 33. 1937.

Report of the Delegation of the United States to the Inter-American Conference for the Maintenance of Continental Peace and Security, Quitandinha, Brazil, August 15–September 2, 1947. Department of State Publication 3016. 1948.

Report on the Claim of Francis P. Ferreira. Senate Miscellaneous Document 55, 36th Congress, 1st Session. 1860.

Report on North Atlantic Coast Fisheries Arbitration at The Hague. Senate Document 870, 61st Congress, 3d Session. 1912.

Report on the Treaty with Spain of 1819. House of Representatives Report 16, 20th Congress, 1st Session. 1827.

Rules of Submarine Warfare. Procès-verbal relating to the Rules set forth in Part IV of the Treaty of London of April 22, 1930. Cmd. 5302. *Parliamentary Papers,* Treaty Series no. 2. 1936.

Salem Claim: Award of the Arbitral Tribunal. Department of State, Arbitration Series 4(6). 1933.

Seventh International Conference of American States, Minutes and Antecedents with General Index. Montevideo: Imprenta Nacional, 1933.

Spanish Treaty Claims Commission: Documents and Opinions. Washington: Government Printing Office, 1904–1910.

To Promote the Defense of the United States (H.R. 1776, Lend-Lease bill). Senate Report 45, 77th Congress, 1st Session. 1941.

Treaties and Other International Acts Series (T.I.A.S.).

Senate Executive D, Treaty with Uruguay. Senate Executive Report 5, 81st Congress, 2d Session. 1950.

Trial of the Major War Criminals before the International Military Tribunal, Nuremberg, 19 November 1945–1 October 1946. 42 vols. Nuremberg, Germany, 1947–1949.

United Nations, Conference on International Organization, San Francisco, 1945. *Documents.* 16 vols. London, New York: United Nations Information Organizations, 1945–46.

United Nations, General Assembly. *Official Records.*

United Nations, General Assembly. *Verbatim Record of the Plenary Meetings.* Second Part of the First Session, 23 October–16 December, 1946.

United Nations, Secretariat. *Survey of International Law in relation to the Work of Codification of the International Law Commission.* Document A/CN.4/1. November 5, 1948.

United States and Germany, Mixed Claims Commission. *Administrative Decisions and Opinions of a General Nature and Opinions in Individual Lusitania Claims and Other Cases to October 1, 1926.* Washington: Government Printing Office, 1926.

United States and Mexico, General Claims Commission. *Opinions of Commissioners, 1927.* Washington: Government Printing Office, 1927.

United States and Mexico, General Claims Commission. *Opinions of Commissioners, 1931.* Washington: Government Printing Office, 1931.

United States and Mexico, Special Claims Commission. *Opinions of Commissioners, 1926–1931.* Washington: Government Printing Office, 1931.

United States and Panama, General Claims Commission. *Comisión general de reclamaciones entre Panamá y Estados Unidos de América.* Panama: Imprenta Nacional, 1934.

United States Statutes at Large.

United States Treaty Series (U.S.T.S.).

Venezuelan Arbitrations of 1903, [Report] by Jackson H. Ralston. Senate Document 316, 58th Congress, 2d Session. 1904.

Wharton, Francis. *A Digest of International Law of the United States.* 3 vols. Washington, 1886. Also published as Senate Miscellaneous Document 162, 49th Congress, 1st Session.

Wharton, Francis (ed.). *The Revolutionary Diplomatic Correspondence of the United States.* 6 vols. House Miscellaneous Document 603, 50th Congress, 1st Session. 1889.

BOOKS AND ARTICLES

Adams, Charles Francis. *Before and After the Treaty of Washington.* New York: New York Historical Society, 1902.

—— *Lee at Appomattox and Other Papers.* Boston and New York: Houghton Mifflin, 1902.

Adams, John Quincy. *The Duplicate Letters, the Fisheries and the Mississippi.* Washington: Davis and Force, 1822.

Allen, Carleton Kemp. *Law in the Making.* 3d ed. Oxford: Clarendon Press, 1939.

Anderson, Chandler P. "The Scope and Character of Arbitration Treaties," *Proceedings of the American Society of International Law,* 1929, pp. 110–119.

Annual Digest of Public International Law Cases. Edited by H. Lauterpacht and others. London, New York: Longmans, Green, 1929 to date. These volumes cover the period since 1919.

Anzilotti, Dionisio. *Cours de droit international.* Paris: Recueil Sirey, 1929.

Assman, Kurt. "Why U-boat Warfare Failed," *Foreign Affairs,* XXVIII (1949–50), 659–670.

Bacon, Ruth. "British and American Policy and the Right of Fluvial Navigation," *British Year Book of International Law,* XIII (1932), 76–92.

Bailey, T. A. "The Sinking of the Lusitania," *American Historical Review,* XLI (1935), 54–73.

Basdevant, Jules. *Les Déportations du nord de la France et de la Belgique en vue de travail forcé et le droit international.* Paris: L. Tenin, 1917.

Bemis, Samuel F. (ed.). *The American Secretaries of State and Their Diplomacy.* 10 vols. New York: Knopf, 1927–1929.

—— *Pinckney's Treaty.* Baltimore: Johns Hopkins University Press, 1926.

Bilsel, Cemil. "International Law in Turkey," *American Journal of International Law,* XXXVIII (1944), 546–556.

Bingham, Joseph W. *Report on the International Law of Pacific Coastal Fisheries.* Stanford University: Stanford University Press, 1938.

Blakeslee, George H. "The Foreign Policy of the United States," in Quincy Wright (ed.), *Interpretations of American Foreign Policy*. Chicago: University of Chicago Press, 1930.

Bluntschli, Johann K. "Opinion impartiale sur la question de l'Alabama et sur la manière de la résoudre," *Revue de droit international et de législation comparée*, II (1870), 452–485.

Borchard, Edwin M. *The Diplomatic Protection of Citizens Abroad*. New York: The Banks Law Publishing Co., 1915.

—— "Armed Merchantmen," *American Journal of International Law*, XXXIV (1940), 107–112.

—— "International Law," *Encyclopedia of the Social Sciences*, VII (1937), 167–173.

—— "The 'Minimum Standard' of the Treatment of Aliens," *Proceedings of the American Society of International Law*, 1939, pp. 51–74.

—— "The Neutrality Claims against Great Britain," *American Journal of International Law*, XXI (1927), 764–768.

—— "The Opinions of the Mixed Claims Commission, United States and Germany," *American Journal of International Law*, XIX (1925), 133–143.

—— "The Place of Force in International Law," *American Journal of International Law*, XXXVI (1942), 628–631.

—— "The Resurrection of International Law," *Proceedings of the American Society of International Law*, 1923, pp. 61–70.

—— "War, Neutrality and Non-Belligerency," *American Journal of International Law*, XXXV (1941), 618–625.

Borel, Eugène. "La Compétence du juge international en equité," *Annuaire de l'Institut de Droit International*, XXXVIII (1934), 182–225.

Bourquin, Maurice. "Règles générales du droit de la paix," *Recueil des cours*, XXXV (1931), 5–232.

Bridgman, P. W. *The Intelligent Individual and Society*. New York: Macmillan, 1938.

Brierly, J. L. *The Law of Nations*. 4th ed. Oxford: Clarendon Press, 1949.

Briggs, Herbert W. "Neglected Aspects of the Destroyer Deal," *American Journal of International Law*, XXXIV (1940), 569–587.

—— "The Settlement of Mexican Claims Act of 1942," *American Journal of International Law*, XXXVII (1943), 222–232.

Brinton, Jasper Y. "Egypt: The Transition Period," *American Journal of International Law*, XXXIV (1940), 208–219.

Brown, Philip Marshall. "The Renovation of International Law," *American Journal of International Law*, XXXVI (October 1942), 631–637.

Brucy, Jean. *Les Traités et la réglementation du droit de la guerre.* Paris: A. Pedone, 1917.

Bulloch, James D. *The Secret Service of the Confederate States in Europe.* 2 vols. New York: Putnam, 1884.

Butler, Geoffrey, and Simon Maccoby. *The Development of International Law.* New York and London: Longmans, Green, 1928.

Callahan, James M. "The Mexican Policy of Southern Leaders under Buchanan's Administration," *American Historical Association, Annual Report for 1910* (1912), pp. 135–151.

Carreño, Alberto M. *México y los Estados Unidos de América.* México: Imprenta Victoria, 1922.

Cass, Lewis. *An Examination of the Question, Now in Discussion, between the American and British Governments, Concerning the Right of Search,* "By an American" (1842). Text of pamphlet may be found in William T. Young, *Life of General Lewis Cass,* Detroit: Markham and Elwood, 1852, pp. 136–166.

Castberg, Fred. "La Méthodologie du droit international public," *Recueil des cours,* XLIII (1933), 313–381.

Chadwick, F. E. *The Relations of the United States and Spain.* New York: Scribner, 1909.

Clark, Keith. *International Communications.* New York: Columbia University Press; London: P. S. King and Son, 1931.

Cobden, Richard. *Speeches on Questions of Public Policy.* Edited by John Bright and James E. T. Rogers. 2 vols. London: Macmillan, 1870.

Collette, Jean. *Les Principes de droit des gens dans la jurisprudence de la Cour Permanente de Justice Internationale.* Paris: Berger-Levrault, 1932.

Corbett, Percy. "Conflicting Theories of International Law," *Proceedings of the American Society of International Law,* 1940, pp.101–104; and remarks, pp. 159–160.

Cowles, Willard B. "Joint Action to Protect an American State from Axis Subversive Activity," *American Journal of International Law,* XXXVI (1942), 242–251.

Cushing, Caleb. *The Treaty of Washington.* New York: Harper, 1873.

Daniels, Paul C. "Influence of Inter-American Relations on U.S. Foreign Policy," *Department of State Bulletin,* XX, 460–463 (April 10, 1949).

Davis, George B. "Doctor Francis Lieber's Instructions for the Government of Armies in the Field," *American Journal of International Law,* I (1907), 13–25.

Davis, J. C. Bancroft. *Mr. Fish and the Alabama Claims.* Boston and New York: Houghton Mifflin, 1893.

Deener, David R. "International Law Provisions in Post-World War II Constitutions," *Cornell Law Quarterly,* XXXVI (1951). 505–533.

Des Gouttes, Paul. *La Convention de Genève du 27 juillet 1929*. Geneva: Comité international de la Croix-Rouge, 1930.
Dickinson, Edwin D. "The Effect of Prohibition Repeal upon the Liquor Treaties," *American Journal of International Law*, XXVIII (1934), 101–104.
—— "Jurisdiction at the Maritime Frontier," *Harvard Law Review*, XL (1926), 1–29.
Doman, Nicholas R. "Postwar Nationalization of Foreign Property in Europe," *Columbia Law Review*, XLVIII (1948), 1125–1161.
Donaldson, John. "Fundamentals of the Foreign Economic Processes and Policies of the United States," *Weltwirtschaftliches Archiv*, XXX (1929), 49–77.
Dunn, Frederick S. *The Diplomatic Protection of Americans in Mexico*. New York: Columbia University Press, 1933.
—— "International Law and Private Rights," *Columbia Law Review*, XXVIII (1928), 166–180.
Eagleton, Clyde. *The Responsibility of States in International Law*. New York: New York University Press, 1928.
—— "The Duty of Impartiality on the Part of a Neutral," *American Journal of International Law*, XXXIV (1940), 99–104.
—— "International Law and the Charter of the United Nations," *American Journal of International Law*, XXXIX (1945), 751–754.
Ellis, Ellen D. "Intervention as a Sanction of International Law," *Proceedings of the American Society of International Law*, 1933, pp. 78–86.
Engelhardt, Ed. P. *Histoire du droit fluvial conventionnel*. Paris: L. Larose et Forcel, 1889.
Esquivel Obrégon, Toribio. *México y los Estados Unidos ante el Derecho Internacional*. México: Herrero hermanos sucesores, 1926.
Fachiri, Alexander. "Expropriation and International Law," *British Year Book of International Law*, VI (1925), 159–171.
—— "International Law and the Property of Aliens," *British Year Book of International Law*, X (1929), 32–55.
Fairman, Charles. "Military Occupation and the Development of International Law," *Proceedings of the American Society of International Law*, 1947, pp. 131–141.
Feller, Abraham H. *The Mexican Claims Commissions, 1923–1934*. New York: Macmillan, 1935.
Fenwick, Charles G. *American Neutrality: Trial and Failure*. New York: New York University Press; London: Oxford University Press, 1940.
—— *International Law*. 3d ed. New York: Appleton-Century-Crofts, 1948.
—— "Intervention by Way of Propaganda," *American Journal of International Law*, XXXV (1941), 626–631.

——— "The Monroe Doctrine and the Declaration of Lima," *American Journal of International Law*, XXXIII (1939), 257–268.
——— "Neutrality on the Defensive," *American Journal of International Law*, XXXIV (1940), 697–699.
Finch, George A. "Secretary of State Hull's Pillars of Enduring Peace," *American Journal of International Law*, XXXI (1937), 688–693.
Flory, William E. S. *Prisoners of War*. Washington: American Council on Public Affairs, 1942.
Freeman, Alwyn V. *The International Responsibility of States for Denial of Justice*. London and New York: Longmans, Green & Company, 1938.
Friedrich, Carl J. *Foreign Policy in the Making*. New York: Norton, 1938.
Garber, Paul N. *The Gadsden Treaty*. Philadelphia: University of Pennsylvania Press, 1923.
Garner, James W. *International Law and the World War*. 2 vols. London, New York: Longmans, Green, 1920.
Garvin, James Louis. *The Life of Joseph Chamberlain*. 4 vols. London: Macmillan, 1932–1934.
Gianni, Gregoire. *La Coutume en droit international*. Paris: A. Pedone, 1931.
Gidel, Gilbert. *Le Droit international public de la mer*. 3 vols. Paris: Sirey, 1932–1934.
——— "Droits et devoirs des nations; la théorie classique des droits fondamentaux des états," *Recueil des cours*, X (1925), 537–599.
——— "La Mer territoriale et la zone contiguë," *Recueil des cours*, XLVIII (1934), 133–278.
Gómez Robledo, Antonio. *The Bucareli Agreements and International Law*. Mexico, D.F.: National University of Mexico Press, 1940.
Gouet, Yvon. *La Coutume en droit constitutionnel interne et en droit constitutionnel international*. Paris: A. Pedone, 1932.
Hackett, Frank W. *Reminiscences of the Geneva Tribunal of Arbitration, 1872*. Boston and New York: Houghton Mifflin, 1911.
Harvard Research in International Law. Draft Convention and Comment on Piracy, in *American Journal of International Law*, XXVI, Supplement (1932), 739–885.
——— Draft Convention and Comment on Jurisdiction with Respect to Crime, in *American Journal of International Law*, XXIX, Supplement (1935), 437–651.
——— Draft Convention and Comment on Rights and Duties of Neutral States in Naval and Aerial War, in *American Journal of International Law*, XXXIII, Supplement (1939), 169–817.
Hazard, John N. "The Soviet Union and International Law," *Illinois Law Review*, XLIII (1948), 591–607.
Higgins, A. Pearce. *The Hague Peace Conferences and Other Inter-*

national Conferences concerning the Laws and Usages of War. Cambridge, England: Cambridge University Press, 1909.
Hill, Charles E. *The Danish Sound Dues and the Command of the Baltic.* Durham, N.C.: Duke University Press, 1926.
Hodges, Henry G. *The Doctrine of Intervention.* Princeton: The Banner Press, 1915.
Hofmannsthal, Emilio von. "Foreign Investments Risky under International Law," a paper presented before the 44th conference of the International Law Association (1950).
Holt, William S. *Treaties Defeated by the Senate.* Baltimore: Johns Hopkins University Press, 1933.
Hudson, Manley O. *International Tribunals.* Washington: Carnegie Endowment for International Peace and Brookings Institution, 1944.
—— "The Membership of the United States in the International Labor Organization," *American Journal of International Law,* XXVIII (1934), 669–682.
Hyde, Charles Cheney. *International Law Chiefly as Interpreted and Applied by the United States.* 3 vols. 2d rev. ed. Boston: Little, Brown, 1945.
—— "The City of Flint," *American Journal of International Law,* XXXIV (1940), 89–95.
Hyneman, Charles S. *The First American Neutrality.* Urbana: University of Illinois Press, 1934.
International Law Association. "'Budapest' Articles of Interpretation of the Pact for the Renunciation of War," *Report of the 38th Conference* (1934).
Jackson, Robert H. Address before the Inter-American Bar Association, Havana, Cuba, March 27, 1941, in *American Journal of International Law,* XXXV (1941), 348–359.
—— "The Challenge of International Lawlessness," *American Bar Association Journal,* XXVII (1941), 690–693.
James, Henry. *Richard Olney and His Public Service.* Boston and New York: Houghton Mifflin, 1923.
Jefferson, Thomas. *The Writings of Thomas Jefferson.* Edited by P. L. Ford. 10 vols. New York and London: Putnam, 1892–99.
Jessup, Philip C. *A Modern Law of Nations.* New York: Macmillan, 1948.
—— "The Anti-Smuggling Act of 1935," *American Journal of International Law,* XXXI (1937), 101–106.
—— "The Growth of the Law," *American Journal of International Law,* XXIX (1935), 495–499.
—— "International Law and Totalitarian War," *American Journal of International Law,* XXXV (1941), 329–331.
—— "The Pacific Coast Fisheries," *American Journal of International Law,* XXXIII (1939), 129–138.

—— "The Palmas Island Arbitration," *American Journal of International Law,* XXII (1928), 735–752.

—— *Neutrality, Its History, Economics and Law.* Vol. IV, *Today and Tomorrow.* New York: Columbia University Press, 1936.

Johnston, H. P. (ed.). *The Correspondence and Public Papers of John Jay.* 4 vols. New York and London: Putnam, 1890–1893.

Jones, Robert L. *The Eighteenth Amendment and Our Foreign Relations.* New York: Crowell, 1933.

Kaeckenbeeck, Georges. "La Protection internationale des droits acquis," *Recueil des cours,* LIX (1937), 321–419.

Kelsen, Hans. *The Law of the United Nations.* London: Stevens, 1950.

—— "Compulsory Adjudication of International Disputes," *American Journal of International Law,* XXXVII (1943), 397–406.

Kiesselbach, Wilhelm. *Problems of the German-American Claims Commission.* Washington: Carnegie Endowment for International Peace, 1930.

Kopelmanas, Lazare. "Custom as a Means of the Creation of International Law," *British Year Book of International Law,* XVIII (1937), 127–151.

Kosters, J. "Les Fondements du droit des gens," *Bibliotheca Visseriana,* IV (1925), 1–275.

Kruszewski, Charles. "Hegemony and International Law," *American Political Science Review,* XXXV (1941), 1127–1144.

Kunz, Josef L. "The Chaotic Status of the Laws of War and the Urgent Necessity for Their Revision," *American Journal of International Law,* XLV (1951), 37–61.

—— "Neutrality and the European War, 1939–1940," *Michigan Law Review,* XXXIX (1941), 719–754.

Lapradelle, Albert G. de, and Nicolas Politis. *Recueil des arbitrages internationaux.* Tome I, 1798–1855 (1905); Tome II, 1856–1872 (1923). Paris: A. Pedone.

Laurens, Adolphe. *Le Blocus et la guerre sous-marine 1914–1918.* Paris: A. Colin, 1924.

—— "La Guerre sous-marine et les neutres," *Revue d'histoire de la guerre mondiale,* IX (1931), 337–368.

Lauterpacht, Hersch. *The Function of Law in the International Community.* Oxford: Clarendon Press, 1933.

—— "Neutrality and Collective Security," *Politica,* II (1936), 133–155.

—— "Restrictive Interpretation and the Principle of Effectiveness in the Interpretation of Treaties," *British Year Book of International Law,* XXVI (1949), 48–85.

Lawrence, Thomas J. *The Principles of International Law.* Boston: Little, Brown, 1895.

Lawrence, W. B. *Visitation and Search.* Boston: Little, Brown, 1858.

Lenoir, James J. "Piracy Cases in the Supreme Court," *Journal of the*

American Institute of Criminal Law and Criminology. XXV (1934–35), 532–553.

Lingelbach, W. E. "The Doctrine and Practice of Intervention in Europe," *Annals of the American Academy of Political and Social Science*, XVI (1900), 1–32.

Lipstein, K. "The Place of the Calvo Clause in International Law," *British Year Book of International Law*, XXII (1945), 130–145.

Lyman, Theodore. *Diplomacy of the United States*. 2 vols. 2d ed. Boston: Wells and Lilly, 1828.

Mably, Gabrielle B. de. *Le Droit public de l'Europe, fondé sur les traités*. 2 vols. Amsterdam and Leipzig: Arkstee and Merkus, 1761–1766.

McNair, Arnold D. *The Law of Treaties; British Practice and Opinions*. Oxford: Clarendon Press, 1938.

Madariaga, Salvador de. *The World's Design*. London: Allen and Unwin, 1938.

Manning, W. R. (ed.). *Diplomatic Correspondence of the United States, Inter-American Affairs, 1831–1860*. 12 vols. Washington: Carnegie Endowment for International Peace, 1932–1939.

Martens, Georg Friedrich von (ed.). *Recueil de traités d'alliance, de paix, de trêve . . . depuis 1761 jusqu'à présent*. Gottingue; Dieterich, 1791–1801; Supp. 1802–1828; 2d ed. 1817–1835.

——— *Nouveau Recueil général de traités et autres actes relatifs aux rapports de droit international*. Continuation du grand recueil de G. Fr. de Martens, par Heinrich Triepel. 3e serie. 40 vols. Leipzig: Dieterich, 1907–1942.

Martin, Percy Alvin. "The Influence of the United States on the Opening of the Amazon to the World's Commerce," *Hispanic American Historical Review*, I (1918), 146–162.

Masters, Ruth D. *International Law in National Courts*. New York: Columbia University Press; London: P. S. King and Son, 1932.

Matsudaïra, K. *Le Droit conventionnel international du Japon*. Paris: Libraire du Recueil Sirey, 1931.

Meng, J. J. (ed.). *Despatches and Instructions of Conrad Alexandre Gérard*. Baltimore: Johns Hopkins University Press, 1939.

Miller, David Hunter. *The Peace Pact of Paris*. New York and London: Putnam, 1928.

Miller, Edward G., Jr. "Non-Intervention and Collective Responsibility in the Americas," *Department of State Bulletin*, XXII, 768–770 (May 15, 1950).

Milne, A. Taylor. "The Lyons-Seward Treaty of 1862," *American Historical Review*, XXXVIII (1932–33), 511–525.

Mirkine-Guetzévitch, B. *Droit constitutionnel international*. Paris: Libraire du Recueil Sirey (S.A.), 1933.

Moliné y Brasés, Ernest (ed.). *Les Costums maritimes de Barcelona universalment conegudes per Llibre del Consolat de Mar.* Barcelona: Estampa D'Henrich, 1914.

Moore, John Bassett. *History and Digest of the International Arbitrations to Which the United States Has Been a Party.* 6 vols. Washington: Government Printing Office, 1898. Also published as House Miscellaneous document 212, 53d Congress, 2d Session.

—— (ed.). *International Adjudications, Ancient and Modern.* 8 vols. New York: Oxford University Press, 1929–1937.

—— *The Principles of American Diplomacy.* New York and London: Harper, 1918.

—— "An Appeal to Reason," *Foreign Affairs,* XI (1933), 547–588.

Morley, John M. *The Life of William Gladstone.* 3 vols. London and New York: Macmillan, 1903.

Mowat, Robert B. *The Diplomatic Relations of Great Britain and the United States.* New York: Longmans, Green; London: E. Arnold and Co., 1925.

Nevins, Allan. *Hamilton Fish: The Inner History of the Grant Administration.* New York: Dodd, Mead, 1936.

Nielsen, Fred K. *International Law Applied to Reclamations.* Washington: J. Byrne and Co., 1933.

Niemeyer, Gerhart. *Law without Force.* Princeton: Princeton University Press; London: Oxford University Press, 1941.

Nolde, B. "Droit et technique des traités de commerce," *Recueil des cours,* III (1924), 291–462.

Nussbaum, Arthur. *A Concise History of the Law of Nations.* New York: Macmillan, 1947.

Oppenheim, Lassa F. L. *International Law, A Treatise.* 2 vols. London and New York: Longmans, Green, 1905–06. Later editions under editorship of Ronald F. Roxburgh, Arnold D. McNair, and Hersch Lauterpacht.

Orfield, L. B. "Equity as a Concept of International Law," *Kentucky Law Journal,* XVIII (1929–30), 31–57, 116–140.

Padelford, N. J. *International Law and Diplomacy in the Spanish Civil Strife.* New York: Macmillan, 1939.

Palmer, Roundell. *Memorials, Part II: Personal and Political.* 2 vols. London and New York: Macmillan, 1898.

Phillips, Ethel C. "American Participation in Belligerent Commercial Controls, 1914–1917," *American Journal of International Law,* XXVII (1933), 675–693.

Phillips, Paul Chrisler. *The West in the Diplomacy of the American Revolution.* Urbana: University of Illinois Press, 1913.

Pierce, Edward L. *Memoir and Letters of Charles Sumner.* 4 vols. Boston: Roberts Bros., 1877–1893.

Potter, Pitman B. *Doctrines américaines de droit international.* Paris: Centre européen de la Dotation Carnegie, 1937.

Preuss, Lawrence. *Article 2, Paragraph 7 of the Charter of the United*

Nations and Matters of Domestic Jurisdiction. Paris: Libraire du Recueil Sirey, 1949.

——— "The International Court of Justice, the Senate, and Matters of Domestic Jurisdiction," *American Journal of International Law*, XL (1946), 720–736.

——— "The Relation of International Law to Internal Law in the French Constitutional System," *American Journal of International Law*, XLIV (1950), 641–669.

Raestad, Arnold. " 'Droit coutumier' et 'principes généraux' en droit international," *Nordisk Tidskrift For International Ret*, IV (1933), 61–84.

Ralston, Jackson H. *International Arbitration from Athens to Locarno*. Stanford University: Stanford University Press; London: Oxford University Press, 1929.

Rasmussen, Gustav. *Code des prisonniers de guerre*. Copenhagen: Levin and Munksgaard, 1931.

Reale, Egidio. *L'Arbitrage international: Le règlement judiciaire du conflit de l'Alabama*. Lausanne: Payot, 1929.

Redslob, Robert. "Considérations sur les fondements du droit des gens," *Revue de droit international et de législation comparée*, XIV, 3e Serie (1933), 488–513.

Reeves, Jesse S. *American Diplomacy under Tyler and Polk*. Baltimore: Johns Hopkins University Press, 1907.

——— "The Codification of the Law of Territorial Waters," *American Journal of International Law*, XXIV (1930), 486–499.

——— "The Influence of the Law of Nature upon International Law in the United States," *American Journal of International Law*, III (1909), 547–561.

——— "The Interrelation of the Domestic and Foreign Policies of the Nation," *Annals of the American Academy of Political and Social Science*, 218 (November 1941), 1–8.

Reid, Helen D. *International Servitudes in Law and Practice*. Chicago: University of Chicago Press, 1932.

Reid, T. Wemyss. *Life of the Right Honourable William Edward Forster*. 2 vols. London: Chapman and Hall, 1888.

Rich, Elihu. *The Brussels Conference and the Universal Alliance*. London, 1874.

Richardson, James D. (comp.). *A Compilation of the Messages and Papers of the Presidents, 1789–1897*. 10 vols. Washington: Government Printing Office, 1896–1899. Also issued as House Miscellaneous Document 210, 53d Congress, 2d Session.

Rippy, J. F. "Anglo-American Filibusters and the Gadsden Treaty," *Hispanic American Historical Review*, V (1922), 155–180.

——— "The Boundary of New Mexico and the Gadsden Treaty," *American Historical Review*, IV (1921), 715–732.

——— "Diplomacy of the United States and Mexico regarding the Isthmus of Tehuantepec," *Mississippi Valley Historical Review*, VI (1920), 503–531.

——— "The Negotiation of the Gadsden Treaty," *Southwestern Historical Quarterly*, XXVII (1923), 1–26.

Röhrig, Georg. *Die Ziele selbständiger Luftangriffe*. Königsberg (Pr.) u. Berlin: Ost-Europa Verlag, 1938.

Rosenman, Samuel I. (ed.). *The Public Papers and Addresses of Franklin D. Roosevelt*. New York: Random House (and Harper), 1938–1950.

Roth, Andreas H. *The Minimum Standard of International Law Applied to Aliens*. Leiden: A. W. Sijthoff, 1949.

Roxburgh, R. F. *International Conventions and Third States*. London and New York: Longmans, Green, 1917.

Rubin, Seymour J. "Nationalization and Private Foreign Investment: The Role of Government," *World Politics*, II (1950), 482–510.

Ryan, James W. *Freedom of the Seas and International Law*. New York: The Court Press, 1941.

Salter, William. *The Life of James W. Grimes*. New York: Appleton, 1876.

Sandifer, Durward V. *Evidence before International Tribunals*. Chicago: The Foundation Press, 1939.

Savage, Carlton. *Policy of the United States toward Maritime Commerce in War*. 2 vols. Washington: Government Printing Office, 1934–1936. Also published in Department of State Publications 331 and 835.

Schwarzenberger, Georg. *International Law*. Vol. I: *International Law as Applied by International Courts and Tribunals*. London: Stevens, 1949.

——— *A Manual of International Law*. London: Stevens, 1947.

——— "The Most-Favoured-Nation Standard in British State Practice," *British Year Book of International Law*, XXII (1945), 96–121.

Scott, James B. *Hague Court Reports*. New York: Oxford University Press, 1916.

Scroggs, William O. *Filibusters and Financiers*. New York: Macmillan, 1916.

Séfériadès, S. "Aperçus sur la coutume juridique international et notamment sur son fondement," *Revue générale de droit internationale public*, XLIII (1936), 129–196.

Setser, Vernon G. *The Commercial Reciprocity Policy of the United States, 1774–1829*. Philadelphia: University of Pennsylvania Press; London: Oxford University Press, 1937.

Shotwell, James T. *War as an Instrument of National Policy and Its Renunciation in the Pact of Paris*. New York: Harcourt, Brace, 1929.

Smith, Herbert A. *The Economic Uses of International Rivers*. London: P. S. King and Son, 1931.

——— (ed.). *Great Britain and the Law of Nations*. 2 vols. London: P. S. King and Son, 1932, 1935.

Snyder, Richard C. *The Most-Favored-Nation Clause*. New York: King's Crown Press, 1948.

Sosa-Rodriguez, Carlos. *Le Droit fluvial international et les fleuves de l'Amérique latine*. Paris: A. Pedone, 1935.

Soulsby, Hugh G. *The Right of Search and the Slave Trade in Anglo-American Relations, 1814–1862*. Baltimore: Johns Hopkins University Press, 1933.

Stoner, John E. *S. O. Levinson and the Pact of Paris*. Chicago: University of Chicago Press, 1943.

Strupp, Karl. *Das Recht des Internationalen Richters, nach Billigkeit zu entscheiden*. Leipzig, R. Noske, 1930.

——— "Les Règles générales du droit de la paix," *Recueil des cours*, XLVII (1934), 259–595.

Sumner, Charles. *Charles Sumner; His Complete Works*. 20 vols. Boston: Lee and Shepard, 1900.

Tansill, Charles C. *The Canadian Reciprocity Treaty of 1854*. Baltimore: Johns Hopkins University Press, 1922.

——— *The United States and Santo Domingo, 1798–1873*. Baltimore: Johns Hopkins University Press, 1938.

Taracouzio, T. A. *The Soviet Union and International Law*. New York: Macmillan, 1935.

Thomas, C. M. *American Neutrality in 1793*. New York: Columbia University Press; London: P. S. King and Son, 1931.

Thomson, Charles A. "Mexico's Challenge to Foreign Capital," *Foreign Policy Reports*, XIII, 126–136 (August 15, 1937).

Trévily, Joseph. *Essai sur l'histoire et la situation du sous-marin en droit international*. Paris: Libraire du Recueil Sirey (S.A.), 1931.

Troyanovsky, Alexander. Address before the Society. *Proceedings of the American Society of International Law*, 1934, pp. 195–197.

Turlington, Edgar. *Mexico and Her Foreign Creditors*. New York: Columbia University Press, 1930.

Van Alstyne, Richard W. "The British Right of Search and the African Slave Trade," *Journal of Modern History*, II (1930), 37–47.

Vidaud, Jean. *Les Navires de commerce armés pour leur défense*. Paris: Picart, 1936.

Voegelin, Eric. "Some Problems of German Hegemony," *Journal of Politics*, III (1941), 154–168.

Walker, W. L. "Territorial Waters: The Cannon Shot Rule," *British Year Book of International Law*, XXII (1945), 210–231.

Walz, Gustav Adolf. *Völkerrecht und Staatliches Recht*. Stuttgart: Verlag von W. Kohlhammer, 1933.

Warren, Charles. "The Mississippi River and the Treaty Clause of the Constitution," *George Washington Law Review*, II (1934), 271–302.
Watrin, Germain. *Le Pacte de la Société des Nations et la constitution française*. Paris: Les Editions internationales, 1932.
Webster, Daniel. *The Works of Daniel Webster*. 6 vols. 8th ed. Boston: Little, Brown, 1854.
Welles, Gideon, *Diary of Gideon Welles*. 3 vols. Boston and New York: Houghton Mifflin, 1911.
—— *Lincoln and Seward*. New York: Sheldon and Co., 1874.
Werner, Auguste-Raynald. *La Croix-Rouge et les conventions de Genève*. Genève: Georg & Cie., S.A., 1943.
Westlake, John, "International Arbitration," *International Journal of Ethics*, VII (1897), 1–20.
Wheaton, Henry. *Enquiry into the Validity of the British Claim to a Right of Visitation and Search of American Vessels Suspected to Be Engaged in the African Slave-Trade*. Philadelphia: Lea and Blanchard, 1842.
—— *Some Account of the Life, Writings and Speeches of William Pinkney*. New York: J. W. Palmer and Co., 1826.
Whiteman, Marjorie M. *Damages in International Law*. 3 vols. Washington: Government Printing Office, 1937–1943. Also Department of State Publications 960, 961, 2005.
Wilcox, Francis. "The United States Accepts Compulsory Jurisdiction," *American Journal of International Law*, XL (1946), 699–719.
Willson, Beckles. *America's Ambassadors to France, 1777–1927*. London: J. Murray, 1928.
Wilson, George Grafton (ed.). *Hague Arbitration Cases*. Boston and London: Ginn and Co., 1915.
—— "The Submarine and Place of Safety," *American Journal of International Law*, XXXV (1941), 496–497.
—— "The United States and International Law," *Proceedings of the American Society of International Law*, 1936, pp. 14–26.
Wilson, Robert R. "A Case of International Responsibility during Martial Rule," *American Journal of International Law*, XXXVI (1942), 657–661.
—— "Clauses Relating to Reference of Disputes in Obligatory Arbitration Treaties," *American Journal of International Law*, XXV (1931), 469–489.
—— " 'Non-Belligerency' in Relation to the Terminology of Neutrality," *American Journal of International Law*, XXXV (1941), 121–123.
—— "Postwar Commercial Treaties of the United States," *American Journal of International Law*, XLIII (1949), 262–287.
—— "Property-Protection Provisions in United States Commercial

Treaties," *American Journal of International Law,* XLV (1951), 83–107.

—— "Reservation Clauses in Agreements for Obligatory Arbitration," *American Journal of International Law,* XXIII (1929), 68–93.

—— "Some Aspects of the Jurisprudence of National Claims Commissions," *American Journal of International Law,* XXXVI (1942), 56–76.

—— "Some Current Questions Relating to Neutrality," *American Journal of International Law,* XXXVII (1943), 651–656.

—— "Standards of Humanitarianism in War," *American Journal of International Law,* XXXIV (1940), 320–324.

—— " 'Treaty-Merchant' Clauses in Commercial Treaties of the United States," *American Journal of International Law,* XLIV (1950), 145–149.

—— "International Law in Treaties of the United States," *American Journal of International Law,* XXXI (1937), 271–288.

Winfield, P. H. *The Foundations and the Future of International Law.* Cambridge, England: Cambridge University Press, 1941.

Winkler, Carl-Heinz. *Vertrage zu Gunsten und zu Lasten Dritter im Völkerrecht.* Leipzig: R. Noske, 1932.

Wolf, Lucien. *Life of the First Marquess of Ripon.* London: J. Murray, 1921.

Woolsey, Lester H. "Government Traffic in Contraband," *American Journal of International Law,* XXXIV (1940), 498–503.

—— "The Taking of Foreign Ships in American Ports," *American Journal of International Law,* XXXV (1941), 497–506.

Woolsey, Theodore D. *Introduction to the Study of International Law.* 5th ed. New York: Scribner, 1878.

Wright, Quincy. "The Transfer of Destroyers to Great Britain," *American Journal of International Law,* XXXIV (1940), 680–689.

—— "International Law and the Totalitarian States," *American Political Science Review,* XXXV (1941), 738–743.

You, Paul. *Le Préamble des traités internationaux.* Fribourg (Suisse): Libraire de l'Université, 1941.

Ziegler, Benjamin M. *The International Law of John Marshall.* Chapel Hill: University of North Carolina Press, 1939.

NEWSPAPERS

Memphis, Tennessee, *Daily Eagle and Enquirer,* June 7, 1853.

The Times (London), August 30, September 2, 4, 1940.

New York Times, October 15, 1936; October 1, 1939; October 13, 27, 30, 1940; June 14, 1941.

Völkischer Beobachter, October 18, 1939; November 14, 1939; January 17, 1940.

INDEX

INDEX

Bei Fragen zur Produktsicherheit wenden Sie sich bitte an:
If you have any questions regarding product safety,
please contact:

Walter de Gruyter GmbH
Genthiner Straße 13
10785 Berlin
productsafety@degruyterbrill.com